The Tokyo Trial

The Tokyo Trial

*War Criminals and Japan's
Postwar International Relations*

HIGURASHI Yoshinobu

Japan Publishing Industry Foundation for Culture

Publisher's Note

This book follows the Hepburn system of romanization, with long vowels indicated by macrons. The tradition of placing the family name first has been followed for Japanese, Chinese, and Korean names.

The original Japanese text has been revised and updated by the author for this English edition.

The Tokyo Trial: War Criminals and Japan's Postwar International Relations
Higurashi Yoshinobu. Translated by the Japan Institute of International Affairs (JIIA).

Published by
Japan Publishing Industry Foundation for Culture (JPIC)
2-2-30 Kanda-Jinbocho, Chiyoda-ku, Tokyo 101-0051, Japan

First English edition: March 2022

Originally published in Japanese under the title *Tōkyō Saiban* by Kodansha Ltd. in 2008.
English publishing rights arranged with Kodansha Ltd., Tokyo.

This publication is the result of a collaborative effort between the Japan Institute of International Affairs (JIIA) and Japan Publishing Industry Foundation for Culture (JPIC).

Jacket and cover design: Francesco Coppola
Jacket and cover photographs: © Mainichi Shimbunsha/Jiji Press (top), © Asahi Shimbunsha (bottom)

Printed in Japan
ISBN 978-4-86658-230-6
https://www.jpic.or.jp/

Contents

Preface   7

Chapter 1 Viewpoints on the Tokyo Trial   11

1. Controversy over Enshrinement at Yasukuni   12

2. Distinguishing between "Class A" and "Class B and C"   20

3. "Civilization's Justice" Theory vs. "Victors' Justice" Theory   30

Chapter 2 How the Framework of the Tokyo Trial Was Formed   39

1. Lessons Learned from the Failure of the Treaty of Versailles   40

2. US Initiative vs. Cooperation among the Allies   49

3. The Decision Not to Charge the Emperor and the Motives of Concerned Countries   57

Chapter 3 What Charges Did the Allies Bring?   67

1. Launching the International Prosecution Section   68

2. Identifying Defendants and Determining Charges   85

3. Logic of the Prosecution   106

Chapter 4 How Japan Responded   129

1. Cooperation and Resistance   130

2. Logic of the Defense   150

3. Defense of State and Defense of Individuals   174

Chapter 5 How the Judgment Was Written   195

1. Disruption of the Bench   196

2. Reorganization of the Judge Group and the Judgment   213

3. How to Interpret Pal's Judgment   240

Chapter 6 Why a Second Tokyo Trial Was Not Held   253

1. International Trial and Subsequent Trial   254

2. MacArthur's Persistence   262

3. Shift toward Completion of the War Crimes Trial   266

Chapter 7 How the Release of War Criminals Commenced   279

1. When and How   280

2. War Criminal Clause in the San Francisco Peace Treaty   295

3. "Serious Domestic Problems" after Regaining Independence   309

Chapter 8 Why Were Class A War Criminals Released?   317

1. Start of Recommendations for Clemency   318

2. Increased Calls for the "Radicalist Approach to Release"   329

3. What Lies beyond the Tokyo Trial   341

Afterword   349

Chronological Table   354

List of References   359

Index   374

About the Author   399

Preface

At the end of World War II, the International Military Tribunal for the Far East (the Tokyo Trial) brought war crimes charges against 28 Japanese leaders. Because there is a direct link between the Tokyo Trial and the evaluation of the war which Japan carried out, the emotional and ideological confrontation in the debate over affirming or dismissing the legitimacy of the trial has become the origin of the ideological division between the right and left wings of postwar Japan. In that sense, the Tokyo Trial acts as both the concluding point of the Shōwa era war period and the starting point of postwar thought.

Within this public debate, the present volume attempts a balanced political history, employing primary materials and bibliographical sources to grasp the international political activities involved in the trial, including the release process for convicted war criminals. It is an attempt at describing extremely dense and complex content in comparatively simple language within a compact format.

This concept was rather successful, and when the volume was published in 2008 it was fortunately awarded the Suntory Prize for Social Sciences and Humanities (History and Civilization category). It was reprinted several times and translated into Chinese by Gusa Press in 2017. For a more detailed account of the trial, I recommend that the reader refer to my *Tōkyō Saiban no kokusai kankei: Kokusai seiji ni okeru kenryoku to kihan* [The Tokyo Trial and International Relations: Power and Norms in International Politics] (Tokyo: Bokutakusha, 2002).

Incidentally, the Tokyo Trial once again attracted attention in Japan on June 7, 2021, when Kyodo News Agency reported the following discovery. Takazawa Hiroaki, assistant professor at Nihon University, had found American army documents in the US National Archives and Records Administration collection. He discovered a report by Major Luther Frierson, US Eighth Army, stating that the remains of the seven executed Class A war criminals, including those of Tōjō Hideki, had been placed onboard a military plane that departed the air station in Yokohama on December 23, 1948. According to this report, the plane turned eastward and approximately 30 miles from the air station scattered the remains of the war criminals over the Pacific.[1]

It had been reported previously by GHQ that, as above, the ashes of the seven condemned prisoners were scattered over the Pacific after cremation.[2] The scattering of the ashes, as was carried out with the executed criminals in the Nuremberg International Military Tribunal, was a measure undertaken to prevent the war criminals from being treated as martyrs.

But the newly discovered US Eighth Army document was significant in that it mentioned the concrete procedure for the handling of the remains, and the general direction in which the ashes were scattered. The Kyodo News Agency article was extensively carried in local newspapers throughout the country, and then by follow-up articles in national newspapers including *Asahi Shimbun* and *Yomiuri Shimbun*. We can draw two points from the fact that this media coverage in June 2021 brought such a large response.

Firstly, that important details of the Tokyo Trial remain largely unknown and in need of elucidation. In the case of the Nuremberg Trial, the details of the decision-making process regarding sentencing and the handling of the remains were fully clarified. In contrast, that could not be said of what occurred during and following the Tokyo Trial.

As one example, consider the handling of the remains. The executions at Nuremberg are recorded to have taken place on October 16, 1946, commencing just after 1:00 a.m. and completing at approximately 2:45 a.m. The remains of eleven convicted criminals, including those of Hermann Wilhelm Göring, who had previously committed suicide by taking poison, were carried by an American military truck to a graveyard in the eastern part of Munich. What happened after that is made clear in a book by Joseph E. Persico.

> When the cremations were completed, including nooses and hoods, the ashes were taken to a white stucco villa in the Munich suburb of Solln. The house . . . was now the U.S. Army's European Theater Mortuary

---

1. *Tokyo Shimbun*, June 7, 2021, and *The Japan Times*, June 8, 2021.
2. Sumimoto Toshio, *Senryō hiroku* [Secret Memoir of the Occupation] (Tokyo: Mainichi Shimbunsha, 1964).

Number One. . . . A group of army officers stood on the bank of the Contwentzbach, a stream running behind the house. They watched the mortuary staff bring down eleven aluminium cylinders. One by one the ashes were emptied into the water. . . . The Contwentzbach carried the ashes into the Isar River, which conducted them to the Danube, which emptied them into the sea.[3]

In contrast with this detailed account, the Eighth Army report taken up by the media in June 2021 gives no concrete details regarding the location of where the ashes were scattered. From the air station, which is in the Kannai area in Yokohama, approximately 30 miles "toward the east" could mean the ashes were scattered either in Tokyo Bay (west of the Bōsō Peninsula) or in the Pacific Ocean (east of the Bōsō Peninsula). All that is certain is that it occurred somewhere to the east of Yokohama. In sum, there are many elements of the Tokyo Trial that remain unclear and research on the trial remains very much at the edge of unknown territory.

Secondly, the response to the media coverage of this discovery shows a high degree of interest in the Japanese Class A war criminals. Because Premiers Tōjō Hideki and Hirota Kōki are broadly recognized names in Japan, and because the term "Class A war criminal" carries such weight, this news drew the public's attention. (In contrast, as noted in chapter 1, the majority of Japanese today say that they do not know the details of the Tokyo Trial.)

While the Tokyo Trial attracts attention in Japan, in the West it remains relatively unknown. Arnold C. Brackman, special correspondent for the United Press (now UPI), titled his 1987 book after a particularly apt phrase for this: "the other Nuremberg." In it, Brackman writes,

the cast of characters was (and is) large and, to most people, virtually unknown. It is doubtful if the average literate person today is familiar with the names of more than one or two of those involved, usually Emperor Hirohito (who was not tried) and Premier Tojo. Nuremberg was different in this respect as in others. At least in the West, the names

---

3. Joseph E. Persico, *Nuremberg: Infamy on Trial* (New York: Viking, 1994).

of the accused Germans are easily remembered. . . . The atrocities hit closer to home, too.[4]

The situation Brackman describes remains much the same today. For this reason, I hope that this English translation will make the details available to an international readership. I would like to take this opportunity to express my gratitude to the Japan Institute of International Affairs (JIIA), for publishing this book as part of their English translation series, and to the Japan Publishing Industry Foundation for Culture (JPIC) for arranging the English publication.

HIGURASHI Yoshinobu

Tokyo
November 2021

---

4. Arnold C. Brackman, *The Other Nuremberg* (New York: William Morrow and Company, 1987).

CHAPTER 1
Viewpoints on the Tokyo Trial

Having been arraigned before the International Military Tribunal
for the Far East, 26 of 28 alleged Japanese war criminals arrive at
Ichigayadai from Sugamo Prison. May 3, 1946.
(National Archives of the Netherlands, Collection 544 B. V. A. Röling)

1. Controversy over Enshrinement at Yasukuni

Some Sixty Years Later

The Tokyo Trial (formally known as the International Military Tribunal for the Far East and commonly referred to as the Tokyo War Crimes Trial) is an international issue.

The Tokyo Trial was an unprecedented war crimes trial held from May 1946 through November 1948, in which eleven Allied countries prosecuted twenty-eight prewar Japanese leaders—the so-called Class A war criminals. The prosecuting countries were the United States, the United Kingdom, China, the Soviet Union, France, the Netherlands, Canada, Australia, New Zealand, India, and the Philippines. After close to two years of hearings, the majority judgment was that Japan's criminal military clique had organized a conspiracy to rule East Asia and the Pacific and initiated an aggressive war in 1928. Twenty-five of the accused were ultimately found guilty.

In Germany, the Nuremberg Trial (formally, the International Military Tribunal) was held from November 1945 through October 1946 by four Allied nations (the United States, the United Kingdom, France, and the Soviet Union) to try Nazi leaders.

These trials in Japan and Germany were unprecedented postwar settlements in which individual leaders of the defeated nations were tried in international courts of justice for crimes against international law that they had allegedly committed.

More than seventy years have now passed since the opening of the Tokyo Trial. According to a 2006 opinion poll conducted in Japan by the daily *Asahi Shimbun* on the sixtieth anniversary of the commencement of the trial, 53 percent of respondents replied that they knew the trial took place but did not know the details, while 17 percent did not even know the trial had occurred. Altogether, 70 percent of respondents said that they did not know much about the trial (*Asahi Shimbun*, May 2, 2006). While it is not my style to fulminate about the dangers of forgetting the Tokyo Trial, I find these figures astonishing.

Due to the fact that the Tokyo Trial has faded from memory over the past two generations (some seventy years), one may expect that it would finally be possible to have a calm discussion regarding the trial. However, that is far from what has happened. In recent years particularly, the so-called Yasukuni issue has become politicized.[1] Prime Minister Koizumi Junichirō paid visits to Yasukuni Shrine for six consecutive years beginning on August 13, 2001. Each visit provoked strong negative reactions from the People's Republic of China and the Republic of Korea. Coupled with Chinese premier Jiang Zemin's repeated attacks on Japan over Japan's interpretation of history since the late 1990s, such key terms as "Class A war criminals" and "Tokyo Trial" have frequently appeared in the Japanese media, and the commonplace debate over approval or disapproval of the Tokyo Trial remains as before.

I, for one, would very much welcome a calm and productive discussion of the trial. In the current approval-or-disapproval debate, however, only stereotypical, and sometimes erroneous, views are exchanged repeatedly. While new facts about the Tokyo Trial have been found since the 1980s, those facts remain known primarily within a narrow circle of experts. The general public does not share this new evidence. That is why I decided to publish this book.

Simple Perception as a Starting Point

To begin with, why are official visits by the Japanese prime minister to Yasukuni Shrine criticized?

China's main complaint is that Class A war criminals are enshrined at Yasukuni Shrine. Public opinion in Japan has been divided over this as well.

---

1. The so-called Yasukuni Shrine issue has multiple elements. First, there is the issue of separation of religion and state, and whether government leaders, especially a prime minister, can legitimately pay respects at a shrine, which is a religious entity. Second, there is the political issue of the arbitrary enshrinement of those who died during various wars despite the fact that they practiced other religions. Third, since convicted war criminals are enshrined there, other nations, especially Asian nations, have made official protests to the Japanese government. The shrine and visits to it have become a perennial source of friction within Japan, and between Japan and other nations.

While this is not a book about the issue of Class A war criminals' enshrinement, I am very much interested in how war criminals were treated after the conclusion of the Tokyo Trial. Thus, let us first look at how war criminals were enshrined at Yasukuni Shrine.

From as early as the Occupation, some bereaved families had hoped that their war criminal fathers or brothers would be enshrined at Yasukuni.

For instance, Imamura Hisa, widow of General Imamura Hitoshi of the Imperial Japanese Army and chairperson of the Tokyo Absentees' Family Society (Tōkyō Rusu Kazokukai), spoke on behalf of the members of the association at the House of Councillors Committee on Judicial Affairs on December 12, 1951: "As for the bereaved families, I feel for them. Those who were executed as war criminals are at present not allowed to be enshrined at Yasukuni, and their surviving families feel stigmatized and deserve our sympathy."[2]

Yasukuni Shrine is "a venue that gives meaning to the death of the war dead,"[3] and war criminals are "victims of the war" who should also be enshrined at Yasukuni. Such was the naïve perception that began the decades-long controversy.

After Japan regained its sovereignty on April 28, 1952, and as a result of legal reforms on governmental assistance passed in 1953–1954, death by execution and death in prison were equated with "death in the line of public duty." Encouraged by these reforms, the Japan War-Bereaved Families Association (Nihon Izokukai, founded in March 1953) and other war criminal advocate groups petitioned for the enshrinement of war criminals at Yasukuni. This prompted the Ministry of Welfare (the present-day Ministry of Health, Labour and Welfare) and Yasukuni to render administrative cooperation in the enshrinement of war criminals beginning in 1956.

The Ministry of Welfare was more positive toward enshrinement of war criminals at that time. For those who wonder why the ministry was accommodating in this regard, let me present the following background.

Under the demilitarization policy of the Occupation authority, the

---

2. Unless otherwise indicated by a direct source citation, translations of direct speech are from the author's Japanese version of the original.

3. Hatano Sumio, "Izoku no meisō" [War-Bereaved Families' Loss of Sense of Direction], in *Kioku toshite no Pāru Hābā* [Pearl Harbor as Memory], ed. Hosoya Chihiro, Irie Akira, and Ōshiba Ryō (Kyoto: Minerva Shobō, 2004).

Imperial Japanese Army and Navy were dissolved and the First Ministry of Demobilization (formerly the Ministry of the Army) and the Second Ministry of Demobilization (formerly the Ministry of the Navy) were established on December 1, 1945, to deal with demobilization and war crimes issues. These two ministries were merged on June 14, 1946, to form the Demobilization Agency. This in turn was integrated into the Ministry of Welfare, and was placed in charge of affairs related to repatriation as the Demobilization Bureau on January 1, 1948. The Demobilization Bureau was reorganized under the extra-ministerial Repatriation Relief Agency on May 31, 1948. After the Occupation, on April 1, 1954, the organization returned to the Ministry of Welfare as the Repatriation Relief Bureau. On June 1, 1961, it was reorganized a final time as the Relief Bureau.

Throughout the evolution of this bureau, it remained engaged in activities on behalf of those who were prosecuted and/or convicted as war criminals. Also, the former Imperial Japanese Army remained an independent entity, occupying a corner of the "Ichigaya office of the Relief Bureau" until it moved to Kasumigaseki on June 27, 1964.

Thus, the former Japanese military came to infiltrate part of the Ministry of Welfare.

Aggressive Former Imperial Military vs. Cautious Yasukuni Shrine

A preliminary meeting to establish the criteria for enshrinement was convened on April 9, 1958. At the meeting were two officials from the Demobilization Division of the Ministry of Welfare's Repatriation Relief Bureau (the former First Ministry of Demobilization, former Army), two from the Second Operation Division of the same bureau (the former Second Ministry of Demobilization, former Navy), and five representatives from Yasukuni Shrine.

The former Imperial Japanese Army representatives requested that Yasukuni consider the possibility of discretely enshrining those war criminals below Class B who would not be too conspicuous. The shrine remained uncommitted, saying it would consult with the representatives of the Yasukuni Shrine Veneration Association, the decision-making organ for its activities.

On September 12, the Repatriation Relief Bureau pointed out that, among the inconspicuous deceased Class B and C war criminals, there were altogether some 200 who had fallen in the line of duty, who had been found guilty on fallacious or forged charges, or who had been victims of mistaken identity. The bureau also requested approval for enshrinement of "as many [victims executed overseas] as can remain inconspicuous. By June of that year, about one-third of Class B and C war criminals who had been arrested overseas but who had died before sentencing had already been enshrined at Yasukuni on the grounds that they cleared the enshrinement criteria of "those deceased overseas after Japan's surrender."

From the viewpoint of the former Japanese military, Class B and C war crime trials were examples of "victors' justice," just like the International Military Tribunal for the Far East. These trials rejected evidence favorable to the accused and showed remarkable disparities in sentencing. For this reason, the former military believed it was only natural for those who had been executed overseas to be enshrined at Yasukuni.

Behind the former military's aggressive attitude were changes in the situation surrounding war criminals. All of the Class A prisoners had their sentences commuted on April 7, 1958, and had already been paroled from Sugamo Prison. The last of the Class B and C war criminals were also paroled by May 30, and they, too, completed their sentences at the end of the year. With the conclusion of the release of war criminals, the Repatriation Relief Bureau made their enshrinement its next goal.

Perhaps due to apprehension about criticism from left-wing elements in Japan, Yasukuni maintained a cautious stance. The shrine claimed that it would be extremely problematic if newspapers reporting on the issue provoked "national repercussions," and suggested that it might request the prior consent of parties associated with the Imperial Household Agency.

On March 10, 1959, three months after the completion of all the war criminals' prison sentences, the Demobilization Division of the Repatriation Relief Bureau first forwarded to Yasukuni the *saijin meihyō*, a list of those Class B and C war criminals who were scheduled to be enshrined. According to the *Yasukuni Jinja gōshi jimu kyōryoku yōkō* (Yasukuni Shrine Guideline on Enshrinement Administration Cooperation), dated April 19, 1956, it was the shrine, upon receipt of the *saijin meihyō*, that made the final decision. While Yasukuni Shrine enshrined 346 Class B and C war criminals executed by overseas military courts as the first group on April 6, 1959, it did not publicize this fact. The shrine hoped that the issue of enshrinement of war criminals would not meet with public opposition, but would "evolve naturally" with gradual changes in public opinion.

From the beginning, Yasukuni had been reluctant to enshrine even Class B and C war criminals. Nevertheless, it is said to have enshrined 479 of them on October 17, 1959; 115 on October 17, 1966; and 44 on October 17, 1967. Enshrined in the four groups were a total of 984 Class B and C war criminals.[4]

"Not Allowing the Enshrinement of War Criminals Means Affirming the Results of the Tokyo Trial"

On February 8, 1966, around the time the enshrinement of the Class B and C war criminals was being completed, a *saijin meihyō* was forwarded to the shrine of twelve Class A war criminals as candidates for enshrinement. The list had to be handled with great caution.

It included the following seven who had been hanged:

Dohihara Kenji
Hirota Kōki
Itagaki Seishirō
Kimura Heitarō
Matsui Iwane
Mutō Akira
Tōjō Hideki

The remaining five had died of sickness after the verdict:

Hiranuma Kiichirō
Koiso Kuniaki
Shiratori Toshio
Tōgō Shigenori
Umezu Yoshijirō

Matsuoka Yōsuke and Nagano Osami, who had died from illness during the

---

4. *Inoue Tadao shiryō* [Inoue Tadao Documents], Yasukuni Kaikō Bunko [Yasukuni Archives].

hearings, were classified as "deceased in Japan during the pendency of verdict." The Act on Special Aid to the Wounded and Sick Retired Soldiers and War-Bereaved Families was not applied to them. Therefore, they were not included in the *saijin meihyō* of Class A war criminals submitted to the shrine.

On January 31, 1969, an agreement was reached between the Relief Bureau of the Ministry of Welfare and the shrine that twelve Class A war criminals and ten defendants "deceased in Japan while awaiting trial," including Matsuoka and Nagano, "were to be enshrined, in consideration of the wishes of the Veneration Association representatives, but that fact would not be publicly announced." It appears, however, that the parties concerned did not intend to carry out the enshrinement immediately, "due to various considerations," and it was put on hold at a meeting between the two parties on June 25, 1970.[5]

Five days later, on June 30, 1970, however, outspoken representatives of the shrine's policy makers decided to move ahead with the enshrinement of the Class A war criminals. The decision was the result of pressure imposed on the Ministry of Welfare as well as on Yasukuni Shrine, both of which remained indecisive, by representatives of the Veneration Association who were frustrated by their inaction.

According to Tokugawa Yoshihiro, former grand chamberlain to the Shōwa emperor from 1936 through 1988, in spite of resistance from some members of the Veneration Association who argued for a more cautious approach, Aoki Kazuo, former minister of Greater East Asia in the Tōjō Hideki Cabinet and a former Class A war crimes suspect (elected to the House of Councillors in 1953), refused to budge. Aoki insisted that "not allowing the enshrinement of war criminals means affirming the results of the Tokyo Trial." From this episode one can conclude that to some people, the enshrinement of the Class A war criminals implied a negation of the Tokyo Trial. At this point, Tsukuba Fujimaro, chief priest of Yasukuni and the third son of Prince Yamashina Kikumaro, had no other option than to concur, stating: "We will follow your plan of action. But we should give careful consideration to the timing of the enshrinement."

---

5. Toyoda Kumao, *Sensō saiban yoroku* [Additional Records of the War Crimes Trials] (Tokyo: Taiseisha, 1986); National Diet Library, Research and Legislative Reference Bureau, ed., *Shinpen Yasukuni Jinja mondai shiryōshū* [Newly Compiled Documents on the Yasukuni Shrine Issue] (Tokyo: National Diet Library, 2007).

Decision to Enshrine Class A War Criminals

While the enshrinement of Class A war criminals had become a fait accompli, the timing was left to the judgment of the chief priest of Yasukuni.

It appeared that Tsukuba, who advocated a cautious approach, intended to postpone the enshrinement as long as possible. When he abruptly passed away in March 1978, however, his successor in July, Matsudaira Nagayoshi (son of Matsudaira Yoshitami, former minister of the Imperial Household), decided to move ahead. On October 17, 1978, fourteen Class A war criminals, including Matsuoka and Nagano, were secretly enshrined.

Tokugawa reminisced, "When I mentioned that enshrinement of the Class A war criminals would be controversial if it became public, Yasukuni assured me, 'Only the relevant bereaved families will be notified,' and 'It will not be openly publicized.'" Matsudaira was a former lieutenant-commander of the Imperial Japanese Navy and a man of strong character, so much so that Prince Takamatsu Nobuhito, who had once served as staff officer in the Naval Department of the Imperial Headquarters, commented that Matsudaira was "the most appropriate person [to succeed Tsukuba], but he will be controversial." Like Aoki Kazuo, Matsudaira was convinced that there would be no spiritual restoration of the Japanese people unless the historical view of the Tokyo Trial (*Tōkyō Saiban shikan*, in Japanese), which blamed prewar Japan for everything, was denied. This illustrates that the argument for enshrinement of the Class A war criminals and negation of the Tokyo Trial were two sides of the same coin.[6]

The enshrinement of the Class A war criminals was conducted without the consent of the bereaved families, and not all of those families had hoped for that enshrinement. The feelings of Tōgō Shigenori's surviving family were representative: they were reported to have been "somewhat taken aback" when they received the enshrinement notification.[7]

The enshrinement of Class A war criminals at Yasukuni became publicly known through the mass media in April 1979. Criticism of the enshrinement

---

6. See Tokugawa Yoshihiro, *Jijūchō no yuigon* [The Last Testament of a Grand Chamberlain] (Tokyo: Asahi Shimbunsha, 1997); Hata Ikuhiko, *Gendaishi no taiketsu* [Confrontations in Contemporary History] (Tokyo: Bungeishunjū, 2003); Hosaka Masayasu, *"Yasukuni" to iu nayami* [Anguish called Yasukuni] (Tokyo: Mainichi Shimbunsha, 2007).

7. See Tōgō Kazuhiko, "Shushō no sanpai ni moratoriamu o" [Moratorium on Prime Ministers' Visits to Yasukuni], *Ronza* (September 2006).

proved to be relatively short-lived. However, six years later, when Prime Minister Nakasone Yasuhiro paid an official visit to the shrine on August 15, 1985, the fortieth anniversary of the end of the Pacific War, fierce protests were made by neighboring countries. The enshrinement of Class A war criminals brought about numerous diplomatic confrontations. While a fierce anti-Japan movement erupted in China, mainly led by students but aggravated by the issue of the trade deficit with Japan, the response of the Hu Yaobang government was generally restrained.[8]

The enshrinement had started with the lesser known but more numerous Class B and C war criminals. This was never considered problematic. This is because, at least in present-day Japan, it is Class A war criminals who are perceived to be the "symbols of Japan's war responsibility." In any event, despite its frequent usage, the term "Class A war criminal" is in many cases misconstrued.

To begin with, what exactly is a war crime, and what is a Class A war criminal? It is essential to define these terms before proceeding.

2. Distinguishing between "Class A" and "Class B and C"

Use of the Term "War Criminal" in Postwar Japan

The term "war criminal" refers to an individual who is responsible for committing war crimes. In Japan today, however, this term is more often used in casual contexts. Take for example the following. "John Terry, who was close to being seen as a 'war criminal,' praised the team's captain, David Beckham, saying, 'Of course everyone looks at his free-kicks and his passing but he tackles back and works hard for the team'" (*Yomiuri Shimbun*, evening edition, June 26, 2006).

In the above quote, John Terry, a defender on the English soccer team whose mistake during the 2006 FIFA World Cup game against Ecuador almost cost the team a goal, showed support for the team's captain, David Beckham, who had saved the team with a vital free kick and dedicated defensive efforts.

---

8. See Itagaki Tadashi, *Yasukuni kōshiki sanpai no sōkatsu* [Summary of the Yasukuni Official Visit Issue] (Tokyo: Tentensha, 2000); Tanaka Nobumasa, *Yasukuni no sengoshi* [Postwar History of Yasukuni Shrine] (Tokyo: Iwanami Shoten, 2002); and Mōri Kazuko, *Nit-Chū kankei* [Japan-China Relations] (Tokyo: Iwanami Shoten, 2006).

"War criminal" in the above quote simply means "a person responsible for defeat and failure who should be denounced." When "Class A" is added to this, the tone of accusation becomes stronger—that is, "a person who bears the ultimate responsibility for defeat." Because most minor errors are forgiven when the game is won, one is labeled a "war criminal" only when the team loses the game. This may be the connotation that the expression "war criminal" has taken on in postwar Japan.

Since it first originated in the tribunals after World War II, the term "war criminal" has deviated from the original meaning of Class A war criminal as someone who is "responsible for starting a war," to one who is "responsible for defeat in a war." Current usage is not completely off the mark. Japanese journalist Tokutomi Sohō once pointed out, "We are dissatisfied with Tōjō and his gang because they led Japan to defeat in a war that had to be won."[9] As this comment indicates, immediately after the end of the war the Japanese perceived Class A war criminals to be "those who bear the ultimate responsibility for defeat." And this responsibility for Japan's defeat was something that Class A war criminals themselves were keenly aware of. Thus, the term "Class A war criminal" in Japan today seems to fundamentally reflect this latter view: it involves responsibility for losing the war.

What Is a Class A War Criminal?

Originally, Class A war criminals were those who were indicted by the prosecution before the International Military Tribunal for the Far East for "crimes against peace" (Class A war crimes) based on the definition that planning, preparing, initiating, waging, and conspiring to accomplish aggressive war were international crimes. It was the term commonly applied to defendants of the Tokyo Trial. Because they were responsible for crimes against peace, or Class A crimes, the defendants were labeled Class A war criminals. Toward the end of 1945, they were already called "A-class heavyweights" among Sugamo Prison inmates.[10]

Theoretically, if a second Tokyo Trial had been convened, its defendants

---

9. Tokutomi Sohō, *Tokutomi Sohō shūsengo nikki* [Tokutomi Sohō Postwar Diary] (Tokyo: Kodansha, 2006), vol. 2.

10. See Mizuno Tetsuo, *Haruka naru heiwa ni* [Toward Faraway Peace] (Tokyo: Tōkō Shoin, 1952).

would also have been called Class A war criminals. As a matter of fact, putative defendants in such a second Tokyo Trial were to be called "Class A war crimes suspects." (Japanese referred to them with the terms "quasi-Class A war criminals" or simply "Class A war criminals.")

Those who were not found guilty should have been freed from the disgrace connoted by this term. Indeed, there has been scarcely any serious discussion as to whether the label "Class A war criminal" should have been removed from Ōkawa Shūmei—whose charges were dropped—or Matsuoka Yōsuke and Nagano Osami—who died of natural causes during the trial. And even if such a discussion were to take place, there would be no substantial change at this point. This is why I have deliberately not included "those who were convicted" in the definition of Class A war criminals. That defendants remained "war criminals" even though they were not actually convicted reveals the idiosyncrasy of the Tokyo Trial.

Because twenty-six of the defendants at the Tokyo Trial, excluding Ōkawa Shūmei and Shiratori Toshio, were also accused of Class B conventional war crimes and Class C crimes against humanity, their crimes were not limited to crimes against peace. In that sense, I believe it is easier to think of the term "Class A war criminals" as referring to the defendants of the Tokyo Trial (i.e., Japan's state leaders).

The Term Class

How did crimes against peace come to be called Class A war crimes?

Originally the use of the term "class" derived from the classifications that were used by the international military tribunals held in Japan and Germany. The lengthy Article 6 of the Charter of the International Military Tribunal (enacted on August 8, 1945) defines each war crime as follows:

> The following acts, or any of them, are crimes coming within the jurisdiction of the Tribunal for which there shall be individual responsibility:
> (a) Crimes against peace: namely, planning, preparation, initiation or waging of a war of aggression, or a war in violation of international treaties, agreements or assurances, or participation in a common plan or conspiracy for the accomplishment of any of the foregoing;
> (b) War crimes: namely, violations of the laws or customs of war. Such

violations shall include, but not be limited to, murder, ill-treatment or deportation to slave labor or for any other purpose of civilian population of or in occupied territory, murder or ill-treatment of prisoners of war or persons on the seas, killing of hostages, plunder of public or private property, wanton destruction of cities, towns or villages, or devastation not justified by military necessity;

(c) Crimes against humanity: namely, murder, extermination, enslavement, deportation, and other inhumane acts committed against any civilian population, before or during the war, or persecutions on political, racial or religious grounds in execution of or in connection with any crime within the jurisdiction of the Tribunal, whether or not in violation of the domestic law of the country where perpetrated.

Leaders, organizers, instigators and accomplices participating in the formulation or execution of a common plan or conspiracy to commit any of the foregoing crimes are responsible for all acts performed by any persons in execution of such plan.

In short, crime types such as Class A and Class B simply correspond to Sections (a) and (b) of the Charter of the International Military Tribunal. As I pointed out in my *Tōkyō Saiban no kokusai kankei* (The Tokyo Trial and International Relations), "A-kyū" is translated into English as "Class A." The term does not indicate a hierarchy of gravity of crimes. In other words, it does not necessarily mean that a Class A crime is more serious than a Class B crime or a Class C crime.

Nonetheless, I suspect that Japanese have mistakenly taken Class A war crimes as being the most heinous. While it is true that in the International Military Tribunals in both Germany and Japan, the greatest emphasis was given to Class A war crimes, this was because the Allied Powers wanted to call attention to that category as the central feature of the trials. In the trials in Nuremberg, testimony about genocide, including the horror at the Auschwitz concentration camp, had such a great impact that Class C crimes, that is, crimes against humanity, became more central than crimes against peace. Yet the ultimate target of the prosecutors was undeniably crimes against peace.

In any event, because "*kyū*" was translated as "class" in the sense of a hierarchy in the Japanese language, instead of "*ruikei* (type)" or "*shurui* (category)," which should have been the terms used, misunderstanding about the grouping known as Class A war criminals persists even today.

Why Special Weight was Given to Class A Crimes

Let us consider why the Allied Powers attached the greatest importance to investigating Class A crimes (crimes against peace), particularly at the Tokyo Trial.

First, the Allied Powers were enthusiastic about punishing those who had committed crimes against peace, a factor seen in the trials in both Germany and Japan. Crimes against peace and crimes against humanity were new crimes in international law that had not been recognized before the Charter of the International Military Tribunal was enacted on August 8, 1945.

While international law is normally developed through a long and evolutionary process, as we will see in the next chapter, the US revolutionized international law in one stroke between the fall of 1944 and August 1945. Simply put, crimes against peace and crimes against humanity are ex post facto law, which is against the principle that punishment must not be retroactive.

The two categories of crimes were created after the fact, but they were not necessarily accusations made in hindsight. For instance, Colonel Murray Bernays, who was in charge of the administrative side of the US policy on punishment of war crimes, was aware by January 1945 that there was a general consensus that starting a war did not constitute a crime under international law. General Dwight D. Eisenhower also stated in the same year, "We are making a new law to punish war criminals."

This indicates that decision makers among the Allies were themselves aware of "the novelty" of these international laws. This is why they felt it necessary to justify what they were doing as "not innovation of law but innovation of law execution." Behind the choice of the neutral term "charter"— as in the Charter of the International Military Tribunal for the Far East—rather than a term such as "code," was apprehension that the document might be criticized as ex post facto law.

Nevertheless it would not be appropriate to denounce the US action as deceitful based only on the background examined above. For instance, behind the Atlantic Charter of August 1941, which advocated Wilsonian internationalism including free trade, self-determination of peoples, and an international peace organization, were such areas of US national interest as assisting Britain in war, destroying the Nazi regime, and providing assurance of postwar peace. But such national interests did not degrade the value of the philosophy of the Atlantic Charter. As far as the international military tribunal was concerned, the US government at the time firmly believed that convening a court to question the individual responsibilities of the Japanese and German leaders for starting a war of aggression would become an effective means to establish the rule of law in international society, which could at that point be likened to a wilderness.

A Term Not Found in German

Second, according to directive JCS 1023/10 (dated July 8, 1945), which was a basic policy document of the US Joint Chiefs of Staff (JCS) on its stance toward trials of German war criminals, those responsible for crimes against peace had to possess the knowledge as well as the authority to participate in conspiracy in a war of aggression. Therefore, according to JCS, those responsible for aggression were limited to "persons who have held senior political, civil or military (including General Staff) positions in Germany or in one of its allies, co-belligerents or satellites or in the financial, industrial or economic life of any of these countries." And, since "those in senior positions"—that is, state leaders engaged in high-level policy matters—would be tried, the tribunal would naturally attract intense public attention. This was one of the reasons Class A was regarded as more important than Class B or C.

Third, in the case of the Tokyo Trial, the US adopted a policy of refraining from indicting Japan's state leaders who could not be prosecuted for crimes against peace (Class A war crimes). In other words, all of the defendants of the Tokyo Trial were suspected of Class A crimes and, therefore, all of them were Class A war criminals. The direct basis for this US decision was SWNCC 57/3, which will be discussed in the following chapter. This policy paper defined the purview of the International Military Tribunal for the Far East in these terms: "For the trial of persons charged with offenses of the type described in paragraph 1.A. [Crimes against Peace], any international court appointed by the Supreme Commander." SWNCC 57/3 also instructed that the prosecution agency "should attach importance to the investigation of the evidence that crimes against peace have been committed." Therefore, in the case of the military tribunal in Japan, from the outset emphasis was placed on punishing those responsible for launching the attack on Pearl Harbor and starting the war.

It is significant that it was only in Japan that the Allies used the term "Class A war criminal." While both the formal designation of "major war criminal" and its common name "Class A war criminal" were used in the Tokyo Trial, only the former was used in Germany. I have never come across an official document that refers to German major war criminals as Class A war criminals.

The term "major war criminal" originated in the Moscow Declaration on Atrocities signed by the US, Britain, and the Soviet Union, which was made public on November 1, 1943 as one of four declarations. The Declaration on Atrocities announced that "major criminals whose criminal offenses have no particular geographical location"—such as the Nazi atrocities—would be punished by "joint decision of the Governments of the Allies." In this case, "major criminals" meant high-level political and military leaders. It was a term created to distinguish them from war criminals guilty of violating the traditional laws of war, who were designated as "minor war criminals."

What Are Class B and C War Criminals?

Let us touch on the definition of Class B and C war criminals.

Class B war crimes are "conventional war crimes," while Class C are "crimes against humanity." Thus, Class B and C war crimes suspects are those responsible for atrocities, guilty of both conventional war crimes and crimes against humanity. Most of the Class B and C war crimes suspects were lower-rank soldiers. Nevertheless, the list of those indicted included such leading figures as General Yamashita Tomoyuki, Lieutenant General Honma Masaharu, and General Imamura Hitoshi, who were no less significant than Class A war criminals.

Class B war crimes, or conventional war crimes, are violations of the laws or customs of war conducted by alien combatants or civilians (including such actions as the mistreatment of prisoners of war and inhabitants of occupied territories, or the wanton destruction of cities, towns or villages). These crimes are, in other words, violations of the traditional laws of war. International laws at that time gave belligerent nations the right to punish individuals

Yamashita Tomoyuki, guarded by military police, returns to his cell at the end of a day in court listening to testimony against him in the war crimes trial at Manila. Nov 1, 1945.
(US National Archives [111-SC-215021])

who committed serious crimes during wartime (wartime felony) in accordance with their own domestic laws until the conclusion of hostilities.

From the First Sino-Japanese War onwards, Japan itself had opened courts-martial (*gunritsu hōtei* in Japanese) after each war it was involved in. During the Pacific War, the Japanese military punished or executed captured Allied airmen and other military personnel in closed-door courts, where defendants were not assisted by defense counsel, and their appeals were not accepted. They were war crimes trials carried out by the Japanese. These proceedings themselves came to be viewed as mistreatment of prisoners of war, and thus were subject to the Allies' Class B and C tribunals after Japan's defeat.[11]

Class C war crimes, crimes against humanity, were also a new category of crime instituted after World War II. This category regarded inhumane acts and persecution committed against any civilian population, before or during the war, as international crimes. But "inhumane acts against any civilian population" could be dealt with within the Class B "conventional war crimes" category alone, and, in fact, the Tokyo Trial tried the Nanjing Incident during the Second Sino-Japanese War as a violation of the laws of war.

What, then, is the essence of a Class C war crime?

---

11. See Kita Hiroaki, *Gunritsu hōtei: Senjika no shirarezaru "saiban"* [Courts-Martial: The Unknown "Trials" of Wartime] (Tokyo: Asahi Shimbunsha, 1997).

The Essence of Crimes against Humanity

Crimes against humanity include "acts against one's own citizens," and "acts preceding a war."

The Nazis persecuted and carried out the genocide of Jewish Germans, debilitated German citizens, and stateless persons. Under existing laws of war, it was not legal to punish those acts against compatriots or actions that preceded the war brought on by the Nazis (although it was possible to try compatriots for wartime treason and espionage).

Sebastian Haffner, a German historian and journalist, and Sakamoto Takao, a Japanese political scientist, both astutely pointed out that the Nazis' "killing for killing's sake" belonged in a category different from war crimes, which from the beginning were committed in the pursuit of victory. Nevertheless, the Allies deliberately called these acts war crimes in consideration of public opinion in the countries where there was strong demand for punishment. Concerning crimes against humanity, and its derivative the crime of genocide, the Rome Statute of the International Criminal Court (the Rome Statute), adopted on July 17, 1998, clearly states that under international law it is possible to punish individuals for these crimes. The International Criminal Court (ICC), established in The Hague in March 2003, however, can try these crimes only when the national courts of the concerned nations do not function properly. In this sense, the international military tribunals in Germany and Japan were significant as precedents in international law.

In the case of the Tokyo Trial, however, the Allies judged that Japan had no intention of annihilating a specific ethnic group, unlike Nazi Germany, and so crimes against humanity were, so to speak, supplementary. Consequently, those responsible for atrocities—the Japanese equivalent of the minor war criminals indicted in Germany, Italy, and Austria—were lumped together in the Tokyo Trial as Class B and C war criminals.

Japanese Minor War Criminals Were All Categorized as Class B War Criminals

Another view of the difference between Class B and Class C war crimes is based on the nature of the crimes. That is, Class B war criminals were military commanders responsible for atrocities, while Class C war criminals were the perpetrators of those atrocities. The demarcation was made on the basis of the nature of the offender's engagement in the crime. Here, too, there was a hierarchical relationship between the two in that Class B suspects were superior to Class C suspects in military rank. At the beginning of the Occupation, this demarcation was communicated by the General Headquarters, Supreme Commander for the Allied Powers (GHQ/SCAP), which did not have an accurate grasp of the policies of the US government at that time, to the Japanese. This inaccurate understanding remained in Japan, nevertheless, where people are sensitive to hierarchies, and took on a life of its own, so to speak, as being "significantly meaningful."

Nonetheless, this demarcation was not an official definition applied by the judging side, the Allies.

For instance, one Japanese diplomatic document states:

> [While] it is correct to demarcate between Class B war crimes, which are violations of the laws or customs of war, and Class C crimes, which are crimes against humanity . . . in actuality, it is customary to designate high-ranking suspects of Class B and C war crimes as Class B war criminals (suspects) and low-ranking perpetrators as Class C war criminals (suspects), because these crimes in fact overlap in most cases and almost all of the accused are prosecuted and tried on both accounts.[12]

This "actual demarcation" applied only within Japan. A US Department of State document of August 1955 stated that, while it had not distinguished between Class B and Class C war crimes as far as Japanese suspects were concerned, all Japanese minor war criminals would have to be classified as Class B if strict criteria were applied. Thus, the charge of crime against humanity in the immediate postwar days was de facto applied only to the Nazi defendants.

---

12. Ministry of Foreign Affairs, *Gaikō kiroku* [Diplomatic Record] (Diplomatic Archive of the Ministry of Foreign Affairs, 1998), 14th Disclosure.

3. "Civilization's Justice" Theory vs. "Victors' Justice" Theory

Endless Conflict

Since the days of the Tokyo Trial, a clash between two theories over the trials has been evident: "civilization's justice" theory (an affirmative argument claiming that civilization was the ultimate plaintiff and that civilization might be destroyed if the judicial undertakings did not succeed in preventing future wars) versus "victors' justice" theory (a negative argument). This was, and continues to be, the basic structure of the controversy over the Tokyo Trial.[13]

"Civilization's justice" theory is an affirmative argument praising as a "virtue" the Tokyo Trial's pursuit of Japan's responsibility for invasions and atrocities in a civilized court of justice. The representative advocate of this theory was Secretary of War Henry L. Stimson, a founding father of the Nuremberg Trial. His argument, which stressed law and justice, had an element of justifying such war measures as the US's indiscriminate bombing of Japanese cities and the atomic bomb attacks on Hiroshima and Nagasaki as unavoidable actions to defeat the Japanese military and minimize the total number of victims. To support his argument, Stimson had to characterize the Allies' war tactics as sanctioned justice against acts of the Axis nations, which were unambiguously "evil."

The "victors' justice" argument denies the right to punish individual leaders for starting a war, because it is the application of a retroactive (ex post facto) law. Applying such a law is unjustified because the actions of the Allies are not called to account, making the proceedings tantamount to mere political retaliation by the victors. From this standpoint, the Allies are no more than a disreputable alliance that does not hesitate to distinguish between virtue and vice, hence making the Tokyo Trial immoral.

Because these two totally opposite arguments are simple and clear, neither have lost their appeal. The controversy between the two positions has now become so hopelessly entangled with nationalism, political ideology, sentimental argument, and moralistic debate on war responsibility that the result is an irreconcilable conflict of sense of values.

---

13. For details of the history of studies on the Tokyo Trial, see Higurashi Yoshinobu, *Tōkyō Saiban no kokusai kankei* [The Tokyo Trial and International Relations] (Tokyo: Bokutakusha, 2002).

The argument on war responsibility advocated by German sociologist Max Weber was about determining the causes of a war. It looks at international relations as a whole from the viewpoint of accountability for the outcome, in terms of which governments pursued external goals that could be realized only through war. Through this lens, it examines the politics, diplomacy, and public opinion in various countries.

The war responsibility debate in postwar Japan, however, has confused the issue of conscience and the issue of politics, as literary critic Etō Jun astutely observed.[14] The discussion on the Tokyo Trial has been no exception. In November 1947, former foreign minister Shigemitsu Mamoru predicted that the Occupation's "indictments of war criminals and implementations of purges of public service positions would ultimately divide the Japanese people into two halves, creating a source of antagonism. Such a policy would do more harm than good both to Japan and the US." Unfortunately, his prediction proved accurate. While the day may come when a dispassionate view of this issue becomes a matter of course, it will be in the distant future. Meanwhile, at present the conflict between these two views remains.

Accumulating "Facts"

That the Tokyo Trial was victors' justice is self-evident. That would be impossible to refute.

While Japan itself had convened courts-martial in wartime to try war crimes suspects for violation of the laws of war, a Class A war crimes trial to question responsibility for starting a war was only possible as "victors' justice." Nevertheless, it would not be proper to deny the validity of the Tokyo Trial outright simply because it was victors' justice. Because norms are very much a part of international politics, the Japanese argument against victors' justice becomes highly problematic if the Japanese side, due to losers' resentment, does not recognize the victors' sense of justice or Japan's own faults.

As for the civilization's justice argument, today there hardly remains any Stimson-like support for the validity of the trial on that basis. Instead, those who are critical of prewar Japan complain that "so-and-so was acquitted and

---

14. See Yamada Munemutsu et al., *Gendai no hakken* [Discovery of Contemporary Times], vol. 6 (Tokyo: Shunjūsha, 1960).

such-and-such an issue was not prosecuted." Some people place too much emphasis on civilization's justice, and use the concept as leverage to criticize Japanese government authorities. Such thinking may be permissible as the basis of a moralistic war responsibility argument, but it is naïve in that it ignores actual incidents and the accompanying constraints.

It should be added that in the present day, emphasizing "Japan-US cooperation" and "Japanese collaboration with the Occupation forces" cannot break the deadlock in the debate between civilization's justice and victors' justice. Recent views assume that the Tokyo Trial was not unilateral victors' justice because Japanese citizens cooperated, and therefore tend to unjustifiably lump cooperation and collaboration together with the civilization's justice premise.

How should we view the Tokyo Trial?

The position of the present volume is quite simple. All it intends to do is thoroughly verify the facts, and maintain a detached perspective. This book has no hidden intention either to condemn or to justify the Tokyo Trial and the actions of prewar Japan.

For instance, when the average Japanese reader comes across gruesome scenes of the execution of Class A war criminals in certain Tokyo Trial books, they cannot help but feel righteous indignation against the Allied Powers. And these readers are liable to reach an extreme and total rejection of the trial, concluding that the trial was out of the ordinary. In itself, this categorization of the trial may be justified. Yet if readers react in this way, their perception will be distorted even when they encounter the facts.

There is no need to accept completely the justification of the Tokyo Trial or to reject outright prewar Japan on the basis of civilization's justice. Conversely, advocates of the victors' justice viewpoint do not have to refrain from recognizing the significance of the Tokyo Trial.

The civilization's justice theory places high hopes on justice and norms, while the victors' justice argument sees a court of justice only in terms of power relations. The difference between the two is the standpoint of their advocates. When attempting to determine which of the two is correct, one realizes that either side can be justified. Both positions were intrinsic to the Tokyo Trial.

Therefore, I take the stance that the Tokyo Trial was a manifestation of international politics, which partook of both civilization's justice and victors' justice. It is not simply one or the other, but rather an amalgam of the two.

The aim of this book is to take all of the above into consideration in order to help readers understand the facts regarding the Tokyo Trial, from pre-trial events through to the release of the Japanese war criminals.

Dreaming of Norms of Justice

It was to punish leaders of the Axis powers that the Allies, including the US, held international military tribunals in Nuremberg and Tokyo.

While the basic purpose of these two courts of justice was to punish Axis leaders, further scrutiny reveals two other objectives: establishing civilization's justice as a norm of justice and establishing victors' justice as an exercise of power. The previously mentioned perspectives on the Tokyo Trial reflect these two objectives.

The following section will attempt to lay out the logic behind the above objectives. (Essentially there was no difference between the Nuremberg and Tokyo Trials because the Allies decided to maintain the unity of the two trials.)

The first objective—the establishment of civilization's justice as the norm of the trials—was to place legal restraints on aggressive wars, and to envision the rule of law as applying to international society. According to this view, war is not only morally evil but also a violation of international law. The Allies intended to make the norm of war deterrence more binding by establishing the precedent of censuring state leaders for starting wars of aggression. According to this logic, the Tokyo Trial was justified as a measure to make international society a safer place under the "norm of justice."

In retrospect, this idealistic logic is self-righteous and naively optimistic. At the time, however, this argument did not seem irrational. In fact, among the Allies the sense of mission and passion behind the creation of such a norm served as a moral backbone to it.

John Lewis Gaddis, an expert on the history of the Cold War, has said that people once trusted the idea of the United Nations and, albeit temporarily, the international legal procedures that back it up.[15] Had it not been for the

---

15. See John Lewis Gaddis, *We Now Know: Rethinking Cold War History* (Oxford: Clarendon Press, 1997).

contemporary intellectual climate, German existentialist Karl Jasper's optimistic declaration that "Nuremberg is, nevertheless, a herald—albeit still uncertain and somewhat weak—of the new world order" based on rule of law would have seemed little more than a misinterpretation of the events.

Hint of Change Seen after World War I

In the nineteenth century, a nation was not denied its sovereign right to wage external wars. Dominant in that period was a perception that war was an extralegal action not restricted by judgments of legality or illegality. This was the most convenient understanding of war in grasping the complicated interests among nations within the European balance of power.

For this reason, the legal regulation of war concentrated on the method of war, *jus in bello*, for example imposing restrictions on weapons and demanding the protection of prisoners of war and noncombatants. At the end of hostilities, probing into war crimes would cease and peaceful relations be restored among the belligerent nations. Such was the forward-looking wisdom intended to maintain stability in the international order.

Nevertheless, during World War I, the view of warfare was, albeit temporarily, on the verge of change. In discussions among leaders of the US, Britain, France, and Italy during the Paris Peace Conference, British prime minister David Lloyd-George and French premier Georges Benjamin Clemenceau insisted that former German emperor (Kaiser) Wilhelm II should be tried at an international court for initiating an "unjust war."

Behind this British and French argument was public opinion in both countries that fervently supported the hanging of the enemy leader. Both countries wanted to guarantee their own security by placing responsibility for the "evil" and "criminal" war on Germany. This was, in a way, a byproduct of the frequent and repeated placement of war responsibility on the enemy during the war and of the unexpectedly heavy casualties of an all-out war.

Clemenceau's Argument

President Woodrow Wilson opposed the British and French argument, asserting that there was no legal precedent for defining the initiation of war as a crime. Nicknamed "Le Tigre" (The Tiger), sharp-tongued Clemenceau, however, retorted, "Nothing is done without emotion." Seeking to defend the lack of legal precedent, he continued by referring abstractly to an imagined first imposition of justice: "The first tribunal must have been summary and brutal; it was, nevertheless, the beginning of a great thing."

The discussions became deadlocked. The following remark by Italian prime minister Vittorio Emanuele Orlando accurately describes the essence of the problem: "It is history that is taking place here; it is no longer law. If we consult the [legal] code, we shall have great difficulty in finding in it what we seek. If we speak only about international morality, it is different."[16]

To break the deadlock, President Wilson adopted the scheme proposed by Secretary of State Robert Lansing to come up with a compromise plan. Consequently, the matter was settled by Article 227 of the Treaty of Versailles, which stipulated that a special international tribunal would be constituted to try William II of Hohenzollern, formerly the German emperor, for a supreme offence against international morality and the sanctity of treaties.

However, it should be noted that this settlement was not directly linked to the post–World War II concept of crimes against peace. This particular article was a compromise scheme in the sense that the winners of World War I intentionally avoided the risk of innovating international laws and resorting to retroactive law and, instead, formed a political tribunal to try an obscure crime described as a violation of international morality.

And yet, because the Netherlands, where the former German emperor had sought asylum, refused to hand him over, the tribunal was not realized. When World War II broke out, the US learned a lesson from this failure, and took the initiative in criminalizing the initiation of aggressive war. This gave idealism a legal standing whilst simultaneously serving the realistic interests of the Allies in constructing a safe international order for themselves.

Make Them Pay for Their Errors

The second objective—establishing victors' justice as an exercise of power—was to to be achieved by determining in a court of justice that Japan and Germany were responsible for the war. For the Allies, this was much more important, realistically, than the objective of the norm of justice.

---

16. Arthur S. Link et al., eds., *The Papers of Woodrow Wilson* (New Jersey: Princeton University Press, 1987), vols. 56–57.

The benefit of this was, first of all, establishment of the legitimacy of the Allies.

If it could be established that the Pacific War resulted from Japan's invasion, and if Japan was subsequently sanctioned by the Allies, this would automatically endorse the justice and legitimacy of the victors. As diplomacy analyst Kiyosawa Kiyoshi has lucidly stated, in international relations it is impossible that one side is completely right and the other side is completely wrong. Still, in actual warfare, out of political and military necessity the countries involved mobilize all the symbols of war responsibility for their own respective benefit. These include national integration, unity among allies, and justification of the punishment of the enemy countries.

In the case of World War II, as well, the Allied Powers interpreted the conduct of the Axis countries in simplified fashion as "the outcome of deliberate planning" and criticized the latter's leaders, on that account. The establishment of international military tribunals was the culmination of this perception, and the trials were a political apparatus whose objective was to record the immoral acts of the Germans and Japanese, and prove the legitimacy of the Allied Powers.

The second benefit of establishing victors' justice was that it rendered Japan harmless. To establish a historical view that pinned war responsibility on Japan was a psychological demilitarization policy, and a psychological security policy, for the Allies.

For instance, Article 4e of JCS 1380/15, a directive issued to General Douglas MacArthur, Supreme Commander for the Allied Powers, at an early stage of the Occupation of Japan had this to say: "By appropriate means you will make clear to all levels of the Japanese population the fact of their defeat. They must be made to realize that their suffering and defeat have been brought upon them by the lawless and irresponsible aggression of Japan."[17] It stated that Japan could be converted into a peaceful nation which would cooperate with the victor nations by reeducating the Japanese people—that is, making them recognize that their war was a crime. Thus, the Tokyo Trial was given the power politics mission of presenting a "good vs. evil historical view" in an open court of justice.

---

17. Article 4e, JCS 1380/15, http://www.ndl.go.jp/constitution/e/shiryo/01/036/036tx.html.

The "Educational" Logic of Punishing One to Warn the Many

Some may wonder whether it was only the Class A war criminals who were tried at the Tokyo Trial. To be sure, the Tokyo Trial only tried the Japanese leaders, and the Japanese people were seen as their victims. Incidentally, it should be noted that the government of the People's Republic of China in Beijing, under the diplomatic judgment of premier Zhou Enlai, distinguished Japanese militarists from the Japanese people as early as the 1950s, and maintained an official fiction that it was the Japanese government at that time—not the Japanese people, who were its victims—that was responsible for the invasion of China.[18] This logic, which was similar to that of decisions of the Tokyo Trial, also made possible the normalization of Sino-Japanese diplomatic relations in 1972.

In short, it was deemed to be in the best interests of the Allies to separate postwar Japan from its prewar days, demarcate the Japanese people from their leaders, and refrain from blaming the people in order to pursue postwar policies toward Japan.

If the truth be told, however, the Allied Powers, through two international military tribunals, did not believe from the bottom of their hearts that the Japanese and German peoples were without responsibility. If the Allies punished both the German and Japanese peoples, however, it would make the people of these two countries in their entirety hostile toward the victors. Facing this dilemma, Secretary of War Henry Stimson, for the sake of convenience, adopted a complex method of penalizing only Japanese and German leaders—"extreme militarists"—in the respective international military tribunals. The tribunals were intended to make the peoples of the defeated countries indirectly realize their guilt. The Judge Advocate General (JAG) of the US Department of War was convinced in January 1946 that making the majority of Germans share responsibility for the Nazi regime and the war would make them remorseful, and this would block a resurrection of Nazism.

This was tantamount to the educational logic of punishing one to warn the many. Using international military tribunals in Nuremberg and Tokyo as a catalyst for democratization, the Allied Powers schemed to defang Japan and Germany.

---

18. See Mōri, *Nit-Chū kankei*.

Link to Connect the Two Logics

What, then, is the link that can connect these two apparently contradictory logics of civilization's justice and victors' justice?

After studying numerous primary sources, I have come to argue that the junction between the two is security, and that the Tokyo Trial was a security policy in international politics for both Japan and the Allies.

For instance, consider the memorandum by the secretaries of the US Departments of War, State, and Justice addressed to President Franklin Roosevelt on January 22, 1945. This memorandum states that, although brutal actions by the Nazis in prewar days were, strictly speaking, not war crimes or violations of existing international laws, the Nazis nevertheless had to be tried and punished for such conduct for the sake of "the demands of justice," "the interests of postwar security," and "a necessary rehabilitation of the German people."[19]

While the document only raised the issue of crimes against humanity, a more comprehensive study of other documents shows that punishment of the Nazis' invasions and atrocities was aimed not only at ordinary retribution but also at reconstruction of the German state during the Occupation, as well as security in the postwar international order. And, as will be discussed in chapter two, these policies toward Germany were also applied to Japan.

Seen from these angles, the Tokyo Trial was clearly part of international politics. Needless to say, the security of the United States and other Allied Powers could not be guaranteed by the Tokyo Trial alone. Their policy was to make use of the international tribunals in Germany and Japan as symbols of the consequences of war crimes, in order to render Germany and Japan harmless by affecting the psychology of the defeated nations. And this policy appeared to be effective in stabilizing the postwar international order.

Taking the Tokyo Trial as a tool of international politics, the ensuing chapters will examine the concrete processes it entailed.

---

19. See Higurashi, *Tōkyō Saiban no kokusai kankei*, and US Department of State, *Foreign Relations of the United States* [*FRUS*]: *Diplomatic Papers, The Conference at Malta and Yalta: 1945*, ed. Bryton Barron, William M. Franklin, and G. Bernard Noble (Washington, DC: Government Printing Office, 1955).

CHAPTER 2

How the Framework of the Tokyo Trial Was Formed

Defendants in the dock at
the Nuremberg trials
(United States Holocaust
Memorial Museum, courtesy
of John W. Mosenthal)

1. Lessons Learned from the Failure of the Treaty of Versailles

In the Atlantic Charter

Klemens Metternich, an Austrian foreign minister in the nineteenth century, was wise enough to incorporate France into the Congress of Vienna, which devised the settlement of Europe after the Napoleonic Wars.

In contrast, following World War I, the Treaty of Versailles, inflicted harsh humiliation upon Germany. And yet, it did not render Germany entirely harmless. This is why some characterize the Treaty of Versailles as pernicious, while others find it to be a halfway measure. In any event, this inconsistent treatment of the defeated Germany eventually invited the rise of the Nazis, eroding the peace settlement of the Treaty of Versailles.

The well-known Fourteen Points proposed by President Woodrow Wilson on January 8, 1918, clearly stated that the German political system would not be changed. After World War II, however, it was believed that victors should occupy the defeated nations and render them harmless and peaceful before letting them return to the international system—a lesson learned from the failure of the Treaty of Versailles. The Potsdam Declaration that Japan accepted on August 14, 1945, was a manifestation of this line of thinking.

Why then was the Tokyo Trial convened, and why was it deemed necessary to punish the Japanese leaders as war criminals? The reasons are that policies toward Germany were applied to Japan, and that Japan surrendered after accepting Article 10 of the Potsdam Declaration. Article 10 clearly stated that "stern justice shall be meted out to all war criminals, including those who have visited cruelties upon our prisoners."

The common philosophy of the international military tribunals in both Nuremberg and Tokyo can be found in the Atlantic Charter announced by US president Franklin Roosevelt and British prime minister Winston Churchill on August 14, 1941. This charter was permeated by a simple, clear view of the justice of the Allied countries versus the evils of the Axis countries. To construct the postwar international order, the Atlantic Charter proposed the practical goal of the "final destruction of Nazi tyranny," and took the stance that Germany's demilitarization was equivalent to the country's rehabilitation.

The Pacific War erupted on December 8 (Japan time), 1941, only a few months after the announcement of the Atlantic Charter. In early January 1942, twenty-six countries (the US, Britain, China, the Soviet Union, and twenty-two others) issued the Declaration by the Allied Nations, reconfirming the principles in the charter.

Roosevelt proposed calling those anti-Axis countries "the United Nations," and thus the principles of the Atlantic Charter came to be applied to Japan, too.

Announcement on War Criminal Punishment without Concrete Measures

Because Churchill announced on October 25, 1941, that punishment of the Nazis' crimes should be included in the Allies' war objectives, the punishment of war criminals, including leaders of the Axis countries, became a policy issue for the Allied Powers.

In order to boost the morale of their soldiers, leaders of the Allied nations repeatedly stated that Nazi war criminals would be punished. This fueled collective zeal for retaliation. One should remember that the term "war criminals" at that time meant almost exclusively "those responsible for atrocities."

The horror amongst people of the Allied countries at atrocities committed by the Nazis turned to impassioned support for the war effort. This widespread fury deprived their governments of a free hand, and drove the Allied countries to punish war criminals accordingly.

Nevertheless, it took some time before concrete punishments were decided.

Even at the time of the Moscow Declaration, announced on November 1, 1943, in which the US, Britain, and the Soviet Union decided to punish war criminals by joint decision by the governments of the Allies, the procedures for implementing such punishment remained unclear. The Allies reached no agreement on what kinds of conduct should be punished or whether Axis leaders should be tried at an international court of justice—or even whether the format of a court of justice should be employed in the first place.

In addition, the Allies were seriously concerned that their nationals who were held as prisoners of war might receive retaliatory mistreatment from Germany and Japan. Therefore they decided that war criminals in World War II would be punished after the termination of hostilities. The US did not immediately apply the Moscow Declaration to Japan; it feared retaliation by the Japanese military because the death rate of prisoners of war was already higher in Japan than in Germany.

Stimson, Founding Father of the Nuremberg Trial

A policy debate within the US government from August through September 1944 put an end to this ambiguous situation. While Secretary of the Treasury Henry Morgenthau, Jr., insisted on the summary execution of the Nazi leaders as a part of the thorough neutralization of Germany, Secretary of War Henry Stimson advocated punishment through "civilized trials."

The power struggle between the two secretaries aggravated the situation, and the two departments fought fiercely. When American newspapers launched a ferocious attack on Morgenthau's policy, President Roosevelt felt that he had no other recourse than to support Stimson. Consequently, US government leaders reached an agreement to try Nazi leaders in a court of justice.

Whether it took the form of judgment by a court of justice or summary execution, the fundamental purpose was to punish the Nazi leaders. But Stimson dismissed retaliation and summary execution as uncivilized conduct on a par with the Nazis, and stressed instead the virtues of trials at a court of justice that guaranteed legal and moral legitimacy. This was the advantage of establishing an international military tribunal.

First, a trial in a court based on law and justice was a measure to suppress the hysterical advocacy of retaliation among the Allied countries and to protect US moral leadership in the postwar world. For Stimson, a trial of war criminals was at the opposite end of the spectrum from retaliation. As a result of his legalistic approach, he was convinced that countries' ambitions could be curbed via legal regulations.

It had its precedents. When the Japanese Kwantung Army advanced into

Right: Henry Morgenthau
Left: Henry Stimson
(Harris & Ewing collection, Prints & Photographs Division, Library of Congress)

northern Manchuria at the time of the Manchurian Incident, the US attitude toward Japan hardened. Stimson, who was US secretary of state at that time, announced the so-called Stimson Doctrine on January 7, 1932. The doctrine endorsed the international policy toward China—commonly known as the "open door policy"—and stressed non-recognition of conditions in violation of the Nine-Power Treaty and the Kellogg–Briand Pact (or Pact of Paris, officially known as the General Treaty for Renunciation of War as an Instrument of National Policy). During a trans-Atlantic phone call, which was extremely rare in those days, Stimson persuaded British foreign secretary John Allsebrook Simon to agree to posit Japan as a violator of the Nine-Power Treaty.[1]

History and Record

Second, quite aside from trying the crimes of individual defendants, the Nuremberg Trial had the special mission of reviewing the history of the war, and establishing a permanent record of the Nazis' war responsibility.

Hartley William Shawcross, British attorney general and the British chief prosecutor at the Nuremberg Trial, stated that the trial would provide an authoritative and impartial record of the war, in which historians in the

---

1. See John K. Emmerson, *The Japanese Thread: A Life in the U.S. Foreign Service* (New York: Holt, Rinehart and Winston, 1978).

Right: John McCloy
Left: Hartley William Shawcross
(Kyodo News)

future would seek the truth, and politicians in the future would seek lessons.[2] Even John Maynard Keynes, the British economist famous for his aversion to lawyers, agreed with Stimson during a conversation in November 1944 that it would be critically important to create a record of "extreme evils," and that this could not be accomplished if the Nazi leaders were summarily executed.

This policy of recording history had important political implications.

Stimson anticipated that the disclosure of the viciousness of the Nazis would have an educational effect on the world and on the peoples of the defeated countries, deterring future aggression and thus contributing to the stability of the international order. John J. McCloy, Stimson's right-hand man who, as assistant secretary of war, was in charge of handling war criminals, went so far as to declare that an international military tribunal would be more important for postwar security than the United Nations. According to Jackson Maogoto, when the Soviet Union and France agreed with the American proposal to form an international tribunal, they saw particular advantages in such trials as a means "to record history, educate the world, and serve as a future deterrent."[3]

---

2. See Martha Minow, *Between Vengeance and Forgiveness: Facing History After Genocide and Mass Violence* (Boston: Beacon Press, 1998).

3. See Jackson Maogoto, *War Crimes and Realpolitik: International Justice from World War I to the 21st Century* (London: Lynne Rienner Publishers, 2004).

Furthermore, recording the evils of the Axis countries would help prove the righteousness and legitimacy of the Allied countries. Thus, an international military tribunal was an alternative to the derogatory Article 231 of the Treaty of Versailles, the so-called "war guilt clause" that attributed the eruption of World War I to the "aggression of Germany and her allies," and which infuriated the Germans.

Because establishment of the victor's righteousness and the enemy's war responsibility becomes a source of energy in a major war, it is essentially a political act. Therefore it was desirable to open an international court of justice, underlining the fact that it was a punishment by the Allied Powers as a whole. That was also why the Allies chose the format of a military tribunal, which was fast and flexible in terms of legal procedures.

From the London Agreement to the Nuremberg Trial

At this point, the US Department of War carried out concrete studies on the methods for holding a court of justice and on related legal issues. The Department of War decided on a scheme to try the Nazis' atrocities and war of aggression in an international tribunal, using the criminal concept of "conspiracy," integral to Anglo-American law (see section 1 of chapter 3 for details).

During this process, the interpretation of the Kellogg–Briand Pact of 1928 was also modified. While that pact prohibited wars of aggression in general, it left the exercise of the right of self-defense to the discretion of the countries concerned. It did not include sanctioning measures against violators of the treaty. In other words, while the pact ensured the "outlawry of war," it failed to criminalize it, thereby making it possible to penalize individuals for starting a war.

Stimson and his associates redefined the pact, which represented the policies of the Republican Party in the 1920s, and insisted that any country that violated the pact would be deprived of its rights under international law and penalized for the crime of committing a war of aggression. They were optimistic about the chance of realizing America's long-sought wish for the "criminalization of wars of aggression" when it seemed almost certain that the Allies would win the war. While the question of treatment of war criminals had previously focused on punishment of the Nazis for atrocities, the US

Department of War shifted the focus of the investigation to responsibility for starting a war of aggression.

There were conflicting views on the criminalization of initiating a war even within the US government. The JAG of the US Department of War argued that the Kellogg-Briand Pact had not criminalized wars of aggression, and that there was no international law prohibiting conspiracy to rule the world. When Americans learned of the Malmédy massacre, however, things changed. This was an incident in which eighty-four American prisoners of war were killed by their German captors near Malmédy, Belgium, on December 17, 1944, during the Battle of the Bulge. News of this massacre enraged the American public, and American policy united along the lines of the argument of the Department of War.

Harry S. Truman, who became US president after the sudden death of President Roosevelt on April 12, 1945, consistently supported Stimson's position. Victory in Europe Day (V-E Day), May 8, 1945, commemorated the one-sided victory of the Allies in the war in Europe. Taking advantage of this situation, Stimson and his associates rushed to reform international law, paying no heed to the long-term implications.

An agreement was reached between the US, Britain, France, and the Soviet Union on the basis of what the American proposed. This culminated in the signing on August 8, 1945, of the London Agreement (the Charter of the International Military Tribunal was attached to the Agreement) for the trial of the major war criminals of the European Axis countries.

After the indictments were served in Berlin on October 18, 1945, five months after the German surrender, the International Military Tribunal (the Nuremberg Trial) was opened on November 20 by the US, Britain, France, and the Soviet Union in the US-occupied territory of Nuremberg. Twenty-four individuals (twenty-two at the time of sentencing) and six organizations were indicted. On October 1, 1946, nineteen defendants were found guilty (thirteen received the death penalty, three received life imprisonment, and four received fixed-term imprisonment), and three individuals were acquitted. Three organizations—the leadership of the Nazi party, the Schutzstaffel (SS), and the Gestapo (State Secret Police)—were judged to be criminal organizations. Indictments against remaining organizations—that is, the Sturmabteilung (SA), the Reich Cabinet, and the General Staff and

High Command of the Oberkommando der Wehrmacht (OKW) (Supreme Command of the Armed Forces)—were dropped.

Article 10 of the Potsdam Declaration

From a longer-term perspective, the US clearly did not refrain from implementing an ideological Far East policy. The US paid no heed to the realistic interests of prewar Japan, as American diplomat George F. Kennan pointed out in 1950. And this policy hurt Japanese sentiment, inviting the rise of "extreme militarists" in Japan.[4] The US confronted Japan, and after winning the war, it eliminated those extreme militarists through Occupation policies, particularly the Tokyo Trial. It is only natural that the US has been criticized for its actions—which could be likened to stirring up trouble in order to get credit for providing the solution. Nevertheless, it would be fruitless to endlessly seek causes of the problem and find fault with them.

From a shorter-term perspective, Japan had been denounced in conjunction with the Nine-Power Treaty and the Kellogg-Briand Pact since the Stimson Doctrine of 1932. When Japan and the US clashed head-on in December 1941, therefore, it was almost inevitable that the American policy of punishing German war criminals would be applied to Japan as well.

On July 26, 1945, the US, Britain, and China issued the Potsdam Declaration (drafted by the US) calling for Japan's surrender. Article 10 of the declaration stipulated that "stern justice shall be meted out to all war criminals, including those who have visited cruelties upon our prisoners" as one term of surrender.

Prior to this, President Roosevelt had implied punishment of Japanese war criminals in his statements in August 1942 and March 1944. There also was the US-Britain-China Cairo Declaration on November 27, 1943, which announced that these three countries "are fighting this war to restrain and punish the aggression of Japan." Neither Roosevelt's statements nor the Cairo Declaration, however, contained real substance. It was only in the Potsdam Declaration that the Allies presented to Japan for the first time a concrete policy regarding punishment of war criminals.

---

4. See George Kennan, *American Diplomacy, 1900–1950* (Chicago: University of Chicago Press, 1951).

On January 19, 1946, the International Military Tribunal for the Far East was established by a special proclamation of General Douglas MacArthur, Supreme Commander for the Allied Powers. MacArthur's proclamation was equivalent to the London Agreement that created the Nuremberg Tribunal. The jurisdiction of this tribunal was derived from Japan's acceptance of the Potsdam Declaration.

On this particular point, Charles L. Kades, deputy chief of the Government Section (GS) of GHQ, testified later that no one in his section thought the legal legitimacy for reforms in Japan, including amendment of its constitution, was derived from a "contract" (meaning the signing of the Potsdam Declaration), because acceptance of the Potsdam Declaration was tantamount to Japan's unconditional surrender.[5]

Reservation of Possibility

But the US Department of State's analysis was completely different.

The State Department held that Japan's acceptance of the Potsdam Declaration established a contractual relationship between Japan and the Allies based on international law. As a corollary, the State Department insisted on a revision of the policy of unconditional surrender, which had been the fundamental principle of the Allies since President Roosevelt's announcement at the time of the Casablanca Conference in January 1943. Unconditional surrender would give the victors considerable discretion, unbound by contractual elements. In brief, it would be more convenient for the postwar occupation as a whole to obtain an unconditional surrender. As far as trying war criminals was concerned, however, it would be more advantageous to use an agreement between the victor and the defeated as legal grounds, which would serve to block objections to the opening of the trial.

One source of complication here was the substance of the "agreement" between the victors and the defeated. Did "all war criminals" in the Potsdam Declaration refer only to those who were responsible for violating the traditional laws of war, or did it also cover state leaders who were responsible for starting war? Defense counsels at the Tokyo Trial took the former interpretation and argued that the court did not have jurisdiction over crimes against

---

5. See Takemae Eiji, *GHQ no hitobito* [People of GHQ] (Tokyo: Akashi Shoten, 2002).

peace. According to a primary source dated August 1945, however, the US government adopted a wider definition of war criminals in Article 10 of the Potsdam Declaration, reserving the option of punishing, through trial, those who were responsible for starting the war.

I take the view that it was Assistant Secretary of War John McCloy who adjusted the wording of Article 10. In my judgment, even before the signing of the Charter of the International Military Tribunal ("Nuremberg Charter," henceforth), McCloy deliberately used ambiguous wording in the article, following the example of the definition of war criminal adopted by JCS 1067 (US Joint Chiefs of Staff Directive to General Dwight D. Eisenhower on Military Rule of Germany dated May 11, 1945), which McCloy himself had drawn up. This directive defined war criminals as "all persons who have participated in planning or carrying out Nazi enterprises involving or resulting in atrocities or war crimes." In this way, the US held in reserve the possibility of punishing Japan's leaders for their war of aggression.

It must have been the intention of the drafter of the Potsdam Declaration to include "those who are responsible for atrocities" in its definition of "all war criminals," including those who are responsible for aggressive warfare.

Thus, when the Japanese government accepted the Potsdam Declaration on August 14, 1945, and subsequently on September 2 confirmed its intention by the Japanese Instrument of Surrender—equivalent to an armistice but so called because it declared Japan's "unconditional surrender"—the international agreement and legal grounds for opening a tribunal to try Japanese war crimes were officially established.

2. US Initiative vs. Cooperation among the Allies

US Basic Policy toward Japan

Application of the same basic policies to Japan as those applied to Germany presented two major problems: that of differences in mode of occupation, and that of differences in domestic situation. As such, one would assume that discussion of these problems would be a prerequisite to deciding whether the exact same policies should be applied to Japan or not. With this in mind, how then was the basic policy of punishment of Japanese war criminals decided?

The Subcommittee for the Far East (SFE), a subordinate agency of the State-War-Navy Coordinating Committee (SWNCC), which decided US Occupation policies, was in charge of drafting policies toward Japan. The SFE launched a full-scale study on the handling of Japanese war criminals close to the time that the Potsdam Declaration was issued.

The major point of contention was whether or not to open an international tribunal on aggressive war against Japan. Some at the US Department of State argued that it would be wiser to punish enemy leaders for their highly political behavior. Nevertheless, the stance of the Department of War took precedence and, consequently, the policies applied to Japan laid out in the SFE 106 report of August 9 were a routine application of those applied to Germany. There were only two differences:

(1) Prosecution of conspiracy was backdated to immediately before the Manchurian Incident; and
(2) It was found pointless to accuse Japan of crimes against humanity because, unlike Germany, there was no organized persecution.

However, at the SFE meeting of August 13 where the definitions of war criminals to be prosecuted were disputed, it was agreed that the categories of war crimes should include those responsible for crimes against peace as well as crimes against humanity. The memorandum of SWNCC 57/1 included this agreement, and was submitted to the SWNCC on August 24, 1945. First, the memorandum aimed to encourage the Occupation forces to arrest suspected Japanese war crimes suspects immediately in order to prevent them from suicide and consequently a form of martyrdom. Second, the memorandum called for the opening of a court of justice on the basis of an international agreement; each country concerned was encouraged to send a chief prosecutor. Third, the authority to approve and modify court decisions was given to General MacArthur by international agreement. In a nutshell, the premise for punishment of Japanese war criminals was the establishment of an agreement among the Allied Powers.

United Nations War Crimes Commission's Policy toward Japan

Colonel R. Ammi Cutter, assistant to Assistant Secretary of War John

McCloy, reported the Japan policy of the United Nations War Crimes Commission (UNWCC) to Washington, DC.

The UNWCC was an international organization established in London by the Allies on October 20, 1943—during a period of intensified rage against the Nazis—to find and prosecute war criminals. Representatives of Australia, Belgium, Canada, China, Czechoslovakia, the French Committee of National Liberation, Greece, India, Luxembourg, the Netherlands, New Zealand, Norway, Poland, South Africa, the United Kingdom, the United States, and Yugoslavia participated in the UNWCC. The Soviet Union did not participate.

The UNWCC's mission was to investigate evidence of war crimes and compile a list of war crimes suspects. It was not endowed with the authority to carry out prosecutions or trials, nor was it entrusted with decision-making power to restrict the governments of the countries concerned. Nonetheless, the UNWCC swiftly took on a life of its own and began to intervene in policy issues.

When the Potsdam Declaration was issued, Lord Wright of Durley, Australian chairman of the UNWCC, stressed that there should be a policy proposal on Japanese war criminals. Subsequently, the UNWCC set up the Special Far Eastern and Pacific Committee consisting of nine countries (the US, Britain, China, France, the Netherlands, Canada, Australia, New Zealand, and India), and adopted the Special Committee's recommendations on August 29.

These recommendations on policy toward Japan, which were based on a draft prepared by V. K. Wellington Koo, chairman of the Special Committee and ambassador of China to Great Britain, basically adopted the policies applied toward Germany. But because Lieutenant Colonel Joseph V. Hodgson, US representative on the UNWCC and concurrently ambassador to Britain, demanded postponement and revision of some of the recommendations so as not to affect US policy decisions, there remained room for divergence from the policies that had been applied to Germany. The recommendations can be summarized as follows:

(1) The suspected leaders of major war crimes are to be tried at an international tribunal in charge of war crimes, crimes against peace, crimes against humanity, and conspiracy.

(2) Japan's criminal planning should be investigated. This was tantamount to adopting the US demand to punish conspiracy.

(3) A prosecutors' structure should be established. The original proposal by Wellington Koo suggested that member countries of the Special Far Eastern and Pacific Committee and the Soviet Union (which did not join the UNWCC) should appoint their respective chief prosecutors, following the pattern of the Nuremberg Trial. This particular portion of the recommendation was deleted due to objections from Hodgson.

(4) While it remained uncertain whether the organizer of the international tribunal would be the Supreme Commander for the Allied Powers, the Control Council, or another organization, justices of the tribunal would be recommended by the above ten countries first before being appointed. Although Wellington Koo's original proposal included detailed prescriptions on this point, they were all deleted by Hodgson, who was attempting to give the Supreme Commander for the Allied Powers, an American, the discretionary power to appoint justices.

The summary recommendations on policy concerning the Japanese war crimes and atrocity were publicly announced shortly thereafter. Reviewing those recommendations, the Japanese government sensed that Japanese war criminals would be treated similarly to German war criminals.

Argument for the US Initiative vs. Argument for Cooperation among the Allies

The UNWCC recommendations for dealing with Japan that Cutter reported to the US government were not final; they took the form rather of a draft proposal of the Special Far Eastern and Pacific Committee issued on August 13. Along the lines of Wellington Koo's original plan, it stipulated that each participating country would appoint respective chief justices and that the international tribunal would be established by international agreement.

The basic US stance was that the tribunal of national leaders of Germany and Japan, which had significant political importance, had to be uniform. It became controversial, however, when both SWNCC 57/1 and the draft proposal of the UNWCC proposed to apply "equality among the Allied countries" even to the tribunal of Japanese war criminals.

The options available to the US at that time were twofold:

(1) To control the court and the prosecutors' organization under US initiative, or
(2) To promote cooperation among the Allied countries by guaranteeing equality among them, as in the case of the Nuremberg Trial.

Let us call the former an "argument for US initiative," and the latter "argument for cooperation among the Allies." The demarcation was not only about the organizer of the court and the prosecutors' organization but also about the composition of the tribunal—that is, whether it was to be a de facto American tribunal or a tribunal jointly organized by the Allies in which governments other than the US could play substantial roles. And the choice between these two would have a bearing on the nature of the Tokyo Trial.

Because it was not firmly established that promotion of cooperation among the Allies would be pursued, the aforementioned SWNCC 57/1 was delivered on August 28 to the SFE, where a sharp confrontation of views emerged. One side insisted that by giving MacArthur the authority to establish a court and an organized prosecution, international negotiations such as those that preceded the Nuremberg Trial could be avoided and MacArthur's authority strengthened. The other camp argued that cooperation among the Allies would enhance the authority of the tribunal, and the US would end up bearing less responsibility.

The point of contention was whether to prioritize an agreement among the Allies or not. In other words, the argument for US initiative conflicted with the promotion of cooperation among the Allies.

Byproduct of Experiences in International Negotiations

It was against this backdrop that Assistant Secretary of War McCloy on September 7 criticized the emphasis that the State Department members of the SFE gave to having each country directly appoint its own justice. He predicted that it would make the tribunal in Japan "difficult to handle" and, instead, stressed the merit of the US initiative as advocated by SFE members from the

US Army and Navy. Hence within the SFE, there was conflict between State Department members who argued for cooperation among the Allies, and the US Army and Navy members who argued for US initiative.

In sum, the War Department's argument was that the US had been "almost entirely responsible" for the Allied Powers' victory over Japan, and therefroe the US should take the leading position in the war crime issue. It was only the US that had been the target of Japan's "dishonest attack on Pearl Harbor," and the US had suffered much more serious damage from Japanese war crimes than from German war crimes. Therefore, the War Department argued, the Supreme Commander for the Allied Powers should assume direct charge of all war crime–related activities, taking full advantage of MacArthur's overall leadership of the Occupation.

To be sure, it is often true that the country contributing most to a victory takes the initiative in postwar occupation and the reconstruction of order. Having been made aware of its own supremacy in the Pacific at the Yalta Conference, the US believed it was only natural for it to assume leadership. Nevertheless, this was not the only reason behind the argument for the US initiative.

In fact, the view of Justice Robert H. Jackson of the US Supreme Court, who was the chief US prosecutor at the Nuremberg Trial, was highly influential in this regard. Based on his experience in negotiations with Britain, France, and the Soviet Union at the time of the London Conference (June–August 1945), Jackson communicated to President Harry Truman and Undersecretary of State Dean G. Acheson how difficult it was for him to handle the Soviet Union, and advised that the court and prosecution for the trial of Japanese war criminals should be promptly established under US initiative. In other words, the argument for the US initiative was a byproduct of the US experience of international negotiations at the London Conference.

SWNCC 57/3

In the end, the argument for cooperation among the Allies lost steam. This was because none other than Undersecretary Acheson argued for the US initiative within the State Department, the last bastion of the argument for such collaboration. The SWNCC approved SWNCC 57/3, the policy memorandum produced by the SFE, on October 2. Their final version was dated October 3. Thus was decided the basic US policy structure toward the trials of Japanese war crimes.

SWNCC 57/3 consisted of two documents: (1) Policy of the United States in Regard to the Apprehension and Punishment of War Criminals in the Far East (henceforth "Policy"), sent on October 18 to all the signatories of the Japanese Instrument of Surrender); and (2) Joint Chiefs of Staff's Directive on the Identification, Apprehension and Trial of Persons Suspected of War Crimes (henceforth "Directive"), submitted to MacArthur on October 6 as JCS 1512. The Directive was comprehensive, covering not only the trials of Class A war crimes trials, but also the trials of Class B and C war crimes trials in each participating country.

The jurisdictions of the Tokyo Trial were, like its predecessor in Nuremberg, crimes against peace, ordinary war crimes, and crimes against humanity. The range of prosecution included the Manchurian Incident, and it was clearly stated that the Tokyo Trial would highlight developments since the Second Sino-Japanese War.

More importantly, MacArthur was given the following broad responsibilities and powers:

(1) Authority to appoint special international military courts;
(2) Authority to prescribe and approve rules of procedure;
(3) Authority to establish a prosecutors' organization and appoint prosecutors from the Allied nations involved; and
(4) Responsibility for carrying out the judgments of international courts, as well as for approving, reducing, or otherwise altering any sentence, but not for increasing the severity thereof.

As for the handling of the emperor of Japan, Article 17 of the Directive only instructed that no action be taken against him as a war criminal, pending receipt of a special directive concerning his treatment.

In sum, it can be said that the argument for the US initiative was clearly reflected in SWNCC 57/3 in the following ways.

First, with this SWNCC 57/3, the influence of the US at the Tokyo Trial became much stronger than at the Nuremberg Trial.

Second, it is noteworthy that the SWNCC 57/3 did not grant MacArthur the right to intervene in the trial. While this might have been the result of respect for the independence of a court of justice, it produced the unexpected outcome that the Tokyo Trial became an independent authority, and had a life of its own beyond the subjective intention of the US.

Third, MacArthur's authority did not necessarily give him carte blanche. In fact, SWNCC 57/3 gave authority to the US government rather than to MacArthur, and restricted MacArthur. Even if MacArthur had hoped for a tribunal by the US alone, SWNCC 57/3 would not have allowed it.

MacArthur's Attitude

Let us examine MacArthur's attitude toward the Tokyo Trial. In the eyes of the Japanese at that time, the approaches of the Tokyo Trial and MacArthur might have seemed to overlap. Actually, however, MacArthur had been skeptical about an international tribunal.

Indeed, in his October 7, 1945, telegram, MacArthur threatened the Department of War saying that if the SWNCC 57/3 were made public he might have to resort to direct military governance of Japan, which would seriously undermine the Japanese government. Instead, MacArthur strongly requested the authority himself to try Tōjō Hideki.

MacArthur also enthusiastically promoted the idea of a trial conducted by the US alone in conversation with Assistant Secretary of War McCloy when the latter visited Japan. On October 31, MacArthur again proposed to the Department of War that members of the Tōjō Hideki Cabinet be promptly tried by an American court for the illegal killing of non-combatant civilians (first-degree murder) during the attack on Pearl Harbor. This argument was not a MacArthur original. It was borrowed from a proposal of the JAG of the Department of War; that is, it was a scheme to try Japan for dishonestly initiating a war with the US in violation of the third convention relative to the opening of hostilities of the Second Hague Conference in 1907. Both MacArthur and the JAG strongly opposed the criminalization of war.

In order to accomplish the successful occupation of Japan, MacArthur preferred to complete the punishment of war criminals as moderately and promptly as possible. No matter how hard the US tried to cultivate democracy in the Japanese people, it would nullify that effort and adversely affect other Occupation policies if it opened an "international" court of justice based on something that could later be denounced as retroactive law. Major General Charles A. Willoughby, head of General Douglas MacArthur's General Staff 2 (G-2, intelligence), stated that his superior opposed the Tokyo Trial because he had been keenly aware of the resentment that remained deeply rooted in the people of the Confederate states after the Civil War.

Having great self-esteem and an inclination to show off, MacArthur resented the fact that the Japanese had attacked Pearl Harbor without a declaration of war and he took it as his duty to punish those who were responsible. To MacArthur, it was important to try the suspects more promptly and, legally speaking, more safely under his direction as in the trial of General Yamashita Tomoyuki by an American military court.

It was utterly unthinkable, however, for McCloy, Stimson's right-hand man, to concur with such a view, and the US government persisted with the plan to hold an international military tribunal as proposed by the SWNCC 57/3.

3. The Decision Not to Charge the Emperor and the Motives of Concerned Countries

Views on the British Argument for Summary Execution

The British government panicked on learning that the US government had determined a basic policy toward Japan. Its hands full with issues related to the trials of German war criminals, it had failed to make any preparation for the trials of Japanese war criminals.

Belatedly, the British government convened a conference on October 16, 1945, for all of the relevant departments and bureaus as well as representatives of the British Commonwealth to discuss the handling of Japanese war criminals. The British government was determined to effect an early settlement of the Class B and C war crime trials. This is clear from the goal set forth by the conference, namely to "complete the trial of at least 500 Japanese minor war criminals by July 31, 1946." As for Class A war criminals, the conference merely agreed to prepare a list of war crimes suspects. Actually, this clearly indicated Britain's stance toward the Class A war crime trials: the

Foreign Office was unenthusiastic about holding an international tribunal to try the Japanese leaders.

From September 1944 under the Churchill wartime cabinet, the British government had strongly argued to the US and the Soviet Union the case for the immediate execution of the Nazi leaders, and had opposed an international tribunal. According to the British argument, an international tribunal would be a prolonged process, invoking legal debates and historical arguments, which would present the Nazis with an opportunity to propagate their views. The punishment of the Nazi leaders was a political issue that should be decided by the governments of the Allied Powers, and so a small number of major Nazi war criminals should be executed immediately to settle the matter, while the traditional war criminals should be dealt with by each country concerned.

This was the British argument for summary execution, but to the other Allied countries it seemed too pre-modern and barbaric. The British government was anyway convinced that by doing this, peace would be restored more rapidly, and resentments would have less chance to fester. The British government was fundamentally at odds with the argument for summary execution by Treasury Secretary Henry Morgenthau, who had aimed for the complete incapacitation of Germany. Incidentally, George Kennan's argument that summary execution by firing squad would have been more fitting for the war criminals drew on the same logic as the British argument.

How Far Do We Go along with the United States?

However, Britain itself changed its position in May 1945; it agreed to an international tribunal on the Nazi leaders. This did not necessarily mean that it also agreed to an international tribunal on the Japanese leaders. Despite a regime change which brought in a Labour Party cabinet under Clement Richard Attlee, there was little change to Britain's basic stance toward the war crime issue.

According to an October 1945 memorandum written by Robert David J. Scott-Fox of the British Foreign Office's War Crime Affairs Bureau, Britain did not want to follow the US lead blindly. While it was unthinkable at that stage to bring up the argument for summary execution again, the British government was afraid that handling the Japanese war criminals would be much more cumbersome than the German case because Japan was more geographically remote, and because more countries were involved. Given these considerations, the Foreign Office came up with the idea of trying Class A Japanese war criminals separately in different Allied countries.

Nevertheless, at this late stage it was already unthinkable that the US would agree to the idea. Besides, given its diminished national strength in the immediate postwar days, it was not likely that Britain could force an important change on the US. Therefore, the British Foreign Office faced the issue of how far it would go along with the US. They agreed with the SWNCC 57/3 in principle, while attempting to "place the burden of work on the Americans."

Even within the British government, however, the Dominions Office strongly argued for Britain's active involvement in the international tribunal on Japanese war crimes. Australia and New Zealand, two of Britain's Dominions, put pressure on the Dominions Office.

Australian Argument for Prosecution of the Emperor

Australia was most enthusiastic about punishing Japan's war crimes.

Australia harbored a strong intention to raise its international position and influence in the postwar world. Herbert Vere Evatt, who was minister for external affairs and attorney general of the Labor government under Joseph Benedict Chifley, insisted that, because Australia had made tremendous contributions to victory over Japan, it was entitled to become a major actor in all Pacific affairs. Australia was not merely being practical. In fact, Australia's "life and fate" hinged on the Pacific.

Because Australia, an isolated continent in the South Pacific, had been obsessed with a deep fear of Japan since the Russo-Japanese War, it hoped to guarantee its security by thoroughly neutralizing Japan. Australia worried that merely imposing superficial reforms through the Occupation would not eliminate the possibility of Japan's militarism reviving in the future.

This was the background to Australia's enthusiasm for punishing Japanese war criminals. External Affairs Minister Evatt announced on September 10, 1945, that it was the duty of Australia to eliminate all Japanese war criminals. Symbolic of the Australian proposals was the prosecution of the emperor of Japan.

The Australian government had already been told by the British government on August 17 that, from the standpoint of lowering the cost of the Occupation, it would be a serious political mistake to prosecute the emperor of Japan as a war criminal. British foreign secretary Ernest Bevin in Clement Attlee's Labour cabinet had stated on July 29, during the Potsdam Conference, that it would be meaningless to destroy the emperor, because he was "the instrument with which one might have to deal in order to control Japan effectively." Recalling the First World War, Bevin commented,

> It might have been far better for all of us not to have destroyed the institution of the kaiser after the last war; we might not have had this [war] if we hadn't done so. It might have been far better to have guided the Germans to a constitutional monarchy rather than leaving them without a symbol, thus opening the psychological doors to a man like Hitler.[6]

But Australia would have none of this type of analysis. Even the Australians had agreed that the Japanese people themselves should decide the future of the emperor system, provided that the political culture of the Japanese was fundamentally altered.

But the people and government of Australia were convinced that the Japanese would never change as long as the Shōwa emperor remained untouched. He must therefore be found guilty, in order to completely destroy the old regime. In short, prosecution of the emperor was a realistic security policy for Australia.

Australia was also worried that MacArthur might take an indulgent attitude toward the Japanese people. The SWNCC 57/3 aimed at granting MacArthur greater power, and so naturally the Australian government could not remain indifferent to that possibility. When the Far Eastern Advisory Commission (FEAC) was founded on October 30, 1945, for governments to discuss the policies for the occupation of Japan, the Australian delegation appealed to the British delegation insisting that the FEAC should give thorough consideration to the SWNCC 57/3. The Australian position was that any modification of decisions by the international tribunal should be made

---

6. See Walter Millis, ed., *The Forrestal Diaries* (New York: Viking, 1951).

not by MacArthur but by a retrial committee composed of the governments concerned. In other words, Australia attempted to restrict arbitrary decision-making by the US through the promotion of cooperation among the Allies.

Britain Undecided

The British Foreign Office made a series of requests to the US Department of State on December 12, 1945: (1) for decisions on technical issues to be left to US discretion; (2) for the addition of an Indian justice to the international judges in response to India's request; (3) for a review of the SWNCC 57/3 at the FEAC, at Australia's request, and for an agreement on general principles; and (4) for the establishment of an advisory committee to modify court decisions.

These British requests were attempts to accomplish partial realization of cooperation among the Allies, made from the viewpoint of protecting Britain's prestige in the British Commonwealth. The proposal to establish an advisory committee was translated from the Australian "retrial committee" idea with its function limited to that of advice. The British Foreign Office, believing it most appropriate to leave "responsibility for making decisions" to MacArthur, wished to retain only a pro forma voice in the handling of the Japanese war criminals.

Differences in the degree of interest were evident not only between the British and Australian governments but also within the British government itself. The British Foreign Office proposed to Attorney General Hartley Shawcross on December 14 that Britain should not get involved too deeply in the US scheme for an international tribunal, and that it should limit its involvement in the Tokyo Trial. In the event that multiple trials were opened simultaneously, the Foreign Office suggested the dispatch of an assistant public prosecutor (instead of a prosecutor) and a few clerical staff members only to those trials that were truly of interest to Britain.

Shawcross, however, refuted the idea five days later, saying that in consideration of Britain's credibility, it was important for Britain to play a substantial role in the Tokyo Trial. At the same time, however, and by way of compromise with the Foreign Office, Shawcross proposed the following cost reduction measures: (1) limiting the number of defendants in an international tribunal to ten to twenty important individuals; (2) limiting prosecutors to those from major Allied nations (while other, minor nations could instead dispatch assistant public prosecutors), and (3) speeding up the trial.

In the face of this argument for Britain's active involvement from Attorney General Shawcross, who had supervised the dispatch of justices and prosecutors and doubled as the British chief prosecutor at the Nuremberg trials, officials of the Foreign Office were obliged to change their position to support full-scale participation in the Tokyo Trial. Foreign Secretary Bevin also approved.

US prosecutors arrived in Tokyo on December 6, 1945, while Britain was still deciding whether to participate in the tribunal. In haste, the British government dispatched Lieutenant General Charles Gairdner, head of the UK Liaison Mission in Japan (UKLIM) to Japan in January 1946 to consult with Joseph Keenan, the US chief prosecutor for the International Military Tribunal for the Far East, in order to convey British views. Keenan, however, remained cool toward the British proposals, insisting that (1) some thirty defendants would be tried in a single court; (2) it would be unrealistic to limit countries dispatching prosecutors as Britain suggested; and (3) MacArthur was skeptical about the establishment of an advisory committee.

At the Far Eastern Commission

As the Australian government hoped, the FEAC included the SWNCC 57/3 in its deliberation agenda. Because the Soviet Union persistently criticized the presence of the FEAC, which had been authorized only to propose recommendations, the committee was disfunctional.

To remedy this situation, the foreign ministers conference held in Moscow in December 1945 attended by the US, Britain, and the Soviet Union decided to establish a Far Eastern Commission (FEC) as the supreme decision-making organ for the occupation policy on Japan. This committee was officially launched on February 26, 1946, in Washington, DC. It was composed of eleven countries: nine signatories of Japan's Instrument of Surrender (the US, Britain, China, the Soviet Union, France, the Netherlands, Canada, Australia, and New Zealand) plus the two non-independent countries of India and the Philippines. These were the same eleven countries that were to comprise the International Military Tribunal for the Far East.

The FEC regarded a decision on the trial of war criminals as a matter of urgency, and decided in March 1946 to examine just the policy element of the SWNCC 57/3.

As amendments, Britain proposed that countries concerned should be invited to select defendants, formulate procedural rules, and modify court decisions. It also proposed, in response to a request from India, that the international bench should include a justice from India.

France added an amendment to Britain's proposal asserting that it should be allowed to participate in the modification of court sentences. Although France had shown little interest in Asian affairs except for issues directly related to its colonies in Indochina (French Indochina), it was exceptionally enthusiastic about participation in the Tokyo Trial and the trials of Class B and C war crimes committed against its own nationals. France hoped for restoration of its prestige as a major power and punishment for Japan's occupation of French Indochina and for the atrocities Japan had committed in the region.

FEC 007/3 as International Policy

The FEC accepted most of the proposals from Britain and France, and adopted the policy statement FEC 007/3 on April 3, 1946. Let us now look into the significance of this policy decision.

First, by accommodating the interests of other Allied nations, even as mere formalities, the SWNCC 57/3, the US basic policy, had now become an international policy shared by the Allies called FEC 007/3.

Second, the FEC 007/3 was conveyed to MacArthur on April 23; this had the legal effect of granting international authority over the Tokyo Trial retroactively. In contrast to the Nuremberg Trial, which was opened by international agreement, the London Agreement, the Tokyo Trial was established by the Supreme Commander for the Allied Powers, an American citizen, on January 19, 1946, based on JCS 1512 = SWNCC 57/3, which was a directive from the US government without international agreement. In fact, there was no awareness of whether this was a unilateral measure by the US government or an international measure representing all the Allies.

Immediately after the completion of the Tokyo Trial, an American defense counsel representing seven Class A war criminals, including former foreign minister Hirota Kōki, submitted a petition for a writ of habeas corpus to the US

Supreme Court. In this petition, he asserted the invalidity of the Tokyo Trial, both domestically and internationally, claiming that the International Military Tribunal for the Far East set up by MacArthur was an "American court."

Having heard the petition, the Supreme Court dismissed it, claiming that the International Military Tribunal for the Far East was "not an American court," and, therefore, could not intervene in its decisions. What was apparent from this petition, however, was the complex nature of the Tokyo Trial, which defied easy characterization as to whether it was an American court or an international court.[7]

US Department of War's Argument for Sparing the Emperor

The third significant aspect of FEC 007/3 was related to the emperor issue.

The Australian government in October 1945 urged the UNWCC to adopt its own list of Japanese war criminals, and that list included the emperor of Japan. While Australians admitted that it was almost beyond doubt that the emperor himself had a liberal outlook and a desire to maintain peace, they found his position problematic, and insisted that Japan's acts of aggression could not have been committed without imperial sanction. Although the US and Britain blocked the adoption of the list, the Australian government attitude remained steadfast.

On August 15, 1945, the US Department of War conveyed its provisional policy to the American Embassy in Britain, of taking no measure against the emperor for the time being. Brigadier General John M. Weir, assistant judge advocate general and director of the War Crimes Office, also conveyed his concern to Joseph V. Hodgson, US ambassador to Britain, that inclusion of the emperor on the list of war criminals would complicate the policy of sparing the emperor. We can assume that at the end of the war, the Department of War was already inclined toward the policy of putting the treatment of the emperor on hold, which led to the decision not to charge him.

Even within the US government, there was debate over whether or not to prosecute the emperor. In Tokyo, however, General MacArthur met the emperor on September 27. That meeting convinced him that the emperor

---

7. See Higurashi Yoshinobu, *Tōkyō Saiban no kokusai kankei* [The Tokyo Trial and International Relations] (Tokyo: Bokutakusha, 2002).

would be indispensable in pursuing the Occupation policy. It is said that MacArthur told former Japanese navy minister Yonai Mitsumasa on November 26 that he had absolutely no intention of altering the position of the emperor.[8] On January 25 of the following year, MacArthur sent a telegram to US Army chief of staff Dwight D. Eisenhower. This was the famous telegram stressing that a major reinforcement of the Occupation forces would become necessary if the emperor were to be prosecuted. This persuasive logic drew on a memorandum dated October 2, 1945, by Brigadier General Bonner Fellers, military secretary to MacArthur.

Thus, through collaboration between the US Department of War and MacArthur, which had about it the character of a pre-arranged accord, the US policy not to prosecute the emperor was consolidated. Of course, this exemption of the emperor from punishment was a measure of convenience based on political considerations. From this viewpoint, the showy activities of the Australian government were simply a nuisance.

International Agreement Not to Prosecute the Emperor

Returning to the FEC's adoption of the policy FEC 007/3 on April 3, 1946, Carl Berendsen, New Zealand's minister to the United States, pointed out that because FEC 007/3 made no reference to the issue of the emperor, it contradicted the policy of putting the handling of the emperor as laid out by the SWNCC 57/3 on hold.

From the beginning, New Zealand was of the view that, depending on the outcome of investigation, the emperor should be prosecuted. (It should be noted, however, that New Zealand had not included the emperor in its list of war criminals.) Because the General Headquarters of the Supreme Commander for the Allied Powers was actually taking advantage of the presence of the emperor for the Occupation of Japan, Berendsen advised his government to remain calm on this issue. Peter Fraser, prime minister cum foreign minister of New Zealand, concurred. In its cautious attitude toward prosecution of the emperor of Japan, New Zealand in early 1946 differed from Australia.

---

8. See Uematsu Keita, *Kyokutō Kokusai Gunji Saiban* [International Military Tribunal for the Far East] (Tokyo: Jinbutsu Ōraisha, 1962).

Regarding Berendsen's remarks, the FEC agreed with the non-prosecution of the emperor in the undisclosed "understanding," and not with the FEC 007/3, which was made public. The understanding was that directives to be issued to the Supreme Commander for the Allied Powers would be "worded as to exempt the emperor from indictment as a war criminal without direct authorization."[9] It was indeed a very important international agreement in the sense that non-prosecution of the emperor was officially confirmed as "a policy common to the Allies." The understanding used the expression "to exempt the emperor," which was more positive than that used by the Directive (JCS 1512 = SWNCC 57/3, on October 6, 1945).

Particularly noteworthy here is the fact that both Australia and the Soviet Union agreed with the policy of exempting the emperor from indictment as a war criminal. At the time, more than six months from the start of the Occupation, the policy of not prosecuting the emperor had become solidified. The international agreement in the "understanding" would bind these two countries. The issue of whether to prosecute the emperor or not was settled when FEC 007/3 was adopted.

---

9. US Department of State, *FRUS: 1946, The Far East, Vol. VIII*, ed. S. Everett Gleason, John G. Reid, and Herbert A. Fine (Washington, DC: Government Printing Office, 1971).

CHAPTER **3**

What Charges
Did the Allies Bring?

Defendants at the Tokyo Trial
(Jiji Press)

1. Launching the International Prosecution Section

Tōjō Hideki's Abortive Suicide Attempt

At noon on August 15, 1945, Matsumura Kenzō, a member of the House of Representatives, listened to the emperor's radio announcement of Japan's surrender at the former Rikken Minseitō (Democratic Party) headquarters. From the window, Matsumura saw white smoke rising here and there in the government office district and tall buildings in the Marunouchi business district. "What is going on?" he wondered. He soon realized that government officials and businessmen were burning confidential documents to prevent their confiscation by the advancing Allied forces. That goes to show, Matsumura reminisced, how panicky people had become. "People were committing suicide by disembowelment facing Nijūbashi Bridge, the entrance to the imperial palace."[1]

For the first time in its history, Japan was faced with military occupation by foreign troops. The sight of General Douglas MacArthur, Supreme Commander for the Allied Powers, arriving majestically at Atsugi Airfield, in Kanagawa Prefecture, is a well-remembered symbol of the Occupation. On August 30, the very day he arrived in Japan, General MacArthur ordered Brigadier General Elliot R. Thorpe, chief of the Counter-Intelligence Corps (CIC), to arrest Tōjō Hideki, and prepare a list of Class A war crimes suspects, under the directive of Chief of Staff George C. Marshall.

Although Thorpe engaged in this task immediately, the work of specifying Japanese individuals proved to be much more time-consuming than

---

1. See Matsumura Kenzō, *Sandai kaikoroku* [Three Generation Memoir] (Tokyo: Tōyō Keizai Shinpōsha, 1964).

expected. Before long, American newspapers started criticizing MacArthur for being too slow in dealing with the Japanese war crimes suspects. This aroused American public opinion, which put pressure on MacArthur.

On September 11, 1945, four days before General Headquarters (GHQ) moved to the Dai-Ichi Seimei Building near the imperial palace, Tōjō was arrested at his private residence in Yōga, Setagaya Ward. While the prompt arrest of Tōjō had been recommended by a directive from the State-War-Navy Coordinating Committee (SWNCC) (see chapter 2, section 2), the timing of the arrest was, more than anything else, a demonstration geared toward American public opinion.

In the midst of the newspaper reporters' jostling and shoving, Tōjō attempted to kill himself. This caused a storm among all who were present. Tokugawa Yoshihiro, grand chamberlain for the emperor, wrote of the incident as follows:

> The former prime minister replied to the messenger that he would comply with the arrest warrant, entered his room, and attempted to kill himself with a pistol. In his agony, . . . Tōjō claimed that the Greater East Asia War was a just war. He also referred to household matters and said that he had requested Hirohashi Tadamitsu, former secretary to the prime minister, to attend to the disposition of the house. Tōjō said he regretted that he had failed to offer an apology to the emperor.[2]

Toward the latter half of August, several "Tōjō myths" surfaced, including one that had Tōjō and his wife fleeing to Manchuria, where they were killed, and a rumor that Tōjō was hiding in Morioka, Iwate Prefecture. By this time, Tōjō's reputation was in ruins.

Later, in April 1946 while he was imprisoned in Sugamo Prison, Tōjō explained his suicide attempt:

> I failed to kill myself because I unexpectedly missed my mark. Had I known that I would be tried at a legitimate court of justice where I

---

2. Tokugawa Yoshihiro, *Jijūchō no yuigon* [The Last Testament of a Grand Chamberlain] (Tokyo: Asahi Shimbunsha, 1997).

could set out my convictions, . . . I would not have attempted suicide. But, remembering what had happened to Mussolini, I thought it would be extremely humiliating if I was made to face Japanese citizens and be lynched, with my body left on public display. Or I could be secretly slain. Either way would be a death in vain, so I decided to commit suicide.[3]

Thus, Tōjō thought execution under kangaroo court–like circumstances would be a meaningless death.

Washington Wanted More Arrests

The list of "the forty-three" designated on September 11, 1945, as the first war crimes suspects to be arrested contained such names as Tōgō Shigenori (foreign minister), Shimada Shigetarō (navy minister), Kaya Okinori (finance minister), Kishi Nobusuke (commerce and industry minister), and Iwamura Michiyo (justice minister).[4] It also included several non-Japanese including Jose Laurel, former president of the Philippines.

But the fact of the matter was that GHQ at the outset of the Occupation intended to limit the number of arrests. One reason was a dearth of investigators. Further, it was decided that if someone were to be on suspicion of commiting a particular crime and then not be prosecuted after all, it would damage GHQ's position. Because Japan had no clear-cut benchmarks against which to determine war crimes as had been the case in Germany, where the criterion was "Nazi party member," it was quite difficult to determine who a suspect was.

In contrast, the US government demanded the arrests of many. For instance, the Basic Initial Post Surrender Directive to Supreme Commander for The Allied Powers for The Occupation and Control of Japan (JCS 1380/15) issued on November 3, 1945, applied broad, routine criteria, and instructed the arrest of all the members of the Supreme Military Council, the Imperial General Headquarters, as suspected war criminals, and the internment of all key members of Dai-Nihon Seijikai (Greater Japan Political

---

3. Mizuno Tetsuo, *Haruka naru heiwa ni* [Toward Faraway Peace] (Tokyo: Tōkō Shoin, 1952).

4. See Toyoda Kumao, *Sensō saiban yoroku* [Additional Records of the War Crimes Trials] (Tokyo: Taiseisha, 1986).

Society) and Taisei Yokusankai (Imperial Rule Assistance Association). This was akin to the denazification that was conducted in Germany to eliminate all who were considered harmful to the Occupation. Assistant Secretary of War John McCloy, who visited Japan in October, exerted additional pressure, stressing that the US government hoped for more extensive arrests.

The US government was deeply concerned about American public opinion. According to the December 1945 census by *Fortune* magazine, more readers found the Japanese to be more barbaric (55.9 percent) than the Germans (38.9 percent).

In the end, the hopes of the home government prevailed and the number of arrests rose. It is estimated that some 25,000 war crimes suspects were arrested, including those overseas, of which some 100 were Class A crimes suspects.

Brigadier General Thorpe himself, who supervised arrests in Japan, considered the Class A trial to be a "fraud," based on ex post facto law, and reminisced that he had suggested to MacArthur that war criminals should be banished to the Ogasawara Islands for life. Charles Willoughby, who had been cautious about arrests of war crimes suspects, also swore that the Tokyo Trial was "the greatest hypocrisy in history." As these examples indicate, there were quite a number of military personnel within GHQ, including Mac-Arthur himself, who were critical of the criminalization of war. They were pressured to arrest war crimes suspects against their will. It should be noted that even John McCloy, a civilian who promoted the criminalization of war, reflected later that the Tokyo Trial was "a total failure."

Japanese Political Elites in Fear

After their arrest, war crimes suspects were detained at Yokohama Prison or Ōmori Prisoner of War Camp before being transferred in mid-November to the infamous Sugamo Prison. (Today, Sunshine City, a commercial complex, stands on that site in Ikebukuro.) Surrounded by barbed wire and watchtowers at strategic points, prisoners had their neckties and belts confiscated, though earlier they had been allowed to keep these items. They faced stern and austere treatment as prisoners.

Others, like Ikeda Shigeaki, Ogata Taketora, Kuhara Fusanosuke, and Tokutomi Sohō, were placed under house arrest due to health conditions. In the case of Ogata, for instance, even though he was formally ordered into domiciliary confinement with no guests allowed, the authorities turned a blind eye to his outings and short trips. The relaxed treatment these people received was in stark contrast to the treatment of those imprisoned at Sugamo.[5]

Political elites in Japan were terrified of being arrested. Desperate to avoid arrest, politicians and military men alike scrambled to convert themselves into self-proclaimed pacifists, and they were seen sending gifts to GHQ and entertaining its officers. Watanabe Kazuhide wrote of this situation:

Inside Sugamo Prison
(Courtesy of the Theodore Akimoto Family Collection)

> While being purged from public office may not take away your life, arrest as a war crimes suspect can lead to, in the worst case, lifetime imprisonment or even execution. Therefore, all those who were designated as Class A war crimes suspects were appalled [at their fate]. They lost their color as well as their appetites, albeit temporarily.[6]

There were some who chose to kill themselves rather than be arrested. Among them were former education minister Hashida Kunihiko, former Kwantung Army commander Honjō Shigeru, and former prime minister Konoe Fumimaro. Thus, an atmosphere of dread spread across Japan after defeat.

Meanwhile, the trials of Class B and C war crimes suspects officially began. The US military tribunal of former general Yamashita Tomoyuki,

---

5. See Ogata Taketora Denki Kankōkai [Ogata Taketora Biography Publishing Committee], ed., *Ogata Taketora* [Ogata Taketora] (Tokyo: Asahi Shimbunsha, 1963).

6. Watanabe Kazuhide, *Kyojin Nakajima Chikuhei* [Nakajima Chikuhei the Giant] (Tokyo: Hōbunshorin, 1955).

commander of the Fourteenth Area Army, opened in Manila on October 8, 1945. Under strong pressure from President Harry Truman, the trial was promptly concluded with a death sentence on December 7.

Yamashita was executed on February 23, 1946. He became the first to be executed as the result of trials of Japanese war criminals. During the trial, Yamashita was accused of "command responsibility of a superior officer who failed to act"—that is, failure to prevent atrocities by his subordinates which constituted violation of the laws of war. The court also judged that Yamashita had failed to exercise effective control over his troops.[7] This new concept of "command responsibility" or the "Yamashita standard" (that is, a commander could be held accountable before the law for crimes committed by his troops even if he did not order them, did not stand by and allow them, or did not even know about them or have the means to stop them) was also adopted during the Tokyo Trial as a charge against defendants.

In Japan, the Class B and C military tribunal by the US Eighth Army (Yokohama War Crimes Tribunals) opened on December 18, 1945. According to the journal of one of the Class B and C war crimes suspects, he had underestimated the trial in the beginning:

> Because nobody had a sense of guilt, we all thought we would probably be released in a year. . . . But when the tribunal began, we were all astonished. Tsuchiya, a civilian employee of the army who was tried first, was sentenced to life imprisonment, while Lieutenants Yuri and Hirate were sentenced to death. . . . We were all appalled and filled with horror. And, belatedly, we regretted that we had surrendered ourselves shamelessly without even trying to escape.[8]

The ordinary citizens of Japan were witnesses to the punishment of war criminals; their daily lives were filled with news of the trials. One may wonder how ordinary Japanese reacted to these events.

---

7. See A. Frank Reel, *The Case of General Yamashita* (Chicago: University of Chicago Press, 1949), and Louis Fisher, *Military Tribunals and Presidential Power: American Revolution to the War on Terrorism* (Lawrence: University Press of Kansas, 2005).

8. Mizuno, *Haruka naru heiwa ni.*

"They Brought It on Us!"

Movie critic Yodogawa Nagaharu once reminisced that, when Japan entered war with the US, he used to marvel at the drills of cadets of the Imperial Japanese Naval Academy at Etajima, Hiroshima Prefecture, as something beautiful; he used to find the Japanese Naval Aviation Preparatory School in Tsuchiura gallant, to applaud kamikaze pilots, and to send care packages and letters of consolation to soldiers on the battlefront. Other Japanese people felt more or less the same. Yodogawa, however, was one of a few exceptional Japanese individuals who during the war were able to watch such Hollywood films as *Waterloo Bridge* and Walt Disney's *Fantasia*, borrowed from the Japanese military unbeknownst to others at the Toho Company Office. All of those who watched those movies were so fascinated that they could barely stay seated, and it is said Yodogawa groaned, "We're gonna lose!"[9]

Subsequently, immediately after the defeat, the Japanese people started to use such terms as *sensō hanzainin* (war criminals), or *senpan* for short, as a matter of course.

In the midst of serious food shortages and inflation, novelist Nagai Kafū deplored the situation, saying:

> When we travel to farm houses in rural areas to procure food, it is rare that we can obtain main staples like rice and potatoes. People say it is only a matter of days before the entire nation plunges into a famine crisis. . . . Only yesterday, we suffered from oppression by the Japanese military. But today we have done a complete turnaround and now flatter former enemies.[10]

It is a sad element within human nature to take out one's anger on someone else. And it was Tōjō and the military clique that became the target of the Japanese people's condemnation in those days. For instance, John K. Emmerson, a specialist on Japan and Northeast Asia who was assigned to

---

9. Yodogawa Nagaharu, *Yodogawa Nagaharu jiden* [Autobiography of Yodogawa Nagaharu] (Tokyo: Chūōkōronsha, 1988), vol. 1.

10. Nagai Kafū, *Tekiroku: Danchōtei nichijō* [Summary: The Danchōtei Diary] (Tokyo: Iwanami Shoten, 1987), vol. 1, September 16, 1945.

the Political Advisor's Office (representative of the State Department at Mac-Arthur's GHQ), was impressed by a room boy at the Hotel New Grand in Yokohama, the first Japanese person with whom Emmerson had a conversation. Emmerson reminisced,

> He exulted at the ending of the war, and his eyes flashed as he spoke angrily of Tōjō and his military associates who had led the nation to catastrophe. "They brought it on us! How could we have beaten a strong country as strong as yours?" These first words were the essence of the Japanese people's reaction.[11]

Many Japanese pressed responsibility for the war on Tōjō and former political leaders and convinced themselves it had nothing to do with them.

Welcoming the Victors' Pursuit of War Responsibility

The same goes for the political elites in Japan.

In late October 1945 on an NHK radio program, Narahashi Wataru, director of the Cabinet Legislation Bureau of the Shidehara Kijūrō Cabinet, responded to the Japanese Communist Party's insistence on the overthrow of the emperor system in this way: "Why did Japan fight such a quixotic war? It was entirely attributable to a segment of the military clique and a few people surrounding the emperor who assumed the imperial prerogative, deceived the emperor, and abused people's reverence for the emperor." This statement elicited a major reaction from the Japanese people.[12]

After hearing this radio broadcast, Tokutomi Sohō satirized Narahashi, saying he was just repeating what the US had claimed.[13] True enough, Narahashi's argument was connected at a fundamental level with the prosecutors' logic at the Tokyo Trial.

I find it interesting that the psychology of the German people in those days

---

11. John K. Emmerson, *The Japanese Thread* (New York: Holt, Rinehart, and Winston, 1978).

12. Narahashi Wataru, *Gekiryū ni sao sashite* [Rowing against the Torrent] (Tokyo: Tsubasa Shoin, 1968).

13. Tokutomi Sohō, *Tokutomi Sohō shūsengo nikki* [Tokutomi Sohō Postwar Diary] (Tokyo: Kodansha, 2006), vol. 1.

was quite similar to that of the Japanese. Lieutenant General Lucius D. Clay, US deputy military governor for Germany, wrote as follows in July 1945:

> No general feeling of war guilt or repugnance for Nazi doctrine and regime has yet manifested itself. Germans blame [the] Nazis for losing [the] war, protest ignorance of [the] regime's crimes and shrug off their own support or silence as incidental and unavoidable. They are however generally cooperative with [the] military government.[14]

Political parties in postwar Japan also rode the tide of the times. They attempted to evade suspicion of war responsibility and, at a House of Representatives session in late November 1945, they demanded a thorough investigation into war responsibility. Prime Minister Shidehara Kijūrō opposed a merciless investigation of Japanese people, and even the endeavor of the political parties lacked seriousness; in the end, it was just posturing.

In short, the Japanese people welcomed the punishment of war criminals by their conquerors, but chose not to pursue their own investigations. It was necessary for the Allies to open a tribunal promptly while public support endured.

Then Came Keenan

Immediately after the start of the Occupation in 1945, the Allied powers set about disarming and demilitarizing:

September 13 Imperial Headquarters abolished
November 17 Military Service Law abolished
November 24 Military Pension Act suspended
November 30 Ministries of Army and Navy abolished
December 1 First and Second Ministries of Demobilization established

On the night of December 6, the American prosecutors and the staff for the Tokyo Trial arrived in Japan.

---

14. Jean E. Smith, ed., *The Papers of General Lucius D. Clay* (Bloomington: Indiana University Press, 1974), vol. 1.

The only chief prosecutor for the International Military Tribunal for the Far East was the American Joseph B. Keenan. Born in January 1888, Keenan, a Democrat, graduated from Harvard Law School. He was 58 years old at the opening of the Tokyo Trial. An early New Dealer, Keenan was highly effective in congressional lobbying as head of the Criminal Division and as assistant to the attorney general, the No. 3 position at the Department of Justice. His success earned him the nickname of "Joe the Key" from President Roosevelt.

On December 7, a day after the prosecution team arrived, MacArthur instructed Keenan to take special care in preventing criticism regarding ex post facto law, convening the court as early as possible, and prosecuting members of the Tōjō Cabinet. The US government was particularly keen on these three points. On December 8, MacArthur established the International Prosecution Section (IPS) as part of GHQ, and appointed Keenan as chief of the section.

According to SWNCC 57/3, the US basic policy, the IPS was an agency that would work under MacArthur's instructions. It was charged with preparing for and managing prosecution, that is the collection of evidence, the selection of defendants and witnesses, and the introduction of evidence. Above all, the IPS paid special attention to investigating crimes against peace.

The IPS, however, faced three problems from the outset.

First, because most of its members were unfamiliar with Japan's history, politics, or customs, it was imperative to collect information urgently and train experts overnight.

Second was the language barrier. For instance, former lieutenant general Ōshima Hiroshi of the Imperial Japanese Army commented on his interrogation: "I was quite at a loss when it came to the terrible interpreter who made so many unthinkable mistakes in translation. . . . When I said, 'my conviction (shinshō),' he mistranslated it as 'credibility (shinyō)'. . . . Although interrogators promised me that they would correct the mistakes, nothing was ever corrected."[15]

---

15. *Inoue Tadao shiryō* [Inoue Tadao Documents], Yasukuni Kaikō Bunko [Yasukuni Archives].

An Act of Sheer Folly: The Incineration of Documents

Third, because government officials incinerated important documents at the time of Japan's defeat, documents that could have served as evidence were far fewer than expected.

Faced with this situation, the IPS searched for documents and interrogated prominent individuals in cooperation with various sections of GHQ, which fortunately achieved a degree of success. The GHQ even searched the homes of high-ranking military officers. Meanwhile, the Shidehara Cabinet helped duplicate and compose documents. Foreign Minister Yoshida Shigeru, too, cooperated by submitting diplomatic records. The former Imperial Japanese Army returned to Tokyo the documents of the Imperial Japanese Army General Staff, which had been evacuated to Ueda City, Nagano Prefecture.[16]

Nomura Masao, an *Asahi Shimbun* judicial correspondent, wrote:

> The Allied forces did whatever they could to dig up half-burned remnants of documents, collected them from here and there . . . and presented them to the court as evidence. The Imperial Army's *Manmitsu dai-nikki* (classified documents on the Manchurian Incident in the possession of the Army Minister's Secretariat) was among them. Also, a large number of conference minutes were retrieved from deep inside the Privy Council.[17]

The journal submitted by Kido Kōichi, former lord keeper of the privy seal, was so valuable that Yabe Teiji, political scientist and former professor at Tokyo Imperial University, marveled, "This is a remarkable document. You can understand the actions of the upper echelon surrounding His Majesty in fine detail."[18] It proved to be a key document for the prosecutors' investigation and introduction of evidence.

Nevertheless, this did not mean that the adverse effect of the incineration of documents—an act of sheer folly—was completely countered.

These imprudent actions irritated not only the prosecutors but also the

---

16. Miyama Yōzō, *Haikyo no Shōwa kara* [From Ruined Shōwa], ed. Kai Katsuhiko (Tokyo: Kōjinsha, 1989).

17. Nomura Masao, *Sabakareta Nihon* [Japan Tried] (Tokyo: Kadokawa Shoten, 1956).

18. Yabe Teiji Nikki Kankōkai, ed., *Yabe Teiji nikki* [Yabe Teiji Diary], vol. 2, *Keyaki no maki* [The Keyaki Volume] (Tokyo: Yomiuri Shimbunsha, 1974).

defense counsels. According to former lieutenant general Satō Kenryō of the Imperial Japanese Army, "Prosecutors and the court spoke ill of this [incineration of documents] as destruction of evidence, but we the defendants also deplored it, imagining how convenient it really would have been if all the evidence had remained intact."[19]

Moreover, a central source of the information was records of interrogations rather than official documents. This meant that the submission of a single document would not do; the information often needed to be verified with time-consuming affidavits, as well as testimonies. This situation contributed to the prolongation of the Tokyo Trial.

Legal Merit of the Conspiracy Argument

The first policy issue for the prosecutors was to determine the span of time they would devote to prosecution.

The American prosecutors paid special attention to the attack on Pearl Harbor. But, at the same time, they found it necessary to comply with the policy of SWNCC 57/3, which instructed them to backdate the prosecution to those responsible for the Manchurian Incident.

Furthermore, another guideline, a "planning memorandum" dated September 11, 1945, of the War Crimes Office, Judge Advocate General (JAG), Department of War, suggested the following policy for prosecuting Japanese war criminals. In order to maintain "coherence with the Nuremberg Trial," prosecutors should charge (1) defendants who, on an unspecified date prior to the attack on Pearl Harbor on December 7, 1941, had started a common plan or scheme to promote Japan's complete rule of Asia and, eventually, Japan's rule of the world; (2) defendants who started an illegal war of aggression based on the above plan or scheme; and (3) defendants who violated humanitarian law, international law, and the laws and customs of war on land and sea in pursuit of the above war of aggression.[20]

Prompted by this planning memorandum, a broad outline of prosecution of Japanese war criminals was adopted as early as December 27, 1945, at an IPS

---

19. Satō Kenryō, *Daitōa Sensō kaikoroku* [Memoirs of the Greater East Asia War] (Tokyo: Tokuma Shoten, 1966).

20. Office of the Judge Advocate General (JAG), *War Crimes Branch Papers: General and Administrative Records 1944–1949*, NARA, II: RG 153, College Park, Maryland.

conference. The conference claimed that a conspiracy to rule Asia territorially, politically, and economically had been started in the 1930s and that defendants had planned, prepared, initiated, and waged a war of aggression as part of this conspiracy.

Special attention should be paid here to the term "conspiracy," which I touched on in chapter 2.

Conspiracy is a criminal concept unique to Anglo-American law. When more than two persons agree to accomplish an illegal goal or a legal goal by illegal means, this constitutes by itself an independent crime. Because the existence of such an agreement can be presumed from circumstantial evidence, evidentiary requirements are less stringent. In reality, the fact of participating in the agreement by attending a meeting would suffice for prosecution. And a defendant is accountable for all conduct until termination of the conspiracy or withdrawal from it.

Once this evidence is acknowledged, even a person who engaged in only part of the scheme will be guilty. At a glance, this "conspiracy" may appear to resemble the concept of an accomplice in Japanese criminal law or civil law. But it differs because complicity in continental law presupposes execution of the crime. Even an attempted criminal act requires initiating the crime.

In September 1944, when suitable ways of dealing with war criminals were debated in Washington, DC, this concept of conspiracy was injected into the war crimes issue. In order to counter Treasury Secretary Morgenthau's argument for summary execution of war criminals, Secretary of War Stimson instructed his department to draft a war crimes trial policy. Colonel Murray C. Bernays (an attorney on wartime duty), director of special planning at the Army General Staff, introduced the notion of conspiracy in his memorandum of September 15, 1944. The hope was that the adoption of this concept would allow the trial of prewar atrocities and the punishment of a number of Nazi war criminals.

Having once served as a prosecutor, Stimson was fascinated by Bernays's argument for the introduction of the concept of conspiracy as a way to fight evil. And in October, perhaps at Stimson's suggestion, it became the War Department's basic policy to apply the conspiracy concept not only to atrocities but also to the starting of a war of aggression. It can be said that, as far as trial and law in international politics were concerned, only the convenient elements of the national legal system were adopted.

Use of the Conspiracy View of History

There were additional merits to the use of the concept of conspiracy during the Tokyo Trial.

First, it was anticipated that the legal characteristic of the concept would be more effective in Japan, where prosecutors were handicapped in terms of evidence, than in Germany.

Second, with the adoption of a framework of "participants in conspiracy," it became easier to identify suspects.

Third, conspiracy was convenient for the prosecutors as a rough summary of the course of Japan's political and diplomatic history. With the political advantage of this "tool of perception and explanation," the prosecutors were able to discern the ultimate goal of a general conspiracy among Japanese leaders to rule the world, based on the notion of ethnic superiority. They were able to construct the fictitious logic of a conspiracy-based historical view, in which Japan, in incremental steps, expanded its ultimate goal of gaining control in Asia, the Pacific, and the world, proceeding from the Manchurian Incident, the founding of Manchukuo, withdrawal from the League of Nations, and the Second Sino-Japanese War and on to the establishment of the Greater East Asia Co-Prosperity Sphere.

This logic was derived from the aforementioned War Department's guideline as well as the Nuremberg indictment, which had recognized that the Nazi conspiracy encompassed everything from the founding of the German Workers' Party in 1919 through the German defeat in 1945. In other words, the logic applied in Japan was analogous to that of the Nazi case.

In fact, this type of conspiracy-based historical view is common enough, regardless of time period and geographical region.

In American political history, for instance, there have been many episodes of conspiracy groups being exposed. And when it was announced that Salman Rushdie, author of *The Satanic Verses*, was to be knighted by Queen Elizabeth II in 2007, the Iranian Foreign Ministry criticized it as "a planned and organized move that enjoyed support of some Western countries."[21] Actions taken by adversaries are liable to be seen as conspiracies. That is why the conspiracy argument is highly convincing.

---

21. *Asahi Shimbun*, June 18, 2007.

Needless to say, there was no conspiracy in Japan to conquer vast areas. George Yamaoka, defense counsel for Tōjō Hideki, gave an easy-to-understand explanation of this subject. He claimed that the so-called conspiracy theory was an exceedingly bizarre, unbelievable argument, because "it consists of nothing more than a collection of isolated and unrelated incidents drawn from at least the last fourteen years."[22] The concept of conspiracy was, nevertheless, introduced into the Tokyo Trial due to its legal and political merits, its consistency with the German case, and the easy analogy with the Nazis. Because of this decision, prosecutors were taxed with the heavy burden of verifying a long-term, consistent intention of aggression. This became another reason for the prolongation of the Tokyo Trial.

Under these circumstances, the IPS decided not to prosecute criminal organizations as was done in Nuremberg. Instead, the IPS chose to prosecute only individual war crimes suspects. Bernays believed that the adoption of conspiracy at the Nuremberg Trial would allow recognition of the Schutzstaffel (SS) and the Gestapo as criminal organizations, which would make it possible to incriminate members of these organizations as conspirators in subsequent trials. Although the IPS in the beginning contemplated the prosecution of criminal organizations, further scrutiny proved that, unlike Nazi organizations, such Japanese groups as Genyōsha (Dark Ocean Society) and Taisei Yokusankai existed merely for propaganda purposes. Britain was also opposed to prosecuting organizations.

Promulgation of the Charter of the International Military Tribunal for the Far East

Along with preparing indictments, prosecutors were also requested to draft the basic law, that is, the charter, of the tribunal. It was unusual for prosecutors, as parties to the trial, to be entrusted with such a task. The drafting of the charter was imposed on MacArthur's representative, i.e., the prosecutors, by SWNCC 57/3.

On January 19, 1946, MacArthur issued a "special proclamation," which was equivalent to the London Agreement, ordering the establishment of the

---

22. Tōkyō Saiban Kenkyūkai, ed., *Kyōdō kenkyū Pāru hanketsusho* [Collaborative Research on the Pal Judgment] (Tokyo: Kodansha, 1984).

International Military Tribunal for the Far East. At the same time, he promulgated the Charter of the International Military Tribunal for the Far East ("Tokyo Charter," henceforth), which stipulated, among other things, the composition of the court, crimes under its jurisdiction, and court decisions. Six American clerical staff members drafted the charter, using the Nuremberg Charter (London Charter) as a model, before delegates of participating countries arrived in Japan. There were, however, differences between the new Tokyo Charter and the Nuremberg Charter:

1. Article 5 of the Tokyo Charter gave the court "the power to try and punish Far Eastern war criminals who as individuals or as members of organizations are charged with offenses which include Crimes against Peace." In other words, defendants would be prosecuted for crimes against peace. There was no comparable constraint at the Nuremberg Trial, highlighting the importance attached to the initiation of war at the Tokyo Trial.

2. The definition of crimes against peace in Article 5 included the planning, preparation, initiation, or waging of an undeclared war of aggression. This was to cover such de facto wars as the Manchurian Incident and the Second Sino-Japanese War in the Tokyo Trial.

3. MacArthur was given authority to appoint a chief justice of the tribunal as well as a chief prosecutor. Any Allied Power with which Japan was at war was allowed to appoint an associate prosecutor to assist the chief prosecutor. (In the case of the Nuremberg Trial, the US, Britain, France, and the Soviet Union each appointed a chief prosecutor.)

4. The alternate justice system, which had been applied in the Nuremberg Trial (with four main justices), was not applied to the Tokyo Trial. There were already nine main justices, and MacArthur himself had argued against the alternate justice system in support of Keenan's view toward the end of the previous year. But because this lineup was susceptible to attack from the defense side, a provision allowing the return of absentee justices to the hearings was added to the revised Tokyo Charter of April 26, 1946.

5. Article 4b of the Tokyo Charter stipulated that "all decisions and judgments of this Tribunal, including convictions and sentences,

shall be by a majority vote of those Members of the Tribunal present." The draft had stipulated that convictions and sentences alone would be determined by a majority vote of all the incumbent justices. But the wording could prompt a debate on whether or not justices absent due to sickness, for example, could be counted as incumbent. MacArthur hoped for a prompt settlement, and so the wording was revised to "Members of the Tribunal present."

6. Perhaps related to the impunity of the emperor, the following statement which appears in Article 7 of the Nuremberg Charter was struck from Article 6 of the Tokyo Charter: "The official position of defendants, whether as Heads of State or responsible officials in Government Departments, shall not be considered as freeing them from responsibility or mitigating punishment."

7. Judicial proceedings were modeled on Anglo-American law. (In the case of the Nuremberg Trial, some were modeled on continental law at the request of France and the Soviet Union.) As stated in Article 13a, however, the "Tribunal shall not be bound by technical rules of evidence." Strict rules of evidence in Anglo-American law were not adopted, in anticipation of a dearth of evidence in Tokyo.

8. Article 9c stipulated that the "trial and related proceedings shall be conducted in English and in the language of the accused [i.e., Japanese], in anticipation of the cumbersomeness of interpretations and translations among multiple languages." (At the Nuremberg Trial, English, French, Russian, and German were all used.)

9. Trials of "criminal organizations," which had been conducted at the Nuremberg trials, were not adopted.

10. While the Nuremberg Charter stipulated that the "Tribunal shall have the right to take proceedings against a person charged with crimes set out in Article 6 of this Charter in his absence," and, in fact, Martin Bormann, head of the Nazi Party Chancellery, had been sentenced to death by hanging in his absence, the Tokyo Charter did not permit absente reo trial.

Most of the above divergences between the Nuremberg Charter and the Tokyo Charter were attributable to the difference in the number of participating countries, Japan's special circumstances, and the argument for US initiative which permeated the SWNCC 57/3.

2. Identifying Defendants and Determining Charges

"A Terrible Job"

After the arrival of the British delegation in Japan on February 2, 1946, prosecutors from participating countries came to Tokyo one after another, making the International Prosecution Section truly international.

What astonished prosecutors from Britain and other British Commonwealth countries upon their arrival was the draft indictment prepared by the American prosecutors. The American draft dated February 4, 1946, took the startling form of the four Allies (the US, Britain, China, and the Soviet Union) and the government of imperial Japan prosecuting Tōjō and others.

Keenan had come up with this idea. First, Keenan understood that, since the Occupation involved preserving the Japanese government, and ruling indirectly, he could protect the emperor from prosecution if he made the Japanese government a plaintiff. Second, Keenan may have been exaggerating here, but the Japanese government also seemed to favor this scheme. This stance would have the additional merit of allowing the Allies to fend off criticism of the trial as "victors' justice."

Nevertheless, Keenan's scheme did not materialize, due to strong opposition from the British Commonwealth countries. Those countries rejected the idea because it could give the wrong impression that Japan as a state was innocent. It would diverge from the Nuremberg Trial, in which Germany had not been one of the plaintiffs. And public opinion in the Allied countries would not tolerate having Japan, the defeated, share equal footing with their own countries.

Prosecutors from British Commonwealth countries were further astonished by the methods of their American colleagues. According to the British Commonwealth delegates, American prosecutors had merely collected unrelated information en masse, apparently without any consideration as to how to use it in prosecuting individual defendants. Records of interrogations were also full of "self-justification by defendants and ambiguous responses typical of Asians."

From left: Canadian Justice McDougall, Chief Prosecutor Keenan, British prosecutor Comyns-Carr (Kyodo News)

British associate prosecutor Arthur Comyns-Carr (King's Counsel, born in 1882) later complained to the British government that he had "a terrible job."

However, we should consider that behind the criticisms from the British Commonwealth countries was the issue of the low status of the "associate prosecutors" they sent. According to a document that Keenan circulated on February 13, all the prosecutors appointed by participating countries other than the US were given "associate prosecutor" status. While they were able to submit the views of their home governments, select defendants, and produce evidence, they were, in the end, mere assistants to Keenan, who had been formally appointed as the single chief prosecutor by the Tokyo Charter promulgated on January 19. Prosecutors from the British Commonwealth countries were displeased by the shadow of MacArthur visible behind Keenan.

Convinced that there would be no progress so long as they relied on the Americans, prosecutors of the British Commonwealth countries began to reorganize the IPS. As a result, an executive committee was established on March 2, with all the prosecutors from participating countries as its members. An indictment committee, an incident and treaty committee, and an evidence and defendant committee were established under the executive committee. It was after this reorganization that drafting of the indictment rapidly gathered momentum.

The Emperor Issue for Prosecutors

On February 11, 1946, Alan J. Mansfield, associate prosecutor from Australia and a puisne judge on the Supreme Court of Queensland (born in 1902 and forty-three years old at the opening of the Tokyo Trial), submitted Australia's list of war criminals (altogether 124 criminals including the emperor) to the IPS immediately after his arrival in Tokyo. That is, Australia still intended to prosecute the emperor.

Keenan, however, opposed the indictment of the emperor, and clearly hinted that MacArthur would intervene. In late November 1948, after the Tokyo Trial was completed, Keenan shared the following with the media corps:

> Because the Emperor had acted on the counsel of his advisors, there was no evidence to support prosecution of the Emperor, who was essentially an advocate of peace, albeit weak-willed. I still considered making the Emperor stand in a court room as a witness, but I met British opposition. General MacArthur basically shared the British view, believing the Emperor would assume all the responsibility himself if he stood at the court.[23]

According to Keenan, exemption from prosecution at the Tokyo Trial was itself proof that the emperor had no responsibility for the war. Incidentally, Mimura Osamu, director of the Cabinet Legislation Bureau who later became justice of the Supreme Court, also used the same logic at the House of Councillors' Committee on the Cabinet on February 14, 1989, to state that the issue of the emperor's war responsibility in international law had already been settled.

The interactions between the various international prosecutors, however, was not that simple.

According to Australian diplomatic records, the emperor issue was informally discussed in the IPS, through which a broad consensus was reached that only by indictment of the emperor could incrimination be possible. Nevertheless, it was only Australia's Mansfield who believed the emperor should be indicted.

Alan Mansfield, prosecutor from Australia
(State Library of Queensland)

---

23. Abe Genki, *Sugamo nikki* [Sugamo Diary] (Tokyo: Tentensha, 1992).

In order to counter the anticipated assertion by the Soviet prosecutor for indictment of the emperor, Keenan tried to persuade Mansfield to change the Australian position in order to secure cohesion among prosecutors from other countries. Nonetheless, Mansfield formally proposed indictment of the emperor at the associate prosecutors' conference on April 8, fully aware that doing so was not feasible. In response, Keenan once again resorted to MacArthur's right of veto and, consequently, the prosecutors agreed not to indict the emperor.

While acknowledging Mansfield's argument for indictment of the emperor, the Australian Foreign Ministry instructed him to "avoid any public protest if decision is against indictment" of the emperor on April 9.[24] This was a demonstration of Australian determination to honor its own argument to prosecute the emperor as well as its intention to refrain from any objections after a decision was made. In other words, by acknowledging the understanding of FEC 007/3 issued a week earlier on April 3, the Australian government, too, accepted the decision not to indict the emperor.

The Soviets' Unexpected Move

On April 30 Soviet Union delegation arrived in Tokyo. Contrary to general expectation, they did not argue for the indictment of the emperor.

Premier Joseph Stalin of the Soviet Union, no stranger to tactical maneuvering, was not the type of man to take daring chances in Japan, which had been recognized by the Yalta Agreement as within the sphere of American influence. Besides, as George Kennan had detected, the Soviet Union at the time was still a weak power, and its policies still retained flexibility.

According to Russian historian Alexey Kirichenko, who analyzed official documents of the former Soviet Union, the Politburo of the Central Committee of the Communist Party of the Soviet Union deliberated before deciding to refrain from proposing that Emperor Hirohito be added to the list of defendants. But the agreed policy also stipulated that, if delegations from other participating countries suggested indictment of the emperor, the Soviet

---

24. Department of External Affairs to Mansfield, April 9, 1946, Department of Foreign Affairs and Trade, ed., *Documents on Australian Foreign Policy 1937–1949, Vol. IX: January–June 1946* (Canberra: Australian Government Publishing Service, 1991).

delegation would support it.[25] It was for this reason that the Soviet Union agreed with the understandings contained in the FEC 007/3.

The international agreement among the prosecutors not to indict the emperor was immediately conveyed to the Japanese side; the defendants were immensely relieved. It was only after the promulgation of the new constitution of Japan, however, that they were fully assured of the safety of the emperor.

Observing the newspaper photo of the emperor and empress "standing in the storm of people's celebratory shouts of 'Long live the emperor!'" at the Tokyo citizens' celebration of the promulgation of the new constitution in front of the imperial palace, Shigemitsu Mamoru, former foreign minister, and Kido Kōichi, former lord keeper of the privy seal of Japan, concurred: "I think it is all right now" (Shigemitsu), and "No need to worry now. I feel as if we have finally ended the war today" (Kido).[26] The Constitution of Japan was enacted on May 3, 1947, exactly one year after the opening of the Tokyo Trial.

Indict Responsible Heavyweights

The second policy issue was who to prosecute.

In the case of the Nuremberg Trial, defendants were selected from ten war crimes suspects listed by Britain and from lists of additional individuals proposed by other countries. Britain suggested that the number of defendants should be limited, but the US, France, and the Soviet Union insisted on adding to the list military personnel and industrial capitalists. After deliberations, the names of twenty-four individuals, including Hermann Wilhelm Göring, former marshal of the Reich, were announced on August 29, 1945. All of the defendants were indicted on October 18.

Prior to the Tokyo Trial, Britain also prepared a list of defendants, using positions responsible for the initiation of war and for atrocities as their benchmark. Britain named ten individuals as defendants in January 1946, the same number as in the Nuremberg Trial. The British criterion was general "renown," and the selection was not based on an examination of evidence.

---

25. Alexey Kirichenko, "Tōkyō Saiban e no Kuremurin himitsu shirei" [Kremlin's Secret Directive to the Tokyo Trial], trans. Kawamura Hide, *Seiron* 398 (July 2005).

26. Shigemitsu Mamoru, *Sugamo nikki* [Sugamo Diary] (Tokyo: Bungeishunjū Shinsha, 1953), vol. 1.

In an International Military Tribunal that attracted the world's attention, renown was an important element.

When the concept of conspiracy was applied, an ordinary worker at a military arsenal could conceivably become a co-conspirator in a war of aggression; there was no limit to the number of possible defendants. However, because the number of defendants that could be realistically indicted in one trial was limited, prosecutors from the British Commonwealth were convinced that the number of defendants should be confined to fifteen to twenty individuals, to ensure a prompt conclusion to the trial. For instance, British assistant prosecutor T. Christmas Humphreys (born in 1901; Humphreys was senior prosecuting counsel at the Central Criminal Court) suggested at the IPS conference convened on March 2 that the years between 1931 and 1945 could be divided into fifteen to twenty incidents, and responsible "heavyweights" could be selected for each incident. It was an attempt to cover the maximum number of incidents with the minimum number of people.

But among the participating countries, there were gaps in the perceptions of "heavyweights" and "those responsible." While the US was keen on indicting members of the Tōjō Cabinet because of the significance of the attack on Pearl Harbor, the British Commonwealth countries, China, the Netherlands, France, and the Philippines were more interested in punishing those responsible for atrocities.

The executive committee's criteria for selecting defendants included:

(1) Those who could be indicted for crimes against peace.
(2) Representatives of each rank and each office.
(3) Those for whom there existed evidence that would definitely lead to incrimination.

Added to these broad criteria, the following individuals were also actually prosecuted:

(4) Those who had enthusiastically taken part in conspiracy for aggression and/or those who had not refused to do so.

Former foreign minister Hirota Kōki, for instance, told his family that, "This is not a trial," confiding to family members the content of pre-indictment inter-rogations. According to Hirota, despite a long search, prosecutors had become frustrated by not finding evidence that pinpointed an individual who had started the war and they had resorted to suspecting him of being the behind-the-scenes string-puller. He had even been suspected of being a secret member of the Kokuryūkai (Black Dragon Society, a prominent ultranationalist right-wing group).[27] Interrogations, nevertheless, failed to produce any information that could point to Hirota as "the agitator of the war of aggression." Admitting this, interrogator Arthur A. Sandusky nonetheless recommended that Hirota, who had revived the rule that only an active military officer could serve as an army or navy minister, should be indicted as a follower of the Imperial Japanese Army. In this process, Hirota was contrasted with another former foreign minister, Shidehara Kijūrō, who had resisted the army.[28]

Why Was Ishiwara Kanji Not Tried?

Here, let me pose a question. Why was Ishiwara Kanji, the mastermind of the Manchurian Incident, not even arrested, while Itagaki Seishirō was actually indicted?

Kido Kōichi, in his January 1946 interrogation, referred to Ishiwara as "a central figure in the Manchurian Incident." Prosecutors were aware that Ishiwara had been hospitalized at the Tokyo Teishin Hospital in Iidabashi, Tokyo. But their investigation itself was inadequate. The fact that Ishiwara's health was so poor that he could not withstand a trial was a major disadvantage to prose-cutors. It is plausible that his demotion to reserve duty due to his confrontation with Tōjō, his senior by four years at the Imperial Japanese Military Academy, played a role. Besides, China's Foreign Ministry had not designated Ishiwara as a war crimes suspect on its second list of suspects dated February 1946.

Near the end of May 1947, a total of some eighty people including lawyers, prosecutors, and newspaper reporters headed by the New Zealand justice,

---

27. Hirota Kōki Denki Kankōkai [Hirota Kōki Biography Publishing Committee], ed., *Hirota Kōki* [Hirota Kōki] (Tokyo: Ashi Shobō, 1992).

28. International Prosecution Section (IPS) Papers, GHQ/SCAP records, RG 331 (National Archives Microfilm Publications, 1991), copies in Modern Japanese Political History Materials Room (Kensei Shiryōshitsu), National Diet Library, Tokyo.

Erima Harvey Northcroft, went to Sakata City, Yamagata Prefecture, where Ishiwara was under medical care, and interrogated him as a witness.

Ishiwara was expected to be a star witness for the defense counsel. When asked by a prosecutor whether he had earlier testified that the conduct of the Japanese troops at the time of the Manchurian Incident was self-defense, Ishiwara replied in the affirmative. He then fended off the hidden intention of the question by saying, "It was the enemy [the Chinese garrison] that charged at us first." Ishiwara's affidavit explained the Liutiaogou Incident (Mukden Incident) of September 18, 1931, as follows:

> We received the first news in the classified military telegram that reported, "After 10:00 p.m. on September 18, ferocious Chinese troops destroyed the South Manchuria Railway to the west of Mukden's Beidaiying, and attacked the garrison to clash with our troops." We then studied appropriate response measures. . . . As the chief officer in charge of operation planning, I offered my opinions to General Honjō Shigeru. After contemplating silently for some five minutes with his eyes closed, Commander Honjō resolutely declared, "All right, let's do it. I will take full responsibility." All of the staff officers were struck with awe and deep emotion.[29]

Today, we know that the Manchuria Incident was created by Ishiwara with meticulous planning and thorough preparation. At the time of the Tokyo Trial, however, this remained unclear.

In short, the prosecutors had no clue about the realities of the Manchurian Incident. When General Honjō Shigeru, commander of the Kwantung Army in Manchuria, committed suicide, they paid closer attention to Colonel Itagaki Seishirō, a senior staff officer of the Kwantung Army, instead of Lieutenant Colonel Ishiwara, a staff officer for the operations of the Kwantung Army. Itagaki had been accused by the Chinese prosecutors, immediately after they arrived in Japan, for masterminding the Manchurian Incident, and for being responsible for the massacre of tens of thousands of Chinese

---

29. Takagi Kiyohisa, *Tōa no chichi Ishiwara Kanji* [Ishiwara Kanji, Father of East Asia] (Tokyo: Tamairabo, 1985).

civilians by playing an active role in the war of aggression serving as advisor to the chief executive of Manchukuo (Puyi), chief of staff of the Kwantung Army, and commander of the Fifth Army Division.

Thus, Itagaki replaced Ishiwara as the supposed man of influence, both in terms of his positions and his involvement in atrocities.

Confirmation of 28 Defendants

The executive committee of the IPS began the task of confirming defendants on March 31. A majority rule was applied and, in case of a tied vote, the prosecutor who proposed the defendant was given the right to decide.

For instance, on March 11, seven individuals including Tōjō Hideki and Tōgō Shigenori, former foreign minister, were designated as defendants, while Eugen Ott was eliminated from the list. Some individuals were considered for indictment, even though they had not yet been arrested. One was Shigemitsu Mamoru, but it was decided on March 20 that he would not be indicted. For the names of individuals who were considered by the executive committee, see the table in chapter 3 of my *Tōkyō Saiban no kokusai kankei* (The Tokyo Trial and International Relations).

As of April 4, the following twenty-nine individuals were listed as potential defendants:

Araki Sadao	Mutō Akira
Dohihara Kenji	Nagano Osami
Hashimoto Kingorō	Oka Takasumi
Hata Shunroku	Ōkawa Shūmei
Hiranuma Kiichirō	Ōshima Hiroshi
Hirota Kōki	Satō Kenryō
Hoshino Naoki	Shimada Shigetarō
Itagaki Seishirō	Shiratori Toshio
Kaya Okinori	Suzuki Teiichi
Kido Kōichi	Tōgō Shigenori
Kimura Heitarō	Tōjō Hideki
Koiso Kuniaki	Ishiwara Kanji
Matsui Iwane	Masaki Jinzaburō
Matsuoka Yōsuke	Tamura Hiroshi
Minami Jirō	

At the associate prosecutors' meeting on April 8, the names of Ishiwara, Masaki, and Tamura were taken off the list, reducing the final number of defendants to twenty-nine. This was reported to MacArthur on April 10.

It should be noted, however, that the Soviet Union did not take part in this decision. Despite concerns that the Soviet prosecutors might reject the list of defendants previously agreed upon by the prosecutors from other countries, the Soviet delegation, which arrived in Tokyo on April 13, proved to be surprisingly moderate.

Ishiwara Kanji, attended by a nurse, undergoes an on-the-spot examination at the Sakata Chamber of Commerce and Industry, Sakata, Yamagata Prefecture. May 1, 1947.
(Kyodo News)

Back in Moscow on March 20, 1946, the Politburo of the Central Committee of the Communist Party had approved recommendations submitted by a secret committee to deliberate on the Tokyo Trial. It was chaired by Deputy Foreign Minister Andrey Yanuaryevich Vyshinsky, infamous as the prosecutor at the Moscow Trials during the Great Purge. Their committee sent the recommendations as a directive to the prosecutor dispatched to the Tokyo Trial.[30] What Associate Prosecutor Sergei Alexandrovich Golunsky (born 1895; director of the Treaty Bureau, people's commissariat for Foreign Affairs, and a delegate to the Dumbarton Oaks Conference) demanded on that occasion was the addition of defendants and accusations related to the Zhanggufeng Incident (Battle of Lake Khasan, 1938) and the Nomonhan Incident (Battle of Khalkhin Gol, 1939).

Most of the names on the Soviet Union's list of recommended defendants were included among the aforementioned twenty-six defendants. At the associate prosecutors' meeting on April 17, Golunsky proposed the addition of Aikawa Yoshisuke (industrialist), Shigemitsu Mamoru, Umezu Yoshijirō, Tominaga Kyōji (lieutenant general of the Imperial Japanese Army), and Fujiwara Ginjirō (industrialist and minister of commerce and industry).

---

30. Kirichenko, "Tōkyō Saiban e no Kuremurin himitsu shirei."

Golunsky was successful in adding Shigemitsu and Umezu to the list. Shigemitsu was loathed by the Soviet Union for his hard-nosed attitude when tending to the Zhanggufeng Incident as the Japanese ambassador to the Soviet Union. Umezu was commander of the Kwantung Army from 1939 through 1944. General Ueda Kenkichi, who was commander of the Kwantung Army at the time of the Zhanggufeng and the Nomonhan Incidents, was deemed inadequate in terms of his position in the central organization of the Imperial Japanese Army. Although Shigemitsu and Umezu had both been removed from the list of defendants in late March, the majority of the prosecutors from participating countries found it in their interest to make a concession to the Soviet Union. Thus, Shigemitsu was relisted by a six to four vote, and Umezu was relisted with a five to three vote.

The twenty-eight defendants of the Tokyo Trial were thus confirmed (see Table 3-1).

Table 3-1. List of Tokyo Trial Defendants

Name	Year of Birth	Academic Background / Year of Entering Ministries	Military Rank / Posts, etc.
Araki Sadao	1877	JMA 9 / AWC 19	General / Minister of the Army
Dohihara Kenji	1883	JMA 16 / AWC 24	General / Head, Harbin Special Agency / Commander of the 7th Area Army
Hashimoto Kingorō	1890	JMA 23 / AWC 32	Colonel, Head of Russian Studies Department, Army General Staff, Commander, 13th Heavy Field Artillery Regiment
Hata Shunroku	1879	JMA 12 / AWC 22	General / Field Marshal / Minister of the Army / Commander-in-Chief of the China Expeditionary Army
Hiranuma Kiichirō	1867	TIU / Ministry of Justice 1888	Prime Minister / President of the Privy Council
Hirota Kōki	1878	TIU / Ministry of Foreign Affairs 1905	Prime Minister / Foreign Minister
Hoshino Naoki	1892	TIU / Ministry of Finance 1917	Director General of the Department of General Affairs, the State Council of Manchukuo, President of the Cabinet Planning Board, Chief Cabinet Secretary of the Tōjō Cabinet
Itagaki Seishirō	1885	JMA 16 / AWC 28	General / Chief of Staff of the Kwantung Army / Minister of the Army / Commander of the 7th Area Army
Kaya Okinori	1889	TIU / Ministry of Finance 1917	Minister of Finance

Kido Kōichi	1889	KIU / Ministry of Agriculture and Commerce	Lord Keeper of the Privy Seal / Minister of Education
Kimura Heitarō	1888	JMA 20 / AWC 28	General / Vice-Minister of the Army / Commander, Burma Area Army
Koiso Kuniaki	1880	JMA 12 / AWC 22	General / Director of Military Affairs Bureau, Ministry of the Army / Prime Minister
Matsui Iwane	1878	JMA 9 / AWC 18	General / Commander of the Central China Area Army
Matsuoka Yōsuke	1880	Univ. of Oregon / Ministry of Foreign Affairs 1904	Minister of Foreign Affairs
Minami Jirō	1874	JMA 6 / AWC 17	General / Minister of the Army / Commander of the Kwantung Army / Governor-General of Korea
Mutō Akira	1892	JMA 25 / AWC 32	Lieutenant General / Director of Military Affairs Bureau, Ministry of the Army / Commander of the Imperial Guard
Nagano Osami	1880	JNA 28 / NWC 8	Admiral / Admiral of the Fleet / Minister of Navy / Chief of Naval General Staff
Oka Takasumi	1890	JNA 39 / NWC 24	Vice-Admiral / Chief of Naval General Staff
Ōkawa Shūmei	1886	TIU	Nationalist ideologue
Ōshima Hiroshi	1886	JMA 18 / AWC 27	Lieutenant General / Japanese Military Attaché in Berlin / Japanese Ambassador to Germany
Satō Kenryō	1895	JMA 29 / AWC 37	Lieutenant General / Director of Military Affairs Bureau, Ministry of the Army
Shigemitsu Mamoru	1887	TIU / Ministry of Foreign Affairs 1911	Japanese Ambassador to Soviet Union and Britain / Minister of Foreign Affairs
Shimada Shigetarō	1883	JNA 32 / NWC 13	Admiral / Minister of the Navy
Shiratori Toshio	1887	TIU / Ministry of Foreign Affairs 1914	Director of Public Information Division, Ministry of Foreign Affairs / Japanese Ambassador to Italy
Suzuki Teiichi	1888	JMA 22 / AWC 29	Lieutenant General / Minister of State / Chief, China Section, Military Affairs Bureau, Ministry of the Army / Chief of the Cabinet Planning Board
Tōgō Shigenori	1882	TIU / Ministry of Foreign Affairs 1912	Japanese Ambassador to Germany and Soviet Union / Minister of Foreign Affairs
Tōjō Hideki	1884	JMA 17 / AWC 27	General / Prime Minister / Minister of the Army / Chief of Staff of the Kwantung Army / Vice-Minister of the Army
Umezu Yoshijirō	1882	JMA 15 / AWC 23	General / Commander of the China Garrison Army / Vice-Minister of the Army / Commander of the Kwantung Army / Chief of General Staff

Note: JMA = Japanese Military Academy, AWC = Army War College
TIU = Tokyo Imperial University, KIU = Kyoto Imperial University
JNA = Japanese Naval Academy, NWC = Naval War College

Imperial Japanese Army and Tōjō-Related Individuals

A glance at the list reveals that most of the twenty-eight defendants were born in the 1880s, and five were born in the 1890s: Hashimoto, Hoshino, Mutō, Oka, and Satō. At the time of the trial, the eldest was Hiranuma (seventy-eight years old), while the youngest was Satō (fifty years old).

All of the listed, except Ōkawa who was outside government, were elite civil or military bureaucrats (senior officials). The listed military bureaucrats were, without exception, graduates of the Army War College or the Naval War College. They were the elite of the elite.

Based on the commonalities among the defendants, the lineup of Araki, Dohihara, Koiso, Hashimoto, Itagaki, Minami, and Ōkawa can be said to reveal the prosecutors' intention to prosecute a general conspiracy that had commenced prior to the Manchurian Incident.

Former prime minister Koiso's indictment was attributed to his involvement with Manchuria when he was director of the Military Affairs Bureau of the Ministry of the Army. Ōkawa, a civilian, was judged to be one of the ideological founders of the conspiracy. It is quite likely that the prosecutors had hoped to present Ōkawa as an ideologue who could be compared to Julius Streicher, publisher of an anti-Semitic newspaper and a defendant at the Nuremberg Trial. In any event, only three naval officers were indicted in contrast with fifteen army officers. Apparently, the Imperial Japanese Army was regarded by prosecutors as the principle axis of the military clique that took the initiative in the conspiracy.

Second, individuals related to the Tōjō Cabinet were particularly conspicuous.

Of these, Matsuoka and Shiratori, who were diplomats, and Ōshima, who was originally an army officer, were indicted as individuals responsible for the Japan-Germany-Italy Tripartite Pact. Kido was a founding father of the Tōjō Cabinet, while Hoshino, Kaya, Suzuki, Tōgō, and Navy Minister Shimada were members of the Tōjō Cabinet when the war erupted. Added to the list were Kimura, Satō, and Mutō, who were all close to Tōjō personally, plus Shigemitsu, who became foreign minister of the Tōjō Cabinet in 1943. That made ten defendants related to Tōjō. This seemed to reflect how important the attack on Pearl Harbor was to the Americans.

The Plausibility of "Replacement Theory"

Concerning the indictment of Shigemitsu and Umezu, war history writer Kojima Noboru advocates what he terms "replacement theory." According to Kojima, when Keenan rejected Golunsky's April 22 demand for the indictment of Shigemitsu and Umezu in addition to the twenty-eight defendants, the latter strongly insisted on replacing other defendants with Shigemitsu and Umezu, and threatened to withdraw from participation in the Tokyo Trial. Bewildered, Keenan consulted with MacArthur, and, as a result, it was decided to yield to the Soviet proposal by replacing Abe Nobuyuki and Masaki Jinzaburō with Shigemitsu and Umezu.[31]

However, there is no record showing that Abe and Masaki were replaced by Shigemitsu and Umezu. Indeed, historian Awaya Kentarō was the first to point out Kojima's misunderstanding. How, then, did Kojima commit this factual error? In my judgment, it was attributable to the entry for June 6, 1947, in Shigemitsu Mamoru's *Sugamo nikki* (Sugamo Diary).

> According to news from the Prosecution Section that we heard from Major General Tanaka Ryūkichi, who frequents the section, prosecutors from the Soviet Union, upon their arrival in Tokyo before the Class A war criminals were indicted, demanded that the emperor be prosecuted as a war criminal. When their demand was rejected by the US prosecutors, the Soviets staunchly insisted that of the twenty-eight Class A defendants Generals Abe and Masaki should be replaced by Shigemitsu and Umezu. I hear that twenty-eight was the maximum that could be seated in the defendants' seats. According to Tanaka, Chief Prosecutor Keenan in the end had to compromise, and accommodate the Soviets.

It remains unknown whether Tanaka Ryūkichi himself believed this rumor, but, in actuality, the Soviet Union did not insist on indicting the emperor, and this "replacement theory" was apparently inaccurate.

To begin with, the information that Tanaka provided behind the scenes was mostly dubious. Ashida Hitoshi, foreign minister in the Katayama Tetsu

---

31. Kojima Noboru, *Tōkyō Saiban* [The Tokyo Trial] (Tokyo: Chūōkōronsha, 2007).

Cabinet, for instance, was informed on October 29, 1947, by Tanaka that he had heard that Keenan, after returning to the US, had been assured by President Truman that it would be problematic to indict the emperor even if he was guilty. It was utterly impossible for Truman to tolerate indictment of the emperor. Another report from Tanaka that British and Dutch prosecutors were tenaciously insisting on indictment of the emperor, relying on Kido's affidavit, which Keenan rejected, was also hard to believe.[32]

There is reason to suspect that Tanaka intentionally brought up the issue of protection of the emperor. And the false information that Tanaka might have knowingly spread found its expression in Kojima's book, via Shigemitsu's prison diary, and was circulated widely.

For What Crimes Should They Be Indicted?

The last policy issue concerned the crimes for which defendants should be indicted. Let us take a look at indictments submitted by British prosecutor Arthur Comyns-Carr to the executive committee on April 5, 1946.

First, conspiracy to commit crimes against peace was divided into the following five sections.

(1) "Overall conspiracy," which covered the entire period from 1931 through 1945 as well as all the prosecuting countries.

And the following four periods of "separate conspiracies":

(2) The Manchurian Incident
(3) The Second Sino-Japanese War
(4) The Tripartite Pact
(5) The war against all of the Allies

Prosecutors decided to divide conspiracy into five segments in anticipation of contention by the defense that the timespan of the indictment was too long. Furthermore, seventeen cabinets were formed over seventeen years, starting

---

32. Shindō Eiichi et al., eds., *Ashida Hitoshi nikki* [Ashida Hitoshi Diary] (Tokyo: Iwanami Shoten, 1986), vol. 2.

with the 1927 Tanaka Giichi Cabinet and continuing through to the 1945 Suzuki Kantarō Cabinet. The prosecution thought the court might support indictments of consecutive separate conspiracies. Incidentally, Comyns-Carr himself, a distinguished barrister in Britain, suspected that crimes against peace might be an ex post facto law.

Second, prosecutors would indict Tokyo leaders—both civilian and military—on the basis of their responsibility for atrocities as conventional war crimes. Behind this was the need, on the part of participating countries, to emphasize atrocities committed by the Japanese troops to satisfy public opinion in the various countries, the difficulty of proving crimes against peace, and concerns regarding the ex post facto law. The US Department of State determined in April 1945 that in order to execute accused Japanese leaders it would be necessary to find them guilty of atrocities. It was also decided in London in January 1946, that, since most people would not approve of the death sentence for crimes against peace alone, the Tokyo Trial should take up violations of the laws of war. Keenan also told MacArthur on March 5 in the same year that even those defendants who were found not guilty of crimes against peace could be sentenced to death if they were found guilty of violating the laws of war. Thus, conventional war crimes were indispensable in justifying potential death sentences.

To Add Murder to the List of Charges

Third, a new charge of murder, a count unique to the Tokyo Trial, was created. Nowhere in the Nuremberg Charter or the Tokyo Charter was there a reference to the "crime of murder." What happened, one may wonder. It was caused by MacArthur's importunate request to add a new, separate charge that could be applied to the attack on Pearl Harbor, which, in his mind, was on a par with murder. MacArthur's original scheme had been to try members of the Tōjō Cabinet for murder, but that was rejected. Consequently, murder was added to the list of charges, and it was made applicable to other countries, including China.

Fourth, crimes against humanity lost their raison d'être, and became a means to back up charges of murder and conventional war crimes. Moreover, through the April 26 revision of the Tokyo Charter, "against any civilian population" was struck from the definition of crimes against humanity.

Crimes against humanity at that time were acts against civilian populations, including those by a country against its own nationals, as well as against stateless persons. As such, they were not considered applicable to Japan. Moreover, when the reference to "against any civilian population" was deleted, there would be no use for the crimes against humanity charge

Xiang Zhejun
(National Archives of the Netherlands, Collection 544
B. V. A. Röling)

at the Tokyo Trial. And yet, it still remained in the Tokyo Charter because of the Allies desire to retain consistency between the Nuremberg and Tokyo Trials. It was also maintained for use as legal backing for the murder charge.

Facing this prosecution policy, prosecutors representing the Netherlands, France, the Philippines, and China and other countries not subject to Anglo-American law, criticized the Tokyo Trial's excessive Anglo-American bias and, as quid pro quo, requested the addition of atrocities to the list of charges. Xiang Zhejun from China (born 1896; graduated from Yale University and George Washington University, and chief prosecutor at the Shanghai High Court), for instance, was not satisfied with prosecuting those responsible for the Nanjing Incident for murder, and succeeded in adding to the list the Japanese troops' atrocities in six other areas including Guangdong and Hankou. The Soviet delegation also insisted that the Zhanggufeng and Nomonhan Incidents were wars of aggression, and succeeded in including them in the crimes against peace.

To summarize the drafting process of the indictment, prosecutors from the British Commonwealth countries, who were critical of what the American prosecutors had done, took the initiative in creating the draft. This resulted in a strong bias toward Anglo-American law, to which prosecutors from non-Anglo-American law countries reacted negatively. Consequently, the final indictment ultimately included more charges in order to reflect the interests of participating countries.

In short, prosecutors dispatched to the Tokyo Trial were agents of their respective governments, making the issuing of the indictments an arena of "diplomatic negotiations" among jurists from these countries.

"An Incredibly Cumbersome Document"

The indictment for the Tokyo Trial was submitted to the court on April 29, 1946, the emperor's birthday. It was delivered to defendants that same day. The indictment consisted of a preamble, which included the famous condemnation that, "The internal and foreign policies of Japan were dominated and directed by the criminal military clique, and such policies were the cause of serious world troubles, aggressive wars, and great damage to the interests of peace-loving peoples, as well as the interests of the Japanese people themselves." It also comprised fifty-five counts (compared with four in the case of the Nuremberg Trial).

As political scientist Yabe Teiji commented with amazement, "This is an incredibly cumbersome document." The indictment had a highly complex structure modeled after Anglo-American law, defying easy comprehension. To begin with, the target of condemnation was obscure: was it the defendants or was it Japan as a whole? That depended on how you read it. What follows is the gist of this hard-to-grasp indictment.

Eleven plaintiff countries pressed charges against twenty-eight defendants for war crimes covering a period of approximately eighteen years and eight months from January 1928 through September 1945. This means that the Zhang Zuolin Assassination Incident (the Huanggutun Incident) in 1928 was chosen as the starting point of Japan's war of aggression.

In this regard, Sugawara Yutaka, one of the defense counsels, stated that the prosecutors took an optimistic view of the trial because they had the so-called Tanaka Memorandum.[33] The Tanaka Memorandum—that is, the Manchuria and Mongolia invasion policy that Prime Minister Tanaka Giichi addressed to the emperor—was a fabricated document that had provoked wariness of Japan in various countries. According to the February 25, 1946, memorandum of Roy L. Morgan, chief of the Investigative Division of the International Prosecution Section, Katō Masuo, a reporter with the Kyodo

---

33. Sugawara Yutaka, *Tōkyō Saiban no shōtai* [The True Nature of the Tokyo Trial] (Tokyo: Jiji Press, 1961).

News Agency (designated manager of the press corps covering the Tokyo Trial) who had been the "confidential informant," had told prosecutors that the Japanese people believed the Tanaka Memorandum was a genuine document written under instructions from Tanaka Giichi himself. Katō also told them that only Matsuoka Yōsuke and Koiso Kuniaki could tell the truth about the instructions given by Tanaka.[34]

In a later court hearing on August 2, 1946, however, Morishima Morito, a Japanese diplomat, replied to a question posed by the defense counsel that he had been aware that the Tanaka Memorandum was a fabrication. The judgment of the court did not refer to this document at all.

In any event, conspiracy is inferred from evidence that there was a common plan or a scheme to commit a crime. For this reason, the prosecutors were confident that they could easily prove that a conspiracy existed between 1928 and 1945.

Fifty-Five Counts

The fifty-five counts contained in the indictment can be divided into three groups. For details regarding each count, see my *Tōkyō Saiban no kokusai kankei* (The Tokyo Trial and International Relations).

The first group, crimes against peace, consisted of war of aggression and war in violation of a treaty. These two were almost synonymous. They included the following counts:

Counts 1–5	common plan or conspiracy;
Counts 6–17	plans and preparations for war against another country;
Counts 18–26	initiation of war; and
Counts 27–36	waging of war.

The second group, murder, consisted of:

Counts 37–38	common plan or conspiracy on murder;

---

34. IPS Papers, GHQ/SCAP records, RG 331 (National Archives Microfilm Publications, 1991), copies in Modern Japanese Political History Materials Room (Kensei Shiryōshitsu), National Diet Library, Tokyo.

Counts 39–43 murders during the attack on Pearl Harbor and at the start of the Pacific War;

Count 44 murder on a wide scale on land and at sea;

Counts 45–50 slaughter of inhabitants during the Nanjing Incident and other atrocities; and

Counts 51–52 murder of inhabitants in the Soviet Union–affiliated territories.

The third group, conventional war crimes and crimes against humanity, consisted of:

Count 53 conspiracy regarding violation of laws or customs of war;

Count 54 execution of such a conspiracy;

Count 55 omission of oversight responsibility, and failing to prevent violation of the laws of war.

Of these fifty-five counts, the fifty-fifth had not been introduced in the Nuremberg Trial. It was first introduced at the trial of General Yamashita Tomoyuki in Manila in 1945, but the idea dated back to the days immediately after World War I. A working group meeting of the Paris Peace Conference submitted a proposal holding civilian, military, and state leaders responsible for failing to prevent violations of laws of war. This proposal was supported by many of the European representatives.

This third group of counts only referred to committing "breaches of the Laws or Customs of War" and, thus, it was, de facto, an indictment of the Class B conventional war crimes. Nevertheless, there remained some element of the Class C crimes against humanity.

In the prosecutor's opening statement, Keenan justified the second group of counts (murder) by stressing that murder was the first item in the definition of crimes against humanity adopted by the Tokyo Charter, which included such crimes as "murder, extermination, enslavement, deportation, and other inhumane acts committed against any civilian population, before or during the war, or persecutions on political or racial grounds in execution of or in connection with any crime within the jurisdiction of the Tribunal." He said that prosecutors intended to hold defendants criminally accountable

Table 3-2. Counts Defendants Were Accused Of

Name	Counts	Total # of Counts
Araki Sadao	1–19, 23, 25–36, 44–47, 51–55	41
Dohihara Kenji	1–44, 51–55	49
Hashimoto Kingorō	1–19, 27–32, 34, 44–47, 53–55	33
Hata Shunroku	1–17, 19, 25–32, 34–36, 44–55	41
Hiranuma Kiichirō	1–47, 51–55	52
Hirota Kōki	1–17, 19–25, 27–35, 37–47, 52–55	48
Hoshino Naoki	1–17, 19–25, 27–35, 37–44, 52–55	45
Itagaki Seishirō	1–19, 23, 25–36, 44–47, 51–55	41
Kaya Okinori	1–17, 19–22, 24, 27–32, 34, 37–47, 53–55	43
Kido Kōichi	1–17, 19–55	54
Kimura Heitarō	1–17, 20–22, 27–32, 34, 37–44, 53–55	39
Koiso Kuniaki	1–18, 26–32, 34, 36, 44, 48–51, 53–55	35
Matsui Iwane	1–17, 19, 25–32, 34–36, 44–47, 51–55	38
Matsuoka Yōsuke	1–17, 23, 25–36, 38–44, 51–55	42
Minami Jirō	1–18, 27–32, 34, 44, 53–55	29
Mutō Akira	1–17, 19–24, 26–34, 36–47, 51, 53–55	48
Nagano Osami	1–17, 20–24, 27–34, 37–44, 53–55	41
Oka Takasumi	1–17, 20–22, 24, 27–32, 34, 37–44, 53–55	39
Ōkawa Shūmei	1–18, 27–32, 34, 44	26
Ōshima Hiroshi	1–17, 20–22, 24, 27–32, 34, 37–44, 53–55	39
Satō Kenryō	1–17, 20–22, 24, 27–32, 34, 37–44, 48–50, 53–55	42
Shigemitsu Mamoru	1–18, 23, 25, 27–35, 44, 48–50, 52–55	37
Shimada Shigetarō	1–17, 20–22, 24, 27–32, 34, 37–44, 53–55	39
Shiratori Toshio	1–17, 27–32, 34, 44	25
Suzuki Teiichi	1–17, 19–22, 24–32, 34–47, 51–55	49
Tōgō Shigenori	1–17, 20–22, 24–32, 34–44, 51, 53–55	44
Tōjō Hideki	1–24, 26–34, 36–44, 48–55	50
Umezu Yoshijirō	1–19, 26–32, 34, 36, 44–51, 53–55	39

Source: Higurashi Yoshinobu, *Tōkyō Saiban no kokusai kankei* (The Tokyo Trial and International Relations)

for the murder of civilians and disarmed troops, and the deprivation of sovereignty through establishment of puppet governments in China, the Philippines, and the Dutch East Indies.

In subsequent hearings, the prosecutors grilled defendants about their roles in the Nanjing Incident and their opium policies in China. The former line of questioning actually could have been pursued together with the violations of the laws of war charge, without resorting to the charge of crimes against humanity. Because the Tokyo Trial indictment included an admix of crimes against humanity and murder, instead of crimes against humanity alone, the issue of crimes against humanity at the Tokyo Trial became complicated. This was one example of failure caused by forcibly applying the framework of the Nuremberg Trial to the Tokyo Trial.

In terms of the total number of counts, Kido topped the list with fifty-four, followed by Hiranuma with fifty-two and Tōjō with fifty. Shiratori was at the bottom of the list with twenty-five counts.

Of those fifty-five counts, twenty-four were applied to all the defendants. They were conspiracy of war of aggression (group one, counts 1 through 5), planning and preparation of war of aggression (group one, counts 6 through 17), execution of the Manchurian Incident and the Second Sino-Japanese War and waging of war against the United States, the Philippines, British Commonwealth countries, and the Netherlands (group one, counts 27 through 32), and conspiracy to murder on a broad scale in territories occupied by Japan (group two, count 44).

Ōkawa and Shiratori alone were not accused of violation of the laws of war (group three, counts 53 through 55) (see Table 3-2).

3. Logic of the Prosecution

As with "the Poorest Japanese Soldier"

On April 22, 1946, the Shidehara Kijūrō Cabinet announced it would resign en masse. Due to continuing confusion, which resulted from the failure to create a coalition with the Nihon Jiyūtō (Japan Liberal Party) and the Nihon Shakaitō (Japan Socialist Party); the purge of Hatoyama Ichirō, president of the Jiyūtō, from public office; and the People's Rally for Obtaining Food on May 19, it was not until May 22 that the first Yoshida Shigeru Cabinet at last formed, as a coalition cabinet of the Jiyūtō and the Nihon Shinpotō (Japan Progressive Party).

On May 3, 1946, during this de facto government vacuum, the Tokyo Trial convened at Ichigayadai. The Nuremberg Trial was held at the venue of the Nazi Party's convention. Ichigayadai, too, was a symbolic site for the Imperial Japanese Army, because it was where the Army Ministry and the Imperial Japanese Army General Staff were established after the Imperial Japanese Military Academy moved out.

The auditorium of the main building of the former Army Ministry was converted into a courtroom. The scene at the convening of the court was as follows:

Defendants transported from Sugamo Prison to the court in a heavily guarded bus. May 3, 1946. (National Archives of the Netherlands, Collection 544 B. V. A. Röling)

Bus transporting defendants to Ichigayadai a day before the verdict. November 11, 1948. (Kyodo News)

Defendants queue to enter the courtroom
Left column from front to rear:
Kimura, Kido, Kaya, Hoshino, Itagaki, Suzuki, Shimada, Shiratori, Tōjō, Oka, Umezu, and Araki
Right column from front to rear:
Dohihara, Hata, Hirota, Minami, Hashimoto, Koiso, Nagano, Ōshima, Matsui, Mutō, Hiranuma, Tōgō, Shigemitsu, and Satō
(Kyodo News)

A little past 10:30 a.m., the Japanese defense counsels entered the courtroom. . . . Behind the justices' bench were eleven colorful national flags of the Allies, arranged in a fan shape and illuminated by bright lights. Facing the press corps seats and elevated one step higher were the VIP seats, which were occupied by some one hundred dignitaries attending this "play within a play." . . . Slightly past 11:00 a.m., Chief Prosecutor Keenan entered the courtroom, followed by a large number of prosecutors. . . . Two minutes later, defendants escorted by MPs made their appearance. . . . It was so quiet that one could hear the sound of camera shutters clicking and a chorus of cicadas. . . . Shortly thereafter, President Webb (of the International Military Tribunal for the Far East) and other justices in black robes took their seats on the bench. Captain Donald S. Van Meter, American Marshall of the Court, stood with a gavel underneath the judges' bench and loudly declared the opening of the trial.[35]

At the time, many predicted that the Tokyo Trial would be completed within a half year or, at the longest, within a year. Chief Justice William F. Webb, from Australia, however, declared at the opening that this would be a rigorous trial in which every defendant, regardless of rank or position, would be treated on an equal footing with the poorest Japanese soldier. And thus began what turned out to be a very long trial.

Dismissal of Defendant Ōkawa Shūmei

Those present on opening day, however, witnessed a sudden comedy in the afternoon. One of the defendants, Ōkawa Shūmei, was barefoot and scribbling something in his seat. All of a sudden, he slapped the head of Tōjō Hideki, who was seated in front of him. Turning around, Tōjō stared at Ōkawa but only smiled wryly.

Half a year earlier, in November 1945, Ōkawa commented, "I humbly surmise that His Majesty will abdicate the throne himself after amendment of the constitution." But in April 1946 he started to behave strangely. For instance, he declared that he was going to see the emperor immediately and make him

---

35. Nomura, *Sabakareta Nihon*.

emperor of China. Another Class A suspect, Sasakawa Ryōichi, once wrote that Ōkawa was different from the normal madman in that he himself admitted that he had gone a little mad. In fact, everyone in Sugamo Prison was well aware of Ōkawa's eccentricity. The day after his inexplicable conduct on the opening day of the court, Ōkawa was hospitalized. The Tokyo Trial therefore lost a defendant just as it was convening.

On April 9, 1947, approximately a year later, the bench of the Tokyo Trial concluded that Ōkawa was

Ōkawa Shūmei being restrained by two MPs (Kyodo News)

mentally ill and dropped the case against him, though he remained in detention. Learning of this decision from the following day's newspaper, Ōkawa noted in his diary that the decision was unexpected. Ōkawa wrote that the medical certificate written by an American medical doctor who had examined him said he possessed "the intellectual capacity and judgment necessary to take reasonable steps in the presentation of his defense."[36]

I assume that the court must have decided to drop the case against Ōkawa in consideration of the need to reduce the number of defendants in order to speed up the trial. A second reason may have been the need to prevent Ōkawa from presenting propaganda in his arguments.

At the arraignment on May 6, 1946, all the defendants except Ōkawa pleaded not guilty. While it was simply customary to plead not guilty at this stage, the Japanese people were not prepared for that. On one radio program, for instance, a daily *Mainichi Shimbun* reporter reviled the defendants as if they had slain his father, saying, "While we expected that all those criminals would be remorseful and truly ashamed of themselves, . . . they all insisted on their innocence . . . [and were determined to] continue insisting on

---

36. Ōkawa Shūmei Kenshōkai, ed., *Ōkawa Shūmei nikki* [Ōkawa Shūmei Diary] (Tokyo: Iwasaki Gakujutsu Shuppansha, 1986).

their innocence . . . [judging from their] defiant attitude." Tokutomi Sohō, a reporter with the *Yomiuri Shimbun*, made a similar critical comment, perhaps representing the majority view of the Japanese people of the day.[37]

Keenan's Opening Statement and Internal Strife within the Prosecution Camp

Approximately a month later, on June 4, Keenan enthusiastically declared in his opening statement before prosecutors began presenting evidence that "this is no ordinary trial, for here we are waging a part of the determined battle of civilization to preserve the entire world from destruction." (For each step in the introduction of evidence, see Table 3-3.)

Keenan referred back to the days of the Russo-Japanese War to criticize the "treacherous and perfidious" tendency of the Japanese. "In 1904, Japan opened the Russo-Japanese War with an attack on the Russian fleet at Port Arthur without notice or warning. The direct result of Japan's 'iniquity' in this case was the Third Hague Convention in 1907 (Relative to the Opening of Hostilities)." Keenan pointed out that Japan remained "perfidious" even at the time of the Manchurian Incident.

Explaining that prosecutors limited the number of defendants at the Tokyo Trial so that "these proceedings would not become impossibly unwieldy," Keenan suggested that "this is not, and will not be, the only trial of Japanese war criminals." Even though defendants were not "a united band, as was the case among the German conspirators," and despite a "sharp difference of opinion between them and fierce rivalries" among them—the fact that Keenan was aware of this is often overlooked—they were "all agreed in a determination to expand . . . the power of Japan." Keenan continued, "nations as such do not break treaties, nor do they engage in open and aggressive warfare. The responsibility always rests upon human agents, the individuals." That is why the individuals must be brought to "punishment for their acts."

In regard to criticism regarding the injustice of ex post facto operations, Keenan declared it should be noted that "every offense charged against these accused was well recognized as a crime in international law long before the dates stated in the indictment. If in the past there have been instances where such

---

37. Tokutomi, *Tokutomi Sohō shūsengo nikki* (2006), vol. 2.

Table 3-3. The Prosecution's Establishment of Facts by Evidence

Date Commenced	Phase of Prosecution's Establishment of Facts	Main Items to be Proved
June 4, 1946	Start of establishment of facts by evidence	Opening Statement
June 13, 1946	General demonstration	State organization, public opinion engineering, assassinations, etc.
July 1, 1946	Manchurian Incident phase	Liutiaogou Incident, Founding of Manchukuo, Japan's withdrawal from the League of Nations
August 6, 1946	Second Sino-Japanese War phase	North China Buffer State Strategy, Lukouchiao Incident (Marco Polo Bridge Incident), Trautmann Mediation, Nanjing Incident, opium problems
September 19, 1946	The Tripartite Pact phase	The Anti-Comintern Pact and the Tripartite Pact
September 30, 1946	French Indochina phase	Advance to French Indochina, Relations with Thailand
October 8, 1946	Soviet Union phase	Plan to attack the Soviet Union, Zhanggufeng and Nomonhan Incidents, and the Soviet-Japanese Neutrality Pact
October 21, 1946	General war preparation phase	Economic policy, industry regulation, South Sea Islands under Japan's mandatory rule, expansion of military power
November 4, 1946	The Pacific War phase	Negotiations with the United States, start of war with the US and Britain, the Southern Expansion Doctrine, occupation of the Dutch East Indies
November 27, 1946	Atrocities phase	Anti-Japan resistance in the Philippines, Malaya, French Indochina, and Dutch East Indies
January 17, 1947	Individuals phase	
January 24, 1947	Prosecution's establishment of facts by evidence	

conduct has remained unpunished, . . . our answer today is that no such neglect can longer be tolerated." In closing, Keenan contended that it was necessary to prevent "not only government but civilization itself from perishing."

After Keenan finished his opening statement, he immediately returned to the United States. His departure was so abrupt that it was not possible to know whether he was actually going to return to Japan, and who had the authority to make decisions during his absence.

The prosecutors from the British Commonwealth railed against the arrogant Keenan as vulgar and incompetent and eager to stand out. William Macmahon Ball, representative of the British Commonwealth at the Allied Council for Japan (ACJ), wrote in his diary, "Most interesting feature of the party was the unannounced and unexpected arrival of Mr. J. B. Keenan a little while before dinner. . . . He was exceedingly drunk, dressed in sports clothes and only in the mood for flying his arms round the necks of those present, and boasting in quite a disgusting way, about his intimacy with President Truman and other great men."[38]

The controversial Keenan publicized the prosecutors' decision to waive the indictment of the emperor in mid-June, while he was still in the United States, without any prior consent. Learning of this grandstanding by Keenan, prosecutors from the British Commonwealth countries initiated a drive to remove Keenan in cooperation with certain members of the American staff, including Carlisle Wallace Higgins, deputy chief prosecutor. This move was blocked by MacArthur, who had a high opinion of Keenan. Although the multilateral group of prosecutors succeeded in compiling the indictment, incorporating the interests of various countries, the internal conflict among them actually became fiercer after the opening of the trial.

Let the Japanese Themselves Try the Defendants

On April 26, 1946, immediately before the commencement of the Tokyo Trial, the committee on evidence of the International Prosecution Section (IPS) confirmed the prosecution's policy to rely more on the establishment of facts through evidentiary materials than witnesses' testimony. In late July that same year, Soviet associate prosecutor Sergei Alexandrovich Golunsky and Indian associate prosecutor P. Govinda Menon insisted on the establishment of facts by relying only on affidavits. In the case of the Nuremberg Trial, witnesses were permitted to submit affidavits without appearing in court. Thus, these two prosecutors hoped that, by limiting court appearances to highly impressive witnesses and by relying, instead, mainly on affidavits, the time required for the prosecution's establishment of facts would be substantially reduced.

---

38. Alan Rix, ed., *Intermittent Diplomat: The Japan and Batavia Diaries of W. Macmahon Ball* (Carlton: Melbourne University Press, 1988).

What, then, was a witness expected to do in court? Wakatsuki Reijirō, prime minister at the time of the Manchurian Incident, offered an easy explanation:

> Before a witness takes the stand, prosecutors examine various facts and compile them into a record of investigation [affidavit]. When I appeared in court, the prosecutor took out this record, and asked me if I had any objection to what was written in the document. When I said no, the prosecutor was able to do away with detailed questions and answers, making the entire process much simpler. But, of course, before this record of investigation was completed . . . I was summoned to the interrogation room in Ichigaya repeatedly. . . . The defense counsel cross-examined me, and I was obliged to answer point by point.[39]

William Joseph Sebald, chief of the GHQ's Diplomatic Section (DS), a graduate of the US Naval Academy, who was critical of the Tokyo Trial, scornfully reminisced that the Tokyo Trial courtroom in the beginning was decorated with vulgar Hollywood-like props, where court spectators were in high spirits as if they were at a ballpark instead of in a courtroom.

The prosecution's presentation, however, began unpretentiously. Before discussing the history of the war since the Manchurian Incident, the prosecution took up such issues as the Meiji Constitution, prewar Japan's governing structure, and the preparation of public opinion for a war (through education, political organizations, police, etc.).

The first witness was Lieutenant Colonel Donald R. Nugent, chief of GHQ's Civil Information and Educational Section (CIE), who had taught in Japanese universities including the Osaka University of Commerce before the war. Nugent was followed by one Japanese witness after another, including Kaigo Tokiomi, associate professor of education, Tokyo Imperial University; Ōuchi Hyōe, professor of finance, Tokyo Imperial University; Takigawa Yukitoki, professor of criminal law, Kyoto Imperial University; Maeda Tamon, former editorial writer with the daily *Asahi Shimbun* who had served the

---

39. Wakatsuki Reijirō, *Kofūan kaikoroku* [Kofūan Memoir] (Tokyo: Yomiuri Shimbunsha, 1975), revised edition.

Clockwise from top left: Kaigo Tokiomi, Ōuchi Hyōe, Suzuki Tōmin, and Maeda Tamon
(All Images on this page and facing from Kyodo News)

Higashikuni and the Shidehara Cabinets as education minister; Itō Nobumi, former director of the Cabinet Information Board; Suzuki Tōmin of the daily *Yomiuri Shimbun*; Shidehara Kijūrō, former prime minister and state minister without portfolio in the first Yoshida Shigeru Cabinet; Shimizu Kōnosuke, a right-wing activist; Tokugawa Yoshichika from the Owari Tokugawa family; and Wakatsuki Reijirō, former prime minister. The tactic of the prosecution was to have the Japanese people themselves try the defendants with Japan's own evidence.[40]

Shouldering Past Misfortunes

Let us now look at some of the witness statements.

Takigawa Yukitoki was cross-examined on June 19 by defense counsel Kiyose Ichirō. (Kiyose also defended Tōjō Hideki, and later became education minister and speaker of the House of Representatives.) Referring to Takigawa's affidavit, Kiyose pointed to Takigawa's testimony that Japan had

---

40. See Nomura, *Sabakareta Nihon*.

Shidehara Kijūrō

From left: Tokugawa Yoshichika, Ōhashi Nami, Shimizu Kōnosuke, and Inukai Takeru in the waiting room

From left: Yonai Mitsumasa, Wakatsuki Reijirō, Tanaka Ryūkichi, and Ugaki Kazunari in the waiting room

prepared students and others for a war of aggression through the educational system and by other means. He admitted that he held that all the wars starting with the Manchurian Incident were wars of aggression. However, when asked if he meant that the education authority in Japan had expected a war of aggression to take place, he evaded the question by stating he had no way of knowing what the education authority was thinking.

Suzuki Tōmin, who appeared in court on June 24, had been forced to give up writing in prewar days, after criticizing the military as a member of the *Yomiuri Shimbun*'s editorial board. Also, Suzuki, as chairman of the labor union, had led the Yomiuri Strike which blamed newspapermen's responsibility for the war and requested democratization of the company in 1945. When censored by the Japanese government, he testified that he would not justify the aggressive purpose of the war. Following the war, he led the labor union strike against the newspaper. In an attempt to damage the credibility of Suzuki's testimony, Kiyose asked if Suzuki was sympathetic with Communist ideology. In response, Suzuki indignantly replied that he was a disciple of Yoshino Sakuzō, forerunner of democracy in Japan.

On June 25 and 26, Shidehara Kijūrō described his experiences as foreign minister. According to his testimony, the Hamaguchi Osachi Cabinet, in which Shidehara served as foreign minister, made an enemy of the Japanese military because it restricted the military budget and signed the London Naval Treaty. This resulted in an assault on Prime Minister Hamaguchi by a right-wing terrorist. The cabinet was forced to resign en masse because of the military's attack on "weak-kneed Shidehara diplomacy." Minami Jirō, minister of the Army at the time of the Manchurian Incident, was not one of the "criminal military clique" and, in fact, he made a personal effort to control the escalation of the incident. But the cabinet and the Foreign Ministry had no choice other than to make its judgment on the basis of the army minister's report that the Liutiaogou Incident was an act of self-defense. While Shidehara's testimony functioned to protect the Ministry of Foreign Affairs and its affiliated defendants, it also tended to subtly criticize the Imperial Japanese Army.

On June 26 and 27, Shimizu Kōnosuke and Tokugawa Yoshichika testified regarding the March Incident, an abortive coup d'état attempt in Japan in March 1931, launched by the radical Sakurakai (Cherry Blossom Society), a secret society within the Imperial Japanese Army. This testimony was the first time that Japanese citizens learned of this coup attempt by mid-level army officers. Central figures in the incident included Hashimoto Kingorō, Koiso Kuniaki, and Ōkawa Shūmei. Ōkawa was particularly noteworthy, because he allegedly declared that Japan had no choice but to destroy the administration that had been corrupted by political parties and the zaibatsu by using the "force of the military." Shimizu, who had been entrusted with 300 dummy cartridges for the coup, testified that he had heard from a drunken Ōkawa at a party that something interesting would happen in Manchuria, even though the attempt in March failed.

Many of the Japanese witnesses who appeared in court in June had experienced misfortunes or failures in the past. For this reason, their testimonies tended to work against the defendants. While some of the witnesses turned out to be of no use, the prosecution's overall strategy was effective.

Tanaka Ryūkichi, an Unusual Witness

On July 5, 1946, a collaborator with the prosecution, Major General Tanaka Ryūkichi, former director of the Military Administration Bureau, Army Ministry, took the witness stand for the first time.

Tanaka was a highly unusual witness who willingly provided all the information that the prosecution wished to obtain. He became a star witness for the prosecution, attracting attention in the early days of the trial. In a meeting of the subcommittee on documents and witnesses of the IPS on May 22, it was reported that all the interrogators who had talked to Tanaka insisted on calling him as a witness. It was decided in the meeting that Tanaka's mental state should be examined in preparation for cross-examination by the defense.[41]

In the courtroom in July, prosecutor Benjamin E. Sackett questioned Tanaka about whether the Manchurian Incident was a premeditated incident. Tanaka replied affirmatively, and identified Tatekawa Yoshitsugu, Chō Isamu, Hashimoto Kingorō, and Ōkawa Shūmei as the key participants in the plot, and Itagaki Seishirō and Ishiwara Kanji as the central players in the Kwantung Army.

The prosecution summoned Tanaka again on January 3, 1947, during the "atrocities phase" (see Table 3-3) to have him explain the Imperial Japanese Army's system of managing prisoners of war in the 1940s. Tanaka's explanation highlighted the heavy responsibility of Minister of the Army Tōjō, Vice-Minister of the Army Kimura Heitarō, and Sato Kenryō, director of the Military Affairs Bureau. During the cross-examination, when defense

Tanaka Ryūkichi on the witness stand
(Kyodo News)

---

41. IPS Papers, GHQ/SCAP records, RG 331.

counsel William Logan, Jr., (in charge of defendant Kido) asked if his testimony on everything that happened after Tanaka's resignation from the post of director of the Military Administration Bureau in September 1942 was based merely on indirectly obtained information, Tanaka readily admitted that was the case. The defense also brought up Tanaka's mental state and his relations with the prosecution in an attempt to discredit his testimony.

Tanaka was often evasive when responding to questions posed by defense counsel George G. Blewett, who had also belonged to the defense at the Nuremberg Trial. He would reply, "I do not know," or "I do not remember," but Tanaka's testimony was advantageous to the Ministry of Foreign Affairs in relation to the prisoners-of-war issue. On that issue, Tanaka testified that the Foreign Ministry had only functioned as a sort of post office. Yet Tanaka was highly critical of Vice-Minister of the Army Kimura Heitarō, who had been teased as "a robot vice-minister," for being only concerned about harmony within the ministry, and had been totally unreceptive to Tanaka's proposals and suggestions.

In late January 1947, Tanaka once again answered questions from prosecutor Comyns-Carr. He testified that Mutō Akira, director of the Military Affairs Bureau had been virtually "a central figure in the Army Ministry" and, when the Imperial Japanese Army was the driving force of the Japan state, measures taken by the army were mostly the creation of the brilliant mind of the director. This testimony delivered a heavy blow to Mutō, against whom Tanaka had held a personal grudge since the former's director days. (During the "individuals phase" in mid-November, Mutō made a frontal rebuttal to Tanaka's testimony.)

Why Tanaka Became a Whistleblower

Based on his testimony, it was no wonder that all the defendants denounced Tanaka as a traitor. Sasakawa Ryōichi, for instance, wrote in his diary,

> Tanaka was in an important position in a special duty military organization in Shanghai, using Kawashima Yoshiko (a female spy) as a tool to advance into China. . . . He was instrumental in launching the Suiyuan Campaign, which became a remote cause of the Second Sino-Japanese War, but escaped from the devastation in Bailingmiao. . . . Everyone

without exception was outraged to learn that, having done all of that, Tanaka wrote a book denouncing the military clique [Tanaka Ryūkichi, *Haiin o tsuku*]. He must have been out of his mind.

Among the Sugamo Prison inmates, it was rumored that Tanaka was an agent of Keenan's and enjoyed the good life.[42]

Tanaka appeared in court three times as a prosecution witness and twice as a defense witness. He was mockingly nicknamed "a professional witness." Nevertheless, he was an exceptionally bold and fearless witness, a rarity among the Japanese. Defense counsel Shimanouchi Tatsuoki (in charge of defendant Ōshima) recalled that Tanaka was interesting to listen to, and he entertained courtroom audiences and the press corps. Former Lieutenant General Kawabe Torashirō, who was two-years senior to Tanaka at the Imperial Japanese Military Academy, defended Tanaka by saying, "Although many people speak ill of him, you have to admit that his testimony is mostly true."[43]

Why, then, did Tanaka become a whistleblower? Eguchi Wataru, a *Tokyo Shimbun* reporter who was personally close to Tanaka, explained that Tanaka might have perceived the Tokyo Trial as an arena for retaliation and as a warning to others by the Allies, and he might have decided to pin the responsibilities on certain individuals to protect the emperor.[44]

However, Tanaka's conduct, which went a little too far, cannot be explained as resulting only from "patriotic" intentions. There was another explanation, namely that Tanaka saw a chance to enhance his own safety by collaborating with the Occupation authorities. Tanaka was, from the prosecution's viewpoint, a convenient collaborator who could be used as a liaison with the defendants. It is obvious that the Tokyo Trial should not be understood only in light of the conflict between Japan and the Allies. Tanaka, too, was an individual embroiled in the tempestuous international politics of the Tokyo Trial.

---

42. Sasakawa Ryōichi, *Sugamo nikki* [Sugamo Diary] (Tokyo: Chūōkōronsha, 1997), and Abe, *Sugamo nikki*.
43. Shimanouchi Tatsuoki, *Tōkyō Saiban* [Tokyo Trial] (Tokyo: Nippon Hyōronsha, 1984).
44. Tanaka Ryūkichi, *Haiin o tsuku* [To Pinpoint the Reason for Defeat] (Tokyo: Chūōkōronsha, 1988).

Puyi on the witness stand
(Kyodo News)

Keenan and Puyi
(Harvard Law School Library, Historical & Special Collections,
Joseph Berry Keenan photograph collection)

Puyi's Vindication

Another, perhaps greater, attraction was the testimony given by Aisin Gioro Puyi, former emperor of Manchukuo (Xuantong Emperor, the last emperor of the Qing Dynasty). Due to the quality of the witness, however, his testimony became a failure for the prosecution.

Puyi, who had been detained in Khabarovsk, appeared in court on August 16, 1946. Appearing tense when he arrived, Puyi was facing the dual threat of (1) being interned in the Soviet Union, and (2) being handed over to China to be tried as a national traitor. (Puyi was later transferred to China in July 1950, and detained as a war criminal by the Beijing government until he was granted special amnesty in December 1959.)

Faced with these double threats and attracting all the attention in the courtroom, Puyi was desperate to vindicate himself on the witness stand. He insisted that Japan be blamed for everything. However, he overdid it, and that caused his failure. The mode of testimony that he employed is symbolized by the following exchange with Keenan:

> Chief Prosecutor Keenan: Did you have any intention to resist the Japanese . . . ?
> Puyi: My true hope was to reject the Japanese requests. But given the military pressure from the Japanese military and recommendations from my own advisors to comply, out of fear for my own life I had no other option than to yield to their demands.

Truth be told, in the beginning the Japanese defense counsels had agreed among themselves not to cross-examine Puyi, out of respect. Witnessing his obvious attempt at shifting the blame to others, they changed their minds. One after another the defense counsels in charge of the Manchurian Incident rushed to cross-examine Puyi.[45]

Nevertheless, Puyi's attempt to evade any responsibility remained unchanged. Chief Justice Webb was so appalled by Puyi's attitude that he said he had heard enough of Puyi's excuses, and that his testimony was no longer necessary.

There also was an unexpected commotion on August 21. Defense Counsel Ben Bruce Blakeney (in charge of defendants Tōgō and Umezu), who was quite knowledgeable about Puyi, held up a piece of paper before the witness. It was Puyi's letter addressed to Army Minister Minami Jirō, accepting the post of the chief executive of Manchukuo.

As soon as Puyi realized what the piece of paper was, he drew himself up and started yelling something. When Webb in a loud voice told him to be seated, Puyi said, "Your honors, this document is totally counterfeit." He flatly denied that the letter or the privy seal on it belonged to him, and would not yield even an inch. According to Shigemitsu Mamoru, Blakeney's cross examination was like watching a star-studded kabuki play.

Tokutomi Sohō read Puyi's mind, saying, "Pathetically weak-looking Puyi all of a sudden turned into a demon woman, carrying on an outrageous performance. . . . I guess life was that dear to him."[46] In his memoir, Puyi himself admitted that his testimony was perjury, and that he had wanted to cover up his criminal acts out of fear of punishment from his home country.[47]

It is interesting to compare the Nuremberg Trial and the Tokyo Trial. "The Nuremberg Trial can be likened to an austere but solemn Wagnerian opera (including the prosecution's elaborative emphasis on the guilt of the defendants vs. the defendants' heroic argument on their innocence), while the Tokyo Trial resembled a vulgar and frivolous third-rate barnstorming

---

45. Shimanouchi, *Tōkyō Saiban*.

46. Tokutomi, *Shūsengo nikki* (2007), vol. 3.

47. Aisin Gioro Puyi, *Waga hansei* [My Life up to Now] (Tokyo: Chikuma Shobō, 1977), vol. 2.

operetta."[48] It seems undeniable that the Tokyo Trial reminded court audiences of slapstick comedy, the typical manifestation of which was Puyi's testimony.

Sejima Ryūzo, Stalin's Witness

The prosecution's "Soviet Union phase," which started on October 8, 1946, was an extraordinary event in many ways.

The opening statement by Soviet prosecutor Sergei Golunsky was unnecessarily lengthy and full of propaganda. He gave top priority to demonstrating Japan's invasiveness and the lawfulness of the Soviet Union.

According to the March 20, 1946, directive of the Politburo, Central Committee of the Communist Party of the Soviet Union, the major task of Soviet prosecutors was to disclose Japan's systematic invasion of the Soviet Union following the Russo-Japanese War and the Siberian Intervention. They were to abide by instructions from the Kremlin regarding strategy during court proceedings and, in the case of emergency, they were to consult with Lieutenant General Kuzma Nikolayevich Derevyanko, Soviet member of the Allied Council for Japan, and other staff. A special secret committee inside the Kremlin studied issues submitted by prosecutors in Tokyo, and gave prior approval to their remarks in court.[49]

On August 23, 1945, Stalin approved the decision of the State Defense Committee to detain some 500,000 Japanese troops. Japanese military personnel who had been engaged in anti-Soviet operations, planning, and intelligence activities were particularly valuable as sources of information and, thus, those who were candidates as witnesses at the Tokyo Trial were detained in Khabarovsk. In January 1946, a committee was set up to select and examine witnesses and, after meticulous consideration, two groups of three witnesses each were formally approved by Stalin. The criteria used to select witnesses were knowledge of Soviet invasion plans, confidence that they would not withdraw their testimonies in court, and their capacity to debate. Those chosen were given special treatment and training in how to

---

48. Ministry of Foreign Affairs, *Gaikō kiroku* [Diplomatic Record] (Diplomatic Archive of the Ministry of Foreign Affairs, 1998), 14th Disclosure.
49. Kirichenko, "Tōkyō Saiban e no Kuremurin himitsu shirei."

memorize the meticulously prepared scenario of anticipated questions and planned answers.

The first group of witnesses, former army lieutenant colonel Sejima Ryūzo, former army lieutenant general Kusaba Tatsumi, and former army major general Matsumura Tomokatsu, were transferred to Haneda on September 17, 1946. Although Kusaba committed suicide by taking poison in the early morning of September 20, claiming it would be too painful to testify against his former comrades, the Soviet prosecutors submitted his affidavit to the court, along with his death certificate. It is said that this conveyed an indescribable sense of pity and eeriness.[50]

Sergei Golunsky
(Kyodo News)

A former staff officer of the Imperial Japanese Army at the Imperial General Headquarters, Sejima was thirty-four at the time of the Tokyo Trial. After giving the prepared testimony, Sejima fended off such questions from Blakeney as to whether the Kwantung Army's strength had been smaller than the Soviet Army when Sejima was with the Imperial Japanese Army General Staff by stating that he had no clear recollection. Sejima thus innocuously completed his witness duty. (Three of the five Soviet-selected witnesses, including Sejima, were subsequently found guilty in Soviet trials and another witness found guilty in Beijing.)

What Was the Tokyo Trial for the Soviet Union?

The Soviet prosecutors used affidavits to condemn the defendants for the Manchuria, Zhanggufeng and Nomonhan Incidents, the zaibatsu's war preparation, and the Research Institute of National Policy. The evidence presented by the Soviet side, however, lacked persuasive power. The scarcity of evidence even regarding Shigemitsu and Umezu Yoshijirō, who had been special targets of the Soviet side, astonished defense counsel George

---

50. Kirichenko, "Tōkyō Saiban e no Kuremurin himitsu shirei"; Tanaka Akira, Kyōdō Tsūshinsha Shakaibu [Kyodo News Social Affairs Department], eds., *Chinmoku no fairu* [Silent Files] (Tokyo: Kyodo News, 1996); and Nomura, *Sabakareta Nihon*.

A. Furness (in charge of defendant Shigemitsu), who had defended Honma Masaharu in the Manila court.

The aims for the Tokyo Trial as set out officially by the Soviet Union included the punishment of those responsible for the war of aggression, the reeducation of the Japanese by eduating them about the true nature of Japan's imperialistic invasions, and, thereby, the deterrence of future Japanese aggression. These were essentially identical with the goals of the Allies. The Soviet Union's goals were somewhat unique, though, in demanding, for instance, that the judgment refer to the Red Army's "heroic role."

In the Soviet political system, the judiciary branch was not independent from the executive and legislative branches. A court of justice in the Soviet Union was subordinate to the administrative authority, and functioned as a tool to protect the interests of ruling elites.[51] During the Tokyo Trial, Soviet prosecutors were sensitive to any "anti-Soviet" remarks from the defense.

Major General Ivan M. Zaryanov, the Soviet justice, went as far as to claim that the court should not permit the defense to propagate its views, which would be harmful to the Occupation and the trial. He pressured Chief Justice Webb not to allow a comparison between Japan and the Allies in the court, because this was a venue for trying Japan's invasion. While no country is willing to be condemned for its wrongdoings, the Soviet Union was abnormally sensitive to criticism from others. For the Soviet Union, the Tokyo Trial was a forum to prove the legitimacy of the country and its Communist Party.

Paradox of the Cold War

In any event, the Soviet Union was handicapped. During the cross-examination on June 4 and 5, 1947, defense counsel Blakeney argued that Soviet participation in the war in violation of the Japanese-Soviet Neutrality Pact amounted to an invasion of Japan. Blakeney relentlessly attacked Soviet weak points. His remarks implied that if the Soviet Union was forgiven for what it did, then Japan's attack on Pearl Harbor would also be permissible.

While this *tu quoque* logic is generally convincing, it was not tolerated in the Nuremberg and Tokyo Trials. They were arenas of international politics.

---

51. The Rt. Hon. Lord Hankey, *Politics, Trials and Errors* (Chicago: Henry Regnery Company, 1950).

American prosecutor Frank S. Tavenner, Jr., refuted them saying, "All the conducts of the Soviet Union were totally irrelevant to this trial. . . . They are out of this court's jurisdiction." Upon this exchange, justices of the Tokyo Trial assembled—the Soviet prosecutors must have fervently argued their position—and decided that the participation of the Soviet Union in the war had no relevance to the trial. While the prosecutors must have anticipated that their decision would further strengthen the image of the Tokyo Trial as a form of victors' justice, the trial itself would not be sustainable if its ideal of cooperation among the Allies lost credibility.

In the past, it has been misconstrued by many that the Cold War impacted the Tokyo Trial in 1947. To be sure, the Truman Doctrine was announced in March 1947, marking the beginning of Cold War in Europe. From the viewpoint of the defeated looking at the US-USSR standoff, the Allies' norm of criminalization of war seems somewhat suspect. That was why the defense counsels regarded the Cold War as advantageous for them in dealing with the Soviet Union. This decision by the defense made it essential for the Allies to collaborate with the Soviet Union during the Tokyo Trial. Even Keenan tried to defend the Soviet Union as much as possible. As Shigemitsu observed, it became all the more necessary for the Allies to complete the Tokyo Trial as promptly as possible in collaboration with the Soviet Union as the Cold War was becoming more intense.

The Tokyo Trial was intended to put an end to World War II. It was the structure and logic of World War II that was consistently dominant throughout the trial.

US-Japan War as Seen by Ballantine

The United States attached the greatest importance to the Pacific War phase of the trial from November 18 through 25, 1946 (see Table 3-3). It was now that Joseph W. Ballantine, former director of the Office of Far Eastern Affairs, Department of State, took the witness stand on six consecutive days.

In a lengthy affidavit, which he claimed to have written mostly on his own, Ballantine reviewed a detailed history of US-Japan relations since the Manchurian Incident, supplemented with multiple diplomatic documents. The defense criticized the affidavit, however, finding that it sounded more like a prosecutor's closing argument than the mere personal conclusion of a witness.

The testimony of Ballantine, who was knowledgeable about Japan and its people, was extremely acrimonious, making him an ideal witness for the prosecution. He stated, for instance, that, in order to make China comply with its directives, the Japanese government produced an egregious document called the Amō Statement in April 1934. After announcing its withdrawal from the Washington Naval Treaty in December 1934, the Japanese government launched an arms buildup in preparation for a war of aggression against China. At the negotiating table with the US, the Japanese government stuck to its policy of invasion and exerting military power. After the formation of the Tōjō Cabinet in October 1941, Japan began ignoring the principles of justice and equality that were essential for the maintenance of peace in the Pacific. On December 7, 1941, Washington time, Japanese ambassador to the United States Nomura Kichisaburō and Special Envoy Kurusu Saburō arrived at the US Department of State to hand a document to Secretary of State Cordell Hull. They delayed the time of their appointment with Hull. The said document was not "a declaration of war with reasons attached" or "an ultimatum"; it was not even "a declaration of intention to sever diplomatic relations." According to Ballantine, "the accusation that the United States had planned to escalate the war was simply absurd." The defense condemned the economic blockade conducted by the US, Britain, and other countries, but for them "it was a measure necessary for self-defense," said Ballantine.

Keenan made the point on another occasion, that the US was attacked by Japan as a result of adhering to a foreign policy that opposed invasions. And this policy had now become the law with which defendants would be punished.[52] The prosecution's evidence about the war between Japan and the US was, indeed, a manifestation of this "prosecution's logic."

Obsession with Proving Atrocities

Proving atrocities was by contrast a bottleneck for Keenan. But the countries concerned would not compromise on the issue of atrocities because that would risk provoking a strong desire for retaliation among those countries' citizens.

In August 1946, immediately after Keenan returned to Tokyo from the

---

52. IPS Papers, GHQ/SCAP records, RG 331.

US, American prosecutors attempted to collectively prove the atrocities relating to both Americans and Filipinos by American prosecutors. Pedro Lopez (born in 1906; member of House of Representatives), prosecutor from the Philippines, which had just gained independence from the US, became indignant. He succeeded in forcing Keenan to allow Filipino prosecutors to carry out their own producing of evidence. However, this made the prosecution more time consuming, and raised the problem of redundancy.

Prosecutor Mansfield from Australia also told Keenan that his government considered the trial of Class B and C war crimes suspects to be one of the most important steps in the Tokyo Trial, and that it would not tolerate any mitigation of that process.

In response, Keenan, who had been urged to complete the trial promptly by both Truman and MacArthur, insisted they should save time by shortening the atrocities phase because the most important objective of the Tokyo Trial was to prove crimes against peace. Having already heard testimony on the Nanjing Incident (Second Sino-Japanese War phase), the majority of the Japanese people were already shocked and ashamed. It was just as Shigemitsu had written in his diary, "The abomination is too monstrous to my ears. Is the Japanese spirit rotten?" Keenan thought that was sufficient. But prosecutors from the British Commonwealth, the Netherlands, and the Philippines fiercely protested that Keenan's suggestion was an arbitrary time restriction, and rejected it at the associate prosecutors' meeting.

Thus, a massive amount of evidence about atrocities conducted by the Japanese military was to be submitted to the court in December.

During the hearing on December 16, Australian prosecutor Alan Mansfield accused Japan of failing to take measures to correct the abuse of prisoners of war even though it had pledged to apply provisions of the Geneva Convention of 1929 correspondingly. He accused the Japanese government, attributing individual atrocities to its general policy. (After this protest, Mansfield returned to Australia early in the new year.)

In late December, details of atrocities committed by the Japanese against Dutch-affiliated people were introduced. Foremost among them were torture, abuse, and the failure to take preventive measures against the spread of disease among detainees in various Dutch East Indies territories. The specific details of these atrocities were more or less the same across the victimized countries. The delay in the completion of the prosecution's introduction of evidence until January 24, 1947, was largely attributable to each country's desire to present the atrocities inflicted on its own people.

In my judgment, Keenan's proposal to speed up the trial was itself reasonable. It was consistent with the policy of the British Commonwealth, which preferred an early conclusion to the trial. Countries that perceived the punishment of atrocities as their national interest were, however, obsessed with proving the brutalities inflicted on their own people, and, for this purpose, prolongation of the trial was unavoidable.

CHAPTER 4

How Japan Responded

Defense counsels. **From left:** Uzawa, Howard, Brooks, Logan, Brannon, McManus, Levin, Yamaoka, and Blewett.
(National Archives of the Netherlands, Collection 544 B. V. A. Röling)

1. Cooperation and Resistance

The Power of the Occupation Forces

The first prime minister of Japan after its defeat in World War II was Prince Higashikuni Naruhiko, whose cabinet was charged with carrying out the demobilization of the Japanese armed forces. When Foreign Minister Shigemitsu Mamoru resigned due to intra-cabinet conflict, Yoshida Shigeru, a former diplomat, succeeded to his post. Yoshida had a reputation for being "a foreign minister who could maintain a good relationship with General MacArthur." However, when the General Headquarters (GHQ) of the Supreme Commander for the Allied Powers (SCAP) ordered the dismissal of Home Minister Yamazaki Iwao (who had told a Reuters' correspondent that anyone advocating any changes in the present political structure, including the status of the emperor, was a communist who should be arrested), and the abolition of the laws and regulations related to human rights suppression, the Higashikuni Cabinet, which had no popular support, chose to resign en masse on October 5, 1945.

The succeeding prime minister had to be someone who would not rouse US antipathy, who was not suspected of war guilt, and who was well versed in diplomacy. Applying these criteria, Shidehara Kijūrō, former foreign minister who was known for his cooperative diplomacy in prewar days, formed a cabinet on October 9. This indicates the influence the Occupation forces had in Japanese politics.

Under the Occupation, Japan's national sovereignty and diplomatic prerogatives were terminated. Diplomat Ōno Katsumi reminisced about those days as follows:

The time has come when GHQ strikes fear in the hearts of the Japanese people. . . . A directive from GHQ reached the Ministry of Foreign Affairs, announcing that henceforth the Japanese government should sever all relations with foreign governments. The directive said relations with foreign countries now would be handled by GHQ instead. What this means is the total loss of Japan's sovereignty in diplomacy. . . . A signboard saying "Central Liaison Office," which is much larger than the signboard of the Ministry of Foreign Affairs, now hangs on the ministry's building.[1]

Under these circumstances, how did the Japanese government deal with the war crime issue? Some claim that the Japanese government dreaded becoming involved in the war crimes issue to such a degree that defendants in the Tokyo Trial had to cope with the prosecution on their own. It appeared this way because, given its acceptance of the Potsdam Declaration, the Japanese government was obliged to cooperate with the war crimes trials by the Allies. Our first task here is to verify if this was actually the case.

While the Ministry of Foreign Affairs maintained a cautious stance so as not to project an image of protecting criminals, it also requested GHQ to show tolerance to those Japanese soldiers who had just followed orders, because in the Imperial Japanese military a superior officer's orders were absolute. Thus, both cooperation and partial resistance were found in the Japanese government's involvement in the war crimes problem.

Nakamura Toyoichi's Suggestion

On September 11, 1945, when Tōjō Hideki was arrested, the Treaty Bureau of the Ministry of Foreign Affairs correctly interpreted Article 10 of the Potsdam Declaration. It was clear to the bureau that Article 10 was not confined solely to the violation of the traditional laws of war, but that it also applied to those who were politically responsible for the war, and included moral condemnation. Based on the London Agreement and the United Nations War Crimes Commission (UNWCC) policy recommendation, the bureau

---

1. Ōno Katsumi, *Kasumigaseki gaikō* [Kasumigaseki Diplomacy] (Tokyo: Nihon Keizai Shimbunsha, 1978).

inferred that policies adopted in Germany would also be applied to Japan.

In question was the scope of "those who were political responsible." The Treaty Bureau made an impressive judgment on this issue. It acknowledged that there were some who insisted on including not only the military clique in Japan but also certain political leaders, right-wing organizations, and business leaders. While in Germany specific individual Nazi leaders were the targets, the bureau predicted that in Japan, where specific individuals did not stand out, organizations—and thus executives of these organizations—would be targeted.

It should be noted that there was actually a scheme to have the Japanese themselves open their own court. Colonel Miyama Yōzō, adjutant general of the Army Ministry (graduate of the '35 class of the Imperial Japanese Military Academy, and later deputy director of the Repatriation Relief Bureau, Ministry of Welfare) wrote in his diary that a Japanese-initiated court would not try the Class A war criminals or commander-level defendants. As Miyama predicted, the proposed tribunal would only try perpetrators of atrocities. Therefore, it was not an attempt to replace the Tokyo Trial.[2] It was only "victors' justice" that could genuinely inquire into Japan's war responsibility, and the Japanese government braced itself for that.

The Central Liaison Office, an extra-ministerial bureau of the Ministry of Foreign Affairs, assumed that the way in which defendants vindicated themselves and the nature of the judgments the court handed down would profoundly affect Japan's future. On November 20, 1945, Minister Nakamura Toyoichi, director of liaison on war criminal issues of the First Department of the Central Liaison Office (son-in-law of Yoshizawa Kenkichi, foreign minister in the Inukai Tsuyoshi Cabinet, and father of Ogata Sadako, United Nations High Commissioner for Refugees), proposed a strategy regarding the war crimes trials. Nakamura advocated the formation of a team of competent defense counsels to support the suspects. Because the defense counsels who were not familiar with the incidents in question needed documents and other information from the administrative secretariat, Nakamura proposed that two committees should be established.

---

2. Miyama Yōzō, *Haikyo no Shōwa kara* [From Ruined Shōwa], ed. Kai Katsuhiko (Tokyo: Kōjinsha, 1989).

One was a provisional investigating committee on war criminals to be headed by the administrative vice-minister of the Ministry of Foreign Affairs and temporary committee members loaned from the Imperial Japanese Army and Navy, the Ministry of Justice, and other bodies. The committee members' role would be to analyze documents and provide them to prosecution and defense lawyers. (This proposal eventually evolved into the "Legal Affairs Councilors' Office," which will be discussed later.)

The second was the smaller War Crimes Trials Countermeasures Committee, which was to be a sort of brain trust, focused on countermeasures for political issues and atrocities. Nakamura said that it was diplomatically advisable to have the committee appear to be independent of the government, devoid of political affiliation, and staffed by civilian intellectuals. In reality, the committee was to provide guidance to defense counsels on behalf of the Japanese government. However, the proposal for the committee was rejected by the Ministry of Foreign Affairs as absolutely unacceptable.

Phantom of a "Unified Opinion" Concept

The way in which defendants were to be defended and how that would affect the future of Japan was a major concern within the Japanese government.

Under the Higashikuni Cabinet, a document styled "Sensō sekinin ni kansuru ōtō yōryō (an)" (Outline of Responses to War Responsibility [draft]) was composed on October 3 as the "unified opinion" of the Japanese side.[3] Apprehensive of the unreliability of suspects' attitudes toward the interrogations, the government passed the task of assisting defendants to the succeeding Shidehara Cabinet. Under the Shidehara Cabinet, Tsugita Daizaburō, chief cabinet secretary; Tajiri Akiyoshi, director of the Foreign Ministry's Political Affairs Bureau; Narahashi Wataru, director general of the Cabinet Legislation Bureau; Yoshizumi Masao, director of Military Affairs, Army Ministry; Hoshina Zenshirō, director of Military Affairs, Navy Ministry; and several others assembled to deliberate "the situation at the start of the war."

As a result, the policy paper "Points of Responses to War Responsibility

---

3. Awaya Kentarō, *Tōkyō Saiban e no michi* [Road to the Tokyo Trial] (Tokyo: Kodansha, 2006).

and so forth" was completed on November 5 by the executive board of the Central Liaison Office (Shūsen Renraku Kanjikai).[4]

The essence of this "unified opinion" was twofold:

(1) To protect the emperor from the pursuit of his war responsibility, and
(2) To simultaneously pursue "defense of state" and "defense of individuals."

By April 1946, some had begun arguing that "the Imperial Japanese Army was responsible for what had happened in the Asian continent, while the Imperial Japanese Navy bore no war responsibility." Concerned about this disunity, Matsumoto Shigeharu, a journalist well versed in the United States, stressed to former colonel Matsutani Sei (graduate of 35th class of the the Imperial Japanese Military Academy), staff member of the First Ministry of Demobilization (former Ministry of the Army), that a state-level collective measure vis-à-vis the Tokyo Trial was indispensable, and that allowing Japanese to throw mud at each other should be avoided by all means. Matsutani, a pro–Anglo-American army officer who had served as secretary to Prime Minister Suzuki Kantarō, was of the same view. The Second Ministry of Demobilization, formerly the Navy Ministry, also strongly hoped to guide defense counsels to prepare for the defense of state. In other words, the former Imperial Army and Navy both found a unified opinion essential.

Former Imperial Japanese Navy colonel Toyoda Kumao (graduate of the 51st class of the Imperial Japanese Naval Academy), who was in charge of the war criminal issue at the Second Ministry of Demobilization, explained that the aforementioned outline was the official view of the Japanese government. Nonetheless, the "unified opinion" was never made an official policy. In my judgment, it was Foreign Minister Yoshida Shigeru and the Ministry of Foreign Affairs that buried this plan.

---

4. Tajiri Akiyoshi, *Tajiri Akiyoshi kaisōroku* [Memoirs of Tajiri Akiyoshi] (Tokyo: Hara Shobō, 1977), and Toyoda Kumao, *Sensō Saiban yoroku* [Additional Records of the War Crimes Trials] (Tokyo: Taiseisha, 1986).

What Did Yoshida Shigeru Think?

Since his appointment as foreign minister, Yoshida Shigeru had been skeptical about the "unified opinion." He believed Japan should refrain from resorting too much to artifice. This was why Nakamura's idea of the War Crimes Trials Countermeasures Committee was rejected. A separate Foreign Ministry document also stated that to distort or suppress facts so as to secure the discharge of specific individuals would lead to disadvantageous results in the long run, and that it was not advisable to guide defense counsels to follow a single policy.

It was not permissible to guide defense counsels directly, and yet it was unacceptable to do nothing. Faced with this dilemma, Yoshida decided to establish a "Legal Affairs Councilors' Office" in consultation with Takayanagi Kenzō, professor of Anglo-American law at Tokyo Imperial University and a legal counsel of the Ministry of Foreign Affairs. Established in mid-December, this office evolved out of Nakamura's plan for a provisional investigating committee on war criminals. The office was headed by Sone Eki (who later became secretary-general of the Democratic Socialist Party), and reported directly to the foreign minister. Its task was to act as liaison for both GHQ and defense counsels and provide them with documents.

On December 14, a meeting to discuss the establishment of the Legal Affairs Councilors' Office was convened among the relevant ministries and bureaus. Okazaki Katsuo, advisor to the Foreign Ministry who later became foreign minister and Japan's ambassador to the United Nations, announced the attempt to work out a policy to provide guidance to defense counsels (unified opinion). Okazaki also told the attendants that "His Majesty's innocence" would be self-evident once the facts were presented.

The Japanese government adopted the following official policy:

(1) In compliance with the spirit of the Imperial Rescript on the Termination of the War, to obey and follow faithfully all directives and memorandums issued by the Supreme Commander for the Allied Powers on the war crimes trials; and

(2) While it is not possible for the government to defend individual war criminals officially . . . the Japanese government shall, with the permission of GHQ, provide such clerical assistance as defenses,

liaisons with defendants' families, and various services by related government organizations in accordance with respective mandates.[5]

This illustrates how the Japanese government would limit the assistance it gave to the defense counsels to the provision of documents and witnesses, and would refrain from providing guidance or exerting control over defenses. Because the government was obliged to collaborate with the Allies' trial on war crimes, provision of "an official defense" was utterly out of the question. The most the government could do was to offer indirect support. In retrospect, because the interests of concerned ministries and bureaus, defendants, and defense counsels were complicated and conflicting, a unified opinion was impossible from the outset.

Acceptance of the Tokyo Trial Was Japan's "Security Policy"

Why, then, did Yoshida actively accept the Tokyo Trial? First of all, that obligation was stipulated by treaty. But that was not the only reason. Shimoda Takesō, a diplomat who later became Japanese ambassador to the United States and Supreme Court justice, recalled the instruction Foreign Minister Yoshida delivered on September 17, 1945, to ministry officials. Yoshida came to the office for the first time that day as foreign minister, "looking like he had lost weight and wearing a now oversized morning coat." Speaking before a gathering of Foreign Ministry officials, Yoshida said, "Gentlemen, our country has lost a war for the first time in its history. Now that we have unfortunately become a defeated nation, let us take it like the Yamato race, and not panic. As the proverb goes, 'When helpless to control your destiny, accept your fate.'" These words inspired the officials.[6]

Yoshida himself welcomed the war crimes trial. Some kind of sacrifice was inevitable for the defeated, and the trial on war crimes fit with Yoshida's reconstruction plan for Japan. Yoshida was convinced that the militarists—"the cancer of Japanese politics"— had messed Japan up from the

---

5. Ministry of Health and Welfare, Repatriation Relief Bureau, ed., *Hikiage engo no kiroku* [Record of Repatriation Relief Activities] (Tokyo: Ministry of Health and Welfare, 1955), vol. 2.

6. Shimoda Takesō, *Sengo Nihon gaikō no shōgen* [Testimonies on Postwar Japanese Diplomacy] (Tokyo: Institute of Public Administration, 1984), vol. 1.

Manchurian Incident onward, and that the country had to steer back to the course it had been taking in the 1920s. In his October 1946 letter to General Douglas MacArthur, Yoshida declared that the war responsibility lay only with the clique composed of military personnel, bureaucrats, right-wing activists, and certain zaibatsu members. When asked to sign a petition to save former foreign minister Tōgō Shigenori, Yoshida said, "Seeing as Tōgō was foreign minister when Japan entered the war, he should have gallantly resigned when negotiations with the United States failed. He should have taken responsibility. It is beyond my comprehension why he idly remained in his post." Yoshida flatly refused to provide his signature.[7]

In Yoshida's view, the war crimes trial was doubly convenient: it could eliminate the Japanese military clique, and establish cooperation with the US. The US Occupation policy turned out to be much milder than expected, and a war crimes trial was a small enough sacrifice to make. The Tokyo Trial was given additional significance as the "protector of the emperor" after February 1946, when the Japanese government received GHQ's draft constitution.

Yoshida was not the only one who found the Tokyo Trial amenable. Those who held the reins of postwar Japanese foreign policy believed that Japan could strengthen its relations with the US by utilizing the Tokyo Trial as a tool for wiping the slate clean. The Tokyo Trial had merit for postwar Japan as a means of consolidating the environment for cooperation with the US. Thus, acceptance of the trial was a "security policy" for Japan. In my judgment, this was the greatest significance of the Tokyo Trial for Japan.

Sectionalism in Bureaucracy

Thus, the Japanese government adopted an official policy of not guiding the defenses during the Tokyo Trial in a unified manner. At the same time, though, individual government bureaus went ahead with preparations for unofficial defenses of the defendants. What follows is a summary of how the Ministry of Foreign Affairs, the former Imperial Japanese Army, and the former Imperial Japanese Navy responded.

Because of its official position, the Ministry of Foreign Affairs could not afford to appear defiant, for fear of projecting an image to the Allies of

---

7. Ōno, *Kasumigaseki gaikō*.

insincerity about war crime issues. A glance at the internal analysis of the indictment, however, reveals how critical Japanese diplomats were of the Tokyo Trial.[8] In reality, the ministry must have exercised significant self-restraint to avoid being torn apart by the gap between its official position and the genuine feelings of its officials.

The Section for War Criminals in the First Department of Central Liaison Office (to which officials of the First and Second Ministries of Demobilization were assigned) was created within the Foreign Ministry to take charge of general war crime–related clerical work as well as the selection of and assistance offered to defendants, witnesses, and defense counsels. The Section for Investigation of War Criminals in the First Department of the Central Liaison Office (formerly the Legal Affairs Councilors' Office) was in charge of providing documents as well as conducting legal and document research. It also answered questions from defense counsels.

In addition, the Naigai Hōsei Kenkyūkai (Research Group on Domestic and Overseas Laws and Politics) affiliated with the Ministry of Foreign Affairs prepared for the trial. Its predecessor organization had been set up around October 1945 at the initiative of Nakamura Toyoichi with donations from business circles, and in February 1946, was reorganized into the Naigai Hōsei Kenkyūkai. It was a non-governmental brain trust tasked with conducting research on defense measures in place of the War Crimes Trials Countermeasures Committee proposed earlier. Its members included Takayanagi Kenzō, Takagi Yasaka, and Kamikawa Hikomatsu of Tokyo Imperial University; Taoka Ryōichi of Kyoto Imperial University; Ukai Nobushige of the former Keijō (Seoul) Imperial University; Shinobu Junpei, a scholar of international law; and critics Baba Tsunego and Ishibashi Tanzan. Committee members compiled high-quality research reports on international law, international politics, and domestic politics, including *Sensō hanzainin shobatsu no hōritsuteki konkyo* (Legal Grounds for Punishment of War Criminals), *Gunbatsu no kaibō* (Anatomy of the Military Clique), and *Tōjō naikaku oyobi gunbu no kaisen sekinin* (The Tōjō Cabinet and the Military's Responsibility for Starting War).

---

8. Higurashi Yoshinobu, *Tōkyō Saiban no kokusai kankei* [The Tokyo Trial and International Relations] (Tokyo: Bokutakusha, 2002).

In the former Imperial Army, the First Ministry of Demobilization set up a research group on the postwar settlement in January 1946. Intellectuals from outside the military including Yabe Teiji, Shinobu Junpei, Matsumoto Shigeharu, Mōri Hideoto (formerly with the Cabinet Planning Board), Irie Keishirō (former correspondent of Dōmei Press), Watsuji Tetsurō (professor at Tokyo Imperial University), and Tsurumi Yūsuke (former member of the House of Representatives from the Minseitō party) were invited to join the research group.

In the former Imperial Navy, an interim research department of the Second Ministry of Demobilization minister's secretariat organized a defense material research team on January 25, 1946, and tasked it with research specifically geared toward defending the Imperial Navy–related defendants. This team, which was also staffed by Takayanagi, Yabe, and others, conducted practical studies such as predicting indictments.

Finally, a liaison committee on the war crimes trials (Sensō Saiban Renraku Iinkai), which was established within the First Department of the Central Liaison Office, was staffed by directors of the General Affairs and Treaty Bureaus of the Foreign Ministry, directors of the General Affairs and Judicial Affairs Bureaus of the First Ministry of Demobilization, directors of the General Affairs Bureau and an interim research department of the Second Ministry of Demobilization, director of the Justice Ministry's Criminal Affairs Bureau, director of the Home Ministry's Police and Public Security Bureau, and director of the Finance Ministry's Budget Bureau as its key members. This indicates that at the time there was a system for director-level officials of the government ministries and bureaus to contact each other. Because the practical operation of defense assistance was unofficially pursued by each ministry independently, however, sectionalism surfaced within the government bureaucracy, further intensifying conflicts within the defense.

Handicaps in Language, Knowledge, Funding, and Human Resources

Let us revisit the issue of defense counsels. Even though giving defendants an opportunity for rebuttal and self-vindication might invite delaying tactics and propaganda on the part of the defeated, it was still an indispensable element of a "civilization's judgment" as proof of justice and a spirit of fairness on the part of the victors. Yoshimoto Takaaki, a renowned poet and literary critic, recalled that while he found the Tokyo Trial granted defendants opportunities for self-vindication, this first exposure to Western legal philosophy came as a pleasant surprise. And this was how effective this measure was for the Japanese people.[9]

GHQ had unofficially permitted Class A war crimes suspects to obtain defense counsels on their own by November 1945 at the latest, and they were matched with Japanese lawyers through various routes including the Ministry of Justice, the Ministry of Foreign Affairs, and the former Imperial Japanese Army and Navy. Compared to the Nuremberg Trial where defense counsels had been selected from the list prepared by the International Military Tribunal, the system for locating defense counsels adopted at the Tokyo Trial was much improved.

Here, I would like to point out various handicaps that Japanese defense counsels had to cope with.

First was the language barrier and the lack of knowledge of Anglo-American law. The Foreign Ministry decided that, since the Tokyo Trial was an international court, prior practice as an attorney in Japan was not required of defense counsels. As a result, diplomats who had been purged by GHQ, including Nishi Haruhiko, Yanai Hisao, and Ushiba Nobuhiko, registered themselves as lawyers in preparation for the indictments of Tōgō, Shigemitsu, and Ōshima.[10] Furthermore, the criterion employed by the Japanese judicial world emphasized experience as defense counsel in domestic criminal courts, whereas competence in English and expertise in foreign law were given only secondary priority.

Second was the shortage of funding and human resources. It was not until July or August 1946, after the Tokyo Trial had already begun, that the Japanese government was able to appropriate the End-of-War Settlement budget to cover expenses of the Occupation forces as compensation for Japanese lawyers under the pretext that they were the Occupation forces personnel as advisors to American defense counsels." Recognizing that a substantial amount of money would be needed to employ lawyers and collect

9. Ian Buruma, *The Wages of Guilt* (London: Vintage, 1994).

10. Sawa Kunio, "Tōkyō Saiban wa haisha e no hōfuku datta" [Tokyo Trial Was Retaliation against the Defeated], *Seiron* (February 2006).

documents, the Foreign Ministry collected donations for the defense of Tōgō.[11] Hozumi Shigetaka, a lawyer in charge of defendant Kido and son of constitutional scholar Hozumi Yatsuka, commented, "Flanked by hundreds of assistants, translators, typists, and others, the prosecution appeared as if they were a million-strong army rushing onto the field. In contrast, the defense was . . . in an extremely disadvantageous position."

Regarding Two Defense Policies

The greatest problem, however, was the various conflicts within the defense. Well-known among them was a conflict over the defense policy. One side argued for the defense of state by stressing the defensive nature of the war. The central advocates of this argument included Uzawa Fusaaki, head of the Japanese defense panel, a lawyer, a graduate of the Law Faculty of Tokyo Imperial University, and a former member of the House of Representatives (Rikken Seiyūkai); Kiyose Ichirō, second in charge of the Japanese defense counsels, a lawyer, a graduate of Kyoto Imperial University's Faculty of Law, and a former member of the House of Representatives (Rikken Minseitō); Hayashi Itsurō and other nongovernmental members of the Dai-Nihon Bengoshikai Rengōkai (a federation of bar associations founded in 1939), which later became the Nihon Bengoshi Rengōkai (Japan Federation of Bar Associations). Before the opening of the Tokyo Trial, Kiyose said, "The defense of former prime minister Tōjō and his cabinet members . . . is not confined to the defense of the defendants as individuals. . . . Public opinion both within and outside of Japan is extremely unfavorable toward the defendants. . . . It is indeed very important to be on an equal footing with the prosecution, and make the trial impartial and fair, and thus stable."[12] One can detect here Kiyose's determination to defend the state against "victors' justice."

The other side stressed the defense of individual defendants. The chief advocates of this stance were Takayanagi Kenzō and former vice-minister of justice Miyake Shōtarō (in charge of defendant Umezu before resigning at an early stage). Members of this group belonged to the aforementioned Naigai Hōsei Kenkyūkai research group on domestic and overseas laws and politics,

11. Ōno, *Kasumigaseki gaikō*.

12. Nomura Masao, *Sabakareta Nihon* [Japan Tried] (Tokyo: Kadokawa Shoten, 1956).

Kiyose Ichirō
(Kyodo News)

Tōjō Hideki and his defense counsels, Blewett (left) and Kiyose (right)
(National Archives of the Netherlands, Collection 544 B. V. A. Röling)

and were regarded as being closely associated with government bureaus. From this angle, it may appear that there were two groups—chiefly nongovernmental advocates of the defense of state and lawyers who were closely associated with the government. In actuality, however, the second group, those emphasizing the defense of individual defendants, was not necessarily united as a faction.

Also, on an individual member basis, the situation was rather complex. Hozumi, who was knowledgeable about Anglo-American law, for instance, advocated the defense of individuals in consideration of the wishes of Kido Kōichi, a distant relative, even though he himself was a private, nongovernmental lawyer. Takayanagi Kenzō, an Anglo-American law expert in charge of defendant Suzuki, placed more value on judicial theory itself and, as such, his argument could well pass for advocating the defense of state, as we will see later.

Because the Allies intended to demonstrate the responsibility of the state as a whole, using examination of defendants' responsibilities as leverage, Japan's two-pronged policy of defending the state and the individuals corresponded to the Allies' subjective goal, albeit accidentally.

Inner Conflict in the Defense

The conflict between the two camps within the defense grew increasingly fierce, and it was never resolved. Elements in this conflict included an intricate entanglement of defense policy, ideology, faction, emotion, and organizational interests.

Ono Seiichirō
(Kyodo News)

In terms of defense policy, ideology was a factor. Takayanagi in later years summarized the situation as "a conflict between the liberalistic group (defense of individuals) and the nationalistic group (defense of state)." Therefore, it might be more accurate to characterize the situation as strife between a group which saw the war as one of self-defense and stressed "defense of state" on the one hand, and a group which, on the other hand, emphasized "defense of individuals," and was unsympathetic toward an excessively nationalistic view.

Regarding factional and emotional aspects, the nongovernmental lawyers group mocked the Naigai Hōsei Kenkyūkai as a body affiliated with the Foreign Ministry. Moreover, Hayashi Itsurō (in charge of defendant Hashimoto) spoke ill of Takayanagi for looking down on Japanese lawyers. Takayanagi, for his part, underestimated nongovernmental lawyers, declaring that "Japan had only one or two qualified lawyers." He chose to work together with American lawyers instead.

To make the situation more complicated, there was rivalry between the Uzawa faction and the Kiyose faction within the advocates of the defense of state. Uzawa Fusaaki, a legal philosopher born in 1872 who had once served as president of Meiji University, was an outspoken person. It is said that he once scolded Ono Seiichirō (born 1881), former professor of Tokyo Imperial University and an authority on criminal law, saying, "You novices have no clue whatsoever!" He also supposedly insulted Kiyose, shouting, "That's why you can't get ahead in your career." The appointment of Uzawa as head of the defense team was also attributable to pro-Uzawa members' engineering the timing of the vote at a time when few pro-Kiyose members were present. Even during the court hearings, precious time was wasted on such trifles as the order of cross-examination and the time slots allotted to defense counsels.

Moreover, the Army, Navy and Foreign Ministries all put their own sectional interests first, meaning that the defense policy for each suspect was totally uncoordinated. By late February 1946, "an increasing number of major Class A figures showed signs of nervous breakdown, and many became unsettled."[13] The possibility of a coordination of views within the defense panel became increasingly remote as worrisome conditions accumulated, to the degree that each ministry, each defense counsel, and each defendant was randomly issuing arbitrary memos and documents. There was also a serious shortage of funds.

It was against this backdrop that the Japanese defense team was formally established on May 4, 1946, the day after the Tokyo Trial opened.

Why American Defense Counsels Were Appointed

Another important point in regard to the defense in the Tokyo Trial was the presence of American defense counsels. Only German defense counsels had been allowed to participate in the Nuremberg Trial, so why did the United States dispatch American lawyers to Tokyo?

The commonly accepted view was that it was a response to demands from the Japanese side. But the fact is that Joseph Keenan, US chief prosecutor for the International Military Tribunal for the Far East, had given thought to appointing American lawyers as defense counsels even before the Japanese government proposed it. As a matter of fact, when Nakamura Toyoichi, the director of the Section for War Criminals, First Department of the Central Liaison Office, visited Keenan on January 9, 1946, the latter declared that either an American or Japanese defense counsel would be appointed for each defendant. With the precedent of the Yamashita trial in Manila and the early days of the Yokohama War Crimes Trials where only American defense counsels had been appointed, Britain also believed that there should be non-Japanese defense counsels for the Tokyo Trial. From the outset, it was the Allied side that took it for granted that the US should dispatch American lawyers.

On January 10, Iguchi Sadao, director of the General Affairs Department of the Central Liaison Office (and later administrative vice-minister of foreign affairs), visited GHQ and sought advice on whether the Japanese government could cover the expenses for Japanese lawyers because suspects'

---

13. Mizuno Tetsuo, *Haruka naru heiwa ni* [Toward Faraway Peace] (Tokyo: Tōkō Shoin, 1952).

families were struggling financially. When Keenan was asked his views on the issue, he admitted it was improper for the Japanese government to do so, which was obliged by the term of surrender to assist the indictment of war criminals and to select and/or employ defense counsels. He nevertheless held that it was a realistic measure to allow the Japanese government to incur the lawyers' expenses. It was feared that rigidly adhering to the original principle would mean that some defendants might not be assisted by defense counsels, and that this could possibly damage the impartiality of the trial.

For whatever reason, this realistic proposal by Keenan was not adopted by GHQ, and the Japanese government was not allowed to pay fees to Japanese lawyers until the summer of 1946. Accordingly, GHQ's prohibition on the Japanese government's involvement in the defense of the Tokyo Trial defendants—which in itself would have been quite appropriate—came to be overly emphasized, and it impressed people with the cruelty of the victors.

Subsequently, by February 14, when he met Counselor Ōta Saburō, who succeeded Nakamura who was transferred to another post, Keenan had changed his mind and decided to rely mainly on Japanese lawyers. He had found it unexpectedly difficult to procure American lawyers. For his part, Ōta stressed the indispensability of non-Japanese defense counsels to Keenan and the justices. It was this reversal of initial positions that fueled the common view that the US had dispatched American lawyers as a result of demands from the Japanese side.

In Order to Avoid Allegations of Victors' Retaliation

We can conclude that American defense counsels were appointed in order to avoid the allegation of "victors' retaliation."

For instance, as John G. Brannon, the youngest American defense counsel (in charge of defendants Oka and Shimada), stated in his closing argument of March 4, 1948, that Japanese lawyers encountered the English term "conspiracy" for the first time, and appeared bewildered about its meaning. In a criminal court based on the adversary system of the Anglo-American law, prosecution and defense counsels face off against one another, and the role of the justice is literally to judge or referee the exchange between the two sides. Because this system relies on jurors, who are laymen in terms of the law, the prosecution's evidence is revealed only after court opens. Defense counsels then have to decide their concrete defense policy, challenge the prosecution, and cross-examine witnesses.

In contrast, in trials based on continental law, which applies the inquisitorial approach, the judge conducts an investigation of the facts. This is why, at the preliminary conference prior to the Nuremberg Trial toward the end of 1945, Soviet judge Major-General Iona Timofeevich Nikitchenko was confused, and had to inquire what cross-examination meant. French judge Robert Falco was shocked to find that the defense side had not been informed of the overall picture of the indictment.[14]

The two court systems are so starkly different that if the Tokyo Trial had relied solely on Japanese lawyers who were not familiar with the English language or the judicial procedures under Anglo-American law, the trial would have been denounced as a "fixed trial," at best. Shigemitsu Mamoru and Maruyama Masao also commented on the impact of employing American lawyers. Shigemitsu wrote in his diary,

> No matter how many times the Chief Justice warned American defense counsels that their defenses were antagonizing their own country, they triumphantly declared that it was their country that had ordered them to defend the defendants. The United States won not only the war.

And prominent political scientist Maruyama Masao acutely observed,

> I think that [employing American defense counsels] was better from the viewpoint of curbing even a little the image of victors judging the defeated. . . . Those American lawyers who had argued on behalf of Japanese defendants, paying no heed to the position of the United States, have made some sort of impression on the Japanese people.

Withdrawal of Coleman's Group

The American defense counsel team was organized on April 1, 1946. Captain Beverly M. Coleman of the US Navy (who had presided over the Yokohama War Crimes Trial) became the chief defense counsel. Navy Captain John

---

14. Telford Taylor, *The Anatomy of the Nuremberg Trials* (London: Bloomsbury, 1993).

W. Guider, another well-known attorney-at-law in the US, came to Japan to defend Tōjō Hideki. Tōgō Fumihiko, son-in-law of Shigenori, who later became the Japanese ambassador to the US, reminisced in later days that American lawyers had hesitated to be assigned to his father-in-law knowing it would be a tough defense. As this episode shows, there were cases of American lawyers being choosy when it came to defending particular defendants.[15]

On May 8, immediately after the opening of the Tokyo Trial, Coleman, through the court, requested that General MacArthur amend the Charter of the International Military Tribunal for the Far East so as to establish an "International Defense Section," which would be under the supervision of a "Chief Defense Counsel" with jurisdiction over all the Japanese and American defense counsels. Partly due to antagonism between Coleman's group and the American lawyers group dispatched by the US Army, Coleman attempted to improve the position of the defense and tighten internal control.

Chief Justice William Webb, however, was furious about this charter amendment proposal and would not accept it. The best that GHQ could do was to make American lawyers affiliates of the Legal Section (LS).

Six American lawyers dispatched by the US Navy, including Coleman, tendered their resignations on May 31, and the next day visited MacArthur for a last-ditch negotiation. MacArthur, however, simply delivered a two-hour monologue, insisting that he had no authority to organize defense counsels. Given this flat rejection, Coleman and his associates returned to the US. They were replaced by lawyers dispatched by the US Army, including Major Franklin Warrant (in charge of defendants Dohihara and Oka), Major Benjamin Bruce Blakeney (in charge of defendants Tōgō and Umezu), an intelligence officer during the war who was fluent in Japanese, and George Yamaoka (in charge of defendant Tōgō). Those American lawyers were made affiliates of the Legal Section in early June and quartered at the Dai-Ichi Hotel in Shinbashi.

The drama of the Coleman group's resignation gives an impression of the trial as being unfair. While it is true that the defense was placed under disadvantageous circumstances, there was an element of an army versus navy

---

15. Tōgō Shigehiko, *Sofu Tōgō Shigenori no shōgai* [Life of My Grandfather Tōgō Shigenori] (Tokyo: Bungeishunjū, 1993).

Franklin Warren   Benjamin Bruce Blakeney   George Yamaoka
(All images on this page and
facing courtesy of the National
Archives of the Netherlands,
Collection 544 B. V. A. Röling)

conflict between the American lawyers. And besides, one must admit that it really was unfeasible to amend the charter after the court had opened.

Unprofessional Conduct

There was also an "American Section" comprised of American lawyers, distinct from the Japanese defense counsel team. Upon his arrival in Tokyo, William Logan (in charge of defendant Kido) expressed regret at accepting an overwhelmingly difficult assignment; he belonged to the American Section's First Defense Division, which was in charge of the general phase of Japan's domestic situation and war preparations. The First Division also functioned as the steering committee for the defense as a whole. The American Second Defense Division was in charge of the Manchurian Incident; the Third Division, the Second Sino-Japanese War; the Fourth Division, Soviet-related matters; and the Fifth Division, the Pacific War. The American Section also had a legal committee.

However, with only a few exceptions, such as Takayanagi, relations between the Japanese lawyers and their American counterparts were not cordial. There was no organizational communication nor any operational cooperation between the two. Kiyose Ichirō (in charge of defendant Tōjō) in particular loathed American lawyers, whom he often badmouthed. The aversion to American lawyers was stronger among the advocates for the defense of state. This was probably attributable to the fact that American lawyers placed

William Logan   Owen Cunningham   Aristides Lazarus

priority on clients' interest, which was close to the conviction of Takayanagi and his associates who advocated the "defense of individual." Among the defendants, though, were some including Shigemitsu and Kido who put their trust in the American defense counsels and did not much appreciate the capability of those who belonged to the "defense of state" group.

When cross-examination by the defense began on February 24, 1947, the conflict between the Japanese and the American defense counsels surfaced for all to see. Logan's remarks, given immediately before Kiyose's opening statement, astonished those present. Logan claimed that, given conflicts of interests, discrepancies of views, and the wide variety of official posts previously held by the defendants, it would not be possible for the defense's opening statement to satisfy all the defendants, and that, in fact, five defendants—Shigemitsu, Hiranuma, Hirota, Dohihara, and Suzuki—opposed the entire content of the opening statement. According to Logan, some found most of the opening statement unacceptable, while others opposed specific portions of it.

When defense counsel Owen Cunningham (in charge of defendant Ōshima) reserved the right to object to a certain portion of the opening statement, Assistant Chief Prosecutor Frank Stacy Tavenner questioned Kiyose relentlessly, asking who the opening statement represented. In response, Kiyose gave an incoherent reply, saying,

Four of the defendants are opposed to the opening statement. No, five defendants because I overlooked Mr. Hirota. All the other defendants are in agreement with it. . . . I hear Mr. Ōshima has a problem with one line. Although I have just said one line, one of the defense counsels called my attention to . . . another one or two lines that Mr. Ōshima is not happy about.

Kiyose was completely incoherent. Matsutani Sei, formerly with the Imperial Japanese Army, observed that the opening statement of defense counsel Kiyose, which began after relentless questioning by American defense counsels, deplored Kiyose's unprofessional conduct, commenting "as expected, his logic was feeble, and his entire manner was immature."

2. Logic of the Defense

Defendants' Motions to Dismiss Prosecution

Immediately after the opening of the court, the defense introduced a number of motions. On May 13, 1946, Kiyose contested two points in the motion concerning the jurisdiction of the International Military Tribunal for the Far East.

First, Japan and Germany differed in the mode of surrender. While Article 10 of the Potsdam Declaration bound both Japan and the Allies, the only war crime that had been known at the time of the issuance of the declaration was violation of the laws of war. Therefore, Kiyose argued, the Tribunal had no jurisdiction over crimes against peace, crimes against humanity, and murders. What is more, the Kellogg-Briand Pact did not criminalize wars of aggression.

Second, it was unreasonable to bring charges concerning the Zhanggufeng and Nomonhan Incidents, which had already been settled by an agreement between Japan and the Soviet Union.

Of these two appeals, it can be said that the first one, on the jurisdiction of the Tokyo Trial, was powerful enough to torment the bench throughout the hearing (see section 1 of chapter 5).

Eight months later, on January 27, 1947, after the prosecution had completed its establishment of facts with evidence, the defense brought forward several motions to dismiss the prosecution. While all of the motions were rejected on February 3, defense counsel David F. Smith (in charge of defendant Hirota) disclosed in court that the defense was considering submitting a motion on MacArthur's authority (from which ten defense counsels abstained) to the US Federal Court. Hearing this, Webb snapped, "Whether you go to Washington, DC, or any place else is of no interest to us." Incidentally, this motion did find its way to the US Supreme Court as a petition for a writ of habeas corpus after the sentencing.

From January 27 through 29, American defense counsels took the podium one after another to submit separate dismissals of the prosecution for each defendant (in the joint names of Japanese and American lawyers). The motions called for the removal of the portion of the indictment pertaining to each defendant and for the defendant's acquittal. Because former foreign minister Matsuoka Yōsuke had died due to illness on June 27, 1946, followed by former admiral Nagano Osami on January 5, 1947, the total number of defendants was reduced to twenty-six, including the hospitalized Ōkawa Shūmei. (The case against Ōkawa was dropped on April 9, 1947.)

From Araki Sadao to Matsui Iwane

The following are summaries of the defenses for each defendant from Araki Sadao through Matsui Iwane.

(1) Although former Imperial Japanese Army general Araki Sadao (Lawrence McManus, defense counsel in charge) was accused of "taking part in conspiracy" in 1928, he was not army minister when the Manchurian Incident occurred. He subsequently became the army minister who brought the incident to a close. No evidence of Araki's engagement in atrocities was presented.

(2) Former Imperial Japanese Army general Dohihara Kenji (Franklin Warren, defense counsel in charge) was always merely "complying with superiors' orders" in the units he was assigned to at the time of the conspiracy on the war of aggression. His involvement in atrocities was not proven.

(3) Former Imperial Japanese Army colonel Hashimoto Kingorō (E. Richard Harris, defense counsel in charge) was head of the Russian

Defendants stand as judges enter the courtroom.
Front row, from left: Tōjō, Oka, Umezu, Araki, Mutō, Hoshino, Kaya, Kido
Back row, from left: Ōkawa, Hiranuma, Tōgō, Matsuoka, Shigemitsu, Satō, Shimada, Shiratori, Suzuki
(All images on this page courtesy of the National Archives of the Netherlands, Collection 544 B. V. A. Röling)

Front row, from left: Hirota, Minami, Tōjō, Oka, Araki, Mutō
Back row, from left: Hashimoto, Koiso, Ōshima, Matsui, Hiranuma, Tōgō

Front row, from left: Hoshino, Kaya
Back row: Shimada

Studies Department, Imperial Japanese Army General Staff, at the time of the Manchurian Incident and a civilian when the Second Sino-Japanese War erupted. It was not proven that the Sakurakai (Cherry Blossom Society), founded in 1930, was party to conspiracy in an external war of aggression. Substantiation of evidence on atrocities was inadequate. The incident of firing at HMS *Ladybird* in 1937 during the Second Sino-Japanese War was attributable to a "mistake."

(4) The name of former Imperial Japanese Army general Hata Shunroku (Aristides Lazarus, defense counsel in charge) hardly appeared in the stenographic record of this trial. Furthermore, he was unrelated to any government agency at the outbreak of the Pacific War. Two months after the fall of Nanjing, he became commander of the Central China Expeditionary Army, when peace and order were already restored in Nanjing.

(5) Hiranuma Kiichirō (Franklin Warren, defense counsel in charge) was unrelated to the conspiracy, and did not take advantage of his official position to facilitate the conspiracy. Although he was indicted for China-related atrocities, there was no evidence to support the indictment. Even "the highly peculiar procedure" of the Tokyo Trial "failed to produce substantial evidence to find him guilty."

(6) It was "extremely odd" that Hirota Kōki (David Smith, defense counsel in charge) was accused of responsibility for the Nanjing Incident. Because of a difference of views with the prime minister on the conduct of Japanese troops in China, Hirota resigned as foreign minister of the first Konoe Fumimaro Cabinet. Japan was peaceful throughout the tenure of the Hirota Cabinet. Hirota never defended Japan's war with the US and Britain as a war for "survival and self-defense." The indictment itself was a grave misjudgment.

(7) Hoshino Naoki (George Williams, defense counsel in charge) was a mere public official throughout his career. The allegation that he was responsible for the economic exclusion of non-Japanese individuals from Manchukuo was based on a misunderstanding of the plan to introduce foreign capital to Manchukuo.

(8) Former Imperial Japanese Army general Itagaki Seishirō (Floyd

Front row, from left:
Araki, Mutō
Back row, from left:
Hiranuma, Tōgō, Satō, Shigemitsu
(All images on this page courtesy of the National Archives of the Netherlands, Collection 544 B. V. A. Röling)

Front row, from left:
Kido, Kimura
Back row, from left:
Suzuki, Itagaki

Front row, from left:
Tōjō, Oka, Araki
Back row, from left:
Hiranuma, Tōgō, Satō

Mattice, defense counsel in charge) only conducted himself in compliance with the decisions and orders of Honjō Shigeru, commander of the Kwantung Army and Itagaki's superior, and of the central leadership of the Imperial Japanese Army during the Manchurian Incident. The fact that he happened to be the army minister at the time of mass murders in Guangdong and Hankou was inadequate grounds for pressing charges of criminal responsibility. The prosecution only implied that Itagaki was "somewhat responsible" for atrocities when he was commander of the Seventh Area Army (in Singapore).

(9) Kaya Okinori (Michael Levin, defense counsel in charge) was merely a "professional administrator." He had already resigned as finance minister at the time of mass murders in Guangdong and Hankou and, furthermore, the finance minister was not responsible for the start of war or atrocities in the first place.

(10) Kido Kōichi (William Logan, Jr., defense counsel in charge) was director of the Minister's Secretariat, Lord Keeper of the Privy Seal, at the time of the Manchurian Incident, and he did not take part in any "conspiracy." When Kido learned of the Imperial Army's plan to gain complete control over Manchuria in 1932, he was appalled by the strikingly different ways of thinking between the army and himself. Since 1936, Kido belonged to a pro-Britain group as a close aide of Matsudaira Tsuneo, minister of the Imperial Household. During his days as education minister, Kido often wrote in his diary that the Second Sino-Japanese War should be settled urgently. Lord Keeper of the Privy Seal was often misunderstood to be a post that "advised the emperor," but actually it was a mere liaison between the emperor and non-cabinet member officials. Kido was not responsible for the Tripartite Pact, and he opposed the war with the United States to the utmost. Kido recommended Tōjō as prime minister because he was convinced Tōjō could avoid the war with the United States through diplomacy, and even suppress young officers in the army and navy should diplomatic negotiations fail. Lord Keeper of the Privy Seal was not a position that could commit atrocities.

(11) Former Imperial Japanese Army general Kimura Heitarō (Joseph

Front row, from left: Doihara, Hata, Hirota, Minami
Back row, from left: Hashimoto, Koiso, Ōshima, Matsui
(National Archives of the Netherlands, Collection 544 B. V. A. Röling)

Howard, defense counsel in charge) did nothing beyond the duty of a military man faithful to his homeland. His only authority over prisoners of war as vice-minister of the army was to communicate instructions from the army minister to all commanders. When Kimura became commander of the Burma Area Army in 1944, the Japanese troops were already on the run, and there was no evidence that Kimura took prisoners of war under his direct control.

(12) Former Imperial Japanese Army general Koiso Kuniaki (Alfred Brooks, defense counsel in charge) did not associate closely with other defendants. He was regarded as neutral within the army and as a fair and mild-mannered moralist among bureaucrats. He was accused of crimes against peace for "extremely complicated reasons," but he was not involved. At the time of the Manchurian Incident, Koiso was director of the Military Affairs Bureau, Ministry of the Army, but he just "complied with orders of Army Minister Minami and carried out missions following Shidehara's policy." As prime minister, Koiso performed his duties, believing that the Pacific War was a lawful war of self-defense. The prime minister in Japan furthermore had no authority to intervene in the treatment of prisoners of war.

(13) Former Imperial Japanese Army general Matsui Iwane (Floyd Mattice, defense counsel in charge) only carried out the attack

on Nanjing under orders from army leadership when he was commander of the Central China Area Army, during the Second Sino-Japanese War. During the operation, Matsui confined himself to the headquarters in Suzhou; he stayed in Nanjing for only a short period of time. There was no sufficient evidence to censure him for his responsibility for the atrocities in Nanjing.

From Minami Jirō to Umezu Yoshijirō

To continue the list:

(14) Former Imperial Japanese Army general Minami Jirō (Alfred Brooks, defense counsel in charge) attempted to suppress the escalation of the Manchurian Incident when he was the army minister. The authority of the army minister in Japan was highly restricted, and it was the chief of the General Staff who had the authority to report to the emperor the dispatch of Japanese troops overseas. Also, Japan had not detained any prisoners of war in March 1936 when Minami resigned as commander of the Kwantung Army.

(15) Former Imperial Japanese Army lieutenant general Mutō Akira (Roger Cole, defense counsel in charge) had mostly been in subordinate positions throughout his military career, and his task was to carry out instructions from his superiors. While a large amount of evidence was submitted to imply that it was the Military Affairs Bureau of the Army Ministry that decided policies related to prisoners of war, the evidence was distorted. While Mutō was commander of the Imperial Guard in Sumatra, the treatment of prisoners was not decided or carried out via the formal chain of command. Therefore, Mutō was not responsible for what happened to the prisoners.

(16) Former Imperial Japanese Navy vice admiral Oka Takasumi (Franklin Warren, defense counsel in charge) was chief of Naval General Staff at the time of the attack on Pearl Harbor, but he was not a decision-maker. He only followed the instructions of a superior. No evidence was found that he had authority to issue orders on the treatment of prisoners of war. To begin with, it was decisive that the Imperial Japanese Navy opposed the war from beginning to end.

(17) Ōkawa Shūmei (Alfred Brooks, defense counsel in charge) had no power or position to enable him to do what he was accused of. Nor did he advocate any personal ambition or criminal intention through his writings. The March Incident and the October Incident in 1931 were no more than banal "political demonstrations." The evidence related to his involvement in the Manchurian Incident was akin to rumor.

(18) Former Imperial Japanese Army lieutenant general Ōshima Hiroshi (Owen Cunningham, defense counsel in charge) played only clerical and mechanical roles. He had never been a policy planner, military commander, or cabinet minister. Usually, indictment of a foreign envoy is prohibited. During his tenure as the Japanese ambassador to Germany, Ōshima never participated in negotiations or gave his signature without the Japanese government's approval or instruction.

(19) Former Imperial Japanese Army lieutenant general Satō Kenryō (James Freeman, defense counsel in charge) was merely a director of section (director, Military Affairs Section, Military Affairs Bureau, Ministry of the Army) and a major general at the time of the attack on Pearl Harbor and, thus, he was not in a position to take part in the planning or instigating of the war of aggression. The prosecution contended that Satō had supervised the Prisoner of War Information Bureau and the prisoner of war camp since April 1942 as director of the Military Affairs Bureau, but both of these bodies were under direct jurisdiction of the army minister.

(20) Shigemitsu Mamoru (Benjamin Blakeney read the argument for defense counsel George Furness) attempted to maintain peace between Japan and China. His remark during the negotiations after the Zhanggufeng Incident, when he was the Japanese ambassador to the Soviet Union, was well within the instruction from the home government. Despite the Soviet prosecutor's groundless accusations, there was no evidence that Shigemitsu demanded the cession of Soviet territory during the negotiation on the boundary between Manchukuo and the Soviet Union. When he was the Japanese ambassador to Britain, Shigemitsu was not involved in the Tripartite Pact

negotiations, and it was in 1943, well into the Pacific War, when he became foreign minister. The only authority over the prisoners of war issue bestowed on the foreign minister was regarding mediation of the exchange of documents between the Japanese and foreign governments.

(21) Former Imperial Japanese Navy admiral Shimada Shigetarō (Edward McDermott, defense counsel in charge) became the navy minister only fifty days before the attack on Pearl Harbor. He took part in the conference which decided on the opening hostilities only three times. Prior to that, he had not been in any position that implemented operational plans. There was a conflict of views within the Imperial Navy, and it was the Naval General Staff that planned and carried out the attack on Pearl Harbor. As for Shimada's involvement in the atrocities, the Navy Ministry could not control outpost fleet commanders, and it was not proven that immoral conduct took place in the few prisoner-of-war camps that the navy managed.

(22) Shiratori Toshio (Charles Caudle, defense counsel in charge) was a professional diplomat whose highest post within the Foreign Ministry was director of the Information Division. During the Manchurian Incident, Shiratori rendered cooperation to Foreign Minister Shidehara's policy to block the invasion. He was the Japanese ambassador to Italy for only a short period of time. The prosecution presented the diary of Italian foreign minister Gian Galeazzo Ciano, which revealed that Ōshima Hiroshi and Shiratori had refused to negotiate through the formal diplomatic channels and threatened that, if Italy did not unconditionally accept the Tripartite Pact, Ōshima and Shiratori would resign from the ambassadorship, and force the Konoe Fumimaro Cabinet to resign en masse. It must be said that it was absurd to talk of a cabinet being shaken up by the resignation of one or two ambassadors. Shiratori had already been dismissed from the ambassadorship to Italy in January 1940 before the signing of the Tripartite Pact in September. On the point of responsibility for the pact, more attention should be paid to the behavior of the "strong-willed and tyrannical" Foreign Minister Matsuoka.

(23) Former Imperial Japanese Army lieutenant general Suzuki Teiichi

(Michael Levin, defense counsel in charge) was a mere army colonel when the Second Sino-Japanese War erupted. The National Mobilization Plan had been mostly completed long before Suzuki became chief of the Cabinet Planning Board in 1941.

(24) The prosecution presented evidence that Tōgō Shigenori (Benjamin Blakeney, defense counsel in charge) guaranteed Japan's compliance with the Geneva Convention and the Red Cross Convention when he was foreign minister. But the Foreign Ministry was not responsible for the handling of prisoners of war; it merely conveyed the Imperial Japanese Army's inquiries and protests "in the manner of a post office." Tōgō accepted the position of foreign minister in the Tōjō Cabinet because he had been requested by the emperor to "peacefully settle US-Japan relations," and he devoted his efforts to successfully conclude negotiations with the US until the conference attended by the emperor on December 1, 1941, which decided on the initiation of warfare with the US. There was testimony that it was due to an order from the Imperial Japanese Army General Staff that the delivery of the emperor's personal telegraph addressed to President Roosevelt was delayed. Because Tōgō officially instructed the Japanese ambassador to the US to deliver the notification before the attack on Pearl Harbor, Tōgō should not be blamed for what turned out to be a delay in delivery.

(25) No legal evidence was found in the prosecution's accusation of former Imperial Japanese Army general Tōjō Hideki (George Blewett, defense counsel in charge) for conspiracy or atrocities.

(26) Former Imperial Japanese Army general Umezu Yoshijirō (Benjamin Blakeney, defense counsel in charge) was accused of signing the He-Umezu Agreement in 1935 during the North China Buffer State Strategy when he was commander of the China Garrison Army. But the task had been entrusted to his chief of staff; and, furthermore, the agreement was merely about suppression of the fray. The vice-minister of the army was a position for carrying out the minister's instructions during the Second Sino-Japanese War. Umezu was not authorized to make important decisions. In 1939, a week before the termination of the Nomonhan Incident, Umezu became commander of the

Kwantung Army; therefore, he was not responsible for it. Evidence presented in conjunction with the Soviet-related allegation was nothing more than an "accumulation of absentee witnesses."

Let us consider the characteristics of the above motions by individual defendants.

Taken individually, the motions for Kido, which denied each and every count and frequently quoted his diary, and Tōjō, which enumerated the invalidity of the prosecution's presentation in a matter-of-fact way without referring to any specific personal circumstances, were particularly conspicuous.

First, taken as a whole, the motions were mostly permeated with the logic that the existence of a conspiracy was not proven, and that even if there had been a conspiracy, there was no evidence that the defendants were involved in it. Second, many motions stressed that defendants were not responsible because they had only "been carrying out their duties," or were "complying with instructions from superior authorities." Some even referred to the identity of those superior authorities. From today's vantage point regarding Japan's political history, some of the motions appear highly dubious. As Ushimura Kei has pointed out, however, arguments by suspects and defendants were in some respects a performance for the sake of evading indictment and/or a guilty verdict.[16] That is, perhaps, what defense of a defendant is all about.

Rebuttal from the Prosecution

From January 10 through 31, the prosecution made the following rebuttals to the defense's motion for each defendant:

(1) Araki took part in the conspiracy and assumed responsibility for the invasion himself in becoming the army minister while the war of aggression progressed.

(2) When Dohihara was head of the Harbin Special Agency, he was reported to be a man who would not hesitate to resort to settlement with force. In the judgment of Qin Dechun, Dohihara was the

---

16. Ushimura Kei, *"Shōsha no sabaki" ni mukiatte* [Facing "Victors' Justice"] (Tokyo: Chikuma Shobō, 2004).

instigator of the Liutiaogou Incident, while Puyi also testified that it was Dohihara who had pulled the strings. As commander of the Eastern District Army, Dohihara was directly responsible for the brutal treatment of prisoners of war. While he was commander of the Seventh Area Army (Singapore), there were thousands of cases of murder and unnecessary deaths.

(3) Hashimoto was the propaganda figure in the conspiracy, and he was directly responsible for the HMS *Ladybird* incident.

(4) During Hata's tenure as army minister, he toppled the Yonai Mitsumasa Cabinet and took the overall conspiracy in a new direction. Immediately after the outbreak of the Second Sino-Japanese War, Hata assumed the position of inspector general of military training, a powerful position that had the capacity to influence policies.

(5) Hiranuma, as president of the Privy Council, could influence important decisions, and he was authorized to object to the government's policies. During his tenure as prime minister, he negotiated with Germany and Italy for the strengthening of the Anti-Comintern Pact.

(6) Although Hirota, when he was foreign minister and prime minister, declared to the Western powers that he would pursue "cooperative" diplomacy, his actual policy as well as its outcome was far from cooperative. The national policy standard of the Hirota Cabinet was the first policy of aggression that the Japanese government adopted. Hirota was an advocate of aggression from beginning to end.

(7) Hoshino supervised and guided Manchukuo's politics and economy, worked together with Tōjō when he was chief of staff of the Kwantung Army, and was the most powerful person in the Manchukuo government as director general of the department of General Affairs, the State Council. It could be conjectured that following his return to Japan and installation as chief of the Cabinet Planning Board, he had attended conferences which decided upon the commencement of the war in 1941. Hoshino agreed with Japan's outward expansion, took part in various conspiracies, and rendered his cooperation to these operations.

(8) Itagaki was one of the first planners of the Liutiaogou Incident. Toward the end of the Pacific War, prisoners of war were treated with atrocious brutality while he was commander of the Seventh Area Army.

(9) Kaya was a financial bureaucrat. Immediately after he became the finance minister of the first Konoe Fumimaro Cabinet, he adopted a five-year plan of economic measures to support the escalation of the Second Sino-Japanese War. Kaya participated in the conference attended by the emperor on December 1, 1941, and agreed to initiating the war. It was unthinkable for such a large-scale construction project as the Thailand-Burma Railway (also known as the Burma-Siam Railway, a railway connecting Thailand and Burma built in 1942–43 by European prisoners of war and Asian laborers, of whom many lost their lives during the construction, under the Imperial Japanese Army) to be undertaken without the consent of the finance minister.

(10) Kido opposed militarism at the time of the Manchurian Incident to comply with the emperor's wish. But he became a full party to the conspiracy in 1937. On top of his role as a key advisor to the emperor as the Lord Keeper of the Privy Seal, he also played a role in offering his opinion about the prime minister's choices to the emperor. When the majority of the government argued for war with the US and Britain, Kido agreed to go along. Kido recommended Tōjō for the prime ministership instead of Ugaki Kazushige, who was the only person who could have prevented the war completely. Kido was a consummate opportunist.

(11) Kimura was vice-minister of the army when the Imperial Japanese Army was in control, which made him much more responsible than ministers of other minor ministries. It was Kimura who decided to mobilize prisoners of war for the construction of the Thailand-Burma Railway, and who ordered the execution of Allied airmen.

(12) Koiso was one of the first leaders of the conspiracy in Manchuria and in Japan. He was also heavily responsible as prime minister for the mistreatment of prisoners of war and others.

(13) Matsui was responsible as commander of the Central China Area Army for the order to fire on the HMS *Ladybird*. Victims of the Nanjing Incident numbered more than either 150,000 or 270,000, depending on estimates, and most of the atrocities must have been ordered deliberately.

Official Posts Equal Criminal Responsibility

(14) Minami contributed to the aggression during the Manchurian Incident as the army minister. As governor-general of Korea, Minami approved the transfer of prisoners of war to Korea for illegal purposes.

(15) Mutō participated in all kinds of aggression both in the army on the ground and in the Army Ministry. A number of atrocity cases occurred while he was commander of the Imperial Guard in Sumatra and chief of staff of the Fourteenth Area Army in Luzon.

(16) Oka participated in the Liaison Conference of Imperial Headquarters and Government, which decided on advances into French Indochina and other matters, as well as in the conferences attended by the emperor on numerous occasions as director of the Navy Ministry's Bureau of Naval Affairs. The Bureau of Naval Affairs was a political bureau corresponding to the Army Ministry's Military Affairs Bureau, where Oka was the top official, comparable with Mutō and Satō in the army. Oka was also responsible for the mistreatment of prisoners of war detained by the Imperial Navy.

(17) Ōkawa was one of the founders of the dangerous ideology that became a hotbed of the conspiracy. He was also an active plotter.

(18) Ōshima took the first step toward the Japanese-German military alliance over the official diplomatic channel's head when he was military attaché at the Japanese embassy in Berlin. He contributed to the realization of the Tripartite Pact in concert with Shiratori "against the Japanese government's intentions."

(19) Satō succeeded Mutō as director of the Army Ministry's Military Affairs Bureau in 1942. According to Tanaka Ryūkichi's testimony, Tōjō placed strong faith in Satō, who stood behind the latter's rise to the office of prime minister. Satō should be blamed as chiefly responsible for the abuse of prisoners of war. As the supervisor of the Imperial Army's budget, he must have approved construction of the Thailand-Burma Railway.

(20) Shigemitsu was the major figure in the conspiracy of aggression following the Manchurian Incident. As foreign minister, he responded to the US and British protests over abusive treatment of prisoners of war with delays and denials. In effect, he tolerated the military's

violation of the laws of war.

(21) Being an active supporter of Tōjō, Shimada became the navy minister in the Tōjō Cabinet and assisted in advancing plans of aggression. He was also responsible for atrocities that took place during submarine warfare.

(22) Shiratori took part in the overall conspiracy from beginning to end, and pushed for the signing of the Tripartite Pact in concert with Ōshima.

(23) Suzuki had been a conspirator since 1931. As chief of the Cabinet Planning Board, which controlled the economy of Japan, he occupied a position of great authority.

(24) Tōgō was involved in the negotiations toward the conclusion of the Tripartite Pact as the Japanese ambassador to the Soviet Union. As foreign minister in the Tōjō Cabinet, Tōgō was in charge of negotiations with the US. He was a party to the deception strategy, and responsible for the decision on the timing of the delivery of the notification to the US government. After guaranteeing *mutatis mutandis* application of the Geneva Convention, Tōgō never looked into the actual situation of compliance.

(25) As a young army officer, Tōjō had planned the conquering of East Asia during the early days of the conspiracy. Occupying an important position throughout the Manchurian Incident and the Second Sino-Japanese War, he became the de facto ringleader of the conspiracy when he became prime minister in 1941. That Tōjō was directly responsible for atrocities was sufficiently proven.

(26) A large amount of evidence revealed that Umezu was responsible for the invasion of North China as commander of the China Garrison Army. As vice-minister of the army, Umezu was responsible for aggressive conduct of the Japanese military during the Second Sino-Japanese War. The military clique he belonged to blocked the formation of the Ugaki Cabinet. As commander of the Kwantung Army, Umezu continued the operation to make Manchukuo a base for attack on the Soviet Union. During his tenure as the chief of the General Staff since 1944, inhumane treatment of prisoners of war were repeated both within and outside Japan.

Naturally, the arguments of the prosecution and the defense clashed completely. Earlier I questioned the defense's interpretations of the motions, but rebuttals by the prosecution were far more dubious. All of the allegations related to conspiracy were irrelevant. But more than that, the prosecution's arguments were notably crude allegations that anyone in a certain position when an incident occurred was criminally responsible.

Opening Statement of Kiyose Ichirō

On February 24, 1947, Kiyose Ichirō made the general opening statement for the defense.

According to Kiyose, the prosecution's allegation that Japan had conspired to rule the world in collaboration with Germany and Italy was a big misunderstanding influenced by the preamble of the Tripartite Pact and the slogan *hakkō ichiu* ("eight corners of the world under one roof," meaning "rendering the entire world a single family under one roof"). Although it appeared that the prosecution regarded the political organization Taisei Yokusankai and the political party Yokusan Seijikai (Imperial Rule Assistance Political Association) as something akin to the Nazi Party in Germany and the National Fascist Party in Italy, this was totally off the mark. There were no cases of crimes against humanity comparable to the Nazi's persecution of the Jews. While the prosecution had contended that the Liutiaogou Incident was a scheme concocted by the Japanese, the Kwantung Army, faced with a military confrontation, had no other option than to defeat the Chinese troops as an act of self-defense and as a duty of the armed forces. The defense would show that the founding of Manchukuo was a movement by residents in Manchuria that arose spontaneously.

The defense would also prove that the Chinese were responsible for the escalation of the unforeseen Marco Polo Bridge Incident (July 1937), and that the Japanese had attempted to settle the problem while it remained a local conflict. While it was regrettable that atrocities by the Japanese troops did occur in China, they were unjustly exaggerated. The Zhanggufeng and Nomonhan Incidents were border disputes that did not fit the pattern of a war of aggression. The Tripartite Pact was not concluded as preparation for the war with the United States. Japan's economic control measures and the military buildup by the autumn of 1941 were all defensive measures.

Regarding the Pacific War, Kiyose declared that the defense would prove that Japan exercised the right of self-defense in unavoidable circumstances.

Kiyose's opening statement was followed immediately by Takayanagi Kenzō. Announcing that the defense would thoroughly refute the prosecution's interpretation of the Charter of the International Military Tribunal for the Far East, Takayanagi began to read out the points in question one by one, only to be interrupted by Chief Justice Webb. According to Webb, while the prosecution did have to explain in its opening statement the applicable laws, the original purpose of an opening statement was to give notice of evidence to be submitted. While the court would not deny the defense's right to argue jurisdiction, Webb said to Takayanagi, "In your closing argument you may, perhaps, refer to all of them." Takayanagi, of course, protested vehemently, but he did not succeed in changing Webb's mind.

Thorough "War of Self-Defense" Argument

How was Kiyose's opening argument received? Many in judicial circles in Japan gave it a passing mark. Japanese newspapers, not to mention overseas media including the *New York Times*, criticized it as being "reactionary." A letter Kiyose received from Tokutomi Sohō, a well-known journalist, on March 2 said,

> Most unpleasant for me was the attitude of the Japanese press toward the Tokyo Trial, and particularly toward your esteemed self. While it may be understandable for our former enemy to be critical, the Japanese press must behave *a little more like Japanese*. The reality is that their tone was like that of the foreign press.[17]

Yabe Teiji, formerly professor of Tokyo Imperial University who assisted the former Imperial Japanese Army and Navy prepare for the Tokyo Trial, suggested that, while almost half of the acts of aggression that Japan was accused of were indefensible, the defense should nevertheless plea that the "Greater East Asia War" was unavoidable due to the Asian policies of the Western

---

17. Kiyose Ichirō, *Hiroku Tōkyō Saiban* [Secret Record of the Tokyo Trial] (Tokyo: Yomiuri Shimbunsha, 1967). Emphasis in original.

powers, the dearth of natural resources and the growth in Japan's population, and the economic blockade of Japan by the US, Britain, China, and the Netherlands (the so-called ABCD encirclement). Obviously, this had to be the basic line of defense.

Kiyose's opening statement, however, presented a complete denial of any aggressive intention on the part of Japan, and instead presented a thorough "self-defense war" argument. This was quite different from the argument suggested by Yabe. Clearly, the "defense of state" faction within the Japanese defense counsels had decided to counter the prosecution's war of aggression allegations with an argument that the war had been a war of self-defense.

On this point, court reporter Nomura Masao made a very interesting remark. In circumstances where defiance of the Occupation forces could mean being purged from public office, the only place where the Japanese could be on an equal footing with the Allies was the Tokyo Tribunal.[18]

Generally speaking, the logic employed by the defense was an excessive denial that Japan had committed a war of aggression. Former Imperial Japanese Army general Ugaki Kazushige commented, "If the basic attitude is to justify everything, no matter how insignificant, would that not weaken the really important elements in the defense?"

Significance of the Dismissal of Defense Counsel Smith

With the opening statement by Kiyose, the defense commenced presenting counterevidence (for each phase of counterevidence, see Table 4-1). On March 5, Defense Counsel David Smith, who was in charge of defendant Hirota, became annoyed by Chief Justice Webb's frequent interruptions during his examination of witnesses and complained that the court was committing "undue interference." While "undue interference" was a commonplace expression in American courts, it was taboo in Australia, Webb's home country.

Infuriated, Webb told Smith to withdraw his remark and apologize, or leave the courtroom. Webb even said he would propose revoking Smith's credentials as a defense counsel to the bench of the Tokyo Trial. Smith explained that he had had no intention of exhibiting contempt of court, but

18. Nomura, *Sabakareta Nihon*.

Table 4-1. Defense's Counterevidence

Commence-ment Date	Phase of Cross-Examination	Main Counterevidence
Jan. 27, 1947	Motion to request dismissal of prosecution	
Feb. 24, 1947	Commencement of the defense's counterevidence	Opening statement
Feb. 25, 1947	General phase	Constitution, government organization, New Order in East Asia, domestic political problems
Mar. 18, 1947	The Manchurian Incident phase	The First Shanghai Incident, Manchukuo
Apr. 22, 1947	The Second Sino-Japanese War phase	Anti-Japanese movement, The Second Shanghai Incident, Nanjing Incident, Wang Jingwei government
May 16, 1947	The Soviet Union phase	Anti-Comintern Pact, Zhanggufeng and Nomonhan Incidents, the Soviet–Japanese Neutrality Pact
Jun. 12, 1947	The Pacific War phase	Tripartite Pact, ABCD encirclement, US-Japan negotiations, treatment of prisoners of war
Sep. 10, 1947	Individual defendant phase	
Jan. 12, 1948	End of the defense's counterevidence	

he nevertheless would not apologize. When Smith was banned from appearing in court by the judges after a fifteen-minute recess, he walked out of the courtroom, saying, "I have no intention of changing my mind."

However, this meant that Hirota lost his American defense counsel, regarding which Smith expressed his deep contrition when he appeared in court six months later, on September 5. Because Webb once again brought up his demand for a formal apology from Smith, however, the two ended up estranged.

Actually, there had been a foreshadowing of the confrontation between the two.

William Webb
(National Archives of the Netherlands, Collection 544 B. V. A. Röling)

David Smith
(Kyodo News)

Webb and Smith had quarreled vehemently since the defense's motion on dismissal of prosecution in late January, and had clashed emotionally. Moreover, Webb was the type of chief justice who threatened the mass media with possible contempt of court. Smith's allegation of "undue interruption" was aimed at Webb, who very much valued "the dignity of the court." The fundamental reason for the dismissal of Defense Counsel Smith was, therefore, a clash of egos rather than "the partiality of the court."

Concerning the Use of Evidence

Immediately after the opening of the trial, the Japanese defense counsels were bewildered by "the theory and the speed" of trial under Anglo-American law. They could barely keep up with the proceedings. One of the defense counsels, Sugawara Yutaka (in charge of defendant Araki), left the following impressive reminiscence:

> American defense counsels frequently raise objections . . . but 80 to 90 percent of these objections are denied by the bench. Nevertheless, they continue to object, and that objection is denied again. Disgusted by such continuous unseemliness, defendants said, "While we can do nothing about Americans, we would like the Japanese defense counsels to be more prudent." As time went by, however, we came to realize that the Anglo-American court manner of the American counsels was actually more appropriate. When we did not speak out against undue remarks made by the court or the prosecution, we learned that it would be interpreted as consent on the part of the defense. . . . Once you raise an objection, it is registered that the defense disagrees, even if the objection is denied. Moreover, it would be entered into the judicial record. . . .[19]

The Tokyo Trial was also an opportunity for the Japanese to learn how a criminal court is conducted under Anglo-American law.

Critics often claim that the evidence adopted by the Tokyo Trial was

---

19. Sugawara Yutaka, *Tōkyō Saiban no shōtai* [The True Nature of the Tokyo Trial] (Tokyo: Jiji Press, 1961).

remarkably unfavorable to the defense. While this is true, to a degree this was attributable to the defense itself.

In particular, the Japanese defense counsels made the crucial mistake of repeating ambiguous remarks without counterevidence for support. This not only made a bad impression on the bench, but it also displeased the defendants themselves. Some defendants were observed disagreeing strongly with their Japanese and American counsels. A reporter with NHK (Japan Broadcasting Corporation) made the harsh observation that the defense, both Japanese and American, was lackluster and only the bulldog tenacity of Kiyose stood out.[20]

The final judgment stated that the Tribunal refused to accept certain evidence submitted by the defense because it was either virtually without support or almost totally irrelevant, so the criticism was not too farfetched. In this connection, it is interesting that Kido Kōichi, who had understood the significance of evidence, concluded that, because the Anglo-American trial practice subscribes to the principle of adjudication based on evidence, the assessment of a case could differ depending on how a defendant was defended. Kido also commented on Hirota, who did not take the witness stand himself: "The defense was entitled to say in court that this was how it really was, and so Hirota might not have been sentenced to death had his defense counsels put him on the witness stand."

Delaying Tactics

One strategy the defense employed was delaying tactics. The Allied representatives in court felt that the defense intended to make the trial a contest of endurance, by scattering about irrelevant pieces of evidence. As a matter of fact, some defense counsels admitted that was a ploy they adopted in order to delay the proceedings. One of the defendants, Kido, testified that "the prolongation of the trial beyond the initial expectation was solely attributable to the presence of American defense counsels," confirming the intentional delaying of the trial by the defense.[21]

---

20. "NHK Hōdō no Kiroku" Kankō Iinkai ["NHK News Record" Publishing Committee], *NHK Hōdō no 50-nen* [Fifty Years of NHK Reporting] (Tokyo: Kondō Shoten, 1988).

21. Arnold C. Brackman, *The Other Nuremberg* (New York: William Morrow & Co., 1988), 2nd edition, and Kido Kōichi Nikki Kenkyūkai, ed., *Kido Kōichi nikki: Tōkyō Saiban-ki* [Kido Kōichi Diary: Tokyo Trial Period] (Tokyo: University of Tokyo Press, 1980).

The defense placed hope on the possibility that the defendants could receive lighter sentences as the Cold War began to affect international relations, or as the excitement of the war wore off over time. They thought the longer the court's judgment was delayed, the more favorable the rulings for the defendants would be.

For every piece of irrelevant evidence that the defense presented, the prosecution raised repeated objections. This alone took up a great amount of time. The defense continued to present similar pieces of evidence. Judging that the defense counsels were refusing to comply with the court decision not to adopt "evidence that is charged with personal opinion," or "documents that were akin to propaganda," Webb warned on May 8, 1947, that by submitting such evidence the defense was in effect deliberately delaying the proceedings. Thus, when it became the turn of the defense to present counterevidence, the delay of the trial became all the more serious.

The prolongation of the Tokyo Trial had actually been controversial ever since the Nuremberg Trial finished in October 1946, some ten months after the trial began.

On December 24, 1946, MacArthur shared his thoughts with fifty-three-year-old British diplomat Alvary Gascoigne, head of the United Kingdom Liaison Mission (UKLIM) in Japan, the British political representative in Japan. MacArthur told Gascoigne that he was annoyed by and worried about the delay of the trial. MacArthur believed that the drawn-out presentation of evidence by the prosecution only benefitted the defense. He deplored the fact that there was nothing he could do beyond what he had already done, which was to criticize the delay, and try informally to persuade the bench to speed up the trial out of respect for President Truman's wishes.

Speed-up Efforts in Vain

Prolongation of the Tokyo Trial was unwelcome due to the fear that its credibility could deteriorate as a result of a decline in interest in the proceedings and the progress of the Cold War.

The Nuremberg Trial, which had tried the Nazis intensively within a short period of time, attracted tremendous attention around the world. The Tokyo Trial, in contrast, was hardly known in the West, and interest in it remained low. While the lack of Western interest might have been inevitable, even the

Japanese people appeared to lose interest in the trial. At first, Japanese people stood in queues overnight to obtain admission tickets. Some tickets were even sold on the black market. From the outset, though, monotonous court hearings could hardly entertain ordinary people, except on such pivotal days as the opening of court, the testimonies of such dignitaries as Tōjō and Puyi, and the final sentencing.

Under pressure from various directions to speed things up, Webb called the Japanese and American defense counsels together on June 24, 1947, to announce that he wished to conclude the trial by the end of the year. This would be accomplished by allotting three weeks to the Pacific War phase, two days to each defendant during the individual defendant phase, and ten days to the prosecution's rebuttal and closing arguments.

That same day, the defendants and defense counsels gathered for the first time since the opening of the trial. Although it was proposed that a consultative meeting among defendants and defense counsels be convened regularly twice a week to eliminate discrepancies among them, Shigemitsu called for the meeting to be held only among the defense counsels, wrecking the plan.[22]

In my view, prolongation of the Tokyo Trial was inevitable due to the following factors, which were entangled in a complex manner.

A number of countries were involved. There were lengthy affidavits and testimonies, not to mention the language barrier. Complex political systems and processes under the Meiji Constitution, which the Westerners were not familiar with, posed another obstacle. The prosecution introduced as many as fifty-five counts to the court, and many of the participating countries pursued atrocities specific to their own nationals. Furthermore, the defense employed delaying tactics. And Chief Justice Webb, in actuality, was more tolerant of the defense's objections and requests for recesses than expected, for fear of being criticized as unfair.

For these reasons, any effort to speed up the trial was destined to fail.

---

22. Shigemitsu Mamoru, *Sugamo nikki* [Sugamo Diary] (Tokyo: Bungeishunjū Shinsha, 1953), and Abe Genki, *Sugamo nikki* [Sugamo Diary] (Tokyo: Tentensha, 1992).

3. Defense of State and Defense of Individuals

Conflicts of Interest among Defendants

Tokutomi Sohō had hoped that Ōkawa, Matsuoka, and Tōjō would speak up and say what had to be said. As mentioned, Ōkawa's case was dismissed. When Matsuoka died of illness in June 1946, Tokutomi lamented that Japan had lost an important, representative voice. What he had hoped for was the "defense of state" argument for Japan's position.

When the individual defendant phase arrived in September 1947, the "defense of individuals" became all the more prevalent. Kodama Yoshio, a Class A war crimes suspect, wrote in June 1947, that "the majority of the Class A war criminals were more ardently attached to what was left of their lives than the future of the mother country."[23] And all the defendants, except Dohihara, Hata, Hiranuma, Hirota, Hoshino, Kimura, Satō, Shigemitsu, and Umezu, decided to take the witness stand themselves.

The pattern of defense of individual defendants was (1) to show that they were pacifists, who had opposed the aggression, and endeavored to avoid war and (2) to point out that they had not been in any position of authority, and that the authority belonged to their superiors or other organizations. This pattern naturally led to conflicts of interest among the defendants, entangled with past personal grudges.

Itagaki, for instance, reacted violently to the defense given by Umezu, who was one-year his senior at the Imperial Japanese Military Academy, and yelled abuse at Umezu within the latter's earshot. When Itagaki found that the evidence Hirota was about to present would be unfavorable to his own defense, he went after Hirota demanding in abusive language that he withdraw his testimony. Morishima Gorō, associate defense counsel in charge of Hirota, was a former China-school diplomat who had been seen as Hirota's only recourse after Smith's resignation. Morishima had been determined to confront the military head on, but was so indignant at Hirota's compromise that he resigned.

---

23. Kodama Yoshio, *Shibafu wa fumaretemo* [Even If Our Lawn Is Stepped on] (Tokyo: Shin Yūkan Shimbunsha, 1956).

"Call Yourselves Men?!"

The conflict over Pearl Harbor between the Foreign Ministry and the Imperial Japanese Navy was quite typical.

Since the opening of the trial, the Foreign Ministry had put its interests ahead of all else. It had remained extremely wary of being considered as on a par with the Imperial Army or Navy and, as such, it was not enthusiastic about coordinating defenses with the military.[24] During the Pacific War phase of counterevidence by the defense in mid-August 1947, Yamamoto Kumaichi, former director of the Foreign Ministry's North American Affairs Bureau, made the following testimony. Itō Seiichi, deputy chief of Japanese Naval General Staff (later commander of the Second Fleet who went down with the battleship *Yamato*) had remarked at the Liaison Conference of the Imperial Headquarters and Government that, "Since, at the opening of the war, . . . it is essential to strike a blow at the US with a surprise attack, we would like the Foreign Ministry not to desist from negotiations with the US, but to keep them going." In response, Foreign Minister Tōgō Shigenori had resisted by saying that notification was absolutely necessary. While Tōgō had intended to announce the termination of negotiations with the US in ample time before the start of war, the Naval General Staff requested that the delivery of the notification to the US be delayed by half an hour. Tōgō had to concur. Defense counsel John Brannon, in charge of defendants Shimada Shigetarō and Oka Takazumi, could endure it no longer and cross-examined Yamamoto.

The indignation of the former Imperial Japanese Navy was clearly recorded in Toyoda Kumao's diary. He wrote that the Foreign Ministry was trying to avenge its grudges in the courtroom; all the defense needed to do was to demand the excision of all references to Pearl Harbor and the ultimatum. Its lack of resources and of thoroughness were deplorable. These defenses, Toyoda wrote, made him wonder what Tōgō might start saying about the Imperial Navy during cross-examination by the prosecution. Toyoda singled out Nishi Haruhiko, Yamamoto Kumaichi, and Tōgō Shigenori, saying "Call yourselves men?!"

---

24. Toyoda Kumao, "Haisōki" [Record of a Debacle], *Chūō kōron* (September 1996).

Shimada Shigetarō's Counterblow

The former Imperial Japanese Navy, which had earlier advocated the "defense of state" position, started its counterarguments with the defense of Oka on November 17. Former captain Shiba Katsuo, formally with the second division of the Ministry of Navy's Bureau of Naval Affairs, gave his testament.

According to Shiba, Oka Takasumi (director of the Naval Affairs Bureau) had repeatedly warned his subordinates that war should be avoided at all cost. And since the draft note to the United States written by the Foreign Ministry was inadequate as an ultimatum, Oka and his subordinates produced a revised version. A representative of the Foreign Ministry, however, rejected it, saying the original version needed no revision.

In response, defense counsel Blakeney (in charge of defendant Tōgō) asked Shiba whether Oka had identified this "representative of the Foreign Ministry." Shiba replied that Oka had not clearly identified him. Convinced that he had succeeded in damaging the credibility of Shiba's testimony, Blakeney concluded his cross-examination.

Shimada Shigetarō took the witness stand on December 5. According to Shimada's affidavit, he joined the Tōjō Cabinet as its minister of the navy, hoping to do his best to carry out diplomatic negotiations with the US. At the time, everyone was occupied with the war with China, and nobody with authority within the government wanted to engage in a war with the US and Britain. The Hull note of November 26, 1941 (the proposal delivered to Japan by US secretary of state Cordell Hull during the US-Japan negotiations), however, was "a bolt from the blue." The note was interpreted as a kind of ultimatum that threatened the very survival of Japan. No one proposed accepting it. Although the Imperial Navy was not at all confident about winning a war with the US, it nevertheless became convinced that Japan would be able to carry out more favorable war preparations at that time than in the future. Accordingly, Shimada and Nagano Osami, chief of Imperial Japanese Naval General Staff, reported to the emperor on November 30 that the Imperial Japanese Navy had completed preparations for waging war with the US.

As mentioned, Shimada found fault with the Hull note. It is true that, in 1941, decision-makers within the Japanese government, including Foreign Minister Tōgō, generally interpreted the Hull note as a US "ultimatum," and viewed negotiations with the US as hopeless. But the actual words and deeds of Navy Minister Shimada Shigetarō, who had been so much in agreement with the army that he was mocked as "Tōjō's aide-de-camp," were quite different from the content of his affidavit.

On October 30, 1941, Shimada told Sawamoto Yorio, vice-minister of the navy, and Oka,

> It appears that the general trend (toward opening of a war) is irreversible. . . . At this point, it is imperative for us to make up our minds to fight a war, ensure that our future diplomacy is internationally justifiable, and lead the Japanese people to be convinced that it is a just war.

Thus, Shimada shifted his position to that of the unavoidability of war. Sawamoto, who had been more cautious about war, was reprimanded for resisting Shimada's views. Oka compromised, saying, "It appears there is nothing we can do."[25]

To Protect the Honor of the Imperial Japanese Navy

Let us return to the court proceedings. When prosecutor James J. Robinson questioned Shimada regarding whether it had been the emperor's view that notification should be sent to the US before the attack on Pearl Harbor, Shimada said, "Yes, that is correct. But it was not only the emperor's view; it was also the policy of the Japanese government."

When asked if he wanted to shift all the responsibility to Foreign Minister Tōgō, Shimada implied that the Foreign Ministry was responsible by stating that it had the sole authority to notify the US and, therefore, there was nothing the Imperial Navy could do. When Robinson pursued Shimada regarding whether the Imperial Navy had from the beginning wished to give the US advance notification, he tried to protect the Imperial Navy's honor by saying, "It has been the pride of the Imperial Navy to comply with international law since the Russo-Japanese War. . . . We would never consider deceiving the enemy."

---

25. Sugimoto Ken, *Kaigun no Shōwa-shi* [Shōwa History of the Imperial Japanese Navy] (Tokyo: Bungeishunjū, 1985).

According to Tōgō Shigehiko, grandson of Shigenori, his grandfather felt that Shimada provoked Tōgō into a fight when the former stressed that the Imperial Navy had never wished to initiate an attack without a declaration of war.[26]

In a meeting of the Taishōkai, a reunion of some twenty former navy admirals, one of the members, Takarabe Takeshi, deplored the situation, saying, "Why does the Imperial Navy not accept responsibility for the notification? I don't like Shimada's testimony at all." To this, former admiral Yamamoto Eisuke complained, "You're an old has-been. You should leave it to the appropriate authorities." This provoked Takarabe to burst out, "Who are you calling an old has-been? Shut up!" And the two came very close to engaging in a fistfight.[27] However, Yamamoto represented the majority position in the Imperial Navy.

Mudslinging Match

When Tōgō Shigenori took the witness stand, the conflict between the Foreign Ministry and the Imperial Japanese Navy turned into a mudslinging match.

When Tōgō's affidavit was read on December 18, even Shigemitsu Mamoru, another diplomat of the Foreign Ministry, severely criticized it, saying, "It is so extremely self-defensive, that it tarnishes others. The entire document is nothing but self-aggrandizement in bad taste."[28]

The next day, Tōgō disclosed the following testimony to John Brannon, American defense counsel in charge of the Imperial Japanese Navy. In Tōgō's recollection, it was Nagano Osami, chief of Naval General Staff, who first started referring to a surprise attack. Subsequently, Itō Seiichi, deputy chief of Naval General Staff, requested that negotiations with the US be continued without modification. When Brannon pointed out that according to Tōjō, Suzuki, Kaya, Hoshino, Oka, Mutō, Shimada, and others, the Imperial Navy had never insisted on an attack without advance notification, Tōgō insisted that their memories could not be trusted. He sarcastically added that they were so good at forgetting anything unfavorable to them that they could not even

---

26. Tōgō, *Sofu Tōgō Shigenori no shōgai.*
27. Toyoda, *Sensō saiban yoroku*, and "Haisōki."
28. Shigemitsu, *Sugamo nikki.*

remember that the conference attended by the emperor had been convened on November 5, 1941.

Tōgō then made a more shocking disclosure.

According to Tōgō, one day in mid-May 1946 in the backyard of the court, Shimada had requested Tōgō not to testify that the navy wanted to launch a surprise attack. Shimada half threatened Tōgō, saying such testimony would be unbeneficial for him. Also, according to Tōgō, immediately before Nagano passed away, he had said he would take full responsibility for the attack on Pearl Harbor.

Tōgō Shigenori on the witness stand (National Archives of the Netherlands, Collection 544 B. V. A. Röling)

Defense counsel Nishi Haruhiko (in charge of defendant Tōgō, who was administrative vice-minister of foreign affairs when the war broke out) tried to persuade Tōgō that it would not be necessary to stress what the navy had said because the notification had been delivered to the US government, and the delay in the delivery had been attributed to clerical errors on the part of the Japanese embassy in Washington, DC. However, Tōgō would not listen.[29]

In a highly unusual development, Shimada was summoned back to the witness stand to testify on January 9, 1947. Shimada once again defended the honor of the Imperial Japanese Navy.

According to Shimada, Tōgō had exaggerated what he had heard, saying that he had been threatened, just to save his own skin. Had the Foreign Ministry delivered the notification to the US government half an hour before the attack, as the Naval General Staff had requested, there would have had been no problem from the perspective of international law. The delay in notification was an error committed by diplomatic officials and, therefore, beyond the Imperial Navy's control.

Ōkawa Shūmei, who was in hospital at the time, wrote the following interesting observation:

29. Toyoda, "Haisōki."

It now appears as if Tōjō started the war singlehandedly. They are saying that the war started even though everyone opposed war, which is
absurd. Those Class A suspects are supposed to be representatives of
Japan, but they are an eternal disgrace.[30]

His Majesty's Procurator

It was Kido Kōichi who most thoroughly pursued the line of "defense of individuals." Since his imprisonment in Sugamo Prison, Kido had maintained his
calm due to his sense of duty to devote himself to the emperor and the country as "His Majesty's procurator."

Kido was also serious about winning the court case. Immediately after the
trial began, he announced, "I am convinced that I have done nothing that
makes me guilty, and I will do my very best to stress this point." When, in April
1947, defense counsel William Logan, who was planning a temporary return
home, suggested that Kido should be the first to take the witness stand during
the individual defendant phase, Kido violently opposed the suggestion, saying:

> It would give people the impression that I was selected to be first
> because the court decided I am more important than Mr. Tōjō. Com-
> bined with the fact that I am charged with more counts than Mr. Tōjō,
> this arrangement would inevitably lead to such a conclusion in people's
> minds. . . . And it would be highly disadvantageous not only to me.
> More importantly, there is a danger it could once again stimulate talk
> about His Majesty's responsibility for the war.[31]

Kido believed that the verdict of the court would depend on what a defendant had done and, he was convinced that "concrete evidence" would be
much more effective than theoretical arguments. Positioning himself as an
imperial court pacifist, and a disciple of the Meiji elder statesman Saionji
Kinmochi, Kido stressed that, although he had attempted to avoid war and

---

30. Ōkawa Shūmei Kenshōkai, ed., *Ōkawa Shūmei nikki* [Ōkawa Shūmei Diary] (Tokyo:
Iwasaki Gakujutsu Shuppansha, 1986).

31. Kido Kōichi Nikki Kenkyūkai, *Kido Kōichi nikki: Tōkyō Saiban-ki.*

attain a peaceful settlement, restrictions imposed by the official authority of his position as Lord Keeper of the Privy Seal prevented him from stopping the war. This "escape to authority," which political scientist Maruyama Masao criticized,[32] was a positive logic intended to prove his innocence.

Thus, Kido persisted with the "defense of individuals" throughout his testimony in October. In his affidavit, which Logan had written, Kido frequently took advantage of his connection with the emperor. Consequently, he became the least liked inside and outside of Sugamo Prison.

According to Abe Genki, another Class A war crimes suspect,

> While he makes all kinds of efforts to vindicate himself, in his affidavit there is no mention of our state's legitimate argument as to why Japan was cornered into fighting the Pacific War. . . . I do not think he can evade his responsibility as Lord Keeper of the Privy Seal. . . . The daily *Mainichi Shimbun* harshly criticizes Kido, while the daily *Yomiuri Shimbun* carries a cartoon with a caption saying, "An eagle insists that it is a dove."

Abe also quoted Shigemitsu's bitter criticism of Kido's affidavit, commenting that it not only hurt his own interests and that of the state and the emperor, but that it also levied tremendous disadvantages on the other defendants.[33] As Nomura Masao pointed out in 1954, Kido Kōichi's diary was "a double-edged sword," which was powerful enough to deliver fatal damage to the military clique, but it could also imply the emperor's responsibility for the war.[34]

Abhorrence and Disillusionment

In 1959, Satō Kenryō, former lieutenant general of the Japanese Army, said this before the Judicial System and Research Department, Minister's Secretariat of the Ministry of Justice:

---

32. Maruyama Masao, "Gunkoku shihaisha no seishin keitai" ["Thought and Behaviour Patterns of Japan's Wartime Leaders"], trans. Ivan Morris, *Thought and Behaviour in Modern Japanese Politics* (London: Oxford University Press, 1964).

33. Abe, *Sugamo nikki*.

34. Tamura Yoshio, ed., *Hiroku Daitōa senshi* [Secret Record of the Greater East Asia War] (Tokyo: Fuji Shoen, 1954), vol. 6.

Around the time Kido recommended Tōjō as prime minister, he noted in his diary that he had done so to suppress the military's strong advocacy of war. Since I had been convinced that the military was extremely cautious about war, I asked Kido for clarification in Sugamo Prison. In reply, Kido informed me that newspaper reporters had been speaking often about the military's strong advocacy of war. . . . The army minister only talked about superficial things, while the Lord Keeper of the Privy Seal hardly had a chance to talk with field rank officers. Therefore, he oftentimes relied on newspaper reporters.

Although Satō admitted that Kido's diary was far more accurate than the Harada-Saionji diary,[35] he nevertheless held that careful examination was called for before adopting personal diaries as evidence.[36]

It is a legitimate right for a defendant to defend himself in a criminal court. In the case of the Tokyo Trial, however, where defendants were mostly representatives of the state, this basic fact was not easily understood. Thus, even though Ugaki Kazushige repeatedly called on defendants to argue boldly that Japan had taken military action for purposes of survival and self-defense, and that as a result, Asian countries had been liberated, they would not listen. Ugaki deplored the fact that what the defendants never went beyond mere self-vindication.[37]

As American diplomat Robert Appleton Fearey reported, the people of Japan felt abhorrence and disillusionment toward their former leaders, as they watched the defendants blaming each other. It was Tōjō Hideki who responded to this set of circumstances by developing the "defense of state" argument, taking on full, singlehanded responsibility for the war, thus becoming the focus of favorable opinion.[38]

---

35. Harada Kumao, *Saionji-kō to seikyoku* [Prince Saionji and Political Situations of the Time] (Tokyo: Iwanami Shoten, 1950).

36. *Satō Kenryō kara no chōshusho* [Hearing on Satō Kenryō], and *Inoue Tadao shiryō* [Inoue Tadao Documents], Yasukuni Kaikō Bunko [Yasukuni Archives].

37. Ugaki Kazushige, *Ugaki Kazushige nikki* [Ugaki Kazushige Diary], ed. Tsunoda Jun (Tokyo: Misuzu Shobō, 1971), vol. 3.

38. Robert A. Fearey, *The Occupation of Japan, Second Phase, 1948–1950* (New York: Mac-Millan, 1950).

The Shadow of the Shōwa Emperor

The de facto non-indictment of the emperor had been decided at the Far Eastern Commission on April 3, 1946 (see chapter 2, section 3). There remained no possibility, therefore, that he would be indicted. Nonetheless, the shadow of the emperor remained on the proceedings of the court throughout the trial.

The prosecution refrained from referring to the emperor in its introduction of evidence, out of fear that careless mention could implicate him. When the process of national decision-making was reviewed, however, reference to the emperor became unavoidable. When the defense began cross-examination, references to the emperor increased in frequency. Regarding the start of war in 1941, historian Tobe Ryōichi has pointed out that "In that the responsible government and military leaders, following proper procedures, decided to start the war, the emperor, as a constitutional monarch, was not allowed to overturn the decision. At least, that was how the emperor perceived it."[39] For those unfamiliar with the decision-making system under the Meiji Constitution, however, the following document, which was submitted to the court as evidence, might imply the emperor's responsibility.

The *Kido Kōichi nikki*, court evidence #3340, related as follows: On November 30, 1941, Lord Keeper of the Privy Seal Kido advised the emperor to determine the true intention of the Imperial Navy directly from Navy Minister Shimada Shigetarō and Nagano Osami, chief of Naval General Staff, because once the imperial decision was made, the momentous decision would be irreversible. Shimada and Nagano, who had an audience with the emperor immediately, reported on the Imperial Navy's readiness with considerable conviction. After that, Kido was instructed to convey to the prime minister His Majesty's wish to convene the conference attended by the emperor as planned.[40]

Witnessing these developments in court, the Allied side became increasingly doubtful about the wisdom of the decision not to prosecute the emperor. Keenan, always a vain individual, decided to demonstrate actively

---

39. Tobe Ryōichi, "Shōwa Tennō to shin Tōjō Hideki" [Emperor Shōwa and His Subject Tōjō Hideki], *Shokun!* (July 2004).

40. Kido Kōichi Nikki Kenkyūkai, ed., *Kido Kōichi nikki* [Kido Kōichi Diary] (Tokyo: University of Tokyo Press, 1966), vol. 2.

in court the rectitude of the argument that the "emperor had no war responsibility," instead of simply hiding the emperor from view.

This type of simplistic logic and method had been prevalent in the US, as well as in GHQ, from the beginning. Brigadier General Bonner Fellers, a military secretary who had served in MacArthur's headquarters as director of psychological warfare against Japan, made the following proposition to former prime minister Yonai Mitsumasa on March 6, 1946, on the eve of the opening of the Tokyo Trial. Because many Allies, including the Soviets, strongly argued for the indictment of the emperor, it would be most effective for the Japanese side to prove in court that the emperor was totally innocent. To this end, the Japanese side should blame Tōjō, and place all the responsibility on him. Yonai wholeheartedly concurred with this proposal and suggested that they should make Tōjō and Shimada fully responsible.[41] In addition, First Lieutenant of the US Marines Aristides Lazarus, one of the American defense counsels, secretly approached Tōjō and persuaded him to protect the emperor, following President Truman's wish.

The logic that the Americans deployed was that, from the beginning, the emperor had no responsibility and, therefore, the emperor could not possibly be indicted.

Keenan, in his questioning of former prime minister Okada Keisuke in late September 1947, bluntly denied the emperor's war responsibility. Keenan also snatched the assignment to question Kido from Comyns-Carr in late October (some say it was MacArthur who ordered Keenan to question Kido) and defended the emperor's conduct so tenaciously that Webb found it necessary to remind Keenan that it was not the emperor who was on trial.

As a result, more attention was placed on the emperor. In other words, Keenan failed to accomplish his objective.

The Last Act of Service

British prosecutor Comyns-Carr sent a highly acrimonious report to Hartley Shawcross, the British attorney general.

According to this report, what Keenan did was to replace an "incompetent" Filipino prosecutor in charge of Itagaki with an "incompetent"

41. Toyoda, *Senso saiban yoroku.*

American prosecutor. Keenan was not capable of questioning Kido in the first place. Keenan took the trouble of taking a detour to the emperor issue and, as a result, proved that the prosecution's policy of evading the emperor issue was wrong. Comyns-Carr told Shawcross that he himself was embarrassed to have lavish meals and stay in the luxurious Imperial Hotel in the war-devastated capital of Tokyo. He confided that he was fed up with Tokyo, where the US Occupation forces acted like kings.

Having learned the hard way from the failure of the questioning of Kido, even MacArthur advised Keenan to refrain from questioning Tōjō. But Keenan would not listen, declaring excitedly that he had to interrogate Tōjō himself. It appears, though, that Keenan was aware that he could not repeat the same mistake. To be fully prepared, he maneuvered behind the scenes, just like an assistant attorney general maneuvering and lobbying congressmen, using Tanaka Ryūkichi to persuade Tōjō to remove all responsibility from the emperor.

But Tōjō, loyal to the emperor, had intended to do exactly that from the beginning. According to Shigemitsu, on January 9, 1947, Tōjō asked for his opinion in the waiting room of the courtroom: "I don't think my oral statement will cause any trouble for His Majesty. What do you think?" Before his attempted suicide in 1945, Tōjō left a message for Foreign Minister Shigemitsu, saying, "I am determined to bear the responsibility for the war myself and not to trouble His Majesty."[42]

In his testimony on December 30, 1972, Tōjō said he "fully understand[s] His Majesty's desire" to find a peaceful resolution to the crisis between Japan and the United States. The testimony was, in this way, his last act of service to the emperor.

On the witness stand on December 30, 1947, Tōjō made a good start, testifying that he had been "well aware of the emperor's wish" to settle the crisis between Japan and the United States peacefully.

Tōjō's Careless Remark

The next day, however, Tōjō blundered. And it was not Keenan but William Logan, defense counsel in charge of defendant Kido, who brought out

---

42. Shigemitsu, *Sugamo nikki.*

Tōjō Hideki
(Both images courtesy of the National
Archives of the Netherlands, Collection
544 B. V. A. Röling)

Joseph Berry Keenan

the careless remark. When Logan asked Tōjō if Kido had ever taken action to thwart the emperor's hope for peace, Tōjō replied, "Of course, there has been no such case. . . . It is absolutely impossible for a Japanese subject to do this or that against His Majesty's wishes. This is all the more so in the case of high-ranking government officials."

This well-known remark of Tōjō's was intended to defend Kido.

At this point Webb interrupted, asking, "Are you aware what your last reply implies?" It has to be said that Tōjō could not have thoroughly considered the implications of what he had said. Perhaps Tōjō let down his guard a little with Logan.

To get Tōjō to revise his comment, Keenan again resorted to behind-the-scenes maneuvering. When the defense touched on Puyi during the cross-examination of Tōjō on January 6, 1948, Keenan intervened, saying that it seemed appropriate to ask the witness a couple of questions regarding the emperor at that point, making a far-fetched connection with the emperor in 1941. Referring to Tōjō's now widely known remark on New Year's Eve of the previous year, Keenan asked Tōjō if his assertion that no Japanese would go against the emperor's orders was correct.

In response, Tōjō explained that with his earlier remark he was merely voicing the Japanese people's sentiment and that the remark had nothing to do with the emperor's responsibility. It was the Tōjō Cabinet that had decided on the war, and the emperor had concurred with great reluctance.

At this point, Keenan asked Tōjō if it was not the emperor who had encouraged the government to give advance notice to the US. When Tōjō replied affirmatively, Keenan followed up by asking, "Did that take the form of a direct order?" Tōjō stated, "It was not an order, but the emperor's counsel. I took responsibility for carrying it out." Thus, the troubleshooting was complete.

Tōjō's Determination

Keenan's cross-examination of Tōjō took place from December 31, 1947, through January 6, 1948. The showdown between the two was the ultimate highlight of the Tokyo Trial, and the Ichigaya courtroom, where empty seats were ordinarily conspicuous, overflowed with spectators.

On August 27, 1945, immediately after the termination of the war, Captain Miyama Yōzō, adjutant general of the Army Ministry, visited Tōjō at his private residence in Yōga, Tokyo. During their conversation, Tōjō said that, unless the emperor's advisors and assistants assumed all responsibility for the war, the imperial family was in real danger of vanishing. During the war, Japan had attempted to fight the US and Britain in cooperation with the Soviet Union, but postwar Japan would have to change its policy, and team up with the US and Britain to counter the Soviet Union. Stressing the importance of anti-communist cooperation with the US and Britain, Tōjō predicted that liberalism would be much more potent than communism, and that the Japanese homeland as well as south Korea would house air bases of the US forces. Furthermore, he said that the greatest efforts should be made to leave for future generations the impression that the Greater East Asia War was in compliance with international moral principles. Thus, while certain people were responsible for the war, there were no war criminals, and the emperor was in no way responsible. Lastly, perhaps with his suicide plan in mind, Tōjō said he would never harm the virtue of the emperor, never betray senior Japanese statesmen to the enemy, never damage Japan's national prestige, and, therefore, would refuse to be tried by an enemy's court.[43]

---

43. Miyama, *Haikyo no Shōwa kara*.

Tōjō, by nature, would not stop until he brought an opponent completely to his knees. When Aubrey S. Kenworthy, principal military police officer in charge of security, who was sympathetic to the Tokyo Trial defendants, advised Tōjō via Shigemitsu not to be fooled by the prosecutor's trick to provoke him, Tōjō admitted his shortcoming, and tried to remain calm throughout the cross-examination.[44]

Keenan Made Sport of

For his part, Keenan continued to ask Tōjō pointless questions, and Tōjō made sport of him. Let us consider several examples.

When Keenan inquired if the Army Department of Imperial Headquarters' announcement that altogether 482,257 spoils of war (weapons) were obtained from China was accurate, Tōjō said, "Let me add a few things here. . . . You see . . . I'd like to talk about the psychology of military personnel in the battlefield. In the battlefield. . ." But he was cut short by Keenan, who said, "But I am not very much interested in psychology."

To this, Tōjō responded that he had no intention of explaining psychology to Keenan. He then spoke of the tendency amongst commanders in battlefields to boast of their accomplishments, and, therefore, their liability to exaggerate to their superiors the number of enemy casualties and spoils of war. Having been asked about the accuracy of the announced number, it was merely that he had wished to inform Keenan of this tendency, Tōjō said.

His tone was cold when he stated this.

To Keenan's question as to whether the US had already been a threat to Japan in September 1940, Tōjō replied that the US had been an economic threat to Japan, particularly after the abolishment of the US-Japan Treaty of Commerce and Navigation in July 1939 (more accurately, the announcement of the abolishment of said treaty).

To the question whether the US had also posed a military threat to Japan, Tōjō replied that it was clear there was a military plan on the part of the United States from exhibit documents #3567 and #3660, and that in fact a large fleet of the US Navy had assembled in Hawaii in May 1940. "A threat

---

44. Shigemitsu, *Sugamo nikki*.

is a threat when the target country feels it as a threat. I felt threatened by the United States, and Japan felt threatened by the United States," he said.[45]

"Do you mean that the United States did not have the right to self-defense against an aggressor nation?" asked Keenan, to which Tōjō replied that, while he would not comment on the right of self-defense of the US, "aggression and tyranny," which were the premises for the US self-defense, did not apply to Japan at all. When Keenan said, "I was speaking of these terms in the past tense, but are you speaking in the present tense?" Tōjō shot back with, "I have no idea what you are talking about." After these exchanges, Keenan gave up on this line of argument, saying, "Since this issue is not important enough to require further questions, I will stop here."

Toward the end of his examination, Keenan asked whether Tōjō had not considered that he had done something legally and morally wrong as prime minister at the start of the Pacific War. Tōjō declared, "I do not think I did anything wrong. I am convinced that I did the right thing."

This exchange, in which Keenan questioned the responsibility for initiation of a war of aggression, and Tōjō defended the war as one of self-defense, typified the logic employed respectively by the prosecution and defense. Many Japanese were thoroughly delighted by Tōjō's attitude.

A Most Serious Blow to the Occupation

Alvary Gascoigne, head of the United Kingdom Liaison Mission in Japan, was deeply impressed by "Tōjō's sharp perception, unambiguous replies, composed behavior, and handling of his opponent." Gascoigne stated that it was obvious to everyone in the courtroom that Tōjō despised Keenan. Most of the courtroom audience felt that it was a clear victory for Tōjō.

While accepting his responsibility for defeat, Tōjō stressed the self-defensive nature of the Greater East Asia War and challenged the prosecution's attempt to criminalize the war. Comyns-Carr also praised Tōjō's testimony as

---

45. Nitta Mitsuo, ed. *Kyokutō Kokusai Gunji Saiban sokkiroku* [Stenographic Record of the International Military Tribunal for the Far East] (Tokyo: Yūshōdō Shoten, 1968). Also available in separate English translation as *The Tokyo War Crimes Trial*, ed. R. John Pritchard and Sonia M. Zaide (New York: Garland, 1981).

"a marvelous performance" to justify the war, while accepting full responsibility for everything.

How effective was Tōjō's testimony?

Sasakawa Ryōichi wrote, "Keenan revealed his true character and in the process made Tōjō a hero." Abe Genki wrote, "The *Nippon Times* carries an article with the headline 'Tōjō's stock has risen sharply, but he is unlikely to become a martyr,' reporting the trend in public opinion. The article was so approving of Tōjō that it is astounding that GHQ allowed it to carry such an article. As a result, public sentiment is favorable to Tōjō."

Furthermore, some testified that Keenan himself acknowledged the sharpness of Tōjō's brilliance, befitting his nickname "razor-sharp Tōjō."[46]

In short, after his testimony, Tōjō, who had been the target of all kinds of abuse, saw his reputation dramatically reversed. Actually, his attitude appeared admirable because other defendants behaved shamefully.[47] Also, Tōjō's brilliance and competence left a strong impression on people, unlike Keenan, who obviously was not capable of questioning and cornering defendants.

In any event, this was a shocking "incident" for the Allies. The Allied side perceived Tōjō's testimony as a most serious blow to the Occupation. MacArthur himself, in dialogue with Gascoigne on January 24, 1948, admitted that Keenan had messed up, and openly expressed his concern that Tōjō's testimony would have a strong impact on Japanese public opinion.

All Depends on the Judgment

It was the Civil Information and Educational Section (CIE) of GHQ, headquartered at the NHK Broadcasting Center in Uchisaiwai-chō, that was in charge of public opinion strategy in Japan. This section gave guidance to news media covering the Tokyo Trial as part of its mission to bring home to the Japanese people the reality of the defeat and war responsibility in a secret operation called the War Guilt Information Program (dated June 3, 1946). It was "the International Military Tribunal for the Far East and news about

---

46. Tamura, *Hiroku Daitōa senshi*.
47. Ōkawa Shūmei Kenshōkai, *Ōkawa Shūmei nikki*.

the cost of living" that GHQ instructed NHK to cover. This was why NHK broadcast a regular radio program called "War Trial Report."[48]

Interestingly enough, CIE made a self-evaluation in the spring of 1948 that it had failed to control Japanese media, and proposed taking the following measures to remedy the situation.

> (1) Suppress such "justifications of the past" as Tōjō's testimony and the "criticism of atomic bombings," in order to prevent a resurgence of ultranationalism in Japan.
> (2) Implement efforts to make the Japanese understand the judgment of the Tokyo Trial.

It was dangerous, however, to launch a frontal attack on the defiant Japanese attitude. Doing so might provoke or reinforce distrust of Japan among Americans, who might oppose economic assistance to Japan and a peace treaty.

Short of a frontal attack, the CIE had to resort to such indirect measures as compilation of a summary of court decisions and the distribution of court admission tickets to well-known Japanese public figures. The order to withdraw from circulation all copies of *Tōjō Hideki Sensei kyōjutsusho* (Tōjō Hideki's Affidavit) published by Yōyōsha in January 1948 was one of the measures taken.

The Tokyo Trial was a battlefield between the prosecution, which hoped to establish a history of "legitimacy of the Allies" and "Japan's war of aggression," on the one hand, and the defense, which aspired to protect Japan from historical stigma by stressing the "legitimacy of Japan" and, on the other hand, the "Japanese war of self-defense." It was quite ironical that it was the vindication of Tōjō, the central target of the prosecution, which conveyed to the Allies a grave sense of crisis. After the Allied side exhausted all means to repel Tōjō's defense, everything depended on the judgment.

Closing Arguments of the Defense

The prosecution made its closing arguments on February 11, 1948.

Keenan's general summation was exaggerated and verbose, finding the

---

48. "NHK Hōdō no Kiroku" Kankō Iinkai, *NHK Hōdō no 50-nen.*

meaning of the Tokyo Trial in the prevention of a third world war, and the provision of warnings to the entire world; he also criticized defendants' evasion of responsibility. Comyns-Carr's legal argument announced a new policy of the prosecution to drop the charge of conspiracy of atrocities—that is, counts 37–38 and counts 44–53. This decision was modeled on the court decision at the Nuremberg trials that the definition of crimes of the Nuremberg Charter did not recognize conspiracy in crimes against humanity and war crimes.

The closing argument of the defense commenced on March 2.

A rather ultranationalistic general summation by Uzawa Fusaaki was followed on March 3 by the two-day-long legal argument that Takayanagi Kenzō, an expert on Anglo-American law, had compiled in cooperation with a British advisor to the Foreign Ministry. (Defendants Matsui Iwane and Hashimoto Kingorō did not agree with the Takayanagi argument.)

Takayanagi argued that a law is something that evolves progressively and, therefore, must not be reformed "abruptly and roughly." Unless ex post facto law was eliminated, Takayanagi warned, defendants would become glorified martyrs for the liberation of Asia. His intention was not so much to achieve a practical effect but to communicate to the world a factual and refined international legal argument, which was the "defense of state" in legal theory.

Defense counsel Logan's argument of the war of self-defense was also the "defense of state." On March 10, 1948, the day the Ashida Hitoshi Cabinet was formed, Logan brilliantly argued that Japan was provoked and cornered into a war of self-defense: "Economic war pressured Japan staunchly and incessantly. Defendants loved their country, Japan. Their decisions were a vital matter of life or death . . . and if their decisions were driven by strong conviction and their patriotism that action was absolutely necessary to defend their fatherland, we argue that the court should not judge them criminal."

Intense Infighting

If the truth be told, there was unseemly infighting inside the defense panel over Takayanagi's argument.

In November 1947, when preparation for the closing argument started, Hayashi Itsurō (in charge of defendant Hashimoto) threatened that, if Takayanagi took up the issue of the Tokyo Trial's jurisdiction, he would boycott it in court. Hayashi argued further that, since they had all accepted the

Tokyo Charter, the charter of the Tribunal, and countered the prosecution based on it within its bounds, it was not appropriate for the defense to attack the lack of jurisdiction after the hearing commenced.

This was an exceptionally bizarre criticism. In the background was the animosity of Hayashi's "defense of state" group (the Uzawa faction) toward Takayanagi, who was, from their viewpoint, a traitor who had pinned all responsibility on the military and rightwing advocates. Takayanagi, to them, pompously looked down on private lawyers as people who could not possibly understand international law. It was intolerable for Hayashi to let Takayanagi elegantly argue about the jurisdiction of the Tribunal.

Around this time, there was a proposal—allegedly made by Takayanagi and some American lawyers—that there should be a unified defense regarding conspiracy. If this proposal had actually been adopted, it would have turned into a genuine "defense of state."

Hayashi refuted the proposal, stressing that this was indeed an issue which each defendant should argue individually. If a unified legal argument was to be attempted, Hayashi argued, it was obvious that a legal theory not based on facts would be utterly worthless. Hayashi insisted that an absolute layman in courtroom dealings and one who would tremble under the pressure should not be the presenter of the general summation. Hayashi instead recommended Uzawa who, in his view, had a thorough knowledge of Japan's politics, military affairs, economy, and general matters.

Ironical Paradox

Hayashi himself made the final defense plea for Hashimoto on March 18, 1948. He argued that Hashimoto should be acquitted, saying, "Hashimoto Kingorō is a master of bushido and a genuine Japanese man. He would never say he had not done things he had done." In the appendix of the defense plea, which was not recited in the courtroom, Hayashi added a superfluous criticism of defense counsel Takayanagi, who he said had not even understood the philosophy behind the Greater East Asia Co-Prosperity Sphere.

It was only natural for Shigemitsu to make the following observation:

> He spoke like a right-wing activist. . . . Loudly dressing down the court, insisting there was no such thing as a military clique, and that it was

Saionji and Makino Nobuaki and the Konoe-Kido group which succeeded them that had misled the country. It was extraordinary that he
singled out Suzuki Teiichi [Takayanagi was in charge of this defendant]
to insult, and pointed out that Shigemitsu, foreign minister in the Tōjō
and Koiso Cabinets, was party to this group.[49]

Shigemitsu's observation makes us realize that the conventional view—that
the "defense of state" faction in the Japanese defense counsels fought a lonely
fight which eventually earned the understanding of American lawyers—has
to be significantly revised.

Hata Shunroku lamented in mid-February 1948 that the total defeat of the
defense was caused by its own disunity. As a matter of fact, throughout the
trial, the defense was permeated by constant, hopeless infighting over factional interests, personal grudges, and attempts at saving face. The "defense of
state" position was diminished to an ultranationalistic argument advocated
by Uzawa and his group.

It is ironical and paradoxical that the closing argument by Takayanagi and
William Logan, champions of the "defense of individuals" position, turned
out to be more significant for the "defense of state" position.

---

49. Shigemitsu, *Sugamo nikki*.

CHAPTER 5

How the Judgment Was Written

Justices of the Tokyo Trial
Front row, from left: William Patrick (UK), Myron Cramer (US), William Webb (Australia),
Mei Ju-ao (China), Ivan Zaryanov (Soviet Union)
Back row, from left: Radhabinod Pal (India), B. V. A. Röling (Netherlands), Edward McDougall
(Canada), Henri Bernard (France), Erima Northcroft (New Zealand), Delfín Jaranilla (Philippines)
(US National Archives [111-SC-251115])

1. Disruption of the Bench

Which Countries Should Provide Justices?

The first point I would like to discuss in this chapter is the appointment of justices for the Tokyo Trial.

The initial point of contention involving the composition of the International Military Tribunal for the Far East was solely concerned with whether "victors' justice" could be impartial or not. In 1943, Austrian jurist Hans Kelsen argued for an "independent and impartial international tribunal" that included the defeated.[1]

The predominant view from this perspective was to open a court of neutral countries to ensure impartiality. A similar argument was heard from Sasakawa Ryōichi in December 1945, although his position was based on a more realistic perception from a different angle.

> If I were American, I would make it a trial by justices from neutral countries instead of a trial by the victors. That way, even if the trial was not truly impartial, people around the world would perceive it as such. If it is a trial by the victors, no matter how impartial it might be, the defeated would refuse to recognize it as impartial because of losers' resentment. If the tried feel that they are unreasonably treated, they will hold grievances.[2]

---

1. Hans Kelsen, "Collective and Individual Responsibility in International Law with Particular Regard to the Punishment of War Criminals," *California Law Review* 31, no. 5 (1943).

2. Sasakawa Ryōichi, *Sugamo nikki* [Sugamo Diary] (Tokyo: Chūōkōronsha, 1997).

While neutral countries may not always be impartial, people in general tend to trust neutral countries. Sasakawa argued that, if judged at a court convened in a neutral country, those who were tried would accept the situation.

Why, then, did the Allies opt to forgo this advantage? John McCloy, who served as assistant secretary of war during World War II, remarked in 1952 that the Allies had failed to obtain any assistance from neutral countries as far as war crime issues during World War II were concerned. What he meant was that the International Military Tribunals were a "continuation of the war," and, for that reason, neutral countries which had not contributed to the Allied victory were not qualified politically or morally to take part in the trial in the first place.

A more central issue in those days was which of the Allies should provide justices for the trial. Initially, following the pattern set by the Nuremberg Trial, to which justices were sent from the US, Britain, France, and the Soviet Union, there had been a plan to limit justices for the Tokyo Trial to the US, Britain, China, and the Soviet Union (see policy paper SFE 106 from the Subcommittee for the Far East [SFE] dated August 9, 1945). If other countries that had fought the war with Japan had wished to send their own justices out of a desire for national prestige and a desire to punish Japan, however, it would have been difficult to turn them down. Thus, it was decided that the nine signatories of the Japanese Instrument of Surrender of September 2, 1945 (the US, Britain, China, the Soviet Union, France, the Netherlands, Canada, Australia, and New Zealand) were to send justices. Accordingly, US secretary of state James F. Byrnes on October 18, 1945, requested each of those countries to nominate justices.

At the beginning, the US Department of War had been thinking of opening multiple trials simultaneously to try fifty to one hundred major war crimes suspects. Irritated by the lukewarm responses from the nations concerned, however, General MacArthur, Supreme Commander for the Allied Powers (SCAP), suggested in December of the same year that (1) a deadline should be set for the appointment of justices and prosecutors; (2) on the basis of advice from Joseph Keenan, the chief of IPS, the chief justice should be appointed by SCAP; (3) there should be no alternate justices, as there had been at the Nuremberg Trial; and (4) there should be "one court and one trial." The US government accepted all of these proposals.

Accordingly, the US government announced that the deadline for the nomination of justices would be January 5, 1946. (India and the Philippines, which were not independent at that time, were requested to appoint only prosecutors.) By early January, Australia, New Zealand, Canada, and China had nominated their own justice and prosecutor.

Maneuvering between the US and the Soviet Union

After the Soviet Union expressed its intention on January 10, 1946 to take part in the Tokyo Trial, it became obsessed with details of how the prosecution would be organized. George Kennan, chargé d'affaires to the Soviet Union, surmised that the Soviets wanted to know details for the practical reason of ensuring that no evidence that was inconvenient for them would be exposed in conjunction with Japan's plan of aggression. This insight by Kennan, who was the most knowledgeable figure regarding the Soviet Union in the State Department, turned out to be accurate. As a matter of fact, when the US, Britain, France, and the Soviet Union consulted on the Nuremberg Trial in May 1945, Sergei Golunsky (Soviet Union associate prosecutor during the Tokyo Trial) expressed the Soviet Union's desire to make some part of the trials a closed-door affair. The Soviets were concerned about Nazi propaganda activities in the courtroom.

On January 18, 1946, the Soviet Union, in compliance with the request of the US government, appointed its own justice and prosecutor to participate in the Tokyo Trial. It also demanded further information about the trial. It was not that the Soviets were reluctant to participate in the trial. In fact, the Tokyo Trial would be an opportune occasion for them to prove the aggressive nature of Japanese militarism. This opportunity was so important that Stalin himself directly ordered the People's Commissariat for Foreign Affairs to prepare for the trial.[3] While it was not unusual for the Soviets to proceed unhurriedly during diplomatic negotiations until they were satisfied, the Soviets in this case were attempting to discern how they might protect their national interest in the trial by "US initiative."

While MacArthur assured the Soviet Union of its right to present its own

---

3. Alexey Kirichenko, "Tōkyō Saiban e no Kuremurin himitsu shirei" [Kremlin's Secret Directive to the Tokyo Trial], trans. Kawamura Hide, *Seiron* 398 (July 2005).

evidence and conduct direct examinations of witnesses, he told Secretary of State Byrnes that at the Tokyo Trial all the major war criminals would be tried in one court. This was a tacit threat to the Soviet Union that, unless it provided a justice and a prosecutor, it could not take part in the Tokyo Trial.

Nevertheless, starting a trial without the Soviet Union was in fact not an option for the US. The absence of the Soviet Union, one of the major powers, would damage the official ideology of punishment of Japan by the "justice" commonly shared by the Allies, which was for appearances' sake a slogan of "cooperation among the Allies." For this reason, the US continued to respond patiently to tenacious inquiries from the Soviets. And the Soviet delegation at last departed Moscow on March 23.

Meanwhile, on January 19, 1946, MacArthur set up the International Military Tribunal for the Far East and proclaimed the Charter of the Tribunal that was to be the basic law of the Tokyo Trial. Article 2 of the Charter stipulated, "The Tribunal shall consist of not less than five nor more than nine Members, appointed by the Supreme Commander for the Allied Powers from the names submitted by the Signatories to the Instrument of Surrender," making it known that the tribunal would be composed of the nine signatories of the Instrument of Surrender.

A Justice from India, Too!

But India, which was not invited to provide a justice, was deeply dissatisfied.

On January 3, 1946, Girija Shankar Bajpai, Indian representative at the Far Eastern Commission (FEC), said to John Carter Vincent, director of the Office of Far Eastern Affairs, US Department of State, "Because India sends a representative to the FEC, logically it should be allowed to provide a justice to the International Military Tribunal for the Far East." He argued that an addition of one justice would not cause any problem.

On January 4, India, in the midst of building national strength to attain independence from Britain, lodged a formal demand with the US Department of State about its right to appoint a justice. India stressed that it was qualified to do so because of the Indians victimized by the Japanese military's atrocities and its own contributions to the victory over Japan.

In fact, prior to this request, the US had been studying the possibility of inviting justices from both India and the Philippines, which had not yet become independent sovereignties. The larger the number of justices grew, however, the more difficult it would be to maintain a unity of views among them, and the longer the trial would last. The nine justices from the signatories to the Instrument of Surrender were already too large in number, and it was open to debate whether colonies could be regarded as belligerent nations. This was the reason Dean Acheson, US undersecretary of state, replied negatively to the request from Bajpai, whom he had come to know personally during World War II. Acheson told Bajpai that a court with as many as eleven justices would be difficult to handle.

Hearing this, Bajpai, in consultation with Edward Frederick Lindley Wood, first earl of Halifax and British ambassador to the United States, recommended his home government entrust the issue to the Far Eastern Commission. From Bajpai's viewpoint, India was much more qualified to provide a justice than France or the Netherlands. In the background was Bajpai's shrewd calculation that (a) the US would be denounced by world public opinion if it rejected India and (b) the Indian government could secure the Indian people's approbation by exhausting all available means to attain what India deserved. It should be remembered that behind India were the British Commonwealth countries. Britain actively took actions to support India's plea as part of its India appeasement policy. New Zealand also announced its support of India, while Canada and Australia did not oppose India's request.

Emergence of an Enormous Tribunal

Even Keenan, who had believed in a limited number of justices, had second thoughts in the face of the real possibility of this issue becoming a hindrance to an early opening of the court. Keenan actively worked to persuade MacArthur to accept India's request. While this was the beginning of a shift in US policy, the decisive moment came on March 1, 1946, when Loy Wesley Henderson, director of the Office of Near Eastern and African Affairs, US Department of State, sent a memorandum to Byrnes.

In this memorandum, Henderson argued that the US should grant India's request because it would be wise to increase the number of Asian justices from outside China. Indians, he said, were quite displeased to find the tribunal to be de facto monopolized by white race nations. Henderson also stressed that opposing India's request would have an adverse impact on

US-Indian relations. Eventually, the State Department decided not to oppose India's request—a passive agreement for which the US did not take responsibility—and also decided to allow the Philippines to provide a justice.

At the Far Eastern Commission on March 4, the British representative proposed that the qualification for a justice stipulated by policy paper SWNCC 57/3 should be revised to "members of FEC." And it was decided by FEC 007/3 of April 3 to give India and the Philippines the right to appoint their own respective justices. Consequently, Article 2 of the Charter of the International Military Tribunal for the Far East (the Tokyo Charter) was revised on April 26 to read, "The Tribunal shall consist of not less than six nor more than eleven Members, appointed by the Supreme Commander for the Allied Powers from the names submitted by the Signatories to the Instrument of Surrender, India, and the Philippines."

Thus, as a result of India's uncompromising demand, the composition of the International Military Tribunal for the Far East perfectly overlapped with members of the Far Eastern Commission.

The moral qualifications required for a country to provide its own justices were "sacrifices" in and "contributions" toward the war with Japan. The central reason for the US policy shift was a decision that it was politically desirable to prevent the Tokyo Trial from being perceived as discriminatory toward Asian countries. With the structural transformation of post–World War II international politics in the background, the Tokyo Trial thus became an enormous court of justice consisting of eleven nations.

Nominated at Long Last Was . . .

Despite having won the right to nominate its own justice at long last, India failed to provide one for quite some time. On April 29, British attorney general Hartley Shawcross in bewilderment commented, "After we made much ado about nothing over appointment of an Indian judge, . . . the Indian government has to date failed to nominate an appropriate one." The Indian government finally conveyed to the US State Department the name of the justice who would represent India.

Radhabinod Pal, acting justice of the Calcutta High Court and a barrister, was appointed. According to a 2007 NHK TV program "Pāru Hanji wa Nani o Toikaketanoka" (What Did Justice Pal Question?), Pal had not been the first pick, but other candidates were reluctant to accept the appointment. Pal willingly agreed to be a justice at the Tokyo Trial when he was approached by the government.

Two and a half years later, Pal submitted a voluminous minority opinion which opposed victors' punishment of Japan's leaders because, under international law, a war was not a crime. Pal's "dissentient judgment" earned him immense popularity among the Japanese people, as symbolized by his decoration with the First Order of the Sacred Treasure when he visited Japan for the fourth time in October 1966. (The prime minister of Japan at that time was Satō Eisaku, younger brother of Kishi Nobusuke, a Class A war crimes suspect.)

It is noteworthy that the Indian government had not wished to provide its own justice to the Tokyo Trial for the purpose of presenting an argument such as "Pal's Judgment." In fact, as British historian Ian Nish pointed out, the Indian government had not expected Pal to express such strong anti-Allies dissent.

In anticipation of imminent independence, the Indian government insisted on the honor of having an Indian justice seated as an equal partner among the Allies. While India had wanted to punish Japanese troops who had brutally abused Indian prisoners of war, a mere associate prosecutor from India was liable to be buried as "one of them" under Keenan. The important thing for India was to have one of its own seated on the bench at the Tokyo Trial.

That was why, once granted the right to provide a justice, the Indian Department of War became nonchalant about the provision of a prosecutor. In fact, in September 1946, it allowed Indian associate prosecutor P. Govinda Menon (prosecutor at the Madras High Court of Justice) a half-year contract and did not bother to provide a successor after Menon returned home.

According to such sources as Indian independence activist Aiyappan Pillai Madhavan Nair (he opened the Nair Restaurant in Ginza, Tokyo after World War II), who had been personally close to General Itagaki Seishirō, a general in the Imperial Japanese Army in World War II, and Rash Behari Bose, an Indian revolutionary leader against the British rule, and Justice Pal, Menon decided to return home because he was weary of cooperating with

Britain and the US to punish Japan.[4] If this was indeed the case, it should be said that there was a significant difference in perception between the Indian justice and prosecutor dispatched to the Tokyo Trial and the Indian government in New Delhi.

Pal's Announcement of Resignation

The first appearance of Judge Pal's great stature occurred on May 17, 1946, the day the justices rejected the defense counsels' motion to challenge the jurisdiction of the Tokyo Tribunal. Although nine justices, except those from India and the Philippines, had agreed in writing beforehand that minority opinions should not be made public, latecomer Pal refused to comply. From that moment on, the risk of minority opinions being made public regularly dogged the bench.

British judge William Patrick deplored the situation, saying, "Pal has made his stance very clear ever since his appointment." Upon his arrival in Japan Pal was already critical of the charge of crimes against peace.

But even to Pal, the prolongation of the Tokyo Trial was unexpected. He arrived in Tokyo assuming that the trial would be completed shortly, but when he realized that this would not be the case, he conveyed his wish to resign to Chief Justice William Webb on October 1, 1946. In other words, from the beginning Pal did not have the resolve to be engaged until the last in a Tokyo Trial that could go on for years. He explained,

> I was explicitly told that my term [with the Tokyo Trial] would be for half a year. . . . With this understanding, I had requested postponement of important cases . . . until the end of a long-term vacation of the High Court, which was granted. [Then] I learned that my task at the Tribunal [Tokyo Trial] was highly unlikely to be completed in half a year. . . . I will have to return home to fulfill my obligations to my client in Calcutta and the court.[5]

---

4. Aiyappan Pillai Madhavan Nair, *Shirarezaru Indo dokuritsu tōsō* [Unknown Struggle for Indian Independence], trans. Kawai Shin (Tokyo: Futōsha, 1983).

5. US Department of State, Central Decimal Files, National Archives and Records Administration (NARA), Archives II: RG 59; 1945–1949, 740.00116, Box 3632, College Park, Maryland.

According to Article 4b of the Tokyo Charter, the Tribunal could render decisions "by a majority vote of those Members of the Tribunal present." And yet, it would look bad if one of the justices left the bench five months after the opening of the trial. MacArthur opposed Pal's resignation. The Indian government tried to dissuade Pal, whose appointment had caused such a tumult earlier.

Ultimately, Pal had to remain as a justice in the Tokyo Trial until its conclusion, despite his wish to resign. Except for court appearances and visits to libraries, Pal spent most of his time confined in his Imperial Hotel room analyzing enormous amounts of trial records and documents, and writing up his argument. Pal's voluminous "dissentient judgment" was produced in this way.

Pal's repeated absences from court hearings were conspicuous to the point of abnormality. He returned to India several times, each for a long period to visit his ailing wife. Pal missed 109 days of the 466 days of hearings. Webb, second in the absentee ranking, was absent 53 days.

Chief Justice Webb Was a Center of Conflict

Pal was not the only source of anxiety for the justices of the Tokyo Trial. In fact, it was Chief Justice William Webb who engendered tension and infighting on the bench by criticizing the ex post facto nature of crimes against peace.

The defense's motion to challenge the jurisdiction of the Tribunal on May 13, 1946, immediately after the opening of the trial, argued that the Tribunal did not have the jurisdiction to try crimes against peace and crimes against humanity. This motion continued to haunt the justices regarding the crimes against peace issue throughout the trial. (There is no evidence that they took the crimes against humanity issue seriously.)

The argument by Justice William Patrick of Britain for the legitimacy of the Tokyo Charter secured a significant amount of support from the other justices. But there was also strong opposition. In the end, after a long quarrel, the justices agreed only that the court did have jurisdiction.

At the hearing on May 17, Webb rejected the defense's motion and announced that the reason behind the decision would be revealed at a later date. Naturally, defense counsels criticized Webb's announcement, saying that denying the motion without stating a justification was unacceptable. But

Table 5-1. List of Judges at the Tokyo Trial

Representing Country	Name	Birth Year	Age*	Previous Post/Permanent Position
Australia	William Webb	January 1887	59	Chief Justice of the Supreme Court of Queensland, and Justice of the High Court of Australia
Canada	Edward McDougall	September 1886	60	Justice on the Court of King's Bench of Quebec
China, Republic of	Mei Ju-ao	1905	41	Chief of the Ministry of Justice
France	Henri Bernard	October 1899	47	Solicitor-General at Bangui
India	Radhabinod Pal	January 1886	60	Acting Justice of the Calcutta High Court, and barrister
New Zealand	Erima Northcroft	December 1884	62	Justice of the Supreme Court of New Zealand
Netherlands	B. V. A. Röling	December 1906	40	Professor of Law, Utrecht University
Philippines	Delfin Jaranilla	December 1883	63	Associate Justice of the Supreme Court of the Philippines
Britain	William Patrick	December 1889	57	Justice of the High Court of Justiciary
United States	Myron Cramer	November 1881	65	Judge Advocate General of the United States Army
Soviet Union	Ivan Zaryanov	November 1894	52	Member of the Military Collegium of the Supreme Court of the USSR

* as of December 1946

the judges could not possibly cite the reason due to the fact that they themselves had not agreed on it.

Because American Joseph Keenan already occupied the post of chief of counsel for the prosecution, MacArthur chose Australian William Webb, who had aided investigations on Japanese troops' war crimes during World War II, as president of the Tokyo Tribunal. (In the case of the Nuremberg Trial, the chief justice was chosen by a vote among the justices.) But this decision proved to be detrimental. The harmony between the justices had begun to collapse from inside the British Commonwealth over the issue of jurisdiction, that is, the criminality of a war of aggression.

The trigger was Webb's argument.

Between June and August 1946, Webb raised the issue of the Nuremberg Doctrine, which held that crimes against peace, perceived as resulting from an aggressive war, were crimes under international law. He argued that the bench for the Tokyo Trial should carefully study this doctrine. Assuming it would be impossible to make war a crime under international law simply by relying on the outlawry of war during the interwar period, Webb argued, the Tokyo Trial should confine itself to trying war crimes that had existed at the time of the signing of the Japanese Instrument of Surrender. If the Tribunal convicted defendants without the backing of an official treaty, the court would be condemned as a "judicial murderer" by the world. If the charter had made a change in international laws, it would be the duty of the justices to ignore any such alterations.

Although Webb's aim was to highlight the dignity of the Tribunal rather than to criticize the trial itself, his earlier discussion of international legal theory closely resembled Pal's dissentient judgment.

Many of the justices—especially those from the British Commonwealth countries—resented the arbitrariness of Webb, whom they considered no more than "first among equals." To make matters worse, Webb was short-tempered and highly strung, and deliberately avoided personal relations with his colleagues. Thus, relations among the justices in the Tokyo Tribunal were riven with edgy animosity.

The Patrick Group United

William Donald Patrick from Britain was a justice of the High Court of Justiciary in Scotland. He was a typical justice with a dignified air, and was a little on the audacious side. Patrick was convinced that it was the duty of justices to apply "criminalization of war and individual responsibility," which was the essence of the Tokyo Charter. He believed those who were reluctant to do this should not remain as justices at the Tokyo Trial.

Patrick joined forces with Erima Northcroft from New Zealand and Edward Stuart McDougall from Canada against Webb. Thus, the internal strife among justices revolved around the rivalry between Webb and Patrick's group.

Three of the Patrick group placed significance on the universality and value of precedent in international military tribunals, and they argued that

Top left: Radhabinod Pal
Top right, from left: Webb, Mei and Zaryanov
Left: William Patrick
(National Archives of the Netherlands, Collection 544 B. V. A. Röling)

a war of aggression had already been established as a crime in international law, and that the Tribunal, as a fact-finding institution, did not have the authority to review the Tokyo Charter. This was the position taken by the majority judgment at a later date.

If the justices had been united in this view, it would have substantiated the charge that "the conclusions of the Tokyo Trial had been predetermined from the beginning."[6] As far as the judgment was concerned, however, it appeared that the view that "conclusions had been predetermined" was a lay opinion based on hindsight. The truth was that the justices had been in sharp conflict with each other over the norm of the criminality of war from the opening of the trial. The outcome of this conflict could have altered and even brought down the judgment itself.

It has been customary for heads of courts in the British Commonwealth to draft a "leading judgment" that would provide the basis for the final

---

6. Tokutomi Sohō, *Tokutomi Sohō shūsengo nikki* [Tokutomi Sohō Postwar Diary] (Tokyo: Kodansha, 2007), vol. 3.

judgment. Accordingly, after witnessing the court rulings at the Nuremberg Trial, Webb on November 27, 1946, distributed his draft to the justices. Quoting Aristotle, Augustine of Hippo, Thomas Aquinas, and Hugo Grotius at length, Webb relied on natural law to explain the outlawry of a war of aggression, and argued for the legitimacy of the Tokyo Charter because it conformed with natural law. Natural law is a universal order—or unwritten law—based on the human reasoning that, for instance, "one should not invade what belongs to others." Natural law is the antithesis of positive law, or laws artificially created, such as statutes and common law.

Webb's written opinion was severely chastised by three justices from the British Commonwealth countries as well as the Soviet Union. Even Mei Ju-ao from China, ordinarily a reserved person, criticized it. Northcroft bitterly criticized it behind Webb's back, saying that the opinion was like a poorly written treatise on international law by a student. In short, Webb's proposal was utterly unusable. Humiliated, Webb became indignant. None of the justices came to his support.

Still, Webb continued to deliver his opinions in writing. Exasperated, Patrick's group told Webb in January 1947 that they would draft the reason for judgment. This made Webb even more furious. He submitted another opinion in writing dated January 20, 1947. While he modified the logic to argue that the aggressive war by Japan was criminalized by the Kellogg-Briand Pact, he still adhered to the natural law argument.

Varied Stances of the Justices

What, then, was the thinking of other justices in early 1947? Below, let me summarize their stances.

Although the stance taken by Mei from China at that time cannot be confirmed, his attitudes before and after early 1947 suggest that he favored the Nuremberg Doctrine.

While Major General Ivan Zaryanov of the Soviet Union generally agreed with the views of the Patrick group, his opinion was that, aside from the issue of the Tokyo Charter, other international legal principles should also be applied.

The Netherlands's B. V. A. Röling, the youngest among the justices, argued in January 1947 that, in the absence of precedents and past records, a war of aggression should not be perceived as a crime under international law. Furthermore, he argued that it would be sufficient to punish the atrocities alone since it was usually atrocities which provoked the desire for retaliation. Röling was an expert in criminal law, and in his own estimation, he had known nothing of international law when he was assigned to the Tokyo Trial.[7] If that was indeed the case, only after he arrived in Tokyo did he become critical of the Nuremberg Doctrine.

Henri Bernard from France advocated natural law, which argued that the legitimacy of the law in the Tokyo Charter was derived from human conscience ("le bon cœur"). On this particular point, he had something in common with Webb.

The following three justices were latecomers to their posts, and were therefore not at court when the trial began.

Pal from India had not hesitated to denounce the norm of the Tokyo Trial following his arrival in Tokyo. The Allies were already wary of him. He distributed his own 260-page legal opinion denouncing crimes against peace. Going his own way, he remained totally oblivious to how others saw him, which left him a little out of place among the justices. Patrick once complained about the Indian government's nomination of Pal and the British government's support of the appointment.

What should not be misunderstood here, though, was that the center of the conflict between the justices was the "Webb vs. Patrick group," not "Pal vs. the others." While the Japanese tend to overemphasize Pal's participation, Pal was only a peripheral figure among the justices. In time, Patrick gave up on Pal, who stubbornly persisted with his own argument.

Delfin Jaranilla of the Philippines first joined the court on June 13, 1946, about a month into the trial. While nobody could tell what he was thinking, it was assumed that he would agree with the guilty judgment because he had been a participant in the Bataan Death March. (The Bataan Death March was the forcible transfer by the Imperial Japanese Army of 60,000–80,000 American and Filipino prisoners of war from Bataan to Tarlac that began on April 9, 1942, after the capture of the Bataan Peninsula, and caused an

---

7. B. V. A. Röling and Antonio Cassese, *The Tokyo Trial and Beyond: Reflections of a Peace-monger* (Cambridge: Polity Press, 1993).

enormous number of deaths of prisoners of war owing to illness, debilitation, and abuse.)

The oldest among the justices, Major General Myron C. Cramer, replaced John Higgins (chief justice of the Massachusetts Superior Court), who had resigned from this appointment in July 1946 due to his distrust of the legality of the Tokyo Trial. Cramer graduated from Harvard Law School and joined the Judge Advocate General's (JAG) Office after serving in World War I. During World War II, as judge advocate general, he severely criticized Secretary of War Henry Stimson's attempt to criminalize war. While he had accepted the Nuremberg Doctrine at the time of his appointment, the American presence among the justices remained insignificant because of the delay in Cramer's appointment as well as his own passive nature.

As shown, the views of the justices of the Tokyo Trial were not unified. They had no other option than to decide on January 30, 1947, to postpone the announcement of the reasons for the Tribunal's decision on its own jurisdiction until the final judgment.

Group of Justices on the Verge of Disintegration

In the case of the Nuremberg Trial, Chief Justice Jeffrey Lawrence from Britain was supposed to draft the judgment, while justices from other countries were requested to make comments. But because it was practically impossible for Lawrence to write all of the judgments singlehandedly, each justice was assigned to write a specific portion of the judgment. An esprit de corps had been nurtured among the justices of the Nuremberg Trial, so the writing of judgments went smoothly. As for separate opinions in writing, only the Soviet justice opposed the sentences, which in his view should have been harsher.

The circumstances that justices of the Tokyo Trial found themselves in were completely different. According to Patrick's report to the British government, "As time went by, the prospect for the Chief Justice of the court to unite the others in order to come up with judgments that everyone could agree on became increasingly remote. The other justices became increasingly critical of everything the Chief Justice did."

In retrospect, having eleven justices with backgrounds in different legal systems made it impossible to handle a new law. By around February 1947, each began to work in his own fashion so it began to appear impossible to produce a unified judgment based on the Nuremberg Doctrine. Paradoxically, it was the view expressed by Yokota Kisaburō, (professor at the University of Tokyo who later became the chief justice of the Supreme Court of Japan) who had represented the Allies' position, which clearly showed how critical the situation actually was. Yokota wrote, "When judgments of the two international tribunals are fully coincident in terms of legal theory, they will take on a decisive value as precedents in international law. And it will have an effect of establishing a new rule under international law."[8] In other words, if the judgment of the Tokyo Trial did not coincide with those of the Nuremberg Trial, the legal and moral legitimacy of the trial itself would be lost completely.

Unable to endure the situation any longer, Northcroft (New Zealand) and McDougall (Canada) tendered resignations to their respective governments between March and April. The New Zealand government tried to dissuade Northcroft from leaving the court, saying his departure would make the British Commonwealth responsible for wrecking the Tokyo Trial. Such was the depth of the crisis that the bench and, more seriously, the Tokyo Trial itself, were facing.

Toward the end of March 1947, Patrick reported the situation to London. Northcroft also told Lieutenant General Charles Henry Gairdner of the British Army in April that because it was predicted that Pal and Röling would submit dissenting opinions, it would be better to discontinue the trial rather than allow it to spoil the accomplishments of the Nuremberg Trial. As soon as Prime Minister Clement Richard Attlee heard this from Gardner, he instructed Foreign Secretary Ernest Bevin to deal with the issue.

Perception Gap with MacArthur

From the British government's viewpoint, the Tokyo Trial was on the brink of collapse.

If the Tokyo Trial were discontinued, it would become a farce and the laughingstock of the world, devastating European prestige completely. It might also give the impression that the Allies had recognized the legitimacy of Japan's militarists.

---

8. Yokota Kisaburō, "Tōkyō hanketsu no kaibō" [Anatomy of Tokyo Sentences], *Nihon kanri hōrei kenkyū* 26 (May 1992).

Facing economic hardship as well as a crisis for the British Empire, Britain explored means to prevent the breakup of the Tokyo Trial in order to defend Britain's prestige if nothing more. In London, those who were concerned about the trial assembled on May 14 at the Lord Chancellor's chamber of the House of Lords. They agreed on the following two measures:

1. To ask for MacArthur's help to solve the problem; or
2. To dispatch Lord Wright of Durley from Australia, Chairman of the United Nations War Crimes Commission (UNWCC), to Tokyo to dissuade the justices from criticizing the Tokyo Charter.

Alvary Gascoigne, head of the UK Liaison Mission in Japan, had already met with MacArthur on May 14 prior to receiving the official directive from Whitehall. MacArthur was furious at what he called "good-for-nothing American lawyers," who, he claimed, had attempted to prolong the trial. As for the infighting among the justices, MacArthur told Gascoigne that he regretted having failed to grant Webb absolute authority. MacArthur predicted that the Tribunal would find those responsible for the attack on Pearl Harbor guilty, and optimistically told Gascoigne that he believed that the sentences did not have to be based on the Nuremberg Doctrine.

After all, the Nuremberg Doctrine was not a matter of significance to MacArthur. Hence, there was a deep perception gap on this point.

It All Depends on Patrick's Maneuvering to Obtain a Majority

In Patrick's view, both measures proposed by Whitehall were nonstarters. As for the first, it was not permissible for MacArthur to interfere in the tribunal. Regarding the second measure—as viewed by Lord Wright—it would only harden the justices' attitudes, and, in particular, Webb would lose his self-restraint, and become even more antagonistic.

On the issue of those justices from Britain, Canada, and New Zealand who wished to resign, British foreign secretary Bevin announced on July 24 that there would be no successors to these three if they actually resigned. And he worried about the possibility of damaging the credibility of not only the Tokyo Trial but also of the Nuremberg Trial, should the judgments of the former fail to be consistent with the Nuremberg Doctrine.

By that time, Patrick, a leading figure among the three justices from the British Commonwealth partly because of his excellent reputation in Britain, had already begun contacting his fellow justices in order to increase the number of adherents to the Nuremberg Doctrine. At this point, it all depended on Patrick's engineering to gain a majority among the justices.

Incidentally, at the British Commonwealth Conference on the Japanese peace treaty held in Canberra in August 1947, New Zealand prime minister Peter Fraser asked Australian prime minister Joseph Benedict Chifley to recall Webb. In early October, due to reasons of "internal conflict in the judiciary," Prime Minister Chifley ordered Webb to return home to reassume his main duties as justice at the High Court of Australia, a post he had taken up in May 1946. The Australian government hoped to fend off a wave of criticism of Webb by calling him back home temporarily.

Webb reluctantly left Japan on November 10, 1947, and returned in mid-December. At the time, Pal had not yet come back from India.

2. Reorganization of the Judge Group and the Judgment

Seven Justices in the Majority

Between February and March 1948, "the majority group" was formed. It comprised the following seven justices:

> William Patrick (UK)
> Edward McDougall (Canada)
> Erima Northcroft (New Zealand)
> Myron Cramer (US)
> Ivan Zaryanov (Soviet Union)
> Mei Ju-ao (China)
> Delfin Jaranilla (Philippines)

William Webb (Australia), B. V. A. Röling (the Netherlands), Henri Bernard (France), and Radhabinod Pal (India) were excluded from the decision-making process, and became "the minority justices."

The "majority" refers to the group of Tokyo Trial justices who affirmed the Nuremberg Doctrine, which regarded an aggressive war as a crime under international law. Patrick started his maneuvering to bring Cramer, Zaryanov, Mei, Jaranilla, and Bernard over into his camp in the spring of 1947. (He failed to win over Bernard.) Although Patrick also contacted Webb, Röling, and Pal, the prospects for winning them were minimal from the beginning.

Thus, the formation of this majority group was due to Patrick's maneuvering. While Britain had taken part in the Tokyo Trial only to maintain its own prestige and punish atrocities, it ended up playing a leading role in the drafting of the indictment and court judgment.

Subsequently, a majority drafting committee was organized with American justice Cramer as its chairman to start drafting the legal argument part of the judgment. At a meeting on March 17, 1948, the justification of the Tribunal's jurisdiction was established. Patrick and McDougall decided not to provide a new justification unique to the Tokyo Tribunal and, instead, borrowed a phrase from the Nuremberg judgment: "The law of the Charter is decisive, and binding upon the Tribunal."

Incidentally, Japanese defense counsel Kiyose Ichirō wrote this in his memoir:

> I hear that a judgment drafting committee has been established. . . . Its members are totally ignorant of the witness hearings or any exchanges in the court. They have produced a composition based on the indictments and a couple of other documents in the absence of any of the Tribunal's members. Yet they call this a judgment.[9]

Kiyose's misinterpretation of the facts was perhaps caused by distorted and exaggerated reports that the justices had had their secretaries and assistants collect documents and produce the preliminary drafts. Nevertheless, it remains an incorrect report.

---

9. Kiyose Ichirō, *Hiroku Tōkyō Saiban* [Secret Record of the Tokyo Trial] (Tokyo: Yomiuri Shimbunsha, 1967).

Writing of the Judgment

Having succeeded in the infighting over the ex post facto law issue, the seven justices of the majority secured control of the drafting of the judgment.

Although one would think that the general line of agreement among the justices would have been discussed with all the justices present, according to Röling, that was not the case.[10] According to Bernard's dissenting opinion, the majority separately wrote portions of legal argument and the finding of facts of the majority judgment. Procedurally, each justice of the majority was put in charge of drafting, with the drafts to be revised and approved by the majority drafting committee. The drafts were also distributed among the minority justices, who could let other judges know their differing opinion in writing.

The only portion that was verbally discussed among all the justices was, according to Bernard, "individual cases." Information by an anonymous justice published in December 1948, however, revealed that all the justices deliberated the verdict of guilty or not guilty for each count, as well as the assessment of culpability. Therefore, the "individual cases" in Bernard's comment must refer to the verdict and assessment of culpability for each defendant.

In open court on April 16, 1948, Webb proclaimed that the judgment would be suspended and the court adjourned until further notice. At this point, the Tokyo Trial of 416 hearings (424 including sentencing proceedings) over a period of roughly two years finally concluded. Altogether, 419 witnesses took the witness stand (109 prosecution witnesses and 310 defense witnesses plus 16 defendants) during the 192 days of the prosecution's introduction of evidence and the 225 days of the defense counsels' presentation of counterevidence. Stenographic records amounted to 49,858 pages.[11]

All that remained to be done was the writing of the judgment. While it took some six weeks for the Nuremberg justices to write their judgment, it took longer in the case of the Tokyo Trial because of the vast amounts of evidence plus the conflicting views among even the justices of the majority. Webb attributed the delay in sentencing to the large number of justices but

---

10. Röling and Cassese, *The Tokyo Trial and Beyond*.
11. David Sutton, "The Trial of Tojo: The Most Important Trial in All History?" *American Bar Association Journal* 36, no. 2 (1950): 93–96.

particularly to the few justices who were excessively sensitive to issues related to their own countries.

Webb continued writing his own opinion, and his May draft stressed that he would no longer put too much weight on natural law. Nevertheless, the majority turned down Webb's suggestions one after another. For instance, Zaryanov brushed off Webb's skepticism regarding the legitimacy of "conspiracy of aggressive war," saying introduction of conspiracy would further develop international laws. He even referred to MacArthur's "supreme authority" to argue against Webb.

For their part, the majority agreed on August 20 to reduce the number of counts in the indictment because there were simply too many. Counts 6 through 26 were eliminated both because it was not necessary to make those who were found guilty of conspiracy doubly guilty for "planning" and "preparation" and because "initiation" could be included in "execution."

Of the five counts of conspiracy, only the count on overall conspiracy (Count 1) was adopted. This was highly significant in comparison with the Nuremberg Trial. The Nuremberg judgment rejected the prosecution's proposal to apply a unitary overall conspiracy count and, instead, recognized the existence of multiple separate conspiracies. The purpose of this was to prevent the timings of formation and execution of conspiracy from departing too far from the interpretation of conspiracy that was close to the theory of complicity in continental law. Compared to this, the majority justices of the Tokyo Trial adopted an entirely different line.

Furthermore, Counts 37 through 52 for "murder" were dropped, because they overlapped with aggressive war and violation of laws of war. Count 53 regarding conspiracy of atrocity was also eliminated from the list.

Final Points of Contention

In the end, the points of contention were narrowed down to three categories of "conspiracy of aggressive war," "execution of aggressive war," and "atrocities." The number of counts adopted was also reduced from 55 in the original indictment to the following 10 counts:

Count 1: Overall conspiracy of aggressive war
Count 27: Waging unprovoked war against China (Manchurian Incident)

Count 29: Waging aggressive war against the United States

Count 31: Waging aggressive war against the British Commonwealth

Count 32: Waging aggressive war against the Netherlands (Dutch East Indies)

Count 33: Waging aggressive war against France (French Indochina)

Count 35: Waging aggressive war against the USSR (Zhanggufeng Incident)

Count 36: Waging aggressive war against the USSR (Nomonhan Incident and war against Mongolia)

Count 54: Ordering, authorizing, and permitting atrocities (violation of laws of war)

Count 55: Deliberately and recklessly disregarding their duty to take adequate steps to prevent atrocities

Some of the judgments were finally decided in a conference between the justices on July 26, 1948. And they were immediately passed on to translators to be put into Japanese. This group of translators—including Yokota Kisaburō, Masaki Hideki (diplomat and son of Masaki Jinzaburō, Ministry of Foreign Affairs), and Nagasu Kazuji (who later became professor at Yokohama National University and governor of Kanagawa Prefecture)—was confined in Hattori House (the private residence of Hattori Genzō, second president of K. Hattori & Co., Ltd.) for three to four months under heightened security to concentrate on the task of translating the judgment. (During the Occupation, private residences were requisitioned on the understanding that they would be rented by the Occupation forces via the Special Procurement Agency.) The

Translators of the Language Division prepare materials to be read during the trial (National Archives of the Netherlands, Collection 544 B. V. A. Röling)

originals of the judgment were delivered to Hattori House one at a time. The portions on the legal argument were the last to arrive, which suggests that the justices were unable to agree on this issue until the last minute.

It is conjectured that around mid-October 1948, half a month before the court was reopened, the majority judgment was completed. According to Yokota Kisaburō, however, "Pal's judgment" had mostly been completed in June of that year and its translation had been making progress at the headquarters of the Occupation forces in Ichigaya.[12]

As has been shown, disagreement among the justices became increasingly serious as the trial progressed. At one point, the court was on the verge of collapse. It was through a reorganization of the justices into majority and minority groups—that is, the substantive compression by the justices themselves of what was once an enormous court comprised of eleven countries—that crisis was avoided. The Tribunal was finally able to complete the majority judgment based on the Nuremberg Doctrine.

A Nuremberg-like Judgment

After the Tokyo Trial concluded in April 1948, protest movements in Japan grew fierce. People protested Cabinet Order 201 of July 31, which prohibited civil servants from participating in labor disputes. Toward the end of August, a suspect in the Teigin Bank robbery incident, in which twelve people died of cyanide poisoning, was arrested. At the same time, the Yokohama War Crimes Trials on Class B & C war criminals pronounced judgment on the case of the Kyushu Imperial University vivisection experiments. (Five defendants were sentenced to death, while four were sentenced to life imprisonment.) Meanwhile, the Shōden bribery scandal continued to escalate, eventually becoming the cause of the dissolution of the Ashida Hitoshi Cabinet and the formation of the second Yoshida Shigeru Cabinet on October 15. Pressured to cover all of these incidents as they unfolded one after another, newspapers had to mobilize even the correspondents assigned to the Tokyo Trial, since there was no way of knowing when the judgment would be announced.

---

12. Yokota Kisaburō, *Watashi no isshō* [My Life] (Tokyo: Tokyo Shimbun Shuppankyoku, 1976).

Mutō Akira, one of the defendants, wrote in his prison memoir, "After three years in prison, I have developed a kind of resigned attitude toward life. Whatever the sentence, I would like to get done with it. I have no hope or expectation regarding the judgment to be announced."[13] That was how long the defendants had been made to wait. On November 2, the defendants were notified of the schedule of rendition of the judgment.

Webb's reading of the majority judgment took seven days, from November 4 through November 12, 1948. The existence of the minority opinions was announced but they were not read in the courtroom.

The "judgment" of the Tokyo Trial was the majority judgment. Article 26 of the Nuremberg Charter reads, "The judgment of the Tribunal as to the guilt or the innocence of any Defendant shall give the reasons on which it is based and shall be final and not subject to review." While the Charter of the Tokyo Trial did not include this "not subject to review" phrase, that was only because MacArthur's power to alter any sentence was referred to as "review" in Article 17. At the Nuremberg Trial, too, the Allied Control Council was granted the power to alter and confirm sentences. By no means did "review" mean that another judicial branch could review the judgment of the Tokyo Tribunal. The prosecution of the Tokyo Trial believed that defendants were not entitled to appeal the review of the court decision. Setting the institutional rule aside, as Tōgō Shigenori observed, "It would be impossible to alter the judgment of the Tokyo Trial . . . because that would be a fiasco for the US government and Supreme Commander for the Allied Powers."[14]

In short, the majority judgment of the Tokyo Trial was final and conclusive. There was no recourse to appeal to an appellate court.

Let us now investigate how the majority judgment of the Tokyo Trial was established. Concerning the issue of jurisdiction of the International Military Tribunal for the Far East, which had disunited the justices, the majority judgment expressed "unqualified adherence" with the position taken by the Nuremberg judgment and certified that "the law of the Charter is decisive and binding on the Tribunal." This was to certify that the sole basis of jurisdiction

---

13. Mutō Akira, *Gunmu kyokuchō Mutō Akira kaisōroku* [Memoir of Mutō Akira, Director of the Military Affairs Bureau], ed. Jōhō Yoshio (Tokyo: Fuyō Shobō, 1981).

14. Tōgō Shigehiko, *Sofu Tōgō Shigenori no shōgai* [Life of My Grandfather Tōgō Shigenori] (Tokyo: Bungeishunjū, 1993).

for the special court was its charter and, conversely, that it was only natural for the Tribunal to judge cases of crimes against peace as stipulated by the charter. Because aggressive war had already been criminalized under international law by the Kellogg-Briand Pact, those who had planned or waged an aggressive war had committed a crime. The principle of *nulla poena sine lege* (the principle of legality) was only a general principle of justice, and it was "unjust" to not punish aggressors who were aware of the criminality of their actions. The majority judgment of the Tokyo Trial justices therefore stressed that the law applied by the International Military Tribunal did not deviate from international law. The foregoing were the Tribunal's reasons for rejecting the defense's challenges to the jurisdiction of the court.

At this point, the judgment of the Tokyo Trial became a Nuremberg-like judgment.

The Judgment's View of History

The portrayal of prewar Japanese history in the finding of facts for the majority judgment reflected a clear anti-Axis ideology. The majority judgment reads:

> [T]he charges in the Indictment directly involved an inquiry into the history of Japan during seventeen years, the years between 1928 and 1945. In addition our inquiry has extended to a less detailed study of the earlier history of Japan. . . . The period covered by the charges was one of intense activity in Japanese internal and external affairs.[15]

The fact-finding of the majority judgment had the following characteristics.

First, it was recognized as fact that there had been an "overall conspiracy" for nearly eighteen years beginning in 1928. This conspiracy aimed at the domination of East Asia, the West and Southwest Pacific, and the Indian Ocean—inclusion of domination of the world in the indictment had been rejected—and had emerged in 1927–1929 under the Tanaka Giichi

---

15. This quotation and those that follow without specific references are taken from the final judgment of the Tribunal, available online at https://crimeofaggression.info/documents/6/1948_Tokyo_Judgment.pdf.

Cabinet, when "a party of military men" collaborated with Ōkawa Shūmei, who had advocated the conquest of Asia, Eastern Siberia, and the South Pacific Islands. The determination of these facts led to the judgment that the overall conspiracy lasted until Japan's surrender in 1945.

The Liutiaogou Incident, which triggered the Manchurian Incident, "was carefully planned beforehand by officers of the Army General Staff, officers of the Kwantung Army, members of the Cherry Society [Sakurakai], and others." The responsible Army figure singled out in Tokyo was Lieutenant General Tatekawa Yoshitsugu. Colonel Itagaki Seishirō was singled out in Manchuria. It was also recognized that Army Minister Minami Jirō had approved actions of the Kwantung Army, while Itagaki and Colonel Dohihara Kenji were the ones who decided to bring forward Puyi, emperor of Manchukuo. Although developments before and after the Liutiaogou Incident were described in detail, Ishiwara Kanji's involvement was not mentioned.

Although the Fundamentals of National Policy (*Kokusaku no kijun*) decided in 1936 by the Kōki Cabinet had only indicated the Northern Expansion Doctrine (*Hokushinron*) advocated by the Imperial Army and the Southern Expansion Doctrine (*Nanshinron*) advocated by the Imperial Navy as possible foreign policy goals, the majority judgment placed excess emphasis on it as a fundamentally aggressive plan that provided the "cornerstone in the whole edifice of Japanese preparations for war."

Subsequently, the majority judgment recognized, those conspirators brought down the moderates one by one. By the time the first Konoe Fumimaro Cabinet was formed, the conspirators had the whole of Japan under their control, and had "carried out in succession the attacks necessary to effect their ultimate object." Thus, the majority judgment concluded, "The conspiracy to wage wars of aggression was already criminal in the highest degree."

In short, the historical view of the majority judgment stressed the consistency of Japan's policy of aggression, conveniently ignoring the fact that altogether seventeen cabinets had been formed between those of Tanaka Giichi and Suzuki Kantarō. The judgment regarded the Imperial Japanese Army as the chief actor in this conspiracy. On this point, in August 1948, after learning that even Foreign Minister Shigemitsu had been convinced that it was the military that had pulled the strings behind these incidents, Mutō Akira complained in his diary, "It is no wonder that foreign countries misunderstood Japan when its own representative of diplomacy was like that."[16]

American defense counsel John Brannon in his summation on March 4, 1948, stated, "Evidence rather shows . . . a lack of leadership among leaders . . . and that there existed no centralized organization which shared a common plan or purpose." As represented by this summation, the Tokyo Trial disclosed the decentralized nature of Japanese politics and conflicts between political elites. Tōgō Shigenori strongly resented that judges with so little knowledge of international politics or Japanese politics could make such "crude" and "irresponsible" judgment.[17]

However, the mission of the judgment was to judge defendants as guilty or not guilty after demonstrating Japan's error-filled past. The mission was not to grasp swings in Japan's politics and diplomacy and give fact-based analyses of them.

The US decided to introduce the concept of conspiracy because it was useful. The charge of conspiracy would make it possible to round up everyone involved. And the concept of conspiracy could provide a tool to explain Japan's history. That was the degree of significance the conspiracy charge held in the establishment of fact. It was not an affair that could be easily dismissed.

Normally, the job of a justice is to hand down a comprehensive judgment after hearing both the prosecution and the defense. In this sense, the majority judgment of the Tokyo Trial justices was extremely close to the prosecution's position. Nevertheless, now that it is known that there were conflicting views among the justices, it is no longer possible to adopt a simplistic "frame-up" theory that the court and the prosecution were identical. After all, the justices held such significantly different and conflicting views that, had it not been for Patrick's maneuvering among the majority, there was danger that no unitary judgment would be reached.

The following review of the second characteristic of the factual determinations makes it apparent that the court and the prosecution were independent of one another.

---

16. Mutō, *Gunmu kyokuchō*.

17. Tōgō, *Sofu Tōgō Shigenori no shōgai*.

Resigned to View It as a Consequence of International Politics

The second characteristic of the Tribunal's fact-finding was the decline in the relative importance of the Pacific War phase, to which the US had originally attached great importance. This was because each phase of the lengthy conspiracy process was given equal treatment. The count of murder in the attack on Pearl Harbor was also eliminated.

The description of the "road to the attack on Pearl Harbor" was set forth in a matter-of-fact manner. It was verified that Foreign Minister Tōgō had indeed sent a wire to the Japanese ambassador in Washington, DC, instructing hand delivery of the notification to the US State Department half an hour before commencement of the attack. In this way, the Tribunal ignored the prosecution's demonstration that Japan had attacked without advance notice. The findings stated as follows:

> Had all gone well they would have allowed twenty minutes for Washington to warn the armed forces at Pearl Harbor. But so anxious were they to ensure that the attack would be a surprise that they allowed no margin for contingencies.

The findings surrounding this portion were far from a unilateral condemnation and, in fact, they were unfavorable to the US. Keenan was furious about the almost complete neglect of Pearl Harbor–related matters. Thus, the Tribunal fell short of the expectations of MacArthur and, for that matter, the US as well.

The third characteristic was the ambiguous depiction of Japan's Soviet policy as "offensive or aggressive." The majority judgment pointed the finger at the insincere policy of the Japanese government noting that, immediately after the signing of the Japan-Soviet Neutrality Pact of April 1941, Foreign Minister Matsuoka Yōsuke had already declared that Japan would attack the Soviet Union if a Russo-German War broke out (June 1941). It also recognized that the attack by Japanese troops during the Zhanggufeng Incident had been "clearly aggressive" and "deliberately planned" by the Army General Staff and Army Minister Itagaki Seishirō. For the Nomonhan Incident, too, "the operation amounted to an aggressive war waged by the Japanese."

While the judgment basically held that such Japanese actions were close to the prosecution's accusations, perhaps in consideration of the Soviet member of the majority justices, it fell short of declaring them an aggression or aggressive war. The result was the purposely delicate description above.

Fourth, the majority judgment found that Counts 54 and 55 for atrocities had been proven to be crimes. Enumerating a number of specific cases of conventional war crimes, the judgment held that leaders in Tokyo (including civil servants) who had failed in their duty to prevent atrocities should be blamed for negligence. The judgment stated that "following so common a pattern in all theaters, [. . .] only one conclusion is possible—the atrocities were either secretly ordered or wilfully permitted by the Japanese Government or individual members thereof and by the leaders of the armed forces."

Crimes against humanity were not mentioned either in the finding of facts or the finding of Count. Röling commented in later years that in the Tokyo Trial crimes against humanity had not been significant, and the accusation and introduction of evidence concerning opium policies were inadequate. The justices ignored this crime category even more than the prosecution had done.

It is oftentimes said that history is written by the victors. Regardless of the location and the time, a government is bound to reject its preceding regime as a dark period and advocate its own legitimacy. The victors of World War II also wrote a history that negated Japan's *ancien régime*.

However, because this type of accusatory history stimulates indignation and a sense of humiliation on the part of the losers, it cannot last long. Confirmation of history is in itself a political act. Seen from this angle, this negation of Japan's past was an extremely dangerous policy for the Allies to adopt.

How did Japan view this portrayal? It is true that the Tokyo Trial provided the Japanese people with an opportunity to confront their own past. Having said that, it should be realized that the history portrayed by the majority judgment was no more than an act of international politics, which was fundamentally different from the discipline of history. However, I do not wish to dismiss the Tokyo Trial as meaningless. I would like to propose instead that as long as one can come to a dispassionate conclusion that the tribunal was the result of international politics, the judgments of the Tokyo Trial can be understood more calmly.

"The Iron Door Was Slammed Shut behind Me"

Judging from the various available documents, it must have been sometime between November 3 and November 12, 1948, just before the passing of the sentence in court, that the sentences were finalized. It is said that the sentences for Kimura Heitarō and Shigemitsu Mamoru were decided at the daytime conference among the justices held on November 12, the very day that the sentences were rendered. According to critic Takeyama Michio, rumor had it that Justice Röling persisted for six long hours to settle on sentences at the conference in chamber.[18]

The passing of the sentences began at last at 3:55 p.m. on Friday, November 12, 1948. Seated among the reporters were such dignitaries as Narahashi Wataru (statesman), Nosaka Sanzō (statesman, Japanese Communist Party), Kawabata Yasunari (novelist), and Osaragi Jirō (novelist).

Matsuoka Yōsuke and Nagano Osami had already passed away and the case against Ōkawa Shūmei had been dropped, putting the total number of defendants receiving sentences at twenty-five.

While normally the justices entered the courtroom after all the defendants were seated in the dock, in this case defendants were called in one by one in alphabetical order. Webb announced the sentences to each defendant respectively. First was Araki.

> Accused ARAKI, Sadao, on the Counts of the Indictment on which you have been convicted, the International Military Tribunal for the Far East sentences you to imprisonment for life.

The next defendant was Dohihara.

> Accused DOHIHARA, Kenji, on the Counts of the Indictment on which you have been convicted, the International Military Tribunal for the Far East sentences you to death by hanging.

When Hirota Kōki, a civilian, was sentenced to death, a wave of shock swept

---

18. Takeyama Michio, *Shōwa no seishin-shi* [Intellectual History of Shōwa] (Tokyo: Shinchōsha, 1956).

through the courtroom. The last defendant to be called in, Tōjō Hideki, was also sentenced to death by hanging. After pronouncing the life imprisonment sentences upon Kaya Okinori, Shiratori Toshio, and Umezu Yoshijirō, who were all absent due to illness, President Webb declared the court adjourned. This concluded the Tokyo Trial.

In the end, seven defendants—Dohihara, Hirota, Itagaki, Matsui, Mutō, Kimura, and Tōjō—were sentenced to death by hanging. Immediately after the sentencing, those seven were separated from the defendants sentenced

Table 5-2. Counts Charged and Sentences by Defendant

Name	Counts Found Guilty	Sentence
Araki Sadao	1, 27	life imprisonment
Dohihara Kenji	1, 27, 29, 31, 32, 35, 36, 54	death by hanging
Hashimoto Kingorō	1, 27	life imprisonment
Hata Shunroku	1, 27, 29, 31, 32, 55	life imprisonment
Hiranuma Kiichirō	1, 27, 29, 31, 32, 36	life imprisonment
Hirota Kōki	1, 27, 55	death by hanging
Hoshino Naoki	1, 27, 29, 31, 32	life imprisonment
Itagaki Seishirō	1, 27, 29, 31, 32, 35, 36, 54	death by hanging
Kaya Okinori	1, 27, 29, 31, 32	life imprisonment
Kido Kōichi	1, 27, 29, 31, 32	life imprisonment
Kimura Heitarō	1, 27, 29, 31, 32, 54, 55	death by hanging
Koiso Kuniaki	1, 27, 29, 31, 32, 55	life imprisonment
Matsui Iwane	55	death by hanging
Minami Jirō	1, 27	life imprisonment
Mutō Akira	1, 27, 29, 31, 32, 54, 55	death by hanging
Oka Takasumi	1, 27, 29, 31, 32	life imprisonment
Ōshima Hiroshi	1	life imprisonment
Satō Kenryō	1, 27, 29, 31, 32	life imprisonment
Shigemitsu Mamoru	27, 29, 31, 32, 33, 55	7-year imprisonment
Shimada Shigetarō	1, 27, 29, 31, 32	life imprisonment
Shiratori Toshio	1	life imprisonment
Suzuki Teiichi	1, 27, 29, 31, 32	life imprisonment
Tōgō Shigenori	1, 27, 29, 31, 32	20-year imprisonment
Tōjō Hideki	1, 27, 29, 31, 32, 33, 54	death by hanging
Umezu Yoshijirō	1, 27, 29, 31, 32	life imprisonment

Source: Nitta Mitsuo, ed., *Kyokutō Kokusai Gunji Saiban sokkiroku* (Stenographic Record of the International Military Tribunal for the Far East), vol. 10 (Tokyo: Yūshōdō Shoten, 1968)

to imprisonment. Upon returning to Sugamo Prison, the seven were placed under close watch in cells with bare floors. Mutō's diary contains this graphic entry for that day: "Once I stepped into the cell, the iron door was slammed shut behind me. That bang brought home to me, for the first time, that I was indeed a condemned man."[19]

Among those who were sentenced to imprisonment, only Tōgō (twenty years) and Shigemitsu (seven years) were sentenced for limited terms; the rest were sentenced to life imprisonment. None of the defendants was found not guilty. (For individual sentences, see Table 5-2.) At the Nuremberg Trial, of twenty-two defendants, twelve were sentenced to death by hanging, three to life imprisonment, four to imprisonment for a limited term, and three were found not guilty.

How did the Japanese people react to the sentences handed down by the Tokyo Trial? The families of those who were sentenced to death were naturally shocked. Some families cried uncontrollably, totally oblivious to others, and complained to the defense counsel who had previously assured them that their fathers and brothers were prime candidates for acquittal.[20] According to newspaper reports, the emperor seemed somewhat shocked upon hearing the guilty sentences for Kido and Hirota.

Major Japanese newspapers accepted the sentences as appropriate and stressed that it was Japan's obligation to espouse peace and democracy. It was noteworthy that even Toyoda Kumao, formerly captain of the Imperial Navy, stated that perhaps Japan should be grateful to the Tokyo Trial for providing the Japanese people with food for thought on their country's past conduct.

No Japanese Backlash

The previous prime minister Ashida Hitoshi wrote in his diary, "There has been no major repercussion domestically." True to these words, the Japanese people showed surprisingly little adverse reaction to the judgments despite their earlier cheers for Tōjō's testimony.

First, most Japanese intellectuals viewed the past war as an "absolute

---

19. Mutō, *Gunmu kyokuchō*.
20. Shimanouchi Tatsuoki, *Tōkyō Saiban* [The Tokyo Trial] (Tokyo: Nippon Hyōronsha, 1984).

evil," and clearly supported the judgment and ideals of the Tokyo Trial. On December 12, 1948, the general assembly of the East-West Study Group, the Colloquium on Peace Affairs (Heiwa Mondai Tōgikai), recognized that the judgment was symbolic of "peace and civilization," which were inseparable from the thorough pacifism embodied in Article 9 of the Constitution of Japan. Intellectuals were filled with remorse, as the US had hoped, and argued that the Japanese as a whole should be made to feel national responsibility for the war. As political scientist Sakamoto Takao accurately pointed out, those Japanese intellectuals shared the international understanding of the Americans in the early stages of the Occupation.

Second, for the political elite (statesmen and bureaucrats), the Tokyo Trial was a taboo subject, so much so that newspaper reporters could not get comments on the judgment from the Japanese government.[21] And as has been pointed out earlier, Yoshida Shigeru and his associates had accepted the Tokyo Trial from the viewpoint of promoting cooperation with the US and Britain.

Third, the reason behind the Japanese people's silence regarding the judgment was the impact of the atrocities on their minds. Osaragi Jirō heard the judgment from the press seats in the courtroom, and felt that it was not only the defendants but also "Japan's modern past" itself and "the Japanese as a whole" that were being sentenced. This was exactly what the Allies had aimed to accomplish. Osaragi felt that way out of shame for the atrocities committed. Atrocities conducted by the Japanese troops alone were "enough for the perpetrators to be sentenced to death, which they must willingly accept in the face of civilization, nay, the honor of Japan that was tarnished."

Still, many Japanese were convinced that only the national leaders should be blamed for initiating the war, and that they themselves were victims who had been deceived by those leaders. At the same time, they also felt shame for the atrocities, leading them to give silent approval to the Tokyo Trial.

Nationalistic Sentiment Underneath

While each of the three types for Japanese people's silent reaction to the judgment was based on a different perspective, all three viewpoints had in

---

21. Nomura Masao, *Sabakareta Nihon* [Japan Tried] (Tokyo: Kadokawa Shoten, 1956).

common a perspective of "denial of war." It would be premature, however, to jump to the conclusion that there was no backlash by the Japanese people.

British philosopher John Stewart Mill singled out "ethnic history" and "shared pride and humiliation, joy and remorse" as the greatest causes of nationalistic sentiment. Setting aside the progressive intellectuals' approval of the Tokyo Trial, daily *Asahi Shimbun* "Tensei jingo" column on December 24, 1948—the day after the execution of Tōjō and other defendants—represented the emotional ambivalence of the Japanese people. The column commented that the Japanese had had enough of war, yet they could not help but feel grief at the executions. While reason told them that those executed only got what they deserved, it was not something that they, as Japanese nationals, could swallow easily.[22]

Japanese on the streets were sympathetic toward the aged Hiranuma Kiichirō and Minami Jirō as well as former diplomats like Shigemitsu and Hirota. They had particularly compassion for Hirota, so much so that they fervently pleaded for his life.

Because of these apparent ambivalences, British diplomat Alvary Gascoigne was not convinced that the Japanese people's acceptance of the Tokyo Trial judgment was purely spontaneous. William Joseph Sebald, chief of the Diplomatic Section of GHQ, also stated in October 1949 that many Japanese people felt that the war crimes trials were no more than an act of revenge on the part of the victors.

All in all, it should be concluded that Henry Stimson's "educational" logic of "punishing one while giving a warning to hundreds"—in other words, indirectly making the people feel guilty by punishing their leaders—was not necessarily successful (see chapter 1, section 3, for more about Stimson's logic). It seems that there were many who simply kept their feelings of resentment hidden.

An even more peculiar sight surfaced. Japanese detainees in the faraway Siberian labor camps "held a feast to celebrate the Tokyo Trial's judgment." Throwing scornful looks at a few former army officers who received the news pensively, the former Japanese soldiers, who had by that time been

---

22. Aragaki Hideo, "Tensei jingo" [Vox Populi, Vox Dei], *Asahi Shimbun*, December 24, 1948.

brainwashed by the Siberian democratic movement and its praise of communism, broke into applause upon hearing the guilty verdicts.[23]

"Life Imprisonment Anyhow Assures the Defendants' Lives"

How were the sentences of the Tokyo Trial decided? In the case of the Nuremberg Trial, the justices gathered to examine the verdicts for counts and sentences. Sentences were decided by a majority vote (three out of four justices). In the case of Rudolph Hess, for instance, he was found guilty by a unanimous decision on the counts related to conspiracy and crimes against peace, while for (conventional) war crimes and crimes against humanity, he was pronounced not guilty because the votes were equally divided. Next, the justices proposed their respective assessments of culpability. In the end, the justices agreed on life imprisonment.

In contrast, information on sentencing for the Tokyo Trial is so scarce that its details have remained unknown. It seems certain, nevertheless, that each justice proposed a sentence for each defendant, after which the sentence was decided by majority vote. Dutch justice Röling commented as follows in 1983:

> It was true that death sentences were decided by majority vote. . . . When the vote was actually taken . . . I suppose that I had an opportunity to protest as one of the justices. I could have said that there were factual errors, or that it was wrong to decide the death sentence by majority vote. When the court was adjourned abruptly [Author's note: Possibly the termination of deliberation by justices in chamber], however, even the possibility of making such objections was taken away from me.[24]

While this quote by itself gives us no clue as to what Röling was trying to say, superimposing it on Röling's testimony in 1982 would lead us to believe that he regretted the short time allotted for assessment of culpability. According to Röling, "in Tokyo it took an unexpected short time to determine the

23. Tanaka Akira, Kyōdō Tsūshinsha Shakaibu [Kyodo News Social Affairs Department], eds., *Chinmoku no fairu* [Silent Files] (Tokyo: Kyodo News, 1996).

24. Hosoya Chihiro, Andō Nisuke, and Ōnuma Yasuaki, eds., *Tōkyō Saiban o tou* [Questioning the Tokyo Trial] (Tokyo: Kodansha, 1984).

penalties. Sir William Webb used as president tactics which were . . . very unusual in Court deliberations," and he did not hesitate to give a death sentence with "only a majority of six to five." Röling argued, "if accused A, a not so notorious person, is dealt with just after the deliberations and sentence concerning a notoriously cruel accused, he will benefit from the fact that the Court will be inclined to give expression to the difference between the two."[25]

Novelist Kawabata Yasunari, who observed the last day of the Tokyo Trial by arrangement with the daily *Yomiuri Shimbun*, wrote:

> Even those "heavyweights" failed to conceal the the level of shock they felt when sentenced to death or to life imprisonment. . . . Witnessing the dramatic difference between a man's life and death right before my eyes, I was deeply moved. . . . Life imprisonment anyhow assures the defendants' lives.

Taking into consideration the process of war criminals being released in the Tokyo Trial, it is beyond doubt that the sentences of death by hanging and life imprisonment were as different as night from day.

Weight of Crimes against Peace

Let us consider what led to the death sentences.

One certainty is that no defendant was sentenced to death for overall conspiracy (Count 1) of crimes against peace. The same thing happened in the Nuremberg Trial. Because Count 1 was the central count to which the justices of the majority gave greater weight than to any other, twenty-three of the twenty-five defendants accused of this count were found guilty. Shigemitsu and Matsui, found not guilty on Count 1, were given the lightest sentence (Shigemitsu, seven years' imprisonment) and the heaviest sentence (Matsui, death by hanging), respectively. When the defendants were found guilty only for Count 1, including Ōshima and Shiratori who both were instrumental in concluding the Tripartite Pact, life imprisonment was the maximum punishment.

---

25. Arnold C. Brackman, *The Other Nuremberg*, 2nd edition, (New York: William Morrow & Co., 1988).

Therefore, the decisive factor for the death sentence can be judged to be "gross atrocities." On the night of the sentencing, Keenan invited reporters of the *Chūbu Nihon Shimbun* to Mitsui House (private residence of Mitsui Takaharu, tenth-generation head of the Mitsui Minami family) in Otowa, Tokyo, and, with a glass of whisky in hand, gave the reporters a piece of his mind:

> What on earth were the justices doing for two years and seven long months? While it is commendable that they determined that an aggressive war is a crime, two-thirds of the defendants accused of this count ended up evading the death sentence. Moreover, all of those who were sentenced to death were found guilty of atrocities. Atrocities could have been handled by the Yokohama War Crimes Trials [on Class B and C war criminals].[26]

Röling, however, confessed in 1960 that he believed it was because the Nuremberg and Tokyo Trials included atrocities in their judgments that the entire world was not tormented by a guilty conscience. Had the International Military Tribunals only tried wars of aggression, people would have felt remorse. I must agree with him on this account. The question about the ex post facto law concerning crimes against peace posed an obstacle to the death sentence. Therefore, British and American planners of the International Military Tribunals had been aware before the opening of the trials that violation of the laws of war had to be included in order to render death penalties.

In the end, what was decisive was the judgment of the Tribunal. On this point, American justice Myron Cramer appealed to Webb in June 1948 saying that while "there is no specific statute in international law saying that those responsible for planning or waging aggressive war shall be sentenced to death," the Tribunal had the authority to render death sentences for violators of the laws of war. Although justices of the Tokyo Trial had attempted to find defendants guilty based on the Nuremberg Doctrine, they nevertheless avoided using the doctrine to issue death sentences.

---

26. Tamura Yoshio, ed., *Hiroku Daitōa senshi* [Secret Record of the Greater East Asia War] (Tokyo: Fuji Shoen, 1954), vol. 6.

From the Viewpoint of Atrocities

Let us consider the death sentences of the Tokyo Trial from the viewpoint of atrocities.

Ten defendants (Dohihara, Hata, Hirota, Itagaki, Kimura, Koiso, Matsui, Mutō, Shigemitsu, and Tōjō) were found guilty for either Count 54 (ordering, authorizing, and permitting inhumane treatment of prisoners of war and others) or Count 55 (deliberately and recklessly disregarding their duty to take adequate steps to prevent atrocities). Of these ten suspects, seven were sentenced to death. Hata, Koiso, and Shigemitsu were the exceptions. It appeared there was no difference between Counts 54 and 55 in terms of the seriousness of offenses. What factor, then, made the difference between those who were sentenced to death and those whose lives were spared?

The first factor that contributed to the death sentence was the severity of the incident for which the suspect was accused.

For instance, the reason for the death sentences for Hirota and Matsui, who had been found guilty only of Count 55, was the so-called Nanjing Incident (Nanjing Massacre). The majority judgment recognized that "the total number of civilians and prisoners of war ordered in Nanking and its vicinity during the first six weeks of the Japanese occupation was over 200,000." On this point, Kiyose Ichirō later contended in his *Hiroku Tōkyō Saiban* (Secret Record of the Tokyo Trial) that Hirota would have escaped the death sentence if it was merely a question of his failure in cabinet meetings to discuss measures to prevent the incident; it was the *Fundamentals of National Policy* of the Hirota Cabinet which played the decisive role in his death sentence. But Kiyose's analysis reversed the order of priority.

Hirota (who had been found guilty on three counts) would have been sentenced to life imprisonment if he had been found guilty only of aggressive war. He was the only civilian defendant sentenced to death because he was found guilty of negligence of duty as the foreign minister at the time of the Nanjing Incident.

"Kido was a member of the cabinet when the atrocities were committed at Nanking. The evidence is not sufficient to attach him with responsibility for failure to prevent them." This judgment was proof of the weight the justices of the Tokyo Trial attached to the Nanjing Incident. Had Konoe Fumimaro, prime minister at the time of the incident, been alive and indicted, it is most likely that he would have been sentenced to death together with—or in lieu of—Hirota.

The only conceivable reason for Matsui's death sentence was his post as commander of the Central China Area Army, at the time of the Nanjing Incident. Matsui himself had regarded the incident as "a major incident in which [he] was involved," and he was prepared for the death sentence.[27] Mutō Akira, Matsui's deputy chief of staff, was judged to have no responsibility for the Nanjing Incident because "in his subordinate position, [he] could take no steps to stop them."

The Nanjing Incident had such a profound impact on people during the prosecution's introduction of evidence that it became a symbol of the Tokyo Trial. Therefore, someone among the defendants had to take responsibility for it. And it was Hirota and Matsui, because of their positions both in the central government and with the expeditionary force, who could provide ideal examples of "responsibility for inaction."

Shigemitsu was also found guilty of Count 55, but he was sentenced to seven years' imprisonment in consideration of the extenuating circumstances that "SHIGEMITSU was in no way involved in the formulation of the conspiracy; that he waged no war of aggression until he became Foreign Minister in April 1943."

It is equally noteworthy that none of the former Imperial Navy defendants were sentenced to death. Among the Sugamo Prison inmates, it was rumored that Tōjō and Shimada had "no hope" of evading that sentence, and those who had been affiliated with the Imperial Navy themselves had accepted that Shimada would be given the death sentence. Shimada's life was spared because he was not found guilty of atrocities. While there were incidents of the navy killing survivors of sunken enemy ships, Shimada was acquitted due to lack of evidence.

Myron Cramer, who as the American justice was presumed to give the greatest weight to the attack on Pearl Harbor, was convinced that atrocity was indispensable for the death sentence. Had Nagano Osami, chief of Naval General Staff, not died of illness before sentencing, his degree of involvement in the atrocities would have determined whether he was sentenced to death.

---

27. Nomura, *Sabakareta Nihon*, and Shimanouchi, *Tōkyō Saiban*.

234   CHAPTER 5 | How the Judgment Was Written

The Navy was fortunate in two ways: that jurisdiction over treatment of prisoners of war lay with the Army, and that there was insufficient evidence to prove the Navy's involvement.

Sniping at Certain Figures

The second factor that contributed to the determination of death sentences was the interests of nations concerned.

Kimura Heitarō, for instance, was such an insignificant defendant that Class B and C inmates of Sugamo Prison wondered "what propaganda value the Allies had found in someone of his small stature."[28] Indeed, he was not a major enough figure to warrant the death sentence. What mattered was that the court found he had approved the mobilization of prisoners of war for the construction of the Thailand-Burma Railway; he was also found guilty of atrocities as commander of the Burma Area Army. And it is conjectured that justices from the British Commonwealth countries insisted on his death sentence.

In the case of Mutō Akira, his conduct during his tenure as director of the Military Affairs Bureau, Army Ministry, alone would have earned him life imprisonment. It was due to his involvement in atrocities in Sumatra and the Philippines that he was sentenced to death.

On this point, Kido Kōichi recalled:

> Toward the last stage of the trial, it was rumored that each participating country pinpointed its own target defendants. The Philippines, for instance, focused on having Mutō executed and did not care what happened to the other defendants. Similarly, China targeted Itagaki, Dohihara, and Matsui. . . . All the other countries followed suit in sniping at certain figures.

Similar information was heard from various sources, and the credibility of the rumors is probably high.

According to the aforementioned anonymous justice, only Hirota's death

---

28. Yoshiura Kameo, *Sugamo Purizun kaiwai* [Round about Sugamo Prison] (Private compilation, 1956).

sentence was decided with a six to five majority vote; the death sentences of the other six were each decided with seven to four majority votes. Votes on Araki, Ōshima, Kido, and Shimada, who were found not guilty of atrocities, were all close contests, but none got the six votes necessary to receive the death sentence.[29] Pal and Zaryanov clearly voted against the death sentence for all the defendants. Webb was also believed to be against the death penalty. Röling once testified that Bernard from France "didn't participate in the vote, as he had misgivings about the whole trial."[30] If that was indeed the case, then the total votes were 10 instead of 11 and, therefore, there could not have been such close decisions as "six to five" or "seven to four," making the anonymous justice's testimony highly dubious.

In any event, the truth will remain unknown unless decisive new evidence can be found. Because Cramer and other justices who had been critical of the death penalty for crimes against peace must have opposed the death penalty for Araki and others, the actual possibility of these suspects being sentenced to death must have been minimal even if the votes had actually been close contests.

Given these facts, it can be concluded that "gross atrocities" played the key role in the handing down of death sentences. The sentences were also influenced by the interests of participating nations as well as by the circumstances surrounding each defendant.

Five Separate Opinions

To the majority judgment of the Tokyo Trial (altogether 1,445 pages in English), five of the eleven justices released separate opinions as follows:

Concurring Opinion:
Delfín Jaranilla, the Philippines (35 pages)

Separate Opinion:
William Webb, Australia (21 pages)

---

29. *Asahi Shimbun*, December 10, 1948.
30. Röling and Cassese, *The Tokyo Trial and Beyond*.

Dissenting Opinions:
Radhabinod Pal, India (1,235 pages)
B. V. A. Röling, the Netherlands (249 pages)
Henri Bernard, France (23 pages)

Of these five justices, only Jaranilla was a member of the majority faction. Ordinarily, a concurring opinion is written when the author is in agreement with the conclusions of the judgment but criticizes the reasoning leading to the conclusions. Being thoroughly pro-American, however, Jaranilla only criticized the fact that the sentences of some of the defendants were excessively lenient. He spent the rest of his opinion openly attacking Justice Pal and defending the atomic bombs on Hiroshima and Nagasaki. He even quoted the US government's view that the atomic bombs had prompted an early termination of the war. This rather unusual separate opinion fully affirming the trial reflected the anti-Japanese sentiment among the Filipinos, which was linked to the war reparation issue. It can be said that Jaranilla's concurring opinion was written to hit back at Pal and the defense.

The three minority justices—Röling, Bernard, and Pal—were excluded from the judgment drafting process. They were not even informed that translation of the judgment was already under way. Röling had to protest to the majority faction that the final judgment had been decided while some justices were not even aware of its content.

Dissenting Opinions of Röling and Bernard

Because of his criticism of the criminalization of war, Röling was seen as problematic by the British government and his own Dutch government, both of which attached weight to crimes against peace. After repeated consultations with the Dutch government, Röling agreed to compromise by submitting a dissenting opinion, but approving crimes against peace on grounds that differed from the majority faction.

His dissenting opinion argued that it was not since the Kellogg-Briand Pact of 1928 but since the Nuremberg Charter of August 1945 that a war of aggression became a crime, and that war victors could ignore the prohibition of ex post facto law because it was merely a policy rule. Still, Röling opposed the death sentence only on counts of crimes against peace and in support of life imprisonment sentences, arguing that, as in the case of the banishment of Napoleon, victors of a just war were allowed by international law to detain individuals who could pose a threat to the postwar order.

Röling also referred to the assessment of sentences of individual defendants, agreeing with all the death sentences, except that of Hirota. He stressed that Oka, Satō, and Shimada should have been sentenced to death for violation of the laws of war, and argued that there was no evidence to support guilty sentences for Hata, Hirota, Kido, Shigemitsu, and Tōgō for either crimes against peace or violations of the laws of war. For instance, Röling took the position that Hirota should not be accused because he had been somewhat against the government's invasion policy, and he had personally negotiated with Army Minister Sugiyama Hajime to stop atrocities at the time of the Nanjing Incident. In short, his interpretation of evidence was different from the majority judgment.

Bernard's dissenting opinion was famous. First, for his disclosure of the inside story of the process of the judgment-drafting and because of his clear hostility toward the majority justices.

Second, resorting to his own theory, Bernard justified the criminalization of aggressive war with "conscience and universal reason," which was the natural law transcending a state.

Third, he argued that no direct evidence of a conspiracy to rule foreign territories was presented and, instead, only the existence of a hope of dominating East Asia was proven. He concluded, therefore, that the defendants could not be found guilty for crimes against peace.

Fourth, Bernard pointed out that, through this trial, it was revealed that the emperor was "one of the suspects," and he regretted the "inequality" manifested by the non-indictment of the emperor. It is relatively unknown that Bernard took a stronger stance regarding the emperor's responsibility than even Webb, and it was his view that the emperor had been a principal instigator of the Pacific War and the defendants were rather accomplices of the emperor.

Webb's Ambivalence

Webb's separate opinion turned out to be the shortest among the minority faction opinions.

First, like the majority faction, Webb approved the binding authority of the Tokyo Charter. This contrasted with Röling, Bernard, and Pal who argued that the justices were endowed with authority to review the Charter. Webb also acknowledged that aggressive war had been rendered illegal and criminalized by the Kellogg-Briand Pact.

Second, Webb referred to the war responsibility of the emperor. Webb said the emperor of Japan was different from ordinary constitutional monarchs in the unique veneration he received from the Japanese people, and yet he did not exercise his authority to stop the initiation of warfare. Nonetheless, Webb went on to say that he was not particularly displeased with the non-indictment of the emperor, and he just wanted to insist that the tribunal should consider a reduction of sentences for the defendants in light of the emperor's responsibility. Webb resorted to a more roundabout rhetoric than Bernard, making his argument a subtle one.

During the court hearing, Webb had given the impression that he wanted to indict the emperor, so the above references to the emperor attracted attention from many quarters. Even the Shōwa emperor himself had to ask Grand Chamberlain Irie Sukemasa "how Webb would react" to the emperor's visit to Australia conducted in 1983.

The fact of the matter is, however, that Webb was ambivalent. During the trial, he made an appeal to MacArthur, saying, "[Before I came to Japan,] I told Dr. Evatt [Herbert Vere Evatt, Australian attorney general and minister for External Affairs] that, if the emperor is indicted, I will not take part in the trial." It would seem that his reference to the emperor's responsibility in his separate opinion was addressed to the Australian government.

Independence of the Tokyo Tribunal

Generally speaking, minority justices of the Tokyo Trial submitted separate opinions in order to protest their exclusion from the judgment decision-making process and express their own positions, which were different from the majority judgment. In Pal's case, however, he had arrived in Japan with a fully formed but unobserved view that was critical of the proceedings, and he retained the attitude that "Allied policy is no concern of mine" throughout the trial.

Also, it should be noted that the majority faction's judgment was not forced on the Tokyo Trial by governments of the participating nations.

American statesman Alexander Hamilton, wrote in the *Federalist Papers* that, "the judiciary is beyond comparison the weakest of the three departments of power. . . . Liberty can have nothing to fear from the judiciary alone but would have everything to fear from its union with either of the other departments." Hamilton, thus, argued that "the complete independence of the courts of justice is peculiarly essential."[31]

Nevertheless, those who affirmed the legitimacy of the Tokyo Trial paid no heed to this wisdom. Those who rejected its legitimacy, on the other hand, suspected a unity between the court, the prosecution, and the governments of the Allies. Judging from what we have seen in this book, however, this suspicion seems quite dubious.

Justices of the Tokyo Trial, like Patrick, were not totally unrelated to their home governments. It was his personal inclination to value his government's intention, which did not necessarily guarantee freedom of the government to control Patrick. Yet the other justices were by no means "agents of the home governments" like the prosecutors. The inability of governments to control the court led, ironically, to the submission of a number of separate opinions owing to the disagreement among the justices. It should be recognized, therefore, that the International Military Tribunal for the Far East was to a considerable extent independent, if not completely so.

3. How to Interpret Pal's Judgment

Not Guilty on All Charges

Let us consider Judge Pal's dissenting opinion, which was unique, even among the minority views.

What came to be known as Pal's so-called "dissentient judgment" belied the legitimacy of the Tokyo Trial. Therefore, those who viewed the Tokyo Trial negatively praised Pal, while those who approved of the trial opposed him. Praise of Pal among right-wing elements in Japan is inseparable from the nationalistic sentiment that "philosopher" Pal defended Japan's honor and the

---

31. Alexander Hamilton, James Madison and John Jay, *The Federalist Papers*, ed. Goldwin Smith (New York: The Colonial Press, 1901).

"self-defensive war" argument about the Pacific War. In contrast, the left wing deeply resented those tendencies and did not want to approve "anti-communist" Pal who had been enshrined by the right wing as Japan's guardian deity. Either way, the arguments were predominantly either political or sentimental.

Ogata Taketora, statesman and former Class A war crimes suspect, met Pal in Calcutta in May 1952, after the termination of the occupation of Japan. Hearing that "Pal returned home temporarily to visit his ailing wife, who told Pal tearfully that he could not return home until he succeeded in making the court understand Japan's position," Ogata was deeply moved and wrote in his diary that, "Dr. Pal's very clear eyes were those of a great man rather than a scholar."[32] There are countless similar commentaries, which are enough to convince us that Pal was indeed a fine man. However, I intend to ignore the sentimental elements, and simply apply political analysis to Pal's judgment.

First, it is essential to clarify what Pal's judgment actually said. Pal contended that the court had to decide whether the conduct that the Tokyo Charter defined as crimes were really crimes. Otherwise it would not be a court of justice but a mere instrument of "ritualized vengeance." Pal argued that victorious nations only had jurisdiction over conventional war crimes and concluded that they were not endowed with the authority to institute a new law—that is, a law regarding crimes against peace.

It is important to clarify that aggression, to begin with, defies easy definition, while the Kellogg-Briand Pact did not change the legal character of war at all. To prepare to dominate other nations is regarded as a grave crime, but it has been common to all the Great Powers since pre–World War II days. There is no Great Power without a blot in its history. But particularly the US, which bore the indelible stain of dropping the atomic bombs, was hardly entitled to talk about humanity. While both the Nuremberg and Tokyo Trials would probably contribute to construction of a "rule of law" in preparation for future world governments, these trials would only present precedents unfavorable to the defeated unless this utopia were to be materialized. Therefore, Pal concluded, it was "premature" to criminalize a war.

Pal also doubted the criterion of the court's acceptance of evidence and

---

32. Ogata Taketora Denki Kankōkai [Ogata Taketora Biography Publishing Committee], ed., *Ogata Taketora* [Ogata Taketora] (Tokyo: Asahi Shimbunsha, 1963).

opposed the finding of facts by the majority judgment. Pal argued that the defendants of the Tokyo Trial were neither Napoleon I nor Adolf Hitler. They were only functionaries in a state that was operating on the basis of the Meiji constitution. Japan participated in World War II as a state.

Pal admitted that there were overwhelming amounts of evidence that Japanese troops had committed atrocities in occupied territories, and that the defense counsels had not denied the occurrence of the Nanjing Incident itself. Pal recognized Japan's violation of the laws of war in this case. According to Pal, the question was how to connect the defendants to criminal responsibility. Reading the evidence, Pal came to the conclusion that atrocities were sporadic incidents. They were not government policies, nor were they ordered or permitted by cabinet members, as the prosecution had alleged. In fact, cabinet members in Tokyo were not authorized to manage the military stationed overseas.

Pal also admitted that "cabinet members' responsibility for nonfeasance" was a concept that could become a code of conduct for future world government. At the same time, Pal admitted that commanders of the troops stationed in the field had been responsible for suppressing information about atrocities by soldiers and, therefore, they were the ones who should be indicted for their inaction and failure to prevent those events. In the case of the Nanjing Incident, although Matsui Iwane's order to maintain military discipline, issued when he learned of the atrocities, was ineffectual, it could not be concluded that Matsui "intentionally and illegally ignored his legal responsibility." Pal argued, therefore, that as far as the evidence was concerned, Matsui was not responsible for atrocities.

Thus, reviewing individual cases, Pal concluded, "I would hold that every one of the accused must be found not guilty of every one of the charges in the indictment, and should be acquitted on all those charges."

Legal Argument Overlapped That of Classical Realists

At this point, I intend to analyze Pal's judgment through two separate lenses: legal theory and fact-finding.

First, Pal's legal methodology was to criticize the majority decision based on legal positivism (a position that recognizes only positive law as the legal norm). On this particular point, I evaluate the Pal judgment highly.

Pal had specialized in Hindu law philosophy, but to criticize him as a layman in international law makes little sense. A person with extraordinary talent can, with half a year of intensive learning, offset the advantage of mediocre experts and easily outdo them.

Pal did not so much as recognize the "illegality" defined by the Kellogg-Briand Pact, although it appears that he did not discriminate "illegality" from "crime" (see chapter 2, section 1). Pal's logic is similar to the logic of classical realism, which regards "equality of national sovereignty" and "exercise of power" as the basic principles of international relations. While Pal did not approve the "exercise of power" as a proper means for a state, his criticism of the ex post facto law paralleled the traditional view of international politics. Therefore, Pal denied the victors' policy of punishing only the defeated by wielding legal justice.

Pal argued that aggression defied an easy definition. In fact, a war of aggression is not a theory invented by scholars but an interpretation applied to actual international relations, so it is, de facto, almost impossible to define.

For instance, the attack on Pearl Harbor in 1941 and, in more recent times, the Iraq War in 2003 were both preventive wars that involved carrying out preemptive attacks against non-imminent threats. While the former was immediately labeled as an aggressive war, the same thing did not happen in the latter case. The concept of aggression was used without definition by the Nuremberg Trial, too. This was due to the fact that a preemptive attack to prevent foreign invasion could be regarded as aggression. Such a hasty definition of aggression could handicap responses to future unexpected contingencies.

Even at the existing International Criminal Court (ICC) in The Hague, in the future when the definition of aggression is firmly established the ICC will finally have jurisdiction over "the crime of aggression" as a crime against peace. In other words, today the crime of aggression effectively remains outside the jurisdiction of the ICC.

Furthermore, Pal argued that charging the crime of aggression was ex post facto law and, therefore, should not be recognized. On this particular point, American historian Richard H. Minear, who pioneered empirical study of the Tokyo Trial in the 1970s, correctly pointed out in that Pal had not disputed that the conduct of the defendants was unjust. He simply argued that such conduct was not illegal.

It is true that Pal's judgment took on a life of its own as a "Japan not guilty" argument. In this case, I believe the term "not guilty" itself is misleading. Although Pal had only explicated his legal argument that "defendants cannot be charged for violation of criminal laws," it was expanded into a broad, moral argument that Japan was absolutely free from fault. Pal's logic is most explicitly manifested in the following statement: "It is certain that the world would not approve of conducts that Japan took in Manchuria. At the same time, however, it would be difficult to criticize those conducts as crimes."

In short, Pal argued that the defendants were not guilty of criminal offenses because the basis for punishment—a law on crimes against peace—had not yet been established. As for the atrocities themselves, even though Pal recognized the existence of the pertinent law, he found all the defendants not guilty, on the grounds that the arguments and evidence presented by the prosecution were inadequate.

Anti-Western Imperialism

Second, Pal's ideological foundation of anti-Western imperialism is strongly reflected in his finding of facts. Pal was not alone among the judges who were favorably disposed toward Japan and had developed a sense of affinity with Japan. Röling felt the same way, and even McDougall, among the majority justices, was sympathetic toward the Japanese people.[33] Thus, favorable feeling toward Japan alone could not be the motive for Pal to write his dissenting opinion. He needed something beyond that, and I believe it was his stance against Western imperialism.

Pal was born in January 1886 in the small village of Nodia, Bengal, in the northeast of the Indian Subcontinent (present-day Salimpur, Kushtia District, Bangladesh), during the Raj, the British rule of India. Unlike Indian nationalist Subhas Chandra Bose (born in 1897), who came from the same neighborhood in an elite caste, Pal came from the Vaishyas caste of farmers, traders, and artisans. Pal grew up in a destitute and fatherless family and experienced firsthand British exploitation and suppression. According to Indian sociologist Ashis Nandy, the Bengal region had been a stronghold

---

33. Sanmonji Shōhei, *Kyokutō gunji saiban* [International Military Tribunal for the Far East] (Tokyo: Asahi Shimbunsha, 1990).

of the anti-British movement and, because of its anti-colonial aspirations, had uniquely strong ties with Japan. Pal also belonged to a generation that believed in "solidarity among Asians."[34] When Japan, an Asian neighbor, won the Russo-Japanese War, Pal rejoiced with genuine pleasure. He looked back at the victory and said, "For the first time, our Asian neighbor defeated the white race's advocacy of aggression."

Pal worked his way through Calcutta University, where he majored in mathematics and graduated summa cum laude. However, the only profession in which an Indian could expect wealth and honor comparable to those of the Caucasian rulers in India during the Raj was a legal career. Pal entered the legal profession due to the strong aspirations of his mother. By the early 1940s, he had attained the positions of acting justice of the Calcutta High Court, lawyer, and vice-president of the University of Calcutta.

When Pal came to Japan for the first time in May 1946 to take part in the Tokyo Trial, GHQ decided against providing him with a suite at the Imperial Hotel, where other justices were lodged, as soon as it learned that Pal was an "Indian nationalist." After Webb protested to MacArthur about this inequality, Pal was provided with an Imperial Hotel suite. It is said, however, that Pal never forgot this humiliation.[35]

From the preceding it is clear that there were sufficient reasons for Pal to pay serious attention to the race factor.

Political Nature of Fact-Finding

The sentiment and position expressed by Pal was quite common among Indians at the time.

In November 1945, the British colonial government brought three military officers of the Indian National Army (INA, Azad Hind Fauj)—an advocate of armed resistance in collaboration with the Japanese military—to military trial for treason. Indian citizens launched fierce protest demonstrations, demanding national independence and cancellation of the trial. There were clashes with the local police force everywhere, leading to tragic bloodshed.

---

34. Ashis Nandy, *The Savage Freud and Other Essays on Possible and Retrievable Selves* (New Jersey: Princeton University Press, 1995).

35. Tim Maga, *Judgment at Tokyo* (Lexington: University Press of Kentucky, 2001).

The Indian National Congress, which advocated nonviolence and criticized the INA, decided to take advantage of the rising anti-British sentiment to further promote its independence movement. It harshly denounced as true war criminals President Harry Truman, who had dropped atomic bombs on Japan, and European suzerain states, which had suppressed anti-colonialism in Southeast Asia as the "true war criminals." A group of elite lawyers organized by the Indian National Congress stressed the injustice of the indictment of the three military officers and the legitimacy of Subhas Chandra Bose's Provisional Government of Free India (azad Hind Sarkar), which had exchanged fire with British troops. These lawyers denounced the military trial as a "suzerain state's justice." Although the three defendants in the INA trial were sentenced to indefinite-term banishment by the end of the year, the British military was cornered into announcing the suspension of the sentence immediately after it was issued.

Subsequently, when a Muslim major was sentenced to seven years' imprisonment for atrocities by a second INA trial, another large-scale protest movement erupted in February 1946. Calcutta was put under martial law, and Indian troops rose in rebellion.[36] This was the turmoil that India had been experiencing when Pal first arrived in Japan.

In the end, British prime minister Clement Attlee announced transfer of sovereignty to India on February 20, 1947, upon which the Islamic state of Pakistan and the Hindu state of India became independent on August 14 and August 15, 1948, respectively.

Anti-Western imperialism had been a mainstream ideology of India. The "victors" that Pal denounced were Western nations, suzerain states. For this reason, Indians viewed Japan, a non-Western neighbor, with an empathy that exceeded favorable attitudes.

Thus, Pal's judgment relativized Japan's actions and came to resemble the defense's logic. For instance, Pal made the following often-quoted remark on the Hull note:

---

36. Fujiwara Iwaichi, *F-kikan* [F-Organization] (Tokyo: Hara Shobō, 1966), and Inagaki Takeshi, *Kakumeika Chandora Bōzu* [Chandra Bose the Revolutionary] (Tokyo: Shinchō-sha, 1986).

Even contemporary historians could think that 'as for the present war, the Principality of Monaco, the Grand Duchy of Luxembourg, would have taken up arms against the United States on receipt of such a note as the State Department sent the Japanese Government on the eve of Pearl Harbor.'

Pal's quotation of another person's strained simile—which comparative culture scholar Ushimura Kei warned was liable to be taken as Pal's own words—concluded that the attack on Pearl Harbor was a "fatal step" that Japan was forced to take.

It was not only the anti-Axis majority decision that was political. The finding of facts in Pal's judgment, which was based on anti-Western imperialism, was also remarkably political. On this point, although I do not hold the majority judgment in the highest regard, I cannot give a high score to Pal's judgment either. However, the latter was much better than the former. Both were biased.

Because of His Strong Personality

I hold that Pal was partially responsible for the popular misinterpretation of his judgment as a "Japan not guilty" argument. I would argue that, because crimes against peace could not be established, Pal should have followed his own logic, and given up on confirming facts in political history. He should have instead concentrated on finding out what actually happened in the atrocities.

A fact-finding based on a criticism of applying ex post facto law only to the defeated would inevitably provoke the logic, "You would do the same if you were the victor," or *tu quoque*. This put Pal's judgment somewhat closer to the defense's counterevidence. This may be one remote cause of Pal's judgment being interpreted, wrongly, as a "Japan not guilty" argument.

More problematic in Pal's seeking to confirm facts was that no Japanese leaders would be blamed for the Manchurian Incident, the Second Sino-Japanese War, and the Pacific War. While there can be no black box in national decision-making, someone must have been responsible for these incidents. It is regrettable that, by offering unnecessary finding of facts, Pal had to call for complete acquittal of all the defendants.

In sum, Pal's judgment had two sides. It was composed of the following two elements:

(1) An elaborate legal theoretical argument criticizing victors' justice from the viewpoint of legal positivism.
(2) Employing political fact-finding based on an ideology of anti-Western imperialism.

As far as the legal theory was concerned, Pal's view was not unique among the Tokyo Trial justices. Pal was not the only judge who questioned the Nuremberg Doctrine. Although they remained the minority among the judges, Webb and Röling shared the same doubts. And anti-Western imperialism and empathy with Japan, which were at the base of Pal's finding of facts, were common among many Indians at the time. In other words, the main thesis of Pal's judgment was not something only Pal could have written.

In consideration of the initial goal of the Occupation of Japan—that is, the "demilitarization of Japan"—denial of the norm and policy of the Tokyo Trial by one of its justices should not have been permitted from the beginning. In retrospect, it was only Pal whose personality could nonchalantly ignore the actual constraints of the Occupation and unaffected by any pressure flatly deny the legitimacy of victors' justice.

Thus, the fundamental reason why Pal's judgment stood out so much is to be found, above all, in his personality.

Distance from the Indian Government

Now let us turn to the position that regards Pal's judgment as "the view of the Indian government." While this view has prevailed since the time of the trial, it is, to jump to the conclusion, a misunderstanding caused by inferring that Pal's judgment was analogous with the Asian liberation ideology and India's nonalignment policy during the Cold War.

In contrast to Southeast Asian countries, which had sought reprisal against Japan immediately after World War II, India appeared tolerant of Japan in the eyes of the Japanese people. In fact, Mahatma Gandhi's nonviolent resistance became idealized in postwar Japan. In 1949, Indira the elephant, which Prime Minister Jawaharlal Nehru presented to Japan, arrived at Ueno Zoo, where it remained the object of children's adoration for many years. In addition, the Japanese government provided the first postwar yen loans to India in 1958. The Japanese affinity with India has been persistent, and Pal is often mentioned when explaining this sentiment.

According to Pal's bereaved family, when Pal returned home temporarily during the trial, he was sharply admonished by Nehru not to defend Japan. Pal refused.[37] In Pal's judgment, perhaps partly due to his anti-communist ideology (which Japanese historian Ienaga Saburō tenaciously criticized), he deliberately took up Nehru's pro-Soviet remarks in order to discard Nehru's argument as utterly useless in achieving the stability of international society.

Pal's judgment was his personal opinion, and it had nothing to do with the Indian government. Although I pointed this out in 1993,[38] I would like to reiterate my conclusion here.

According to Narasimha Murthy, while the Indian government had been critical of Japan from the 1930s through the immediate postwar days, it shifted its policy to a "let bygones be bygones" stance when it accomplished independence in August 1947. Behind this shift was, of course, calculation of realistic interests, such as India's prestige in international politics and trade relations with Japan.

Along the way, India became concerned about the possibility of Pal's judgment being viewed as the government's official view, and on August 3, 1948, it asked the British whether it should make some sort of announcement that Pal's judgment was unrelated to the government. Judging that an announcement would draw unnecessary attention to Pal's judgment, the British advised the Indian government that it would be wiser at that point to remain silent.

For India, it was especially important to uphold its honor as "a member of the Allied Powers." Having finally obtained the right to send a justice to the Tokyo Trial after much ado, India ended up with Pal, who would not listen to

---

37. Toyoda Kumao, *Sensō saiban yoroku* [Additional Records of the War Crimes Trials] (Tokyo: Taiseisha, 1986), and Satyabrata Pal, "Mago ga akasu Tōkyō Saiban: Pāru hanji no kigai" [Tokyo Trial Disclosed by Pal's Grandson: Justice Pal's Grit], trans. Tagawa Yasugo, *Seiron* 417 (December 2006).

38. Higurashi Yoshinobu, "Pāru hanketsu saikō" [Rethinking Pal's Judgment], in *Nihon kindaishi no saikōchiku* [Reconstruction of Japanese Modern History], ed. Itō Takashi (Tokyo: Yamakawa Shuppansha, 1993).

the government, jeopardizing its position as a result. In this case, according to the logic of international politics, the proper solution would be to deny the government's connections with Pal's judgment.

A "Bat-like" Position

When Pal's judgment was made public, however, public opinion in India identified with it.

At this point, the Indian government faced a dilemma over Pal's judgment. Externally, India held a position as a member of the Allied Powers, which was the complete opposite of Pal's judgment. Domestically, however, the people of India shared Pal's sentiment.

In the face of this dilemma, first of all, the Indian government decided to refrain from any official "statement" denying its connection with Pal's judgment, while secretly giving "notice" to concerned nations. According to a document uncovered recently, Nehru sent the following telegram to the governor of the West Bengal state on November 29, 1948:

> I have consulted with my colleagues in the cabinet and we agreed that there is no need to send any telegram to General MacArthur [about Pal's judgment]. Setting this decision aside, our conduct on this issue will inevitably connect Judge Pal's dissenting opinion at the Tokyo Trial to the Indian government. The said judgment was permeated with misguided and sweeping descriptions, most of which we cannot agree with. We were obliged to notify governments concerned that, concerning the suspicion that the Indian government had solicited Justice Pal to write it, we officially assume no responsibility whatsoever.[39]

Thus, the Indian government chose the option of secretly notifying nations concerned through diplomatic channels that it had nothing to do with Pal's judgment. Being a thorough realist, Nehru was satisfied with this solution. Open publication of the "statement" would have unnecessarily stirred up public opinion in India.

---

39. Naitō Masao, "Pāru Hanji 'igi hanketsu' no kyokō" [Myth of Justice Pal's "Dissentient Judgment"], *In-Pa kai kaihō* [Indo-Pakistan Society, Tokyo University of Foreign Studies] 16 (2006).

Secondly, the Indian government instructed B. N. Chakravorty, head of the Indian Liaison Mission in Japan who had provided assistance to Pal while he was in Japan, to recommend to an advisory board on the Tokyo Trial sentences convened by MacArthur on November 22, 1948, that all the death sentences be reduced to life imprisonment.[40]

Due to the popular image of India as magnanimous, this proposal tended to be understood to be of the same nature as Pal's judgment.

India's recommendation, however, was different from both Pal's judgment and the policy of the Allies. Here one can detect the cleverness of the Indian government. It was a bat-like recommendation, after Aesop's fable "The Bat, the Birds, and the Beast," to please both its domestic population and the Allies. Domestically, the proposal was meant to impress the Indian people with the government's magnanimity and closeness to Pal's judgment, while externally it sought to impress the Allies that the Indian government's position was different from Pal's judgment.

"The Indian Government Has Never Changed Its Position"

Reviewing the reactions of Japanese mass media to these separate opinions, we find that while the *Nippon Times* (an English-language paper) and several local papers paid due attention to Pal's dissenting opinion, major dailies did not devote much space to it. This indicates that the impact of Pal's judgment in Japan was smaller than expected.

As soon as Japan regained its sovereignty on April 28, 1952, however, excerpts of Pal's judgment began to be published in succession, including *Nihon muzairon* (The "Japan Not Guilty" Argument), edited by Tanaka Masaaki (Taiheiyō Shuppansha, May 1952); *Senshi o yaburu* (Breaking War History), translated and edited by Yoshimatsu Masakatsu (Nihon Shoseki Insatsu Tōkyō Shisha, June 1952); and *Zen'yaku Nihon muzairon* ("Japan Not Guilty" Argument, Complete Translation) (Nihon Shobō, November 1952).

Also, when the Japanese government applied for clemency to Class A war criminals in early November 1952, Nehru supported their release. Furthermore, in December, the foreign undersecretary of India shamelessly

---

40. For this advisory council, see Higurashi Yoshinobu, *Tōkyō Saiban no kokusai kankei* [The Tokyo Trial and International Relations] (Tokyo: Bokutakusha, 2002).

told Nishiyama Tsutomu, the first Japanese ambassador to India, that, "As is obvious from our Justice Pal's argument for acquittal of all the war crimes suspects at the time of the Tokyo Trial, the Indian government has never changed its position."[41]

For the Indian government, its position as a member of the Allied Powers was important at the time of the Tokyo Trial. As Indian diplomacy shifted its weight toward neutralism and non-alignment in the 1950s, however, the utility value of Pal's judgment increased after the fact. And this was what was behind the adroit change of attitude by the Indian government.

41. Ministry of Foreign Affairs, *Gaikō kiroku* [Diplomatic Record] (Diplomatic Archive of the Ministry of Foreign Affairs, 1998), 14th Disclosure.

CHAPTER **6**

Why a Second Tokyo Trial
Was Not Held

Joseph Berry Keenan and
General Douglas MacArthur
in front of GHQ
(Harvard Law School Library,
Historical & Special Collections,
Joseph Berry Keenan photo-
graph collection)

1. International Trial and Subsequent Trial

What to Do about Post-Nuremberg Trials

The International Military Tribunal for the Far East (Tokyo Trial) was concluded with the rendition of judgment. But what about the other Class A war crimes suspects? General Headquarters, Supreme Commander for the Allied Powers (GHQ), had arrested more than 100 Class A suspects, and so theoretically it would make sense for a second Tokyo Trial to be held. But we know for a fact that no such trial was held. Why was it not convened?

On this point, Kishi Nobusuke, a former Class A war crimes suspect, commented:

> The progress of the Cold War was our only hope in Sugamo Prison. When the Cold War became more serious, we thought our lives might be spared. . . . Around 1946, when the focus of our concern was whether there would be a second round of indictments, we learned of the Cold War. . . . It was because of the Cold War between the US and the Soviet Union that there was only one round of indictments for the Tokyo Trial with no second one to follow.[1]

In Kishi's analysis, when the conflict between the US and the Soviet Union grew fiercer, the US would terminate punishment of the Japanese war criminals in order to incorporate Japan into the Western bloc. While his logic makes sense, one wonders whether the Cold War was the only reason a

---

1. Hara Yoshihisa, ed., *Kishi Nobusuke shōgenroku* [Testimonies by Kishi Nobusuke] (Tokyo: Mainichi Shimbunsha, 2003).

second Tokyo Trial was abandoned. To understand this basic policy issue, we should first examine the US policy toward Germany.

From an early stage, the Allied forces in Germany had been considering how to treat major war crimes suspects who had not been tried in the Nuremberg Trial and what to do about a second major war crimes tribunal.

Charles Fahy, legal advisor to the US military government for Germany (Berlin), and Brigadier General Edward C. Betts, judge advocate, at the headquarters of the European Theatre of Operations (Frankfurt), had studied "post–Nuremberg Trial" options since the autumn of 1945 in consultation with Robert H. Jackson, chief US prosecutor of the Nuremberg Trial. Toward the end of the year, they reached the conclusion that the chief prosecutor should continue to try major war criminals in a subsequent trial even after the conclusion of the Nuremberg Trial, and to try minor war criminals in trials convened in the US occupation zone. President Harry Truman approved this proposal on January 16, 1946, thus formalizing the decision to hold a subsequent trial of German major war criminals.

The remaining question was whether to make this subsequent trial an international tribunal or a series of national trials by the various nations. Because Jackson was scheduled to resume his duties as Justice of the Supreme Court of the United States after the Nuremberg Trial, Colonel Telford Taylor (promoted to brigadier general in April 1946) was appointed to succeed Jackson toward the end of March 1946. Taylor went ahead with preparations for the follow-up trial. Taylor himself was of the view that at least industrial capitalists should be tried in an international tribunal. This hope was said to be shared by the Soviet Union and France.

Establishment of the Subsequent Nuremberg Trials

Jackson had led an "argument for US initiative" in the Tokyo Trial (see chapter 2, section 2). Still, he remained so averse to an international tribunal that he advised President Truman in mid-May 1946 that the remaining major war crimes suspects should be tried by a series of national trials in the respective countries. Indignant that the Soviet Union had been using the Nuremberg Trial for political purposes, Jackson had deepened his anti-Soviet sentiment. Lucius D. Clay, deputy military governor in Germany, who excelled at managerial affairs, emphasized to the US Department of War that, if a second international tribunal were convened after August, it would highlight the ideological conflict between the US and the Soviet Union, thus betraying the purpose of the trial.

In the summer of 1946, the Departments of State and War considered the possibility of convening a new international tribunal. Fahy, who had returned from Germany to become a legal advisor in the State Department, was skeptical about a second international tribunal because it would be, in his judgment, ineffectual. Secretary of State James Byrnes, however, was of the view that, if other nations demanded a second international tribunal, the US could not refuse. The Department of War also preferred an international tribunal to try German industrial capitalists so as to prevent a resurgence of German militarism. Intra-governmental consensus on a second international tribunal was, thus, not readily achieved. It was tentatively decided that the final decision on this issue should await the judgment of the Nuremberg Trial.

On October 1, 1946, the Nuremberg Trial judgment was announced. Immediately after the sentencing, in early October, the four powers—the US, Britain, the Soviet Union, and France—judged that a precedent had been established with the Nuremberg judgment. They agreed among themselves to forgo a second international tribunal, and that each nation's trial of major war criminals should be continued. For the Western nations, the difficulty of managing relations with the Soviet Union seemed to be a decisive reason for abandoning a second international tribunal.

Given these developments, the US military government for Germany singlehandedly set up a "Control Council Court" on October 18, 1946. It had jurisdiction over four crimes: crimes against peace, war crimes, crimes against humanity, and membership in criminal organizations. On October 24, Jackson resigned, and Taylor succeeded him as chief prosecutor.

The uniqueness of this US unilateral Subsequent Nuremberg Trials lay in its authority to indict major war criminals for crimes against peace. The first indictment was delivered on November 5, 1946, and a court to try twenty-three medical doctors was convened on December 9. Until the Subsequent Nuremberg Trials were concluded on April 14, 1949, a total of twelve courts were convened to try a total of one hundred eighty-five indicted suspects including civilians, military personnel, industrial capitalists, legal professionals, and others who took part in decision-making.[2]

At the same time, Britain and France also set up similar courts of their own in their respective occupation zones. (Whether the Soviet Union followed suit is unknown.)

Scheme for a Subsequent Trial of Japan

What about the treatment of the remaining Japanese Class A war crimes suspects? Following the opening of the Tokyo Trial, setting aside Arima Yoriyasu and Ikeda Shigeaki—the latter who was under house arrest—and others who were exempted from prosecution and released, there were still fifty Class A war crimes suspects as of June 26, 1947. According to historian Awaya Kentarō, while Charles Willoughby, head of G-2 (intelligence), GHQ, frequently argued for their release, the International Prosecution Section and Legal Section of GHQ remained cautious about their early release.[3] Meanwhile, Chief Prosecutor Joseph Keenan and Colonel Alva C. Carpenter, chief of GHQ's Legal Section, announced the possibility of convening a second Class A war crime trial in the latter half of 1946.

Upon hearing this announcement, the British government sounded out the US State Department's intentions in February 1947. It preferred not to be involved in the trial of "minor" Class A suspects that GHQ had arrested, most of whom had only slight responsibility for the war plan.

On March 18, 1947, after the British government's contact, it was proposed at the War Crimes Branch of the Civil Affairs Division (CAD), US Department of War, that Class A suspects should be tried at an American national subsequent trial, modeled after precedents in Germany. On May 5, the following provisional policies were formed:

(1) To examine Class A suspects and transfer those who were found to belong to Class B and C to GHQ's Legal Section.

(2) To establish three American subsequent tribunals of Class A suspects.

---

2. Telford Taylor, *Final Report to the Secretary of the Army on the Nuremberg War Crimes Trials under Control Council Law No. 10* (New York: William S. Hein, 1997).

3. Awaya Kentarō, *Tōkyō Saiban e no michi* [Road to the Tokyo Trial] (Tokyo: Kodansha, 2006).

(3) To appoint only Japanese lawyers to defense counsels and have American lawyers function as advisors.

(4) To open the subsequent trials on October 1, 1947, without waiting for the conclusion of the Tokyo Trial.

The US Department of War in the spring of 1947 had envisioned the application of the US policy toward Germany to Japanese Class A suspects and the opening of a unilateral American national subsequent trial of Japanese war crimes suspects instead of an international trial.

MacArthur's View on a Class B and C War Crimes Trial

The War Department's proposals notwithstanding, MacArthur warned in his May 12, 1947, telegram to the Joint Chiefs of Staff that it would be "disadvantageous" for the Occupation of Japan to continue to detain some fifty Class A suspects and raised the following issue of interpretation of FEC 007/3. According to MacArthur, it was not permissible to try crimes against peace in a single-nation tribunal such as the "Subsequent Nuremberg Trials" in Japan, which was under the control of FEC 007/3. In other words, MacArthur argued that only an international tribunal could try the accused for crimes against peace in Japan.

MacArthur requested his government to give him the authority to try Class A suspects at a Class B and C court. The intention behind this alternative idea was quite obvious. MacArthur loathed international tribunals and crimes against peace so much that he proposed a Class B and C trial that he could control.

It is certainly true that the US had particularly stressed the need for "an international tribunal on crimes against peace" as part of its policy toward Japan. Therefore, in the end, the US government agreed that it was up to the interpretation of the authorities concerned, and accepted MacArthur's interpretation.

Thus, while the CAD of the Department of War and MacArthur were in agreement about avoiding another international tribunal, they were in direct confrontation as far as the convening of a Class A war criminal court was concerned. The only thing that the War Department could decide for the moment was early implementation of the screening of Class A suspects.

The directive on this screening was issued on June 17, 1947, to the prosecutors of the Tokyo Trial by Joseph Keenan, in Washington, DC, whose responsibility and authority it was to indict Class A suspects. The directive instructed that the screening should be divided among American prosecutors and prosecutors from other countries, and that the results and related documents should be submitted to the War Crimes Branch of the Department of War.

Nightmare of the Second International Tribunal

Keenan's directive surprised prosecutors from the British Commonwealth countries in Tokyo. They had no idea that Class A suspects had been detained for such a long time. British Commonwealth prosecutors protested to the American prosecutors and reported on the situation to their respective governments.

Frederick Everson of the British embassy in the United States visited Katherine B. Fite, assistant to the legal advisor of the US Department of State, on August 6, 1947, to hint subtly that Britain did not wish to share responsibility for the prolonged detention of the Class A suspects, and that it did not intend to take part in a second international tribunal. The British Foreign Office was terrified by the prospect of a second international tribunal and was of the view that if the US wished to convene such a trial, it should do so singlehandedly.

Keenan, who had returned to Tokyo, revealed in a press conference on August 11 that the Department of War had ordered the prompt opening of the trial on the remaining Class A suspects. As a matter of fact, the War Crimes Branch there had examined documents on forty-eight Class A suspects that the International Prosecution Section had submitted and singled out six of them, including Kishi Nobusuke, as indictable as Class A war crimes suspects, pending additional evidence.

The British Foreign Office took this news as an indication that a nightmarish second international tribunal was now imminent. Thus, it decided to propose that Class A suspects be tried by an American Class B and C trial, adopting the advice of the prosecutors of the British Commonwealth countries (Comyns-Carr's proposal). More specifically, the British Foreign Office concluded that it was due to lack of evidence that Class A suspects had failed to be indicted by the Tokyo Trial, and predicted that a second indictment would not be successful because some defendants of the ongoing Tokyo Trial would be found not guilty for crimes against peace. Thus, since the ongoing International Military Tribunal for the Far East would be hopelessly slow and inefficient, any secondary trials should be convened by each nation unilaterally. At this point, the methodology of the British Commonwealth coincided perfectly with that of MacArthur.

On October 9, 1947, the British government formally conveyed its position to the US Department of State, rejecting participation in any second international tribunal that might be convened. By that time, the British government had already abolished the war crime bureau of its Foreign Office as of September 30, 1947, and was settling into its own Class B and C war crime trial.

Avoidance of a Class A Trial

On August 20, 1947, Colonel Edward H. Young, director of the War Crimes Branch of the Department of War, Alva Carpenter, chief of GHQ's Legal Section who temporarily returned home, and Ernest A. Gross, legal advisor of the Department of State for the Occupation zone, gathered in Washington, DC, to discuss the issue of how to handle the Class A suspects. They came to a general agreement (albeit not an official decision) that "it was desirable to avoid further international trial." In other words, they agreed to convene an American national subsequent Class A war criminal trial.

As mentioned, the American government's inclination to open a new international trial had almost completely dissolved by the summer of 1947. There were two alternative methods for dealing with the Class A suspects:

> (1) subsequent Class A war crimes trials (advocated by the Department of War, Department of State, and Joseph Keenan); or
> (2) a Class B and C war crimes trials (advocated by MacArthur and the British Commonwealth)

Therefore, if a second Tokyo Trial were to open, it would take the form of a national trial like the one in Germany, and not an international trial.

Ten days later, on August 30, fifteen Class A suspects, including Aikawa Yoshisuke (president, Manchurian Industrial Development Company), Shōriki Matsutarō (president, *Yomiuri Shimbun*), and Masaki Jinzaburō (inspector general of military training, Imperial Japanese Army) as well as eight suspects under house arrest including Ogata Taketora (minister of state of the Koiso Cabinet), Kuhara Fusanosuke (president of the political party Rikken-Seiyūkai), and Tokutomi Sohō (chairman, Dai-Nihon Genron Hōkokukai [Japanese-Speech Patriot Association]) were all exempted from prosecution and released. Thus, the number of the remaining Class A suspects was reduced to approximately twenty.

Until returning to his post in Tokyo in August, Keenan, like the Department of War, had supported an American national subsequent Class A war crime trial. But the former Japanese Navy obtained a "Keenan information" document in September 1947 that said, "[Class] A would no longer be pursued. (Class A war crimes trial ends in Ichigaya.)"[4] Upon his return to Tokyo, Keenan was converted to advocacy of a Class B and C trial for Class A suspects by MacArthur. The final authority to decide the treatment of Class A suspects rested with Keenan, and so this conversion was highly significant.

The final blow was a telegram that MacArthur sent to the Department of War on January 13, 1948. It said that Keenan "strongly suggested" that "a further Class A trial should not be convened" because it would inevitably be a long-term affair. Keenan also suggested, according to MacArthur's telegram, that of the nineteen Class A suspects (sixteen in Sugamo Prison and three under house arrest) those who were indictable as Class B and C war criminals should be transferred to the jurisdiction of the Legal Section of GHQ, while the rest should be released.

This MacArthur-Keenan joint proposal was approved by the Departments of War and State. On January 31, 1948, this news was communicated to MacArthur through the Department of War. In other words, the American policy of abandoning both further international trial and a Class A subsequent trial was confirmed in January 1948. In mid-February, the Department of War and GHQ announced that there would be no second international trial. It also implied that Class A suspects might be tried for Class B and C war crimes.

---

4. Toyoda Kumao, *Sensō saiban yoroku* [Additional Records of the War Crimes Trials] (Tokyo: Taiseisha, 1986).

2. MacArthur's Persistence

Trial on Former Cabinet Members

As of March 8, 1948, the sixteen Class A suspects in Sugamo Prison were:

Aoki Kazuo, Minister of Greater East Asia, Tōjō Cabinet
Abe Genki, Home Minister, Suzuki Cabinet
Amō Eiji, Director, Cabinet Information Bureau
Andō Kisaburō, Minister of Home Affairs, Tōjō Cabinet
Ishihara Hiroichirō, President, Ishihara Industry, Co. Ltd.
Iwamura Michiyo, Minister of Justice, Tōjō Cabinet
Kishi Nobusuke, Minister of Commerce and Industry, Tōjō Cabinet
Kuzuu Yoshihisa, President, Kokuryūkai (Black Dragon Society)
Kodama Yoshio, Founder, Kodama Kikan (Kodama Agency)
Gotō Fumio, Minister of State, Tōjō Cabinet
Sasakawa Ryōichi, President, Kokusui Taishūtō (Patriotic People's Party)
Admiral Takahashi Sankichi, Vice Chief, Naval General Staff
Tani Masayuki, Minister of Foreign Affairs, Tōjō Cabinet
Terashima Ken, Minister of Communications, Tōjō Cabinet
Admiral Toyoda Soemu, Chief, Naval General Staff
General Nishio Toshizō, Commander, China Expeditionary Army

Additionally, three Class A suspects were under house arrest:

Suma Yakichirō, Director, Information Department, Ministry of Foreign Affairs
General Tada Hayao, Commander, North China Area Army
Honda Kumatarō, Japanese Ambassador to China

Altogether, there were nineteen Class A suspects. Another list included twenty-one suspects, in which Ōkawa Shūmei and Lieutenant General Tamura Hiroshi (Director, Prisoner-of-War Information Bureau, Ministry of the Army) were included.

On September 27, 1948, MacArthur expressed his intentions of trying eight former cabinet members of suspected Class A crimes for Class B and C crimes. This included Aoki, Andō, Iwamura, Kishi, Gotō, Tani, and Terashima of the Tōjō Cabinet and Abe of the Suzuki Cabinet. This indicates that MacArthur persisted in punishing the Tōjō Cabinet.

At this point, MacArthur declared he wished to open the trial of former cabinet members within about forty-five days of the Tokyo Trial sentencing. He even said that if permission was not granted, he intended to release all the Class A suspects. His proposal was approved by Secretary of War Kenneth Claiborne Royall.

GHQ Trials

Furthermore, GHQ actually indicted former admiral Toyoda Soemu and former lieutenant general Tamura Hiroshi for Class B and C crimes on October 19, 1948, immediately after the formation of the second Yoshida Cabinet. The trials of the two former generals are known as the "GHQ trials."

The trial of former cabinet members and these GHQ trials shared several characteristics. GHQ attempted to invite justices from concerned nations to both courts, to make them "mixed military courts." A mixed military court was, like the Yokohama War Crimes Trials, an American Class B and C trial in which representatives of other nations participated. Institutionally, it was different from an international military tribunal such as the Tokyo Trial. As a matter of fact, in the official directive on the GHQ trials, they were simply referred to as a "military tribunal" with no reference to "international." GHQ, nevertheless, attempted to make it appear as if those former Class A suspects were tried by an "international

Top: Toyoda Soemu
Bottom: Tamura Hiroshi
(Kyodo News)

tribunal" rather than in a mere Class B and C trial. To place the trial under the "direct jurisdiction" of GHQ was also a form of "stage direction," intended to make this trial of previously Class A suspects look more prominent.

But only Australia and the Soviet Union expressed any intention of participating in the GHQ trials. Australia dispatched its judge to the trial of Toyoda on the condition that it would not be an international tribunal. The Soviet Union ended up not participating after all, following a disagreement with GHQ over the delay in appointing the judge of the court.

As a result of these hearings, Tamura Hiroshi was sentenced to eight years of heavy labor for allowing his subordinates to abuse prisoners of war. (He was released on parole in December 1951.) Toyoda Soemu was accused of atrocities during his tenure as commander-in-chief of the Combined Fleet and chief of Naval General Staff; he was acquitted on September 6, 1949.

Disadvantageous Precedent

With the opening of the GHQ trials, the number of remaining Class A suspects was reduced to nineteen. Of those, Amō, Ishiwara, Kuzuu, Suma, Takahashi, Tada, Nishio, Honda, Ōkawa, Kodama, and Sasakawa were found unindictable for Class B and C crimes and were released. The remaining eight, i.e., Aoki, Abe, Andō, Iwamura, Kishi, Gotō, Tani, and Terashima, were to be tried before the former cabinet member proceedings in January 1949.

Let us take a look at the diary Kishi kept during his imprisonment.

On October 20, 1948, when Kishi heard that the Legal Section of GHQ was examining the possibility of trying him and his inmates for Class B and C crimes, he was puzzled because, "It would go against common sense for us to be indicted for crimes which are classified as Class B or Class C crimes."

As the GHQ trials progressed, however, Kishi recognized the likelihood of his being indicted as a Class B and C suspect. On November 13, his fifty-second birthday, he had become resigned enough to say, "Deducing from the judgment of the Tokyo Trial, it appears that before long we, too, will be indicted. . . . In the past, I became hopeful several times that I would be released, but now, there is no hope whatsoever."[5]

---

5. Kishi Nobusuke et al., *Kishi Nobusuke no kaisō* [Memoir of Kishi Nobusuke] (Tokyo: Bungeishunjū, 1981).

Considering MacArthur's persistence, there was a real possibility that Kishi and other inmates would be tried in January 1949. But we now know that those eight former cabinet members were not indicted. Why, then, were their indictments abandoned?

The answer can be found in the judgment of the Tokyo Trial. The Legal Section of GHQ decided for the following reasons that the judgment would set a disadvantageous precedent for the proposed former cabinet members' trial.

First, the prosecution of the Tokyo Trial had indicted Kaya Okinori, Shigemitsu Mamoru, Suzuki Teiichi, and Tōgō Shigenori, civilian cabinet members during the war, on Counts 54 and 55 for violation of the laws of war. Nevertheless, only Shigemitsu was found guilty on Count 55. Therefore, the eight former cabinet members, for whom the prosecution could only present evidence similar to that for non-military cabinet members, were likely to be found not guilty.

Second, all of the defendants who were found guilty on Counts 54 or 55 were Imperial Japanese Army officers, except Shigemitsu and Hirota Kōki, who was found responsible for the Nanjing Incident. Therefore, the Legal Section became pessimistic about the success of a trial of the former cabinet members.

Bound by Its Own Standards

The Cold War was not the only reason that a second Class A war crimes trial or a subsequent trial was abandoned. Internal affairs within the Allies, such as Britain's and MacArthur's aversion to international tribunals played a part, even though the assessment was that only an international tribunal could try Japanese Class A war crimes.

Nevertheless, a Class B and C trial of Class A suspects (former cabinet members) remained a real possibility. The Department of War had already endorsed it, and it would not take too long for an American national court to try only eight suspects. If these eight suspects were indicted for Class B and Class C crimes, however, they had to be found guilty. If winning a guilty verdict was not guaranteed, GHQ might as well forgo the attempt completely in order to avoid losing face.

It should be clearly understood then that, although GHQ had seriously considered trying the former cabinet members, it had to abandon that course of action due to the impact of the Tokyo Trial judgment. Because the Allies had overemphasized the judiciary nature of the Tokyo Trial, they were constrained by its judgment. In other words, ironically, the Allies ended up being bound by their own norm.

At midnight on December 23, 1948, seven death-row prisoners including Tōjō Hideki were executed at Sugamo Prison. It was reported that the Shōwa emperor, in a dark mood that day, confined himself to his room.

The media learned that Lieutenant General Walton Walker, commander of the US Eighth Army, who had jurisdiction over Sugamo Prison, had visited MacArthur on December 21, and so they crowded into the Public Information Section of GHQ beginning on the evening of December 22.

At noon on December 24, all seventeen Class A suspects were released. (Tada Hayao and Honda Kumatarō had passed away by mid-December.) Alva Carpenter, chief of GHQ's Legal Section, declared that, with the ongoing GHQ trials and release of these seventeen prisoners, "The handling of former major war crimes suspects in Japan has been completed." Christmas Eve was chosen for the release of the seventeen prisoners in an attempt to mitigate the impact of the executions on the previous day.

3. Shift toward Completion of the War Crimes Trial

George Kennan's Argument for Completion of the Trial

Hugh Borton, chief of the Northeast Asian Affairs Division, the Office of Far Eastern Affairs, Department of State, compiled a draft peace treaty with Japan dated August 5, 1947. The so-called "Borton draft" assumed a "hard peace," which exercised surveillance over Japan, and proposed that the Allies should be able to try war criminals, with Japan being responsible for assisting the court and carrying out the sentences, even after Japan regained its sovereignty. The authority to grant clemency to prisoners was to be monopolized by the Council of Allied Ambassadors to Japan (a surveillance organization comprised of member countries of the Far Eastern Commission), and Japan would not be entitled to intervene.

But George F. Kennan, director of the new Policy Planning Staff (PPS) of the State Department (established on May 5, 1947), criticized the Borton draft for failing to respond to the new international environment under the Cold War. Kennan submitted his own policy paper PPS 28 to Secretary of State George Marshall toward the end of March 1948.

PPS 28 proposed a shift in policy from "defanging" Japan to establishing Japan's "economic recovery" and "political stabilization." It also proposed an early completion of the war crimes trials. It suggested that an "early deadline" should be set for Class A trials (the abandonment of any second Class A

George Kennan
(Harris & Ewing collection, Prints & Photographs Division, Library of Congress)

trial had already been confirmed in January 1948), and that suspects unlikely to be indictable for Class B and C trials should be screened for early release, after which trials of the remaining suspects should be held promptly.

From the beginning, Kennan had been skeptical about the effectiveness of a war crimes trial in terms of international relations because it was a typical manifestation of the legalistic approach of which Kennan was critical. Diplomacy is an ongoing process to mitigate conflicts between nations; it is the art of persuasion and compromise. The war crimes trials that followed World War II were, in contrast, guided by the illusion that international problems could be solved by legal regulations and indignation toward the violators of law. To be sure, the law does have a certain mystical power, and people tend to think it is unconditionally right to suppress barbaric conflicts with civilized law. It was Kennan's view, nevertheless, that this formula could not be automatically applied to the realities of international politics.

Furthermore, Kennan warned, the prosecution and the defense in war crimes trials are actually working within the world of international politics, not the world of law, and only experts in history and international relations will feel comfortable in this kind of environment. According to Kennan, what people believed to be a court of justice was actually an arena of international politics in which the interests of nations are negotiated as they are at a diplomatic conference, where legal professionals are of little use. Kennan brought to the surface the difficulty of handling the causes of war through legal procedures.

Kennan also pointed out that political trials of Japan would be detrimental to the interest of the Allies. He was most apprehensive about the adverse psychological effects of the trials, namely the emergence of anti-American sentiment among the Japanese people. Kennan was of the view that, even though the Japanese did not show bare animosity toward the humiliating test of endless war criminal punishment, deep inside they sympathized as compatriots with their nation's war criminals.

As a matter of fact, GHQ's Legal Section and the Japanese government were in agreement in 1949 on the following analysis. If the proceedings were seen to be unfair, the tribunal would lose its "educational value" and, moreover, it would become "harmful" to future international relations. Most of the convicted war criminals and their families were devoid of a sense of guilt; instead, they attributed their "misfortunes" to defeat in the war or to retaliation by the Allies, and deplored the powerlessness of the Japanese government. A director of the War Trials Division, Third Department of the Liaison Bureau, Prime Minister's Agency, was fearful that those war criminals and former military persons could become easy prey to ultranationalist and communist ideology.[6]

In his diary in June 1949, Ugaki Kazushige openly expressed his sympathy with war criminals:

> The execution of war criminals is quite a cruel affair. The treatment of the relatives of the military personnel, including purgees, is also extremely severe, much more so than in the case of those who had defied the imperial court at the time of the Meiji Restoration. . . . Thus, many of the Shōwa-era ronin [lordless samurai] resent the relentlessness of the Japanese state and people, and their ill thoughts have been exacerbated day by day.[7]

---

6. Ministry of Foreign Affairs, *Gaikō kiroku* [Diplomatic Record] (Diplomatic Archive of the Ministry of Foreign Affairs, 1998), 14th Disclosure.

7. Ugaki Kazushige, *Ugaki Kazushige nikki* [Ugaki Kazushige Diary], ed. Tsunoda Jun (Tokyo: Misuzu Shobō, 1971), vol. 3.

The Situation in Germany

The situation in Germany was actually quite similar. According to the November 1948 report of Telford Taylor, chief prosecutor of the US Subsequent Nuremberg Trials, people's interest in the war crimes tribunals had dwindled, and the German people were beginning to come out of their "insensible and indifferent mental state." It had been the intention of the Allies to use the war crimes trials to force a sense of guilt on the German people, which was supposed to help spread democracy in the country. But the reality did not turn out to be that simple. Taylor concluded that, of all the Occupation policies, nothing irritated the spirit or the rubbed the conscience of the German people the wrong way more than the war crime trials. When the defeated overcame their lethargy, their resentment toward the war crimes trials strengthened.

In Germany, a policy to complete war crimes trials promptly had been pursued as early as March 1947. The US military government for Germany wanted to set the completion date of the Dachau Trials (America's trials for German minor war crimes) by June 1948. Directive JCS 1779 of July 15, 1947, which shifted the goal of the German occupation to reconstruction of the country, also instructed prompt completion of the war crimes trials. Consequently, the Dachau Trials were completed before August 1948.

When the London Six-Power Conference between the US, Britain, France, and the Benelux countries recommended the creation of a democratic and federal government in the US-, British-, and French-occupied zones of the country in March 1948, the Soviet Union started the Berlin Blockade. Under these circumstances, Britain's Labour Party cabinet in March 1948 decided to terminate the German major war crimes trials on the grounds that punishment of war criminals would deprive the future generation of hope.[8]

Incidentally, leader of the Conservative Party Winston Churchill criticized the Tokyo Trial on November 12, 1948, as noted in the following extract:

> Americans are going to need Japanese cooperation in the years ahead, and at this juncture, three years after the end of the war, to hang

---

8. Irwin Cotler, ed., *Nuremberg Forty Years Later* (Montreal: MacGill-Queen's University Press, 1995).

prominent people in that country seems to him [Churchill] stupid. . . .
No ruler of a country can control the actions of his troops. On the same
theory, both Roosevelt and himself would have been executed if the
Allies had lost the war.[9]

While Churchill was the first to demand punishment of the Nazi leaders
in 1941, what he advocated was their immediate execution. The prolonged
Tokyo Trial, which had become an obstacle to "unity of the West," was loath-
some to Churchill as well as to Kennan.

Policy Shift of the United States

On May 28, 1948, an early termination of the purge of public offices and war
crimes trials in Japan was agreed upon by the British and American diplomatic authorities on the grounds that they created a poor impression and were
psychologically unjust. Based on Kennan's PPS 28, the basic policy toward
Japan in the National Security Council (NSC), NSC 13/2, was decided on
October 9, 1948. Article 18 of NSC 13/2 on war crimes trials reads as follows:

> The trial of Class A suspects is completed and the decision of the court
> is awaited. We should continue and push to an early conclusion the
> screening of all "B" and "C" suspects with a view to releasing those
> whose cases we do not intend to prosecute. Trials of the others should
> be instituted and concluded at the earliest possible date.[10]

Directive NSC 13/2 recommended early conclusion to the punitive war
crimes trial, because it hindered the stabilization of Japan and provoked
anti-American sentiment. However, the document did not give a deadline for
the completion.

At this point, American policy on the punishment of war criminals shifted
toward early termination—not a reversal of policy, but a shift toward the

---

9. Walter Millis, ed., *The Forrestal Diaries* (New York: Viking, 1951).

10. US Department of State, *FRUS: 1948, The Far East and Australasia, Vol. VI*, ed. S. Everett Gleason, Frederick Aandahl, John G. Reid, and David H. Stauffer (Washington, DC:
Government Printing Office, 1974).

concluding stage. How did these factors lead the United States to shift toward conclusion of the trials?

The primary factor, needless to say, was the international situation of the Cold War. In order to cope with this new situation, NSC 13/2 proposed a shift of US policy from defanging Japan to establishing political stability and terminating the trials.

Second, it was deemed necessary to minimize the adverse psychological effect inherent in war crimes trials—that is, the resentment of the defeated. For Kennan especially, the development of the Cold War environment was an opportunity finally to implement his long-cherished theory. He did not argue for an early conclusion of the trials because of the Cold War.

Third was the issue of the federal budget of the US, as political scientist Amakawa Akira astutely pointed out. While war crimes trials were funded from the budget allotted to the Department of War, the US Congress, with a Republican Party majority since 1947, criticized the war crimes trials because of their burden on taxpayers. Due to the single-fiscal-year budget system, the Department of War was requested to complete most war crimes trials before the end of fiscal 1948.[11] From the department's viewpoint, this budgetary obligation was much more compelling than NSC 13/2.

New Zealand's Proposal and Completion of the Class A Trial

Common sense tells us that war crimes trials held by the victors could not continue forever. In January 1948 the possibility of a second Tokyo Trial disappeared at the decision of the US government. It should be noted, however, that this was not a decision of all of the Allied Powers; in fact, Class B and C trials by Allied nations other than the United States were still ongoing. How, then, did the Allies as a whole deal with this issue of the termination of the war crimes trials?

One element was a movement inside the Far Eastern Commission (FEC) to terminate Japanese war crimes trials by the Allies. It was triggered by FEC 314, which New Zealand submitted on July 29, 1948. FEC 314 proposed that "no further trials of Japanese war criminals should be initiated in respect of

---

11. Igarashi Takeshi and Kitaoka Shinichi, eds., *Sōron, Tōkyō Saiban to wa nan datta no ka* [Contestation, What Was the Tokyo Trial] (Tokyo: Tsukiji Shokan, 1997).

offenses classified under paragraph 1(a) [crimes against peace]" (Class A clause), that "no investigation in respect of offences classified under paragraph 1(b) and 1(c) [conventional war crimes and crimes against humanity] . . . should be proceeded with after 31 December and that all trials . . . should be completed by . . . 30 June 1949" (Class B and C clause).[12]

In this document, New Zealand, informed by the opinion of the justice and prosecutor it had dispatched to Tokyo, argued that aimlessly prolonging a war crimes trial would provoke negative reactions among the Japanese people, which would be detrimental to the interest of the Allies. Therefore, New Zealand could not feel at ease until an international agreement was reached on concluding those trials. Also, because this less prominent member of the Allies had not held its own Class B and C trial, it was able to freely argue for an early completion of Class B and C war crimes trials. The method of setting a deadline for conclusion of war crimes trials had been talked about in occupied Germany since the previous year, so it is possible that New Zealand obtained pertinent information from Britain and followed suit.

In any event, this FEC 314 became the topic of FEC deliberations from October 11, 1948.

At first, only Britain, France, and the Soviet Union fully supported New Zealand's proposal, including the "Class A clause" and the "Class B and C clause." Many of the other FEC member countries found the Class B and C clause problematic, and they did not like being forced to terminate their own Class B and C trials. (The positions of Canada and India are unknown.)

In contrast, it is noteworthy that there was almost no disagreement on concluding the Class A war crimes trials. No nation demanded its own national Subsequent Class A trials. On February 24, 1949, FEC decided to continue deliberating FEC 314's Class B and C clause, and adopted only the Class A clause as FEC 314/8 with nine in favor and two (Philippines and the Soviet Union) abstentions. Its text reads as follows:

The Far Eastern Commission decides as a matter of policy that: No

---

12. FEC 314, "Trial of Japanese War Criminals New Zealand Policy Proposal," July 29, 1948, GHQ/SCAP records, National Archives and Records Administration (NARA), Archives II, College Park, Maryland, microfiche in National Diet Library, Tokyo.

further trials of Japanese war criminals should be initiated in respect of offenses classified under paragraph 1 a [crimes against peace] of the policy decision of the Far Eastern Commission [FEC 007/3].[13]

Thus, FEC 314/8 (delivered to General MacArthur on March 8, 1949) confirmed the termination of Class A Japanese war crimes through international agreement. Accordingly, on February 24, 1949, the arena of international politics known as the International Military Tribunal for the Far East was also officially closed.

"Crimes against Peace" Recede

This smooth decision to terminate Class A war crimes trials came about due to a loss of interest in further Class A indictments among the governments concerned. China's Kuomintang (KMT, the Chinese National Party) government, which had previously expressed interest, both inside and outside the FEC, in Class A indictments, had converted its policy toward termination of war crimes trials because of the escalation of the Chinese Civil War and the recapture of Yan'an by the People's Liberation Army in April 1948. The Kuomintang government could no longer afford to indict Japanese war criminals.

In the end, the Tokyo Trial became the only court in Japan in which Japanese leaders' responsibilities were pursued.

Seen from the perspective of international society as a whole, this decision to conclude Class A war crimes trials was not totally unrelated to the reduced significance of the norm of crimes against peace. The attractiveness of the criminalization of war had already waned even within the US government as early as mid-1949, to the degree that some in Washington openly questioned whether crimes against peace could be used in international society other than in trials of the defeated.

At the United Nations, work had begun immediately after the completion of the Nuremberg Trial to codify the Nuremberg principles and establish an international criminal court. Having suffered many difficulties, including

---

13. FEC 314/8, "Trial of Japanese War Criminals: Policy Decision No. 55," February 25, 1948.

failure to reach an agreement on the definition of aggression, this effort fell through in December 1954.[14]

Today, because acts of aggression are harshly condemned on moral grounds, national leaders must act very cautiously. On this point, one Japanese political scientist in 1980 highly praised the effect of the Tokyo Trial's norm, saying, "After the international military tribunal was convened and leaders were executed, it became enormously difficult to wage a war of aggression."

But is that really the case?

The tendency in the years since World War II for countries to avoid aggression as a means of solving conflict owes a lot to realistic factors such as the emergence of nuclear weapons and profits from free trade. It was the Charter of the United Nations, which banned all use of armed might except for wars of self-defense and the exercise of collective security, that was hugely influential in "changing norms."

While the two international military tribunals—Nuremberg and Tokyo—contributed to the development of international law in the realm of atrocities, their contribution regarding the deterrence of war was limited to "exceptional criminalization" in the days immediately following World War II. In my judgment, they were not very influential.

All the Trials Should Be Terminated

What remained to be settled was the termination of Class B and C war crimes trials. NSC 13/2 had authority only over American trials and did not specify the deadline for termination, which is why the international agreement on the termination of Class B and C trials would be highly significant.

Nevertheless, perhaps because of these factors, the Class B and C clause of FEC 314 met fierce resistance. Class B and C war crimes trials belonged to the sovereignty of each nation-state and were inseparable from domestic politics because they were strongly affected by emotional public opinion. It was thus in a country's national interest to continue trials until people's eagerness for the punishment of war criminals receded.

Although three years had passed since the end of the war, zeal for

---

14. See Higurashi Yoshinobu, *Tōkyō Saiban no kokusai kankei* [The Tokyo Trial and International Relations] (Tokyo: Bokutakusha, 2002).

retaliation persisted in the Philippines, the Netherlands, and Australia. At the same time, it seemed inevitable that the Yokohama War Crimes Trial would be delayed. Under these circumstances, the important issues for each nation concerned were how to deprive the Class B and C clause of its binding power, and how long to postpone the deadline for termination of the trials.

After heated exchanges over various amendment proposals, on March 31, 1949, about a month after the adoption of the Class A clause, FEC 314/15 on the Class B and C clauses was adopted by FEC. The vote was six in favor (the US, Britain, France, Australia, New Zealand, and India), one against (the Philippines), and four abstentions (China, the Soviet Union, the Netherlands, and Canada). As the vote showed, it was a close race. The text of FEC 314/15 reads as follows:

> The Far Eastern Commission makes the following recommendations to member governments of the Commission. . . . If possible, investigations in connection with offenses falling under paragraph 1 b and c [conventional war crimes and crimes against humanity] of the policy decision of the Far Eastern Commission [FEC 007/3] . . . , including such offenses alleged to have been committed by persons suspected of offenses falling under paragraph 1 a [crimes against peace] of the said policy decision, should be completed before 30 June 1949, and all trials thereof should be concluded if possible before 30 September 1949.[15]

Let us compare this FEC 314/15 (sent to MacArthur as "information" on April 1, 1949) with the original proposal submitted by New Zealand.

First, its format was downgraded from "policy decision" to "recommendation," and it was deprived of any binding power over participating countries.

Second, the deadline was postponed to September 30, 1949, and the expression "if possible" was added to allow loopholes.

Third, the phrase "such offenses [Class B and C war crimes] alleged to have been committed by" Class A suspects was intended to include cases of indicting Class A suspects for Class B and C crimes within the framework of FEC 314.

---

15. FEC 314/15, "Trial of Japanese War Criminals: Policy Decision No. 57," April 7, 1949.

Signpost to the Shift in Occupation Policies

Table 6-1 shows the status of Class B and C trials conducted by seven countries as of the early 1950s. The table was constructed on the basis of the order of completion of said trials, and it shows that Australia was the last to complete its trial. (I would like to correct the date of completion of trials in France, which I erroneously gave as 1949 in my previous publication, *Tōkyō Saiban no kokusai kankei*.)

Australians regarded the Japanese as "subhuman monsters," and animosity toward Japanese showed no sign of decreasing. Therefore, on June 5, 1950, Robert G. Menzies' Liberal Party government, which had just been formed, started a Class B and C trial on Manus Island in northeast New Guinea.

Meanwhile, the Soviet Union abruptly opened the Khabarovsk Trial on December 25, 1949, to try suspects for the case of biological weapon warfare. Only five days later, twelve defendants, including General Yamada Otozō, former commander of the Kwantung Army, were found guilty of the "preparation and use of bacteriological weapons."

Furthermore, in February 1950, the Soviet Union demanded that the British and US governments open an "international military tribunal" to try five suspects on charges of biological weapon warfare, including the emperor and Lieutenant General Ishii Shirō, a medical officer. These two governments

Table 6-1: Class B and C Trials by the Allied Countries

Country	Opening Date	Date of Completion	Major Venues of Court	Number of Defendants
United Kingdom	Jan. 20, 1946	Dec. 20, 1948	Hong Kong, Singapore, Malaysia, etc.	865
Kuomintang China	Apr. 1946	Jan. 26, 1949	Nanjing, Taiwan, Shanghai, Guangdong, etc.	517
United States	Aug. 1945	Oct. 19, 1949	Yokohama, Manila, Guam, etc.	1,344
Netherlands	Aug. 5, 1946	Dec. 24, 1949	Java, Batavia, Sumatra, etc.	995
Philippines	Aug. 1, 1947	Dec. 28, 1949	Manila	151
France	Jun. 1946	Mar. 29, 1950	Saigon (Hanoi)	181
Australia	Dec. 2, 1945	Apr. 9, 1951	Hong Kong, Singapore, Manus Island, etc.	777

Sources: Ministry of Health and Welfare, Repatriation Relief Bureau, ed., *Hikiage to engo 30-nen no ayumi* (Thirty-Year History of Repatriation and Relief), and Toyoda Kumao, *Sensō saiban yoroku* (Additional Records of the War Crimes Trials)

believed the demand to be retaliation for British and American criticism of the detention of Japanese prisoners of war in Siberia, and nothing but a ploy to divide public opinion in Japan, so they decided to ignore it.

Thus, only Britain and China had completed war crimes trials by September 30, 1949. Clearly, FEC 314/15's recommendation was powerless concerning countries such as Australia and the Soviet Union that had no intention of terminating their trials. Nonetheless, the majority of the countries did complete all the war crimes trials before the end of 1949, indicating that this recommendation was, to a certain extent, significant as a way of applying pressure for an environment amenable to concluding the war crimes trials.

The Japanese Ministry of Foreign Affairs detected in FEC 314 a major departure from punitive Occupation policy. In fact, the direction of the Occupation policy as a whole was beginning to change as can be seen in the relaxation of the US reparation policy toward Japan in the same year.

CHAPTER 7

How the Release of War Criminals Commenced

Left: Shigemitsu bidding farewell at the Sugamo Prison gate
Right: Shigemitsu bows in the direction of the imperial palace
(Kyodo News)

1. When and How

Transfer of War Criminals

Due to Australia's war crimes trial on Manus Island, the trials of the Japanese war crimes suspects were not completed until April 9, 1951. One would naturally assume that the completion of the trials marked the end of the war crimes issue.

In actuality, that was not the case. What happened was that procedures entered a phase of release of the war criminals, and the focus shifted to managerial aspects, such as detention and commutation. We now know that convicted Class A prisoners were released from Sugamo Prison during this phase. Why and how were Class A war criminals set free? The final chapters of this book will investigate this issue.

Clemency for war criminals itself was not conceived of as part of the so-called "reverse course" of US Occupation policy. Within the US government, the possibility of commutation due to good conduct had been raised as early as August 1946. The War Crime Branch of the Department of War had started studying "post-trial measures including clemency and social rehabilitation" toward the end of 1948 at the latest. The US government took these measures because it believed that, by taking steps to assist prisoners in obtaining clemency, it would enhance the people's view of the fairness of the trial, proving to them the high moral standards of a democratic country. In short, clemency was an integral part of the US war crimes trial scheme from an early stage.

The question was when and how to begin granting clemency. What triggered this issue were, once again, developments in Germany. In 1948, petition appeals from convicts of the Dachau Trials flooded American courts of justice. It should be recalled that in the Malmédy massacre case (in which, of 73 indicted, 43 were sentenced to death, 22 to life imprisonment, and 8 to imprisonment for determinate terms), torture was used to extort confessions. The Republican Party denounced the Department of War in the US Congress for this abuse.

Consequently, Secretary of War Kenneth C. Royall ordered the temporary suspension of executions in the summer of 1948, and dispatched an investigation mission led by Gordon Simpson, justice of the Texas Supreme Court, to Germany. While the report of this Simpson committee dated September 14 concluded that the Dachau Trials had been "essentially fair," it also recommended instituting a permanent clemency (commutation) plan.

Along with the clemency issues, the Department of War and the US military government for Germany also studied the issue of detention of war criminals. As a result, the War Department in 1949 came up with a method of entrusting detention of war criminals to the German and Japanese authorities within a year, while retaining its control over them. This was part of a policy to transfer the power of the Occupation authority to the Japanese government—a "de facto peace" policy to cut the cost of the Occupation.

When sounded out by the Department of War, the concerned sections of GHQ on May 16, 1949, concurred with the idea of entrusting detention of war criminals to the Japanese side. More noteworthy, however, was the view of the Judge Advocate Section (JAS) of the General Headquarters of the Far East Command that, since "the question of clemency was apparently under consideration in the US Zone in Germany," a similar measure for the Japanese war criminals should also be explored. In the end, sections of GHQ reached agreement that "the question of clemency was a problem that should be discussed at some other time and made the subject of a separate study for the Chief of Staff, and that it was a problem, which could be determined at the SCAP level." Within ten days of this agreement, GHQ agreed that Class A convicts should be transferred to detention by the Japanese authorities in the near future.[1]

---

1. Government Section (GS) Papers, GHQ/SCAP records, National Archives and Records Administration (NARA), Archives II: RG 331, College Park, Maryland, microfiche in Modern Japanese Political History Materials Room (Kensei Shiryōshitsu), National Diet Library, Tokyo.

Thus, the US Department of War created a plan to transfer war criminals with which the US military government for Germany, GHQ, and the US Departments of State and Justice agreed. The high cost of the detention of war criminals was a decisive factor. Nevertheless, the transfer of war criminals was never realized either in Japan or Germany before the sovereignty of both nations was restored. General Thomas T. Handy, commander-in-chief, US European Command, remarked in February 1950 that it would be unwise to entrust important figures of the Third Reich to West Germany because it was highly dubious whether the German people really regarded these prisoners as war criminals. On the basis of these observations, Handy insisted that the Occupation forces supervise war criminals. His argument dissuaded the War Department from following through on the policy.

Commutation System in Germany

Let us turn to the issue of commutation.

As the Cold War in Europe became increasingly fierce, the Federal Republic of Germany (West Germany) was formally founded on September 7, 1949, integrating the occupation zones of the respective Western powers. The first cabinet of Konrad Adenauer was formed on September 20, 1949. This was accompanied by a shift in the style of occupation from military government to civil government. Henry Stimson's right-hand man, John McCloy, who had been president of the World Bank, was appointed as US high commissioner. This office was under the jurisdiction of the State Department.

These developments made jurisdiction over German war criminals somewhat complicated.

First, the responsibility for supervision of major war criminals convicted by the Nuremberg Trial—who were detained at Spandau Prison in West Berlin under the joint management of four major Allied Powers—was transferred from the military governor of the American occupation zone to the high commissioner. In Washington, DC, responsibility was transferred from the secretary of war to the secretary of state. Furthermore, the US high commissioner shared the responsibility with Britain, France, and the Soviet Union.

Second, major war criminals of the Subsequent Nuremberg Trials by the US also came under the jurisdiction of the high commissioner. These prisoners were detained at the US-controlled Landsberg Prison.

Third, the commander-in-chief, US European Command, and the secretary of war continued to exercise jurisdiction over minor war criminals from the Dachau Trials. The Dachau-related prisoners were the dominant majority at Landsberg Prison.

In response to the report of the Simpson committee and pressure by the US Congress, a "good-conduct credit" system was introduced on December 20, 1949. This merit system targeted prisoners with fixed terms at Landsberg Prison who had been convicted by the Dachau Trials and the Subsequent Nuremberg Trials. If a prisoner complied with all the rules, and if he was judged to be of good attitude, five days per month would be reduced from his prison sentence. That would be sixty days per year. If the term of imprisonment was six years, 360 days (sixty days times six years)—nearly a year—would be struck off from his prison term. In short, a de facto commutation system was adopted.

Furthermore, a body was created to screen individual prisoners and advise whether commutation should be granted. According to historian John Mendelsohn, American trials tended to hand down a wide variety of sentences for the same crime. It was decided that the screening of individual prisoners would be conducted by the commander-in-chief, United States European Command, and the high commissioner separately. Accordingly, General Handy of the US European Command established a War Crimes Modification Board (composed of five high-ranking military officers) in November 1949 for the Dachau Trials convicts. John McCloy, US high commissioner, set up the War Criminal Clemency Advisory Board (composed of three civilians) in March 1950 for the Subsequent Nuremberg Trials convicts. While Handy rejected most of the recommendations from the War Crimes Modification Board, McCloy approved most of what the War Criminal Clemency Advisory Board recommended.[2]

McCloy announced the final decision on clemency on January 31, 1951. Declaring that he had tried to mitigate "justice" with "mercy," he reduced ten of the fifteen death sentences to life imprisonment. The remaining five were

---

2. John Mendelsohn, "War Crimes Trials and Clemency in Germany and Japan," in *Americans as Proconsuls: United States Military Government in Germany and Japan, 1944–1952*, ed. Robert Wolfe (Carbondale: Southern Illinois University Press, 1984).

executed as sentenced. McCloy also granted commutation to sixty-four out of the total seventy-four prisoners with life and fixed-term sentences.

Adenauer's Position

These commutations provoked a fierce backlash from Jewish organizations as well as the populations of the Allied powers. Whereas such major American newspapers as the *New York Times* and the *Washington Post* expressed understanding, saying that as unpleasant as the decision might be, it was probably desirable to make West Germany a member of the Western camp.

West Germany as a whole welcomed the decision. According to Kai Bird, "No other decision McCloy made in his years in Germany aroused greater furor than this mass clemency. Most Germans strongly approved the commutation of sentences and criticized the decision to hang five of the prisoners, all of whom had directly participated in mass murders. Adenauer himself called upon McCloy to reconsider the executions."

The McCloy family was troubled by threats, including a promise to take revenge on their children if the executions were conducted. A panicked Mrs. McCloy felt called upon to express her sympathy to the war criminals.[3] McCloy, thus, experienced tremendous pressure from German society.

If left unattended, this episode would have tarnished West Germany's image terribly. Therefore, Adenauer had to stress the "[self-]reflection of the German people" to the press in March 1951. He also told McCloy that those who had violated international humanitarian law and the laws of war (that is, those responsible for atrocities) did not deserve sympathy or mercy, and the federal government would not defend them. At the same time, Adenauer stressed that there were only a handful of war criminals, and they would not affect the honor of the Reichswehr, the unified German defense force.[4]

While the Nazi's atrocities were inexcusable, German honor had to be defended. This was Adenauer's position, and it was highly subtle.

M. Cherif Bassiouni observed that, "unlike in Germany, where those accused and convicted of war crimes became, for the most part, pariahs in

---

3. Kai Bird, *The Chairman: John J. McCloy* (New York: Simon & Schuster, 1992).
4. Office of the Judge Advocate General (JAG), *War Crimes Branch Papers: General and Administrative Records 1944–1949*, NARA, II: RG 153, College Park, Maryland.

their society, the Japanese did not view such persons as criminals but as victims. For the Japanese, the trials were victors' vengeance couched in terms of Victors' Justice."[5] In light of the realities in Germany, this observation seems to have been a little too careless. Having said that, I do not intend to simplify the situation by saying that Germany and Japan were identical. Beyond doubt, Germany, which had been exposed to the severity of international politics, dealt with war crime issues much more skillfully than Japan. However, to stress only the differences between the two nations, ignoring changes over time and the true state of affairs, would be akin to the idolization of Germany in prewar Japan.

I hold the view that there were more commonalities than differences in the responses of Japan and Germany into the 1950s. I submit that the backlash was the ordinary impact of war crimes trials on the defeated.

Christmas Present from MacArthur

When the ripples of US policies toward Germany were felt in Japan, the process of releasing war criminals began. On December 19, 1949, two months after the conclusion of the Yokohama Trials, Major General Edward Almond, chief of staff, GHQ, instructed the Legal Section to prepare a plan to commute the sentences of all the war criminals. Almond instructed that, following the German precedent, the good-conduct credit and confinement credit (to include days of pre-sentencing confinement in the term of imprisonment) of the US federal law system should be applied. Almond also added that MacArthur hoped for an early implementation of these measures.

In three days, the Legal Section replied to Almond that it had been studying a comprehensive clemency system including the introduction of parole, which was not part of the policy applied to German war criminals. Anyone could have thought of the parole. For instance, when Kimura Shiroshichi, director of the Foreign Ministry's Liaison Bureau, met Alva C. Carpenter, chief of GHQ's Legal Section, and several others in October 1949, Kimura sounded out Carpenter about whether GHQ intended to adopt the parole system employed in the US. On that occasion, Carpenter fended off the

---

5. Jackson N. Maogoto, *War Crimes and Realpolitik* (London: Lynne Rienner Publishers, 2004).

Left: Class B and C war criminals released
Right: A released prisoner picking up his child after a long separation
(Kyodo News)

question, saying the parole system could not be applied to war criminals because it called for probation. GHQ told Kimura that it would perhaps not be applied until the signing of a peace treaty, considering how difficult it would be to achieve an agreement among the nations concerned.

It appears that GHQ decided to introduce parole due to MacArthur's positive attitude toward the release of war criminals, as well as the need to prevent overcrowding at Sugamo Prison due to the increasing number of prisoners returning home from abroad. In fact, MacArthur started taking action before the completion of the Legal Section's plan. On December 24, 1949, he instructed the commanding general of the Eighth Army to implement commutation based on good-conduct credit and confinement credit in order to launch a prompt commutation. The press release issued on December 25 reads as follows:

> General MacArthur announced today that Japanese war criminals serving less than life sentences in Sugamo Prison will be entitled to reductions in sentences for good conduct while in confinement. The

announcement also stated that a parole system is under study which will be applicable to all prisoners serving sentences including life sentences. Today's statement will result in the immediate release of approximately 46 prisoners who have been serving four years or less for minor war crimes. Under the new policy, war criminals sentenced to less than life terms will receive credit for all pre-trial confinement.[6]

It was, so to speak, a Christmas present from MacArthur.

Show of "Magnanimity"

Thus, the good-conduct credit (a reduction of five to ten days per month depending on the prison term) as well as the confinement credit were applied to those war criminals not facing life imprisonment. The future institution of a parole system was also announced.

While the good-conduct credit applied in Germany reduced prison terms by five days per month across the board, GHQ's system reduced prison terms by five to ten days. In the case of a prisoner whose prison term was longer than half a year but shorter than a year, for instance, five days per month were deducted from the prison term, making a 60-day commutation, which was the same as in Germany. In the case of a prisoner whose prison term was more than ten years, however, ten days per month, or 120 days per year, would be deducted, which would be double the commutation for a German prisoner with the same prison term. (Influenced by this Tokyo system, the good-conduct credit in Germany was revised on August 25, 1950, to a ten-day-per-month commutation.)

Before this system was adopted, the situation at Sugamo Prison was such that Kido Kōichi lamented, "Early this morning, four prisoners were executed. . . . It has already been four years since the end of the war. I wonder why they still have to continue this capital punishment."[7] Thus, it was only

---

6. Press release, December 24, 1949, Legal Section (LS) Papers, GHQ/SCAP records, National Archives and Records Administration (NARA), Archives II: RG 331, College Park, Maryland, microfiche in Modern Japanese Political History Materials Room (Kensei Shiryōshitsu), National Diet Library, Tokyo.

7. *Kido Kōichi kankei monjo* [Documents Related to Kido Kōichi], in *Kido-ke monjo* [Kido Family Documents], microfilm, Chiba National Museum of Japanese History, August 20, 1949.

natural for the prisoners to see some hope in this newly instituted commuta-tion system. The last execution at Sugamo Prison was on April 7, 1950.

One may wonder why MacArthur was so positive regarding the release of war criminals. When MacArthur conferred with President Harry Truman and others on Wake Island in the North Pacific on October 15, 1950, in the middle of the Korean War, he said, "Don't touch the (North Korean) war criminals. It gets nowhere. You should leave it to the local commanders. Both the Nuremberg trials and the Tokyo Trial were absolutely no deterrent."[8] Gravely concerned about the adverse effect of the prolongation of the war crimes trial, MacArthur intended to demonstrate his "magnanimity" to the Japanese people with an early release of war criminals.

Incidentally, unlike the Nuremberg Trial, GHQ did not publish the records of the Tokyo Trial. When the Soviet Union published the Tokyo Trial record in Russian, some in Britain and the US felt pressure to publish an English version. This spurred the US War Department to decide in May 1950 to publish such basic documents as the majority judgment, separate opinions, and indictment (with the exception of the exhibits and court proceedings). Having concurred with this decision once, GHQ, however, abruptly changed its attitude and declared on May 22 that publication of the trial record would hardly present any intrinsic benefit of its own. GHQ also opposed publica-tion of the record in its May 29 telegram, citing budgetary problems.

Because these telegrams regarding GHQ's decision against publication of the trial record had been issued before the eruption of the Korean War on June 25, the turmoil on the Korean Peninsula could not have been the real reason for the decision, while it might have provided an excuse for ex post facto justification. In my view, it was the combination of MacArthur's low estimate of the Tokyo Trial and budgetary constraints that led to the collapse of the plan to publish the record of the Tokyo Trial.

Launching of the Parole System

The Supreme Commander for the Allied Powers (SCAP) issued Circular No. 5, Clemency for War Criminals, dated March 7, 1950. It called for the

---

8. Ushida Kumi, trans., "Uēkutō kaidanroku" [Record of the Discussion on Wake Island], *Seiron* 417 (December 2006).

creation of a uniform system of reducing the sentences and parole of all individuals confined in Sugamo (encompassing commutation as well as parole). The dominant characteristic of this system was adoption of American-style parole.

Let us examine its details. The newly established Parole Board (composed of three members chaired by George Hagen, director of the Prosecution Division of GHQ's Legal Section) examined individual prisoners' trial records, behavior during confinement, age, health, and other factors. Depending on the results of these examinations, the Parole Board would recommend that SCAP grant parole to particular prisoners. It was the prerogative of SCAP to make the final decision on whether to grant parole or not. Once a prisoner with a prison term of less than forty-four years had served one-third of his term of imprisonment, he was eligible to apply for parole. Prisoners serving life sentences or prison terms longer than 45 years were eligible for parole after serving fifteen years. (Incidentally, the conditions for parole stipulated by Article 28 of the Criminal Law of Japan are having served one-third of a sentence in the case of those with limited prison terms, and having served ten years in the case of life imprisonment.)

Article 1 of Circular No. 5 stipulated that commutation and parole would be granted to "all war prisoners now or hereafter serving prison terms in Japan."[9] This means, first, that these allowances would also be granted to Class A prisoners. And, second, that war criminals sentenced by courts of nations other than the US would also be eligible if they had served prison terms in Sugamo Prison. In fact, when one of the governments concerned requested the transfer of war criminals to Japan, GHQ asked that government to acknowledge that these prisoners would go under the full jurisdiction of MacArthur and, as a corollary, be subject not only to detention but also to clemency. In this connection, while the Philippines and Australia detained Class B and C Japanese prisoners abroad even after the effective date of the peace treaty, all the Class B and C prisoners that Australia repatriated to Japan after August 8, 1953, served their terms at Sugamo Prison.

In contrast, as of March 1950, in Germany the parole system was still

---

9. Legal Section (LS) Papers, GHQ/SCAP records, microfiche in National Diet Library, Tokyo.

"under consideration." In other words, at that point, the clemency policy in Japan had already overtaken that in Germany.

It should be noted, however, that the position of GHQ was the "gradualist (judicial solution) approach to release." This position emphasized a gradual progression toward granting commutation and parole completely within the judicial framework.

On the other hand, there was the "radicalist (political solution) approach to release." For instance, American career diplomat William J. Sebald, chief of the Diplomatic Section of GHQ, had agreed with the Japanese request for amnesty, and insisted on the "radicalist approach to release," which was a political rather than a judicial solution, including prompt mass amnesty and pardons.

However, GHQ's Legal Section strongly opposed political amnesty because wiping away "crimes of the past" would reduce the value of the war crimes trial.

The issuance of Circular No. 5 was a unilateral action on the part of the US, which had not sent prior notice even to Britain. Only Kuomintang China and the Soviet Union, however, officially protested this act in the FEC. The Kuomintang government representative complained that MacArthur was "not in a position to grant parole to those prisoners [Class A war criminals] without authorization and direction from the Commission [FEC]."

The Soviet Union, with Shigemitsu Mamoru in mind, denounced the illegality of Circular No. 5 in May 1950, saying that GHQ was attempting to liberate Japanese major war criminals from the sentences decided by verdict of the international tribunal. In response, the US in June contended:

> [T]he parole system . . . does not in any way involve a modification, that is, a reduction or alteration of any sentence imposed by a war crimes tribunal. . . . [The] parole system merely prescribed one aspect of the administrative methods which are employed and constitute the practice in enlightened democratic countries.[10]

---

10. FEC 314/21, "US statement of 18 May 1950 regarding Parole of War Criminals," May 18, 1950.

Here Come the Celebrities

On May 1, the first parole was granted. Class B and C prisoners at Sugamo Prison overestimated Circular No. 5, and were optimistic about their future. The same was true for Class A prisoners, as represented by Kaya Okinori, who wrote in his diary as follows:

> Mr. Shigemitsu will be paroled toward the end of this month, while Tōgō is rumored to be given parole toward the end of this year. Although other Class A prisoners under life imprisonment are required to have served fifteen years before becoming eligible for parole, the fact of the matter is that parole is granted quite promptly. I heard this good news should be spread to all the inmates.[11]

According to Kido Kōichi, the general feeling among the imprisoned at Sugamo Prison was one of doubt that "the punitive policy toward our war criminals would go for nothing now that the world has been under tremendous stress due to the Korean War."[12]

The optimistic mood, however, was short-lived. Screening by GHQ's Parole Board turned out to be much more stringent than expected, betraying the hope of the prisoners. In fact, it was the Japanese attitude that was behind the unexpected strictness. As the Parole Board's chairman, Hagen once complained to the Japanese side about the treatment accorded to released prisoners. In Hagen's view, former Sugamo prisoners were treated with excessive indulgence to the extent that the Demobilization Bureau of the Repatriation Relief Agency, which had strong ties with the former Japanese military, went as far as organizing welcoming parties and other fêtes for a large number of released war criminals.[13]

As demonstrated by such special treatment, the Japanese authorities did not treat war criminals as "ordinary criminals," so the Parole Board decided to be strict in order to defend the "legitimacy of the trials." The US, the victor, adhered to the "gradualist approach to release," which was a judicial solution,

---

11. Kaya Okinori, *Uzu no naka* [Inside the Whirlpool] (Private compilation, 1979).
12. *Kido Kōichi kankei monjo*, December 31, 1950
13. Legal Section (LS) Papers, GHQ/SCAP records.

War criminals enjoying a sumo match
Seated in the front row, from left: Shimada, Ōshima, Satō, Suzuki, Kido, and Hata
(Kyodo News)

in order to defend the "justice" and "legitimacy" of the Allied war crimes trials.

Nevertheless, measures to appease prisoners were attempted after the issuance of Circular No. 5, including improvement in the treatment of prisoners at Sugamo Prison. In a letter addressed to his wife, Kido wrote, "Lately, they often serve Japanese food. The other day, I savored a Japanese breakfast including miso soup with tofu, dried seaweed, pickled plum, and bancha tea for the first time in a long while. They stopped serving cheese, too."[14] A half year later, Kido wrote, "We enjoyed entertainment again today, and I had a big laugh at Yanagiya Kosan's *rakugo*, the Swing Combi, and others. Since star entertainers have come to entertain us, I think I have seen and heard more attractions than when I was not in prison."[15]

In fact, after the signing of the peace treaty, such celebrities as Fujiyama Ichirō, Misora Hibari, Hasegawa Kazuo, Tatsumi Ryūtarō, Yanagiya Kingorō, and Ichikawa Ennosuke II (Ichikawa Enō I), sumo grand champions including Chiyonoyama and Tochinishiki, and professional baseball players such

14. *Kido Kōichi kankei monjo*, May 1, 1950.
15. *Kido Kōichi kankei monjo*, January 14, 1951.

as Chiba Shigeru, visited Sugamo Prison to entertain war criminals. Araki Sadao coolly concluded that the main audience for those entertainers were Class B and C prisoners. That may be so, but those entertainers also served as evidence of the Japanese people's sympathy with war criminals. Such a rush of celebrities would certainly not have occurred if prisoners had been seen as atrocious fiends. This was a phenomenon that symbolized how Japanese society at the time saw war criminals.

Parole of Shigemitsu Mamoru

As of September 1949, some grimly observed that "in light of international relations, the handling of Class A war criminals [commutation, etc.] would be more difficult than Class B and C."[16] The reference to international relations implies that this must have been an observation with the Soviet's opposition in mind.

Nevertheless, GHQ's parole system also applied to the Class A war criminals. Because most of the Class A prisoners had been sentenced to life imprisonment, they would have had to serve fifteen years in prison to become eligible for parole, which means that they would have had to wait until 1960 or later. And the good-conduct credit was not to be applied to those with life imprisonment. Therefore, the only Class A prisoners eligible for parole for the time being were Tōgō Shigenori (sentenced to twenty years) and Shigemitsu Mamoru (sentenced to seven years). Incidentally, it should be added that Tōgō died of illness in July 1950.

Shigemitsu applied for parole in March 1950 together with sixty-seven Class B and C prisoners. He wrote as follows in his diary regarding the hearing conducted on October 31:

> This is a courtroom, complete with the witness stand and gallery seats. . . .
> Hagen: The Parole Board was not interested in anything other than the prosecutor's Count 55 on ill treatment of prisoners of war. . . .
> Shigemitsu:The responsibility for the prisoners of war management lay

---

16. Shigemitsu Mamoru, *Sugamo nikki* [Sugamo Diary] (Tokyo: Bungeishunjū Shinsha, 1953), vol. 2.

with the military, and that the Ministry of Foreign Affairs
had no authority over this issue. . . .

Hagen: What did you intend to do after you obtained parole?[17]

After the hearing, the Parole Board decided to grant parole to Shigemitsu on
November 2. The instruction to parole Shigemitsu was issued to the commander of the US Eighth Army on November 10.

Normally, Shigemitsu would have completed his full sentence in April
1953. Even with the good-conduct credit, he would not have been released
from prison until November 1951. Thanks to the newly instituted parole system, however, he was able to leave Sugamo one year earlier on November 21,
1950. On that particular day, Shigemitsu wrote as follows in his diary:

> When the main gate opened, newspaper photographers, news agency
> correspondents, radio broadcasters rushed in. . . . The only thing I
> could do was murmur brief words of thanks through a microphone and
> nothing more, unable to move in the crowd of people. . . . When my car
> started moving, I saw a lot of people leaning out of windows of the main
> building of Sugamo Prison to send me off with applause. . . . It was at this
> moment that I felt deep in my heart that I was released from the prison.[18]

In July 1951, after Shigemitsu was paroled, Murray Grey of the Parole Board
told Shigemitsu that, having completed his sentence, he would be completely
free and GHQ would welcome it if he became prime minister of Japan
or anything else he wished to be.[19] Shigemitsu completed his sentence on
November 7, 1951. After the clearing of the purge in public offices in March
1952, he became president of the Kaishintō party, was elected to the House
of Representatives, and assumed the posts of foreign minister and deputy
prime minister of the Hatoyama Cabinet in December 1954. While in office,
he engaged in the war criminal release issue.

---

17. Shigemitsu, *Sugamo nikki*.

18. Shigemitsu, *Sugamo nikki*.

19. Itō Takashi et al., eds., *Shigemitsu Mamoru shuki* [Shigemitsu Mamoru's Personal
Notes] (Tokyo: Chūōkōronsha, 1988), vol. 2.

2. War Criminal Clause in the San Francisco Peace Treaty

Prison without Bars

Nishimura Kumao, former head of the Treaty Bureau of the Ministry of Foreign Affairs, looked back on the days when Japan was under the Occupation as follows:

> On top of being deprived of all of our freedoms, we were constantly instructed to do this that way and that this way. We never knew when and how we would be punished. It is not fun to be told to do something, even if it is a good thing. I cannot forget those six years of suffering when both the government and each and every one of the Japanese people suffered anxiety.

And he went on to describe the Occupation days as a "prison without bars," borrowing an expression from another diplomat.[20]

No matter how generous the Occupation forces might have been, the reality of being a country under occupation was harsh. The longer the Occupation continued, the greater the sense of humiliation became. Therefore, from the late 1940s to the early 1950s, the Japanese ardently hoped to bring the Allied Occupation to a close.

How to manage war criminals and clemency for them after Japan regained its sovereignty remained an important issue for Japan and the Allies. Article 11 of the San Francisco Treaty (the war criminals clause) was the result of deliberations on this matter. Let us next consider how this article came about.

On September 14, 1950, President Truman announced that he had instructed the US State Department to start unofficial negotiations on the peace treaty with Japan with twelve members of the Far Eastern Commission (eleven original members plus Pakistan, which had separated itself from India to become an independent nation). With this development, the signing of a peace treaty with Japan finally became a realistic prospect.

In response, a team of officials at the Ministry of Foreign Affairs, centered around Director of the Treaty Bureau Nishimura urgently prepared an action

---

20. Etō Jun, *Mō hitotsu no sengo* [Another Postwar Era] (Tokyo: Kodansha, 1978).

policy ("Task A"), and submitted it to Prime Minister Yoshida on October 5. Dated October 4, 1950, Task A read, "Requests that Our Government Should Submit Regarding the US Draft of the Peace Treaty with Japan." Three points were listed: termination of further indictment of war criminals, a request for amnesty of imprisoned war criminals, and the hope that the US would leave the execution of sentences to the Japanese government after the peace treaty came into effect.[21] Task A was turned down by Yoshida, but by making an utterly unacceptable request for amnesty, the Treaty Bureau attempted to draw out favorable conditions for Japan from the US. According to Nishimura, Foreign Ministry officials at that time were obsessed with a fear of the "hard peace" to come.

The State Department's Draft

What John Foster Dulles, who had become consultant to the secretary of state in charge of the peace treaty with Japan in May 1950, aimed at was, however, not a "hard peace" but a "soft peace." The seven principles of the peace treaty with Japan that the State Department released to the press on November 24 that year also clearly announced its "soft peace" policy. How then was the war criminal issue to be handled within this basic policy? The original thinking of the State Department can be found in the article on war criminals (Article 14) of the peace treaty draft compiled on August 9, 1950, after the outbreak of the Korean War, by Dulles and John Allison, chief of the Northeast Asian Affairs Division. The draft read:

> 14. Japan will respect the sentences imposed by military tribunals of the Allied and Associated Powers on persons who are incarcerated in Japan. The power to grant clemency, reduce sentences, parole and pardon may be exercised by Japan only with the approval of the Government or Governments which imposed the sentence in each instance. In the case of the persons sentenced by the International Military Tribunal for the

---

21. Ministry of Foreign Affairs, Treaties Bureau, Legal Affairs Division, ed., *Heiwa Jōyaku no teiketsu ni kansuru chōsho* [Protocol of the Signing of the Peace Treaty] (Diplomatic Archive of the Ministry of Foreign Affairs, 1967), vol. 3. *Chōsho* hereafter.

Far East, such power may be exercised by Japan upon the approval of a majority of the Governments represented on the Tribunal.[22]

First, "respect the sentences imposed by military tribunals" was a clause that imposed on the Japanese side the duty for carrying out sentences. While it appeared that, at that stage, it did not necessarily imply "approval of judgments" in the future, the phrase "respect the sentences" indicates the intention to protect the "legitimacy of the trials."

Second, Article 14 gave Japan the power to grant clemency "only with the approval of the Government or Governments which imposed the sentence." Moreover, it also implied the possibility of "pardon," which in this case was synonymous with amnesty. If the truth be told, the US State Department had contemplated the future provision to Japan of comprehensive authority for clemency even before this draft.

It should also be recalled that the "Borton draft" of August 1947 (see chapter 6, section 3) had given all authority for clemency to the Allies; the Japanese side had not been allowed to intervene. As the Cold War grew increasingly intense, however, the State Department came to value relations with Japan highly and decided to give Japan considerably more authority.

Now let us look at the draft dated September 11, 1950. First of all, the entire first sentence—"Japan will respect the sentences imposed by military tribunals of the Allied and Associated Powers on persons who are incarcerated in Japan"—was deleted. It was, perhaps, an attempt to obscure Japan's war responsibility as part of a "soft peace." The drafter might also have decided that the intended result could be obtained without this sentence.

Second, lest the wording be criticized for being too tolerant toward Japan, the sentence beginning "power to grant clemency" was revised to read "may be exercised jointly by Japan and the Government or Governments which imposed the sentence." As the State Department went on to negotiate with the Allies and consult with the US Senate Foreign Relations Committee, Japan's "power" in this regard became increasingly limited.

In October 1950, the State Department instructed the Japan side to allow

---

22. US Department of State, *FRUS: 1950, East Asia and the Pacific, Volume VI*, ed. Neal H. Peterson et al. (Washington, DC: Government Printing Office, 1976).

the Japanese government to depurge. At the same time, it affirmed that the execution of sentences on war criminals would be maintained even after the conclusion of the peace treaty. From the viewpoint of the Allies, a judicial court judgment carried much more weight than an administrative sanction. It was unthinkable to give Japanese war criminals political amnesty (in line with the "radicalist approach to release") because that would wipe out their past crimes.

Impact of the War Guilt Clause

More threatening to a "soft peace" was Britain's draft of the peace treaty. Borrowing from the preamble of the peace treaty with Italy (February 1947), the British draft introduced an article on Japan's responsibility for aggressive war. Having learned of this in April 1951 from the US, Prime Minister Yoshida and high-ranking officials at the Ministry of Foreign Affairs were stunned.

As of early January 1951, Britain had in fact attached more importance to unity in the Western camp, believing that communism was a much more realistic threat than resurgence of Japan's militarism. It was due to anti-Japanese sentiment among the British people and the pressure from the Commonwealth countries that Britain, nevertheless, included the "war guilt clause" in its peace treaty draft.

In particular, Australia and New Zealand regarded the Potsdam Declaration and the judgment of the International Military Tribunal for the Far East as evidence of Japan's war responsibility, as they had stressed to Dulles in February 1951. It was unthinkable for these two nations to give Japan even a portion of the power to grant clemency. From their viewpoint, what was truly needed was a long-term guarantee against the resurgence of Japanese militarism.

The British provisional draft dated April 20, 1951, provided the "war guilt clause" in its preamble as follows:

> Whereas Japan under the militaristic regime became a party to the Tripartite Pact with Germany and Italy, undertook a war of aggression and thereby provoked a state of war with all the Allied and Associated Powers and with other United Nations, and bears her share of responsibility for the war.

Also, the article on war criminals (Article 21) stipulated as follows:

Japan undertakes to accept the judgments and carry out the orders of the International Military Tribunal for the Far East, and of all other duly constituted Allied War Crimes Courts both within and outside Japan, respecting convictions and sentences imposed upon Japanese nationals. The power to grant clemency, reduction of sentences, and parole, shall, in the case of Japanese nationals sentenced by the International Military Tribunal for the Far East, be exercised jointly by the Government of Japan and a majority of the Governments represented on the Tribunal; and in the case of war criminals sentenced by any other of the above-mentioned War Crimes Courts and undergoing punishment in Japan, shall be exercised jointly by the Government of Japan and the Government or Governments which constituted the Courts having imposed the sentences in each instance.[23]

The latter half of the article differed only slightly from the American draft, except for the deletion of "pardon," the inclusion of which could lead to the release of all convicted war criminals. The British draft's uniqueness lay in the stipulation of the first half that Japan "undertakes to accept the judgment." Most of all, it was an effective stipulation that would oblige Japan to carry out the sentences of the Tokyo Trial. For the British Commonwealth countries, particularly Australia and New Zealand, carrying out the sentences was a matter of course. The stipulation for Japan to "accept the judgments" shared the same value with the war guilt clause, and it aimed at making Japan recognize the legitimacy of the Tokyo Trial as well as Japan's war responsibility.

Finalization of Article 11 of the Treaty of Peace with Japan

Fully aware of Japan's anxiety, the US strongly opposed the proposed war guilt clause, and negotiated with Britain to accomplish a "non-punitive" peace treaty. The result was a US-Britain joint draft treaty dated June 14, 1951. As John Allison told Iguchi Sadao, vice-minister for foreign affairs, on June 25 during his visit to Japan, the war guilt clause was the first to be struck out, followed by the reference to pardon. I see the stipulation to "accept the

---

23. Robin Kay, ed., *Documents on New Zealand External Relations, Vol. 3: The Anzus Pact and the Treaty of Peace with Japan* (Wellington: Government Printer, 1985).

judgments," which Britain insisted on adding, as a substantial quid pro quo.

The US accepted the stipulation "accept the judgments" after it struck out the strongly worded "undertakes to." With the elimination of the accusatory war guilt clause, the stipulation that Japan must "accept the judgments," which was connected to it, would also be diluted, allowing for more flexible interpretations. The US must have found it acceptable to make a compromise on that.

As for the "power to grant clemency," the hitherto existing "[to be] exercised jointly by Japan and the Government or Governments which imposed the sentence" was also reworded so that the power to decide clemency was monopolized by the Allies, and Japan's power was downgraded to that of recommendation.[24] Thus was accomplished a compromise between Britain and the US.

Article 11 of the final version of the Peace Treaty with Japan (commonly known as the San Francisco Peace Treaty; signed on September 8, 1951) reads as follows:

> Japan accepts the judgments of the International Military Tribunal for the Far East and of other Allied War Crimes Courts both within and outside Japan, and will carry out the sentences imposed thereby upon Japanese nationals imprisoned in Japan. The power to grant clemency, to reduce sentences and to parole with respect to such prisoners may not be exercised except on the decision of the Government or Governments which imposed the sentence in each instance, and on recommendation of Japan. In the case of persons sentenced by the International Military Tribunal for the Far East, such power may not be exercised except on the decision of a majority of the Governments represented on the Tribunal, and on the recommendation of Japan.

It is worth noting that, in early 1952, the US, Britain, and France sounded out the intentions of Chancellor Konrad Adenauer of West Germany, informing him that if West Germany accepted the judgments of the war crimes trials

---

24. Ministry of Foreign Affairs, *Gaikō kiroku* [Diplomatic Record] (Diplomatic Archive of the Ministry of Foreign Affairs, 1982), 7th Disclosure.

and agreed to carry out the sentences, the Allies were prepared to transfer the power of detention of war criminals to the Bundesrepublik.[25] It was a statement modeled on the peace treaty with Japan. It must have been judged to be sufficient to request the German side to carry out the sentences. The Allies deliberately added the acceptance of judgments in order to prevent West Germany from raising an objection to the legitimacy of the Allied trials.[26]

On the Stipulation Regarding Acceptance of Judgments

Article 11 of the peace treaty can be divided, roughly, into the first half on acceptance of judgments, and the latter half on power over clemency. What can be confirmed from the first half is that Japan was obliged to accept the judgments of the Tokyo Trial and Class B and C war crimes trials, and to carry out the sentences of prisoners detained in Japan even after the restoration of its sovereignty.

While the legal grounds for the trials of Japanese war criminals derived from Article 10 of the Potsdam Declaration, subsequent concrete policies were decided at the discretion of the Allied Powers. Unlike the purge from public offices, which was later converted to Japan's domestic law, the Allied war crimes trial was a sanctuary in which the Japanese government could not interfere. Article 11 of the San Francisco Peace Treaty had the function of making the Japanese government confirm the state of these trials in international law.

The wording of this article was particularly obscure, however, allowing a variety of interpretations. A treaty is interpreted on the basis of "what the countries concerned (the signatories) want to accomplish." Because both Japan and the US did not want to confirm an exact interpretation of Article 11, no official interpretation of the first half of this article exists, allowing the following two interpretation problems.

One had to do with "mistranslation." Because the Ministry of Foreign Affairs had translated "judgments" as *saiban* (trials) instead of *hanketsu* (judgments), right-wingers in Japan contended that it appeared as if Japan had accepted the trial in its entirety. They insisted that Japan had only

---

25. US Department of State, *FRUS: 1952–1954, Western European Security, Volume V*, ed. John A. Bernbaum et al. (1983).

26. Subsequently, West Germany had not officially accepted the judgments of war crimes trials by treaty with the Allied Powers.

accepted the judgments, which were "the results or part of the trials." Conversely, some left-wingers suspected that the Foreign Ministry had deliberately used *saiban* in order to soften the impression of a guilty verdict, which use of the word *hanketsu* might have projected.

What, then, does this *saiban* that appears in the Foreign Ministry's translation mean? At the Committee on the Cabinet of the House of Representatives on August 19, 1986, Chief Cabinet Secretary Gotōda Masaharu (of the Nakasone Cabinet) presented the government view on Article 11 of the San Francisco Peace Treaty as follows: "It is a fact that the Japanese government, in its relations with countries in the world, has accepted this *Kyokuto saiban* [Tokyo Trial]. . . . Therefore, we have also accepted the results of this trial."

Gotōda's reply was already ambiguous, but subsequent government views became even more cryptic. For instance, in response to a written question submitted to the cabinet by Noda Yoshihiko, a Minshutō member of the House of Representatives and later prime minister, on October 17, 2005, the government's written reply from the Koizumi Cabinet only repeated that, as written in Article 11 of the peace treaty, Japan had accepted the trial but would not elaborate on the meaning of the trial.

Perhaps, this response could not be helped, because the meaning of *saiban* was cryptic, even if the documents from around the time of the signing of the treaty had been reexamined. Or, perhaps it was assumed that it was preferable to maintain the ambiguity.

Strictly speaking, translating the original term "judgments" as *saiban* was not accurate. The Foreign Ministry, nevertheless, appears to have deliberately used the word *saiban*, thus implying some hidden intention on its part. According to the ministry's official interpretation in those days, *hanketsu* (judgments) of the Tokyo Trial referred to the verdict of guilty or not guilty and the sentences given by the majority judgment. How meaningful it is to apply the domestic Code of Criminal Procedure to a war crimes trial is open to question, but a verdict normally includes finding of facts.

What can be pointed out here is that, if Japan had indeed accepted the "judgments" in that sense, then the dissenting opinions of Radhabinod Pal and B. V. A. Röling as well as counterevidence from the defense would have been excluded, making the judgments unfavorable to Japan. In my view, the Foreign Ministry—its Treaty Bureau under Nishimura Kumao—deliberately translated "judgments" as "*saiban*" so that the Japanese people could read into it the ministry's criticism of the Tokyo Trial.

The second interpretation that was controversial was that accepting the judgments only guaranteed the *validity* of the judgments—that is, the execution of the sentences—by the Japanese government even after the peace treaty came into effect. It did not recognize accepting "the justness or legitimacy of the Tokyo Trial." A representative example of this interpretation was the *Kihon kenkai* (Basic View) that the Jinja Honcho (Association of Shinto Shrines) issued on June 9, 2005.

According to Nishimura Kumao of the Foreign Ministry, most of the articles included in the San Francisco Peace Treaty would lose their raison d'être if the Japanese government met the stipulation that they carry out the sentences even after the peace treaty came into effect. Considering Article 11 as one such article, its raison d'être would de facto vanish when the release of war criminals was completed. Personally, Nishimura himself was looking forward to the arrival of "an era in which it is no longer necessary to refer to or quote the San Francisco Peace Treaty either in terms of popular memory or in diplomacy."[27]

It should be kept in mind, however, that a treaty has a life of its own. Just as the Kellogg-Briand Pact was ex post facto redefined as the legal ground for the criminalization of war, the San Francisco Peace Treaty, too, could someday be used after reinterpretation. In that sense, the first half of Article 11 is a long-forgotten Pandora's box. Prime Minister Nakasone Yasuhiro's official visit to Yasukuni Shrine in 1985 carried the hidden meaning of opening up this box.

British Commonwealth Countries as the Greatest Factor

I, too, once believed that the first half of Article 11 of the San Francisco Peace Treaty was an expression of the Allied Powers' strong will to make Japan carry out the sentences and restrict Japan's arbitrary release of war criminals after restoration of its sovereignty.

After World War I, pressured by stiff reaction from the German side, the

---

27. Nishimura Kumao, "Sanfuranshisuko no omoide" [Reminiscences of San Francisco], *Chūō kōron* (May 1957).

Allies decided to delegate to Germans war crimes trials on violations of the laws of war. But the Leipzig War Crimes Trials thus opened turned out to be something of a "farce." Hearings were botched, and the few defendants who were found guilty by this court were quickly released. Traumatized by the "fiasco of the Leipzig war crimes trials," it was only natural for the Allied Powers of World War II to make sure they carried out the sentences of the war crimes trials.[28]

After studying primary sources from various countries, however, I came to realize that it might not be enough to interpret the first half of Article 11 solely as a guarantee for the Tokyo Trial sentences to be carried out. Had the peace treaty been a bilateral treaty between Japan and the US, the provision of acceptance of the judgments would not have been adopted, no matter how tenaciously the US Congress had pushed it. The inclusion of this stipulation was, in my judgment, aimed at appeasing the British Commonwealth countries, who had ardently demanded explicit reference to Japan's war-guilt clause. In other words, this stipulation was an alternative to the war guilt clause, a missing piece from the viewpoint of the British Commonwealth countries. If the wording were adopted only to make sure that the sentences of the war crimes trials were carried out, it would have been enough to write "respect the sentences," as proposed by the Dulles-Allison draft of August 1950. But this would not have been enough for Britain to satisfy Australia.

We should confirm that the fundamental reason behind Australia and New Zealand's agreement to a tolerant or "soft peace" was the guarantee on mutual defense in the form of the ANZUS Pact (a security treaty between Australia, New Zealand, and the United States, concluded in 1951), not the war criminals clause.

In any event, it should be recognized that, from the viewpoint of the Allied Powers, the first half of Article 11 not only requested that the Tokyo Trial sentences be carried out, but also accommodated the Allies' resolute will not to tolerate any move on the part of Japan to abolish the judgments or to challenge them. In other words, this stipulation connoted the Allies' wish to confirm the "legitimacy of the trials."

---

28. See Higurashi Yoshinobu, *Tōkyō Saiban no kokusai kankei* [The Tokyo Trial and International Relations] (Tokyo: Bokutakusha, 2002).

After all, "carrying out of the sentences" and the "legitimacy of the trials" could not be unrelated. They were inseparable. While the Japanese people may feel repugnance when they hear the phrase "justness of the trial," it was only natural for the Allies to protect the justice and legitimacy of the Tokyo Trial, considering that the Allied Powers had gone out of their way to avert criticism of "victors' justice." It would have been unthinkable for the US to admit the "injustice of the Tokyo Trial," if it were to maintain its moral leadership, and the same is true today.

For the Sake of International Good Faith

Japan's Ministry of Foreign Affairs, the other party to the negotiation on the peace treaty, commented that the article on war criminals in the US-British joint draft treaty "is not an amendment that the Japanese side is in a position to launch a protest over."[29]

It is clear from this comment that the Foreign Ministry did not find it particularly problematic that Japan's power was limited to that of recommendation. The Foreign Ministry also refrained from arguing against the stipulation on the acceptance of the judgments. As a matter of fact, the ministry had been prepared for quite some time to accept the provision to carry out the sentences. A memorandum of the Legal Division of the Foreign Ministry's Treaty Bureau dated January 21, 1949, stated that, because Japan had accepted the Potsdam Declaration, it was a matter of course for the Japanese government to acknowledge the validity of the judgments resulting from the trials.[30] Therefore, there is no doubt that the Foreign Ministry accepted the stipulation for Japan to carry out the sentences.

What then was the Foreign Ministry's view on the "legitimacy" of the trials? The Foreign Ministry has remained quiet on this issue, which of course does not mean it was unaware of the issue. When the Demobilization Bureau questioned whether acceptance of the Tokyo Trial judgments left any leeway for Japan to raise an objection to the trials, Yoshimura Matasaburō, director of the Research Division, Liaison Bureau of the Ministry of Foreign Affairs, replied as follows on August 17, 1951: "You should not think that no leeway is

---

29. Ministry of Foreign Affairs, Treaties Bureau, Legal Affairs Division, *Chōsho*, vol. 6.
30. Ministry of Foreign Affairs, *Gaikō kiroku* (1982), 7th Disclosure.

left for us to raise an objection to any part of the trial." Yoshimura added that he believed Japan could demand a remedy for an obvious mistrial based on mistaken identity, torture, or other factors.[31]

The objection that the Foreign Ministry approved here was limited to wrongful Class B and C war crimes trials. The ministry showed no readiness to challenge the "victors' justice" itself. The Foreign Ministry highly valued "international good faith" here. In fact, there were several internal documents in the ministry that were critical of the Tokyo Trial indictments.[32] However, the Foreign Ministry showed absolutely no signs of dissatisfaction to the outside. After all, it was obliged by the Potsdam Declaration to cooperate with the war crimes trials. Even the hardline Demobilization Bureau refrained from requesting the retrial of war criminals—that is, it refrained from challenging the imbalance or legality of sentences—due to "doubtful feasibility and attentiveness to irreverent conduct towards the Allies."

As explained, even though the Foreign Ministry was secretly dissatisfied with the Tokyo Trial, it remained cautious so as not to step on the landmine of "legitimacy" of the trial. "The charm of a treaty lies in its obscurity with a lot of space for interpretation. It is better not to scrutinize details at this stage." This was the strategic position that the Foreign Ministry opted for on this issue.[33]

Minister of Justice Inukai Takeru's reply in the House of Councillors plenary session on February 2, 1953, was, in substance, as follows: The continued confinement of Japanese war criminals by the Japanese people is most unfortunate. However, as long as we continue to acknowledge the validity of the decisive judgment that has already been firmly established under, so to speak, a supra-constitutional legal order, it cannot in legal terms be considered a violation of the Japanese Constitution. Rather, the most significant issue in terms of international good faith is that (should Japan challenge the legality of the judgments) Japan will be perceived as a country that, once a peace treaty or any international treaty has been concluded, does not take that agreement seriously.

Again, it is international good faith that matters.

---

31. Ministry of Foreign Affairs, *Gaikō kiroku* (1998), 14th Disclosure.
32. See Higurashi, *Tōkyō Saiban no kokusai kankei.*
33. Ministry of Foreign Affairs, *Gaikō kiroku* (1998), 14th Disclosure.

The Price of Restoring Peace

When former justice Radhabinod Pal from India visited Japan for the second time in October 1952, he told Shigemitsu Mamoru, president of the Kaishintō party, that it was a "duty" for Japan to release war criminals, and that he was disappointed by Japan's acceptance of Article 11 of the San Francisco Peace Treaty without any resistance.[34] In its written request to the Diet in 1953, the Japan Federation of Bar Associations also lamented the fact that "such stipulation as Article 11 of the Peace Treaty should never have been accepted."[35]

Indeed, as shown by President Ronald Reagan administration's refusal to accept the judgment of the International Court of Justice (ICJ), which found the US mining of Nicaragua's harbors in the 1980s illegal, in international politics it is possible to reject the judgment of a court.[36] However this is the case only under normal circumstances.

Japan, the defeated, had no other choices than to accept Article 11 with the restoration of peace. Particularly in light of relations with the British Commonwealth countries, a peace treaty without Article 11 would have been utterly unimaginable, which makes Pal's complaint highly unrealistic. In any event, the fact that Japan accepted the article carried significant weight.

Judging from this background, it is unwise on all counts to politicize Article 11 from the argument of a denial of the Tokyo Trial. While compliance with international laws stipulated by the second clause of Article 98 of the Constitution of Japan carries meaning in actual international relations, we should probably listen to the following profound argument by political scientist Sakamoto Takao:

> It is a rule in international law to settle issues with an agreement between nations lest an issue linger endlessly. . . . There were, admittedly, a number of false charges and unjust proceedings in the Class B

---

34. Radhabinod Pal, *Heiwa no sengen* [Declaration of Peace], ed. Tanaka Masaaki (Tokyo: Tōzai Bunmeisha, 1953).

35. Tamura Yoshio, ed., *Hiroku Daitōa senshi* [Secret Record of the Greater East Asia War] (Tokyo: Fuji Shoen, 1954), vol. 6.

36. See Joseph Nye, Jr., *Understanding International Conflicts* (New York: Pearson Longman, 2008).

and C war crimes trials. . . . Nevertheless, it should be recognized that in international relations, the issue has been settled, including those unfortunate cases.[37]

Needless to say, it is important to review the Tokyo Trial critically and explore the meanings of Article 11. This is significant as a policy evaluation of the Tokyo Trial, and I take the view that it is not wise to politically rehash what has already been settled in international relations.

The Provision of Clemency

The latter half of Article 11 stipulates that the power "to grant clemency, to reduce sentences and to parole with respect to such prisoners [Japanese war criminals] may not be exercised except on the decision of the Government or Governments which imposed the sentence in each instance," and limits Japan's power to that of recommendation. This was an embodiment of the Allies' "gradualist approach to release," and, at least at a glance, it seems a harsh stipulation.

If the truth be told, however, those concerned on the Japanese side placed hopes on the broad scope of the concept of clemency. Toyoda Kumao, who was with the Demobilization Bureau at that time, wrote:

> I judge that, since such a versatile and suggestive term as clemency is used, not only amnesty and special pardon but also general recommendations for all kinds of benevolence have been made possible. (The Ministry of Foreign Affairs, prominent American lawyers, and scholars of international law also subscribe to this interpretation.)[38]

The Ministry of Foreign Affairs was also of the view that Japan could consult with the US on such matters as parole and commutation, enabling Japan to obtain favorable results through diplomatic negotiations with the US. While it is true that Article 11 was far from a tolerant article, it was not as inflexible

---

37. Sakamoto Takao, *Rekishi kyōiku o kangaeru* [Thinking about History Education] (Tokyo: PHP Institute, 1998).
38. Ministry of Foreign Affairs, *Gaikō kiroku* (1998), 14th Disclosure.

and unfavorable as to warrant the indignation of the Sugamo prisoners.

The significance of Japan being granted the power to recommend reprieves should not be underestimated. While it was a significant setback from the earlier draft, which included the passage saying, "power to grant clemency, reduce sentences, parole and pardon may be exercised by Japan only with the approval of the Government or Governments which imposed the sentence in each instance," it was still better than nothing. Those concerned about war crime issues in Japan found a way out through the power to recommend.

3. "Serious Domestic Problems" after Regaining Independence

Is Class A More Advantageous than Class B or C?

First, let us confirm the number of war crimes prisoners.

Through GHQ's parole system, 892 prisoners were paroled by the effectuation of the peace treaty on April 28, 1952, including Class A prisoner Shigemitsu. (See Table 7-1 for the breakdown.) A total of 1,244 war criminals remained detained after Japan regained its independence, including those who were detained overseas.[39] Among Class A war criminals, seven had been executed, including Tōjō; four had died of illness (Umezu in January 1949, Shiratori in June 1949, Tōgō in July 1950, and Koiso in November 1950); and Shigemitsu had been paroled. Therefore, there remained after Japan's independence thirteen Class A life imprisonment prisoners, including Araki,

Table 7-1. Parole during the Occupation Period (March 1950–April 1952)

Year	Class A	US	Australia	NLD*	UK	China**	France	Total
1950	1	56	0	54	1	55	5	172
1951	0	111	2	128	48	45	16	350
1952	0	140	15	95	82	28	10	370
Total	1	307	17	277	131	128	31	892

Note: * The Netherlands ** Kuomintang China
Source: Hōmu Daijin Kanbō Shihō-Hōsei Chōsabu [Judicial System and Research Department, Secretariat of the Minister of Justice], ed., Sensō hanzai saiban gaishi yō [Summary of Historical Overview of War Crime Trial] (Tokyo: Ministry of Justice, 1973)

---

39. Hōmu Daijin Kanbō Shihō-Hōsei Chōsabu [Judicial System and Research Department, Secretariat of the Minister of Justice], ed., Sensō hanzai saiban gaishi yō [Summary of Historical Overview of War Crime Trial] (Tokyo: Ministry of Justice, 1973).

Hashimoto, Hata, Hiranuma (deceased in August 1952), Hoshino, Kaya, Kido, Minami, Oka, Ōshima, Satō, Shimada, and Suzuki.

According to Article 11 of the peace treaty, clemency could be granted to Class B and C prisoners (including Taiwanese and Korean prisoners) who had been tried in a national military court on the decision of the government which imposed the sentence. Thus, Japan had to negotiate bilaterally with Australia, Britain, the Netherlands, France, Kuomintang China, the US, and the Philippines (which had not ratified the treaty) through diplomatic channels. Clemency for Class A prisoners required the decision of the majority of the Tokyo Trial participant nations, foreclosing the chance to settle the matter bilaterally. Trends among the Allies would also influence clemency for Class A prisoners—something beyond Japan's reach.

Interestingly, however, Yoshimura Matasaburō of the Foreign Ministry predicted at a liaison conference of the relevant ministries and agencies in September 1951 that it would be easier to win concessions from the Allies on Class A prisoners than on Class B and C prisoners. Although this prediction was the opposite of the Japanese people's sympathy with Class B and C prisoners, it was by no means a peculiar prediction.

For instance, Benjamin Bruce Blakeney, former American attorney at the Tokyo Trial, also believed that, as of 1951, Class A prisoners were in a more advantageous position than Class B and C prisoners. From the American viewpoint, crimes against peace committed by Class A prisoners were "old occurrences which were bound to be forgotten," while the atrocities for which Class B and C prisoners had been accused of were "heinous and uncivilized crimes which are hard to pardon or forgive."[40]

Development of War Criminals Relief Movement

Former Japanese Army colonel Matsutani Sei observed that the Japanese people's sentiment toward Class A war criminals gradually shifted from animosity in the immediate postwar days to sympathy, while Class B and C war criminals continued to receive people's sympathy.[36] Nonetheless, there were quite a number of pitiful cases involving the families of Class B and C prisoners who were stigmatized by their neighbors and with whom marriage

---

40. Ministry of Foreign Affairs, *Gaikō kiroku* (1998), 14th Disclosure.

engagements were cancelled. People sympathized with Class B and C prisoners because it was, after all, somebody else's problem. It is likely that most Japanese people were simply indifferent.

In April 1953, one year after Japan regained its independence, Abe Kōbō, novelist and recipient of the Akutagawa Prize, visited Sugamo Prison and wrote the following: "We must break the habit of being indifferent and should cooperate more closely with Class B and C prisoners. The movement for the release of these prisoners was, originally, a peace movement."[41]

Thus, the core of the war prisoner relief movement during the Occupation period were the absentees' family societies organized by prefecture. While some families severed their ties with prisoners because of the blemish they had placed on the family name, most put up with destitution, believing in the prisoners' vindication that "everything they had done had been for the homeland." These family societies gradually expanded their organization, made pleas for the cancellation of executions, called for the repatriation of war criminals from overseas, submitted petitions for clemency, and promoted mutual help among member families with the help of the Demobilization Bureau. Several religious groups also participated in war criminal relief activities.

The Legal Section of GHQ was alarmed by these trends as shown in a February 1950 document:

> The movement in behalf of war criminals partakes of the nature of political activity because of the pressure it is exerting on Japanese agencies and officials. . . . It further appears that continuation of the movement will tend to glorify and martyrize the war criminal. The crimes committed by these men were crimes according to the accepted international standards and organizations on their behalf should not be permitted. It is doubted that the Japanese Government would permit such organizations and activity on behalf of the felons held in Japanese jails.[42]

---

41. Abe Kōbō, "Uragirareta sensō hanzainin" [Betrayed War Criminals], *Kaizō* (April 1953).

42. Legal Section Document, "Organized Activity on Behalf of War Criminals," February 27, 1950, GS Papers, RG331, GHQ/SCAP records, microfiche in National Diet Library, Japan.

The peace treaty's coming into effect became the turning point in regard to war criminal relief activities. The devoted efforts of former Japanese Navy vice-admiral Hara Chūichi, who had completed his prison term as a Class B and C war criminal, culminated in the establishment of the Sensō Jukeisha Sewakai (Aid Society for War Prisoners) on April 24, 1952, as a "powerful private organization" after consultation with the former Imperial Army and Navy. (It was formally inaugurated on May 10, 1952, and dissolved on April 30, 1958.) The association's leader was Fujiwara Ginjirō, who was assisted by its board of directors. These posts were filled by such former Class A suspects as Aoki Kazuo, Aikawa Yoshisuke, Kishi Nobusuke, and Shōriki Matsuratō. Such prominent figures as Arita Hachirō (former foreign minister), Ichimada Hisato (governor, Bank of Japan), Ugaki Kazushige (former Japanese Army general), and Fujiyama Aiichirō (businessman who later became foreign minister), and Yamanashi Katsunoshin (former Japanese Navy admiral) also joined the association.

Prince Takamatsu, a former Japanese Navy captain, had long hoped for the release of Class B and C prisoners and was pleased to hear from Hara about the founding of the association. Prince Takamatsu advised Hara that the first thing to accomplish toward settlement of the war criminal issue was to deepen the Japanese people's understanding of the issue. Prince Takamatsu also warned Hara that the utmost caution should be paid to prevent any adverse reactions, because it was a delicate issue.[43]

The Aid Society for War Prisoners, in close coordination with its local chapters—local chapters and similar groups had been organized in thirty-two prefectures by the end of 1952—strongly appealed to the Ministries of Legal Affairs and Foreign Affairs as well as to other relevant organizations for the prompt release of prisoners and for aid to war criminals.

At the Japan Federation of Bar Associations, too, former defense counsels of the Tokyo Trial, including Hayashi Itsurō, Sanmonji Shōhei (in charge of defendant Koiso), and Kiyose Ichirō, decided to promote a "national move-ment" calling for the release of war criminals, and set up the Senpan Shakuhō Iinkai (Committee for the Release of War Criminals) on May 27, 1952.

---

43. Toyoda Kumao, *Sensō saiban yoroku* [Additional Records of the War Crimes Trials] (Tokyo: Taiseisha, 1986).

(Hayashi Itsurō was chairman and Sanmonji Shōhei and Katō Takahisa were deputy chairmen.) Insisting that the Tokyo Trial had suppressed the defense's arguments and labeled the Japanese people as aggressors, the committee worked on the government, the Diet, and mass media to sell their arguments denying the validity of the Tokyo Trial. Toward the end of the year, the committee hosted two national conventions to demand "the immediate release of war criminals" in Tokyo and Osaka.[44]

These actors on behalf of the war criminal relief movement took the position of requesting clemency for the prompt release of prisoners, or "victors' mercy," which was a call for a political, rather than judicial, settlement. Their ultimate goal was to attain amnesty when the San Francisco Peace Treaty came into effect. For instance, Enomoto Shigeharu (an official of the Liquidation Department of the Second Demobilization Bureau, who was formerly in charge of international law in the Imperial Japanese Navy) argued that it was the nineteenth-century international custom to grant "amnesty" to war criminals who had violated the laws of war at the time of restoration of peaceful relations in order to "forget the past war . . . and prevent rekindling of animosity." Enomoto added that if the peace treaty did not include an express provision denying amnesty, war criminals would be automatically given "amnesty" with the coming into effect of the treaty.[45]

But this would not apply to the two "all-out" wars of the twentieth century. While provisions on the punishment of war criminals were included in the Treaty of Versailles after World War I, prosecution of the ex-kaiser did not materialize, and the trial on violations of the laws of war only resulted in the "fiasco of the Leipzig war crimes trials." It was based on the "lesson" from this complete failure of policies on war criminals adopted after World War II. This "past war" (World War I), thus, was not forgotten because of its scale and the damage it had brought.

Prisoners Taken to Kōrakuen Ball Park

On April 28, 1952, when effectuation of the San Francisco Peace Treaty put an

---

44. Tamura, *Hiroku Daitōa senshi*.

45. House of Representatives Legal Affairs Committee, *Senpan kankei shiryō* [War Criminal–Related Documents] (Tokyo: Committee on Judicial Affairs, n.d.).

end to the state of war as defined by international law, directive SCAPIN 550 (Removal and Exclusion of Undesirable Personnel from Public Office) was lifted, and jurisdiction over Sugamo Prison was completely transferred to Japan.

Due to delays in the responses of the nations concerned, however, not only amnesty but even parole was put on hold for a while after independence. This led Sugamo prisoners to conclude that the Japanese government had abandoned them in order to please foreign governments. As a result, Sugamo Prison overflowed with anti-government sentiment.

After Japan regained independence, the Japanese people's sympathy for war criminals heightened, resulting in a rush of written petitions to various embassies in Tokyo. British ambassador to Japan Esler Maberley Dening expressed his displeasure with those written petitions, saying they had become "more threatening and arrogant," compared to letters before the independence which retained at least "a minimum sense of remorse."

And it was, indeed, natural for resentment to become prevalent among the Allies. On November 26 of the same year, 629 war crimes prisoners wearing khaki inmate uniforms with the letter *P* (for prisoner) on the back were taken by bus to Kōrakuen Ball Park in Tokyo. This trip was widely covered by Japanese and foreign newspapers with photos, including one of Shimada Shigetarō, former minister of the Japanese Navy, beaming as he admitted his enjoyment of professional baseball.

The outing was arranged at the invitation of the secretariat of the Commissioner of Japanese Professional Baseball, which Kawakami Isamu, warden of Sugamo Prison, accepted at his own discretion. When the US Embassy protested to Kawakami the following day, he successfully fended off the protest, citing "the Prison Law" to be in compliance with "the law on execution of sentences and clemency based on Article 11 of the Peace Treaty with Japan (Act No. 103 of 1952)" (we will return to this domestic law in chapter 8, section 1).[46] Hearing complaints about increasingly audacious Japanese attitudes from its embassy in Japan, the British government instructed its mission to issue a warning to the Japanese government.

On the political party level, the Kaishintō, an opposition party, used the

---

46. Sanematsu Yuzuru, *Sugamo* [Sugamo] (Tokyo: Tosho Shuppansha, 1972), and Kawakami Isamu, "Sugamo Purizun hōkokusho" [Report from Sugamo Prison], *Bungei shunjū* (December 1955).

release of war crime prisoners as a tool in political contention, urging some members of the governing Jiyūtō to criticize what they saw as the "idleness" of the Yoshida Cabinet. All of these movements culminated in the joint resolution of both the House of Representatives and the House of Councillors on release of war criminals in June 1952. Incidentally, the two houses had passed war criminal–related resolutions nine times by July 1955.

The House of Representatives resolution of June 12, 1952, can be summarized as follows. First, although the resolution had been jointly proposed by the Jiyūtō, the government party, and the Kaishintō and both the Saha Shakaitō (Leftist Socialist Party) and the Uha Shakaitō (Rightist Socialist Party), each party's motivation for backing the resolution was different. The Jiyūtō and the Kaishintō had the political aim of denying the justness of the war crimes trials. At its core, support from both socialist parties was based on humanitarian sympathy for Class B and C prisoners.

Second, Sasakawa Ryōichi, who had been active in war criminal relief since his own release from Sugamo Prison, proposed to the chief secretaries of the Jiyūtō and the Kaishintō as well as to the secretary-generals of the two socialist parties that they should submit a resolution on release of war criminals.[47]

Third, there was a precedent in West Germany. According to a report by the American High Commissioner dated February 12, 1952, the West German Bundestag (Federal Diet) adopted a resolution on speeding up commutation and the "release all war criminals who were not sentenced to imprisonment for crimes in their traditional meaning."[48]

Hope for Rebirth

The war criminal issue thus ended up being a serious domestic problem in newly independent Japan.

A popular song, *Aa Montenrupa no yo wa fukete* (Night in Muntinlupa), composed by two Japanese war criminals on death row in the Philippines longing for their homeland became a smash hit in the latter half of 1952. The song was sung by Watanabe Hamako and made into a film in October that

---

47. Satō Seizaburō, *Sasakawa Ryōichi kenkyū* [Study of Sasakawa Ryōichi] (Tokyo: Chūōkōronsha, 1998).

48. US Department of State, *FRUS: 1952–1954, Western European Security, Volume V.*

same year starring Uehara Ken. As indicated by the voters' rejection of the rearmament of Japan, and as shown in the results of general elections in 1952 and 1953, the Japanese people were not particularly nationalistic. They simply took pity on the victims of victors' justice.

On May 19, 1952, on the eve of the Diet resolution, Shirai Yoshio, a boxer who had been trained according to scientific methods by Dr. Alvin Cahn of the Natural Resources Section of GHQ, contended in the world boxing flyweight championship in a specially built boxing ring at Kōrakuen Ball Park. At ringside were such dignitaries as Prince Takamatsu Nobuhito and Prince Mikasa Takahito. Asanuma Inejirō, secretary-general of the Rightist Socialist Party who was remotely related to Shirai, also attended. Watched by an audience of 40,000, Shirai defeated American contender Salvador "Dado" Marino by decision, and became the first Japanese world champion. It was not only a monumental achievement for the Japanese sports world, but also a historical incident that gave the Japanese people of the immediate post-independence period "self-confidence" and "hope for rebirth." Incidentally, the West German people went wild with excitement over the miraculous first tournament championship at the 1954 FIFA World Cup in Switzerland.

On the occasion of the ceremonial investiture of Crown Prince Akihito in November 1952, there emerged what could be termed a "Crown Prince boom" among the Japanese people. The next year witnessed superheated coverage of the Crown Prince's overseas tour, hinting that the emperor's war responsibility issue was no longer a concern to ordinary people. And after champion Shirai's televised bout to defend his title in October 1953, it became commonplace for people to gather in front of street televisions to watch live coverage of sports events. The beginning of the period of "high economic growth" in Japan was just around the corner.

It was under these circumstances that the view of war criminals as "a remnant of the war and the Occupation" became increasingly powerful.

CHAPTER 8
Why Were Class A War Criminals Released?

Party at Sugamo to celebrate the release of all war criminals. June 21, 1958.
Seated on the left side of the table are Arita Hachirō **(third from the left)**, Araki Sadao **(right of Arita)**, and Hoshino Naoki **(two right of Araki)**.
Standing behind Araki are Aichi Kiichi **(glass raised)** and Kaya Okinori.
Seated on the right side of the table is Tani Masayuki **(second from the right)**.
(Kyodo News)

1. Start of Recommendations for Clemency

Two Arguments for Release of War Crimes Prisoners

On April 28, 1952, the very day that the San Francisco Peace Treaty came into effect, "the law on execution of sentences and clemency based on Article 11 of the Peace Treaty with Japan (Act No. 103 of 1952)" was promulgated and came into force immediately. It was a domestic law to provide for the supervision of and clemency for war crimes prisoners after Japan regained sovereignty.

Drafted by the Hōmufu (Ministry of Legal Affairs, which became the Hōmushō, or Ministry of Justice in August 1952) under "guidance" of the Legal Section of GHQ, the law followed suit with SCAP Circular No. 5 (repealed on the same day) in terms of the good-conduct credit and the parole system. Recommendations on parole were to be submitted by the National Offenders Rehabilitation Commission, an extra-ministerial bureau of the Ministry of Legal Affairs, to governments of concerned countries via the minister of legal affairs or attorney general (later the minister of justice) and the minister of foreign affairs. Whether these recommendations would be accepted or not was left to the nations concerned. (The National Offenders Rehabilitation Commission was incorporated into the Ministry of Justice in August 1952.)

There was a discrepancy among Japanese ministers and agencies in the degree of their enthusiasm. The Demobilization Bureau of the Repatriation Relief Agency, staffed with former military personnel, and the Ministry of Justice as well as the National Offenders Rehabilitation Commission, which were both sensitive to discontent among war criminals, insisted on the prompt release of the prisoners, or the "radicalist approach to release." On

August 14, 1953, the document "Senpan no kaishō hōsaku (an)" (Ways and Means to Resolve the War Criminal Issue [draft]), which was believed to have been drafted by the Ministry of Justice, stressed the "strong wishes of the entire Japanese people," and proposed various measures, including overseas dispatch of official/non-official dignitaries. And in the event that the war criminal issue was not settled by the tenth anniversary of the end of the war, the document called for "bold measures," including house imprisonment of war criminals and declaration of the abolishment of Article 11 of the Peace Treaty. From the viewpoint of those who advocated the "radicalist approach to release," the war criminal issue was "a remnant of the war and the Occupation" that was inappropriate for an independent nation.

By contrast, aware of the unforgiving attitude of the nations concerned, the Ministry of Foreign Affairs and Prime Minister Yoshida Shigeru subscribed to the argument for gradual release of war criminals, the "gradualist approach to release." Yoshida was convinced that the handling of war criminals called for much more caution than that of ordinary criminals. He took special care not to be viewed with suspicion domestically or abroad. Pressured to show some concrete action before the general election, however, in June 1952 Yoshida instructed Hori Shigeru, his chief cabinet secretary, to proceed with recommendations to nations concerned with the possible release of prisoners. On this issue, Foreign Minister Okazaki Katsuo sent a telegram, saying,

> as public opinion in Japan has heightened remarkably [in favor of releasing war criminals, particularly those of Class B and C], our government has first devoted its efforts to obtaining parole and clemency for the Class B and C war criminals. . . . Regarding recommendations on Class A war criminals, this calls for delicate consideration in various regards, and requires further careful study."[1]

Accordingly, the Foreign Ministry began to make parole recommendations for Class B and C war criminals from late June 1952.

---

1. Ministry of Foreign Affairs, *Gaikō kiroku* [Diplomatic Record] (Diplomatic Archive of the Ministry of Foreign Affairs, 1998), 14th Disclosure.

Moreover, the National Offenders Rehabilitation Commission also recommended amnesty for all Class A prisoners on the occasion of the ceremonial investiture of Crown Prince Akihito in October 1952. It pleaded for compassion for distressed families of Class A prisoners, who had been imprisoned for seven years, and presented the Diet resolutions and "ten million" petition signatures as proof of the deep sympathy of the Japanese people.

After careful deliberation, the Yoshida Cabinet approved the recommendations on clemency for Class A prisoners. In the background was the result of the October 1952 general election following Prime Minister Yoshida's surprise dissolution of the House of Representatives. Some 30 percent of the elected seats were occupied by lawmakers who had made a comeback subsequent to the depurging of public offices. At a plenary session of the House of Representatives toward the end of 1952, Justice Minister Inukai Takeru reported on the recommendations that the government had sent, and his report was met with applause from the whole house. Newspapers in Japan openly approved the Japanese government's recommendations for clemency for Class A prisoners. As these episodes indicate, recommendations immediately after the establishment of independence were mainly a demonstration geared toward the Japanese people.

Interestingly, Joseph Keenan, former chief prosecutor of the Tokyo Trial, supported the prompt release of prisoners—that is, the "radicalist approach to release." (Keenan passed away in December 1954.) Claiming that the main purpose of the Tokyo Trial was to convey the facts of the Pacific War to the Japanese had already been accomplished, Keenan was agreeable to the release of war criminals in April 1952.[2]

These developments notwithstanding, criticism of Class A criminals lingered. For instance, when an act to revise the Public Officials Pensions Law in order to reinstate pensions for war criminals was introduced to the plenary session of the House of Councillors on July 30, 1953, Naruse Banji of the Leftist Socialist Party voiced his opposition. While Naruse could not help but sympathize with Class B and C war criminals, he found it highly regrettable

---

2. Suetsugu Ichirō, *"Sengo" e no chōsen* [Challenge to "Postwar Era"] (Tokyo: Rekishito-sho-sha, 1981).

that the war responsibilities of Class A war criminals had not been disclosed simply because they had not been tried by Japanese domestic law.

In any event, imprudent agitation from Japan on this issue would certainly irritate public opinion in the nations that had taken part in the Tokyo Trial. Thus, the Bureau of Far Eastern Affairs of the US State Department requested the Japanese government to restrict mass media reporting, while British foreign secretary Anthony Eden advised Satō Eisaku, who had just resigned as chief secretary of the Liberal Party (Jiyūtō) in the wake of a shipbuilding scandal (Zōsen Gigoku), that Japan should not be too vocal about the release issue.

Responses of Nations Concerned

Immediately after the peace treaty came into effect, the US responded promptly to Japan's recommendations on Class B and C war criminals. On September 4, 1952, President Harry Truman organized a three-member Clemency and Parole Board for War Criminals made up of representatives of the Departments of State, Defense, and Justice. Conrad Snow, a former deputy legal advisor to the secretary of state, was chairman. The purpose of the board was to examine recommendations from Japan and advise the president. This indicates that the US rejected "amnesty," which would overlook crimes that prisoners had committed, because it would be a political solution. Instead, the US decided to apply individual judicial screenings, which allowed it to uphold its view of "justice." In other words, the US adhered to the principle of the "gradualist approach to release"—that is, a judicial settlement rather than a political settlement.

In the Treaty of Peace Between Japan and the Republic of China that took effect on August 5, 1952, the Kuomintang China government left the handling of Japanese war criminals to the discretion of Japan, in consideration of its relations with the People's Republic of China government in Beijing. This was a de facto granting of amnesty. Owing to the treaty, all of the Kuomintang-related Class B and C prisoners were released. The Philippines granted a pardon to all Class B and C prisoners in December 1953 in consideration of war reparations from Japan. France also gave amnesty to Class B and C criminals in June 1953 to support the Yoshida Cabinet; all of them were intermittently released by April 22, 1954. The issue of the release of Class B and C war criminals in the Kuomintang China government, the Philippines, and

France ended up being settled relatively promptly, although it was motivated by practical considerations.

As far as Class A prisoners were concerned, however, it had not yet been determined how to handle recommendations from the Japanese government itself. While parole for Class A prisoners called for decisions by the majority of the participating nations in the International Military Tribunal for the Far East, how would the Soviet Union, the Kuomintang China government, and India, which did not sign the peace treaty, be treated? What about the Philippines, which did not ratify the treaty until July 1956? Would Pakistan, separated from India as an independent nation, be included?

The US and Britain discussed these issues, and in February 1953, the following procedure was agreed on among the nations concerned. Representatives of the US, Britain, France, the Netherlands, Canada, Australia, New Zealand, and Pakistan stationed in the US were to bring their own decisions on recommendations from the Japanese government to an informal conference convened by the US Department of State, where their decisions would be put to a vote. The results (approved when five out of eight nations voted affirmatively) would be communicated to the Japanese government by the legations of each country. The Soviet Union, the Kuomintang China government, India, and the Philippines would not be invited to participate in this decision-making process.

In response to this decision of the former Allied Powers, the Japanese government in April 1953 first recommended parole for prisoners Hata, Minami, and Araki, who were more than 70 years old. It submitted parole recommendations for all the Class A prisoners by 1954.

The eight governments gathered on November 5, 1953, to review recommendations on the first three prisoners. Because Hata had been found guilty on Count 55 (atrocities), seven countries except the US insisted on putting his case on hold. The votes on Minami and Araki, both of whom had been found guilty on Count 1 (overall conspiracy) and Count 27 (execution of the Manchurian Incident), were split four to four. (The US, France, Pakistan, and the Netherlands voted for parole, while Britain, Canada, Australia, and New Zealand voted against it.)

The "just cause" cited by those who voted affirmatively was humanitarian consideration for the prisoners' advanced age and illness. Behind the US decision, however, was coolheaded calculation. Secretary of State John Foster Dulles of the Eisenhower Republican administration (formed in January 1953) held that paroles for Class A prisoners would contribute to the stabilization of US-Japan relations, and function as a countermeasure against the Soviet "peace offensive"; the Soviet Union had hinted in 1953 that it would return 1,274 Japanese "war criminals" to Japan. Should Western nations refuse parole for the aged Minami and Araki, Dulles feared that the US would become the target of international criticism, providing neutralist elements and communists in Japan with an instrument for propaganda.

The four British Commonwealth countries were more concerned about the counts on which those Class A prisoners had been found guilty. Britain took Araki's responsibility for war of aggression seriously, while the Australian government was constrained by fierce anti-Japan public opinion at home.

So as Not to Make Japan Anti-American

The release of war criminals was a low priority for Yoshida Shigeru.

Yoshida adhered to the principle of the "gradualist approach to release," being skeptical of amnesty and of the early release of prisoners. He was more concerned about the war criminal issue complicating US-Japan relations. He opted to cut the request appealing to the humanism of the Allies to its bare minimum and leave things to chance. Even when he was directly approached by the Sensō Jukeisha Sewakai (Aid Society for War Prisoners), which included Aikawa Yoshisuke, a member of the House of Councillors since 1953, Yoshida said, "Everything has a proper timing and, besides, we have to take the other party into consideration." Disappointed, Aikawa lamented Yoshida's lack of compassion, saying, "Yoshida has no heart."[3]

It appears, though, that the emperor conveyed his hopes for the release of war criminals to Yoshida. Perhaps owing to this, in his policy speech before the Diet in January 1954, Yoshida expressed his wish to settle the war criminal issue, which was both "a memory and a wound of the past war." In May, Yoshida told US ambassador John Allison that the continued existence of war criminals was "a grave national problem" which could curb Japanese enthusiasm for international cooperation. During his tour through Europe and the

---

3. *Aikawa Yoshisuke monjo* [Aikawa Yoshisuke Papers], Tokyo, National Diet Library.

US in September, too, Yoshida lobbied for prompt parole with each government that he visited.

It was in 1954 that the "first change" appeared. In January that year, US ambassador Allison entreated the State Department to carry out an amnesty or mass paroles for Class B and C Japanese war criminals. This entreaty was fully supported by the department's Northeast Asia division, which believed that the war criminal issue could provoke anti-US sentiment among the Japanese, and hamper Japan's sense of independence as well as its awareness of being a member of the Western camp. Unlike the defense issue and the return of Okinawa, argued the Northeast Asia division, the war criminal issue could be settled instantaneously. Allison and the division argued for the "radicalist approach to release," that is, the prompt release of war prisoners, in the interests of better US-Japan relations.

On March 1, 1954, the Japanese fishing boat *Daigo Fukuryūmaru* from Shizuoka Prefecture was contaminated by nuclear fallout from the US Castle Bravo thermonuclear weapon test at Bikini Atoll. The incident triggered a nationwide movement against atomic and hydrogen bombs, and an increase in anti-US sentiment among the Japanese people accompanied the movement. Worried about this potential damage to Japan's inclination toward neutrality, in May Allison pressed Secretary Dulles even more forcefully to parole Class B and C prisoners en masse on the occasion of Yoshida's visit to the US, saying it would benefit the US greatly if they were to offer to settle the war criminal issue from the US side. Allison stressed that Yoshida's visit might be the last chance for the US to deprive Japan of an issue of contention that could be utilized to their advantage.

Thus, the release of Japanese war criminals was perceived to be a "less expensive gift" to visiting Prime Minister Yoshida.[4] While Allison thought it better to grant amnesty to Class A prisoners as well as Class B and C criminals, he decided to act quickly by concentrating on paroles for Class B and C prisoners because they did not require an international agreement.

---

4. Allison to Dulles, May 21, 1954, et seq., Department of State records, Central Decimal Files, 694.0024-694.0026, Boxes 3020–3022, 1950–1954, National Archives and Records Administration (NARA), Archives II, College Park, Maryland.

A New Policy: The Ten-Year Rule

Allison's proposal met fierce opposition from the Office of Legal Advisors as well as the Bureau of European Affairs of the State Department, the Clemency and Parole Board for War Criminals, the Department of Defense, and the Department of Justice. They were all in favor of the "gradualist approach to release." They feared strong opposition from the US Congress and American public opinion, the crumbling of the "justice" of the war crimes trial, and heightened demands for the release of German war crimes prisoners in West Germany.

The Northeast Asia division of the State Department, which prioritized good US-Japan relations, proposed to the Clemency and Parole Board for War Criminals that the eligibility for parole be shortened from fifteen years to nine years. This was Allison's breakthrough idea. The division took the position that the war criminal issue could have an adverse effect on Japan's expansion of its defense capabilities. It chose to seal the argument for amnesty and, as an alternative, proposed moving paroles forward.

At the time, the Eisenhower administration was adopting a "New Look" policy that aimed to reduce the burden on its defense budget by having its allies share the financial costs of ground forces. As a part of this policy, the administration, through the negotiations on the Mutual Defense Assistance Agreement between Japan and the United States of America (negotiations on military and economic assistance based on the Mutual Security Act of the United States), had pressured Japan since the summer of the previous year to increase its defense capabilities. Thus, the rise of anti-US sentiment among the Japanese propelled the argument for application of the "radicalist approach" to the Northeast Asia division, which impacted the defense issue.

Subsequently, the Clemency and Parole Board for War Criminals proposed an amendment of the rule so that Class B and C prisoners who had served ten years would be eligible for parole. This "Ten-Year Rule" was approved by President Eisenhower on July 12, 1954, and implemented in August. In response, on August 9 the Japanese government promulgated and executed Decree 238 based on the Ten-Year Rule. Under the new policy, all Class B and C prisoners with prison terms longer than thirty years would become eligible for parole toward the end of 1957, instead of 1961 as was set by the older rule.

This was the first change in the US policy of "judicial solution." It should be noted, however, that the change only made those Class B and C prisoners eligible to apply for parole, and it did not necessarily mean they would be paroled. As a matter of fact, Eisenhower, who was personally interested in the war criminal issue, reacted strongly to the proposal of the Clemency and Parole Board for War Criminals. He even exercised his veto power occasionally to restrict any hasty release of war criminals.

Meanwhile, the parole of Minami Jirō (79 years old) for medical reasons was approved by unanimous decision. This decision was communicated to Japan's Ministry of Foreign Affairs on January 3, 1954, and Minami returned home soon thereafter. However, the recommendation on Araki Sadao (77 years old) was deadlocked in a tie vote. Britain requested unanimous approvals on paroles from all the countries concerned and postponement of parole for Araki in 1956. For the US, negotiations with the other related countries turned out to be a difficult obstacle to overcome.

Peace Offensive from the Eastern Camp

It was a change in the international situation that proved fortunate for the US in these negotiations. After Premier Joseph Stalin died in March 1953, the Soviet Union, seeking to take advantage of the rise of anti-American public opinion in Japan, announced commutations for Japanese "war criminals" to visiting Japanese Diet members in July 1954. In October the Communist China government in Beijing, for its part, pardoned forty-seven Japanese "war crimes suspects" and promised to return 1,069 "war crimes suspects" to Japan. Furthermore, the Chinese and Soviet governments jointly appealed for normalization of diplomatic ties with Japan.

These actions by communist countries functioned as catalysts. Fearing that these "peace offensives" from China and the Soviet Union might bedazzle the Japanese people, the nations of the West began to reconsider the Class A war criminal issue from the viewpoint of their relations with Japan. More concretely, Britain made a compromise on medical parole for Class A prisoners. Australia followed suit, hoping to redirect its people's antipathy toward Britain. New Zealand also fell in line with these two countries.

Consequently, Hata Shunroku (75 years old) and Oka Takasumi (64 years old) were granted medical paroles in October 1954. A US State Department official in charge informally told Japanese Ambassador to the United States Iguchi Sadao that the US planned to consult again with the countries concerned on parole for the remaining nine Class A prisoners. It seems that the US government was positive toward this issue.

At this juncture, allow me to touch on the special Chinese and the Soviet definition of "war criminals." The Soviet Union in 1949 announced that some 10,000 Japanese detainees in the country were "war crimes suspects," of which some 3,000 were conjectured to be indicted as "war criminals" between 1948 and 1951. Most of them were accused of espionage and anti-Soviet activities, which were violations of Article 58 of the Soviet Criminal Law.

One recruit, for instance, was indicted at the military court, and then abruptly sentenced to twenty-five years' imprisonment, which at that time was the heaviest punishment, although he had only anticipated a routine interrogation. This was a uniquely Soviet method called "written document trial," which called for no hearing or defense counsel. It was a summary decision trial that took only a few minutes.[5]

Sejima Ryūzō, a former staff officer at the Imperial General Headquarters, was arrested by the Soviet Union in May 1949 after his testimony at the Tokyo Trial. After being detained at the Ministry of Interior prison in the Soviet Union, he was indicted on July 8, and sentenced to a twenty-five-year term of imprisonment on July 18.

The Communist Party of China's Policy toward Japan

In the case of the Communist Party of China, it is said that a number of Japanese officers or soldiers were executed as the result of the "people's court" of the Eighth Route Army (Bālù-jūn) immediately after the war. After the founding of the People's Republic of China, the Communist Party attempted "thought-remolding" on its own 140 "war crimes suspects" (detained at the Taiyuan War Criminals Management Center in Shanxi province), and on 969 suspects turned over by the Soviet Union in July 1950 (detained at the

---

5. Sengo Kyōsei Yokuryū-shi Hensan Iinkai [Committee for Compilation of the Postwar History of Forced Internment], ed., *Sengo kyōsei yokuryū-shi* [Postwar History of Forced Interment] (Tokyo: Public Foundation for Peace and Consolation, 2005), vol. 5, and Shida Yukio, *Shiberia yokuryū o tou* [Questioning Detention in Siberia] (Tokyo: Keisō Shobō, 1987).

Fushun War Criminals Management Center in Liaoning province) were held in the name of "admission of guilt" or "re-education."

What happened to detainees in Communist China can be detected from the diary of Aisin Gioro Pujie, who was detained at Fushun War Criminals Management Center together with his brother Aisin Gioro Puyi. Pujie wrote on May 20, 1954:

> A general meeting was convened at the center. First, Furumi Tadayuki [deputy director of the Department of General Affairs, the State Council of Manchukuo, who later returned to Japan in 1963] admitted his guilt to the Chinese people. . . . He also disclosed in detail the content of his "thought struggle". . . . It was indeed an denunciation session consisting of passion, tears, and anger. Hirose Saburō [former Imperial Japanese Army lieutenant colonel], who remained defiant regarding the accusations against him, was handcuffed and taken out of the hall. Even yesterday's enemies were inspired by the fairness and selflessness of the Chinese People's Government to accuse, disclose, and admit their guilt.

On January 26, 1955, Pujie wrote:

> We enjoyed traditional Japanese dances and musical drama performed by Japanese war criminals. They were all about how our People's Liberation Army took good care of the Chinese people . . . and the Japanese people's struggle against an atomic war based on true stories. No small number of the Japanese war criminals made teary protests about the monopoly of atomic power by American imperialism, and vocally expressed appreciation for the magnanimous policy of our people's government.[6]

In its Japan policy document of March 1, 1955, the Politburo of the Communist Party of China established a few principles including normalization of diplomatic relations with Japan, opposition to a resurgence of Japanese

---

6. Aisin Gioro Pujie, *Fuketsu jiden: "Manshūkuo" kōtei o ikite* [Autobiography of Pujie: Life as Imperial Brother of the Emperor of Manchuria], trans. Maruyama Noboru (Tokyo: Kawade Shobō Shinsha, 1995).

militarism, and making an ally of the Japanese people. Settlement of the war criminal problem was included as one of the concrete issues to be tackled. Because of this basic policy toward Japan, toward the end of the same year the Politburo adopted Premier Zhou Enlai's proposal to try only a few "war criminals" in court and give no death or life sentences.[7]

Following this decision, representative Japanese "war criminals"—military personnel, Manchukuo bureaucrats, military police, and so on—were tried by the special military courts of the Supreme People's Court in Shenyang (thirty-six defendants) and Taiyuan (nine defendants) from June 9 through July 20, 1956. They were accused of atrocities, bacteriological warfare, and espionage, amongst other counts. Preparation of the indictments was supervised by Zhou Enlai. Mei Ju-ao, former justice at the Tokyo Trial, provided legal advice.

After giving statements of self-criticism, forty-five defendants were given prison terms of eight to twenty years with forced labor, but they were pardoned in sequence from 1956 before their prison terms ended. The last three returned home on April 9, 1964. In my view, the true significance of this public trial was to point a finger at Japan's militarism.

The remaining 1,017 suspects were exempted from indictment and released immediately in three groups from June through August 1956 soon to be returned to Japan as examples of the "peace offensive."[8]

2. Increased Calls for the "Radicalist Approach to Release"

The Real Truth of Medical Parole

It was only "humanitarian" medical parole, for which understanding was easily obtained amongst ordinary people, that the Allies had allowed for Class A prisoners. For instance, an official of the British embassy in Washington, DC, commented as follows in February 1955:

---

7. Mōri Kazuko, *Nit-Chū kankei* [Japan-China Relations] (Tokyo: Iwanami Shoten, 2006).

8. Hata Ikuhiko, *Gendaishi no taiketsu* [Confrontations in Contemporary History] (Tokyo: Bungeishunjū, 2003), and Arai Toshio Shiryō Hozonkai [Arai Toshio Materials Preservation Society], ed., *Chūgoku Bujun senpan kanrisho shokuin no shōgen* [Testimonies of Officials at the Fushun War Criminals Management Center] (Tokyo: Nashinoki-sha, 2003).

According to medical reports, Shimada is suffering from incurable heart disease and his overall health condition has deteriorated due to advanced age. Shimada is also suffering from cataracts. . . . Under these circumstances, the British Foreign Office is prepared to discharge Shimada promptly on special medical parole under the same conditions [release only for a period that was medically required] as prisoners Minami, Hata, and Oka.[9]

According to those who knew the situation surrounding Shimada and with whom this author had a chance to speak, Shimada was not so gravely ill. When Shimada (71 years old then; he survived until 1976) was released from Sugamo Prison in April 1955, the daily *Asahi Shimbun* attributed his early release to "high blood pressure and aggravated eye trouble," but reported he had "steady steps for a 71-year-old man."[10]

When Hata Shunroku was unofficially told by Hara Chūichi, advisor to the Ministry of Justice, about the decision on his parole in October 1954, he said, "I have decided to check into a hospital tonight, forthwith."[11] In any event, he was not seriously ill.

Minami Jirō was secretly hospitalized in July 1951 at Nihon University Hospital in Iidabashi. He was heard to say,

> I am free to see anyone I like, and I am free to eat and drink as I like. . . . Friends send me sake, and I get to see my favorite sumo wrestlers, such as former *yokozuna* Futabayama and Kagamisato . . . and my subordinates also visit me one after another. So I have gradually recuperated."

Although Minami did not appear to be in a serious condition, his visceral functions "continued to deteriorate day-by-day." He passed away in December 1955, the year after he was paroled.[12]

The recommendations from the Japanese government were just an

---

9. Hata, *Gendaishi no taiketsu*, and Arai Toshio Shiryō Hozonkai, *Chūgoku Bujun*.

10. *Asahi Shimbun* (evening edition), April 8, 1955.

11. Komiyama Noboru, ed., *Gensui Hata Shunroku gokuchū gokugai no nisshi* [Field Marshal Hata Shunroku's Diary in and out of Prison] (Private compilation, 1992).

12. Mitarai Tatsuo, ed., *Minami Jirō* [Minami Jirō] (Private compilation, 1957).

expediency to obtain "medical parole," the only parole that the Allied government approved, and the Allied side did not dare to scrutinize each case. This method was employed until June 1955 for Araki (78 years old), and reviews of the medical paroles—a parolee was supposed to be imprisoned again once he recovered his health—were intentionally avoided.

The Ten-Year Rule was also of great significance in the paroles of Class A prisoners. Applying this new rule to Class A prisoners, Satō Kenryō, the last Class A criminal to be arrested, would become eligible for parole in March 1956. The US government sounded out the countries concerned about application of the Ten-Year Rule to Class A prisoners starting in the autumn of 1954. Moreover, in anticipation of Foreign Minister Shigemitsu's visit to the US, the government put forth a more proactive proposal that Class A prisoners be automatically paroled after ten years of imprisonment.

France in October 1954 concurred with the application of the Ten-Year Rule to Class A prisoners on the condition that Class A parolees stayed out of political activities. France in particular had Hashimoto in mind. France was alarmed by the communist bloc's use of pardons for "war criminals" as propaganda. (France also agreed with the American proposal in the summer of 1955.)

In December 1954, the Netherlands showed a positive response to the proposed parole for Class A prisoners, stating that the government could justify its stance to the parliament and the Dutch people because the Class A issue was the collective responsibility of the nations concerned. Nevertheless, the Netherlands refused even to consider prompt parole for Class B and C prisoners, until it obtained compensation for the detention of Dutch nationals by the Japanese military during the war.

Changes under the Hatoyama Ichirō Cabinet

In November 1954, in the aftermath of the political turmoil caused by the shipbuilding scandal, the Hatoyama and Kishi factions defected from the Jiyūtō party, and merged with the Kaishintō and Nihon Jiyūtō parties to form the anti-Yoshida Nihon Minshutō party. The next month, the Yoshida Cabinet resigned en masse in the midst of public criticism, leading to the formation of the first Hatoyama Ichirō Nihon Minshutō Cabinet.

Shigemitsu Mamoru, a former Class A war criminal, was appointed to serve as the Hatoyama Cabinet's foreign minister cum deputy prime minis-ter. Former foreign minister Tani Masayuki, a former Class A suspect, was appointed as advisor to the Foreign Ministry. In this position, Tani exer-cised significant power as one of "the three disciples of Shigemitsu." Such was Tani's power that it was rumored that no document could be stamped with the Foreign Minister's seal unless it had been signed by Tani. In 1956, Tani was appointed Japanese ambassador to the United States.[13] The chief secretary post of the governing Minshutō party was filled by another former Class A suspect, Kishi Nobusuke. Kiyose Ichirō, a Minshutō member of the House of Representatives and former defense counsel at the Tokyo Trial, was appointed as education minister in the third Hatoyama Cabinet.

For those government officials who had been involved in the Tokyo Trial in one way or another, the war criminal issue was naturally not some-one else's problem. They could still hear resentful complaints from Sugamo Prison. And because the Minshutō government stressed "sovereign indepen-dence," it was obliged to differentiate itself from the Yoshida Cabinet, whose US-dependent diplomacy had been criticized as a stumbling block to the war criminal release.

Thus, the Hatoyama Cabinet shifted its axis to the "radicalist approach to release," the argument for prompt release of war criminals, and began to appeal aggressively to the countries concerned to approve early releases. In January 1955, immediately after he became foreign minister, Shigemitsu met Admiral Arthur W. Radford, chairman of the Joint Chiefs of Staff, and Ambassador Allison. Shigemitsu argued that the detention of war criminals was hampering Japan-US cooperation, and benefiting the communist camp, which had used the release of "war criminals" as a tool of political propa-ganda. Shigemitsu strongly pleaded that the time had come to forget the past and heal the war wounds.

On July 19, 1955, on the occasion of the tenth anniversary of the end of World War Two, the House of Representatives adopted a "resolution regard-ing the request for the immediate release of war prisoners." The reasoning behind the appeal of the "radicalist approach to release," aiming for the pris-oners' prompt release, was that "our national sentiment has already reached

---

13. Saitō Shizuo, *Gaikō* [Diplomacy] (Tokyo: Simul Shuppankai, 1991).

the limit regarding further continuation of detention." The gist of this proposal is as follows:

> As was apparent in Justice Pal's "Japan not guilty" argument, the tribunal after the world war contained a number of questionable points from the perspective of world history. For instance, regarding the use of the atomic bombs, international public opinion finds it problematic as an act in defiance of humanity. As calm has been restored to people's minds around the world, people have started to doubt whether the war tribunal unilaterally opened by the victors was justifiable from the viewpoint of international legal theory. (applause) It has to be said that the fact that the countries concerned cannot open again a war tribunal after the end of the Korean War and the turmoil in French Indochina reveals how flimsy the rational grounds for a war tribunal are. (applause)[14]

Even though a Diet resolution on various national political issues is simply a declaration of intent in Japan, it is still noteworthy that the Japanese legislators blatantly denied everything about the Allied war crimes trials. The National Offenders Rehabilitation Commission also decided to propose clemency for all Class A and Class B and C prisoners, hoping to settle the past, and make a fresh start on the august occasion of the tenth anniversary.

"Much Easier than Life in Gakushuin's Dormitory"

At Sugamo Prison, "de facto release measures" were being carried out in order to appease the prisoners. For instance, by taking advantage of the provision on "temporary release from prison" included in Act No. 103 of 1952, it became possible for prisoners to visit their hometowns, and make secret visits to their homes. The Ministry of Justice's proposal to extend the duration of temporary release from five days excluding transportation to fifteen days (maximum thirty days), drafted by House members for diplomatic reasons, was passed by the Diet as a legislation, and became effective on January 22,

---

14. The full Japanese transcript can be found online via the National Diet Library website's Kokkai Kaigiroku Kensaku [Parliamentary Record Search]. 22nd Diet Session, House of Representatives, Plenary Session No. 43, July 19, 1955, https://kokkai.ndl. go.jp/#/detail?minId=102205254X04319550719&current=3

1953. The US embassy filed a formal complaint to the Japanese government, but that was all.

Thanks to these measures, by early 1954 it became a rarity for all of the Class A prisoners to be found in Sugamo Prison on a given day. Kido Kōichi reminisced as follows:

> If the truth be told, life at Sugamo became rather comfortable since jurisdiction over it passed to the Japanese government. I even went home occasionally. . . . In the beginning, we were not permitted to stay at home overnight. . . . But soon enough, we were allowed to stay three or four nights. . . . I often came back to Sugamo to stay overnight, and then went back home again the next morning. Life in Sugamo was much easier than life in Gakushūin's dormitory.[15]

It appears that, to Kido, the boundary between the inside and outside of the prison no longer meant much.

When the Japanese government unofficially approved employment of prisoners outside the prison under the pretext of "vocational guidance" as stipulated by the Prison Law in 1953, one Class B and C prisoner commuted every day to Yamaichi Securities Co., Ltd.[16] When Aikawa Yoshisuke that same year requested that Prime Minister Yoshida provide war criminals with allowances, Yoshida dismissed the request with a laugh, saying, "I hear prisoners at Sugamo nowadays have found employment outside the prison and send their salaries home." It appears that the US embassy, too, turned a blind eye to this practice "as long as it is not reported by major newspapers."[17]

But Araki Sadao boldly wrote as follows in the November 1955 issue of the monthly *Bungei shunjū* after being paroled:

---

15. Tatai Yoshio, *Ketsudan shita otoko: Kido Kōichi no Shōwa* [A Determined Man: Shōwa Era of Kido Kōichi] (Tokyo: Bungeishunjū, 2000). Author's note: Gakushūin was an educational institution for the imperial family and the nobility in the prewar period.

16. Sanematsu Yuzuru, *Sugamo* [Sugamo] (Tokyo: Tosho Shuppansha, 1972).

17. Nishida Shunichi, "Bōrei to natta Sugamo senpan" [Sugamo War Prisoners Who Became Ghosts], *Kaizō* (February 1954).

Prisoners leave Sugamo Prison in the morning, work at their respective jobs, and return to Sugamo in the evening. It just goes to show that Sugamo Prison has become something like an apartment where prisoners come back to at night to sleep. . . . Who can blame them if some of the prisoners were to open a bar or pachinko parlor?[18]

Diplomats of the Tokyo legations of the concerned countries were upset by this exposé, but it shows how farcical the carrying out of the sentences were becoming.

Parole for Class A Prisoners

NSC (National Security Council) 5516/1, the US-Japan policy decided on April 9, 1955, set out a plan to strengthen Japan's political and economic powers in order to prevent Japan becoming a non-aligned country. As far as the war criminal issue was concerned, NSC 5516/1 established the immediate goal of speeding up paroles, and settling the issue by the beginning of 1956.

On May 16, 1955, President Eisenhower approved a compromise proposal that the presidential authority to decide paroles should be entrusted to the Clemency and Parole Board for War Criminals in order to speed up the process.

This was the "second change" in the US policy toward the Japanese war criminals. Three months later, Foreign Minister Shigemitsu visited the United States and had discussions with Secretary of State John Foster Dulles. In the Japan-US joint statement announced on August 31, 1955, while Shigemitsu requested "the early release of war prisoners," Dulles "described the complexity of the problem and indicated that the question of the release of war criminals will be kept under continuous and urgent examination." Nevertheless, in contrast to his cold attitude toward the defense issue, Dulles promised Shigemitsu that, although releasing all of the war criminals at a single stroke would be impossible because it would invite violent opposition from the American people, the US should continue its efforts toward releasing them. He also confessed to Shigemitsu that the Class A war criminal issue was

---

18. Araki Sadao, "Sugamo danchō no ki" [Heartbreak Diary of Sugamo], *Bungei shunjū* (November 1955).

expected to be settled "within the near future."[19] (Shigemitsu suddenly passed away in January 1957 immediately after Japan joined the United Nations.)

On September 7, 1955, eight countries that had participated in the Tokyo Trial came to a unanimous agreement that, while retaining the system of examining each case individually—the Netherlands opposed an automatic across-the-board parole—Class A prisoners should be paroled after they had served ten years in prison. At the same time, paroles for Hashimoto Kingorō, Kaya Okinori, and Suzuki Teiichi were also unanimously agreed upon (they were paroled on September 17), while the remaining four Class A prisoners would also be "reviewed," meaning paroled, after they had served ten years of their sentences. The British Foreign Office feared a worsening of its relations with the United States and isolation in the international community, but decided nonetheless to confer benefits on Japanese prisoners in order to outmaneuver the Soviet Union. The eight-country, unanimous agreement was also a product of labored efforts by countries in the West to keep up with others in the Cold War environment.

Thus, Hoshino Naoki was paroled on December 13, 1955, and Kido Kōichi and Ōshima Hiroshi were paroled on December 16. They walked out of Sugamo Prison about a month after the Jiyū Minshutō party (Liberal Democratic Party, LDP) was formed by a merger of the conservative parties. The last remaining Class A prisoner, Satō Kenryō, was also paroled on March 31, 1956.

Double Standard Concerning War Criminals

Around this time, Araki, Suzuki, and Hashimoto, who should have maintained low profiles during their parole, shared their thoughts on a radio program. They put forth an irresponsible argument akin to a "national confession of Japanese war guilt" that was unbecoming of former national leaders. They said, "We must restore the glory of Japan. The war responsibility lies with the entire nation, not just us [who were convicted of war crimes]. If the Japanese people really had not wanted the war, they should have resisted us." The daily *Yomiuri Shimbun* harshly criticized the trio and declared that

---

19. US Department of State, *FRUS: 1955-1957, Japan, Vol. XXIII, Part 1*, ed. John P. Glennon and David W. Mabon (Washington, DC: Government Printing Office, 1991).

they should repent during their prison terms and apologize to the Japanese people.[20]

The irresponsible remarks, however, did not stop with Araki. Kiyose Ichirō, who was appointed education minister in the third Hatoyama Cabinet, the first LDP government after the merger of conservative parties, reiterated the historical perspective that the Pacific War was an act of self-defense and a "holy war" to liberate Asia.

Irritated by this, the US Department of State denounced this trend in the media, saying, "As long as Japan's major newspapers show common sense (as in the *Yomiuri Shimbun*'s criticism of the conduct of Araki), the United States will not censure the Japanese people for what a few disgruntled old men say or do."[21]

Before being paroled, Hata went to an *oden* restaurant in Ginza, the first time he had visited Ginza at night and saw the attractive but somewhat flashy neon lights.[22] To these released prisoners, postwar Japan looked like an "American colony," and they found that unforgivable.

During his parole, Hashimoto ran for the House of Councillors in July 1956 as an independent candidate in the national constituency. He had been elected to the House of Representatives from the fourth electoral district of Fukuoka prefecture with the largest number of votes in the 1942 general election without the voicing of dissent (*yokusan senkyo*), but in 1956 he was too unprepared and underfinanced to get elected. Soon after the election, he was diagnosed with lung cancer; he died the next year.[23]

It should be recalled that the Public Offices Election Act of 1950 denied political suffrage to those who had been sentenced to imprisonment or more. And yet, the prisoners detained in Sugamo Prison exercised their right to vote, and Hashimoto was allowed to run for a Diet seat during his parole. They were allowed to do so because domestic laws in Japan did not regard them as "criminals."

Besides, Shigemitsu and Kaya ran for office after completion of their prison terms. And the only thing that had blocked the political ambitions of

---

20. Ministry of Foreign Affairs, *Gaikō kiroku* (1998), 14th Disclosure.

21. *Yomiuri Shimbun*, April 25, 1956.

22. Komiyama, *Gensui Hata Shunroku*.

23. Tatamiya Eitarō, *Hashimoto Kingorō ichidai* [Life of Hashimoto Kingorō] (Tokyo: Fuyō Shobō, 1982).

former Class A suspects Aoki Kazuo, Aikawa Yoshisuke, and Gotō Fumio (all of whom were elected to the House of Councillors in 1953) as well as Kishi Nobusuke (elected to the House of Representatives in 1953) was the purge during the Occupation period.

In the beginning, the Ministry of Legal Affairs announced in a July 8, 1950, notification that "those who were found guilty by the Allied military tribunal will be treated in the same way as those who are sentenced by Japanese courts of justice." This was, however, proven to be a temporary policy decision valid only during the Occupation. As soon as Japan regained its sovereignty, the minister of Legal Affairs declared on May 1, 1952, that it was appropriate to assume that the validity of the previous July 8, 1950, notification had expired with effectuation of the peace treaty.[24]

In short, a double standard was applied to the Japanese war criminals, in that externally they were criminals under international law but domestically they were not criminals as defined by Japanese law. This situation was unprecedented and peculiar.

Psychological Point of Contention

The root cause of everything was the exceptional circumstances of the Occupation. The double standard on war criminals was convenient for Japan immediately after restoration of its independence. The enshrinement of the Class A war criminals at Yasukuni Shrine, which was discussed in chapter one, should be understood as an extension of this double standard. From a position that values international relations, the enshrinement is a target of criticism. (Incidentally, I share this position.) Yet seen from a position that almost exclusively values domestic relations, enshrinement was an act that should be approved as a matter of course. Things cannot always be decided in terms of black or white. Even if you sympathize with war criminals, you will have to take a critical stance toward such occurrences as the enshrinement, if you value "international good faith."

Former chamberlain Urabe Ryōgo wrote in his July 2001 diary that the emperor was displeased with the enshrinement of Class A war criminals at

---

24. *Inoue Tadao shiryō* [Inoue Tadao Documents], Yasukuni Kaikō Bunko [Yasukuni Archives].

Yasukuni Shrine.[25] If that was indeed the case, it should be understood that the Shōwa emperor had reached this view as the result of his decision to value "international good faith"—a decision attained through complicated emotions and anguish. By no means should the decision be understood in the context of a simple dichotomy. The problem is, simply, that postwar Japan then employed—and still employs—a double standard that demands complicated thinking and judgment.

The release of war criminals was a troublesome "psychological issue" that simultaneously stimulated nationalism in the Japanese people and a punitive sentiment among peoples of the former Allied Powers.

On the Japanese side, the movement to promote prompt release of war criminals, or the "radicalist approach to release," was on the rise in the mid-1950s.

From its viewpoint, the US could not approve the request for prompt release of war criminals because it needed to defend the legitimacy of the Tokyo Trial, and to fend off criticisms from the public in the US. But this attitude of the US might have led to worsened relations with Japan, making it difficult to keep Japan in the Western bloc. Furthermore, if nationalistic ideology regained momentum in Japan, it would obstruct the US Cold War strategies. In short, the essence of the dilemma between "the logic of World War II" and "the logic of the Cold War" was apparent in the issue of releasing Japanese war criminals.

In the end, the US decided to make efforts toward the paroling of Class A prisoners while persisting with the principle of "judicial settlement." The following four reasons can be cited for the rapid progress in the paroles of Class A war criminals.

First, it was atrocities, including the case of vivisection experiments at Kyushu Imperial University, that were regarded as truly repugnant crimes in the US, and there was a limit to the parole of Class B and C war crimes suspects even when the Ten-Year Rule was applied. There was, however, no similar constraint on Class A prisoners, and their paroles could be handled within the boundary of "judicial measures." This was all the more an issue

---

25. Mikuriya Takashi et al., eds., *Urabe Ryōgo jijū nikki* [Diary of Grand Chamberlain Urabe Ryōgo], (Tokyo: Asahi Shimbunsha, 2007), vol. 5.

because the norm of crimes against peace had long disappeared from the international arena. This also held for the United Nations' termination of the study on codification of the Nuremberg principles on December 14, 1954.

Second, it was easier to justify parole for Class A prisoners on such humanitarian grounds as advanced age and deteriorating health.

Third, because parole for Class A prisoners was subject to votes by all the concerned nations, the responsibility was dispersed among participating countries, reducing the pressure from domestic public opinion.

Fourth, it was deemed most appropriate, in terms of relations with Japan, to parole highly visible Class A prisoners because that would ensure the maximum impact with the minimum number of releases.

Political Advantage of Life Imprisonment

The German war criminals who had been sentenced to prison terms by the Nuremberg International Military Tribunal were detained in Spandau Prison in West Berlin under the international supervision of four Allied Powers (Britain, France, the Soviet Union, and the US). Prison guards were provided by each of the four countries on a monthly rotation basis. Release of prisoners required international agreement among the four countries, which was a different situation from that of the Japanese war criminals. Thus, only three of the seven prisoners in Spandau were paroled for serious medical reasons before completion of their respective prison terms: Konstantin von Neurath in 1945 (sentenced to fifteen years; passed away two years after parole), Erich Raeder in 1955 (life imprisonment; passed away five years after parole), and Walter Hunk in 1957 (life imprisonment; passed away three years after parole).

Of the remaining four, Karl Dönitz (sentenced to ten years) in 1956, Albert Speer (sentenced to twenty years) in 1966, and Baldur von Schirach (sentenced to twenty years) in 1966 all completed their prison terms before being released. Rudolf Hess (life imprisonment) became "the sole remaining inmate in Spandau" after 1966; he died in 1987 at the age of ninety-three, completing his forty-six years of imprisonment. Unlike the case of the Japanese prisoners, "the logic of the Cold War" worked against the German war criminals sentenced by the Nuremberg Trials when it came to their release.

In any event, when we realize that all twelve Class A Japanese prisoners were paroled by 1956, our thoughts go out to those who were executed as the result of the Tokyo Trial. Although I do not believe in the abolition of the death penalty, I find myself regretting the death sentences rendered by the Tokyo Trial as a tool of international politics. The irreversible harshness manifested in the death penalty only provoked a grudge against victors' justice.

It would have been wiser politically for the Allies to limit the maximum penalty to life imprisonment. If the maximum penalty had actually been life imprisonment, all the surviving Class A war criminals would have been paroled in the mid-1950s, including even Tōjō Hideki. It is hard to imagine that the US would not have allowed parole for Tōjō alone, given its emphasis on impartial justice.

The deaths due to illness of Umezu Yoshijirō about two weeks after the executions of Class A war criminals, and of Shiratori Toshio about half a year later hardly attracted attention, and the same is true even today. The impact of a natural death during imprisonment would be far milder than "execution at the hands of the victors." Refraining from execution alone would have diluted to some degree the notoriety of victors' justice.

3. What Lies beyond the Tokyo Trial

The United States Left Behind

Ironically, it was the US, which had taken the leadership in the release of the Japanese war criminals, that found itself in the most disadvantageous position among the Allies in 1956.

First, voices rose in Japan denouncing the US double standard. The Japanese people found it unreasonable for low-ranking Class B and C soldiers to continue to suffer while Class A heavyweights were released.

Second, feeling pressed by the "second change" in the US policy of 1955, the Netherlands, Australia, and Britain sped up their release of Class B and C prisoners. Consequently, as of the end of 1956, eighty-five of 115 Class B and C prisoners in Sugamo Prison (about 74 percent) were US-related prisoners.

The Netherlands paroled its last Class B and C prisoner on August 15, 1956, as a compensatory measure. Britain commuted the last two remaining prisoners and released them on January 1, 1957. When Prime Minister

Robert Menzies of Australia visited Japan on April 11, 1957, he conveyed to Prime Minister Kishi Nobusuke his intention to release Class B and C prisoners. True to his words, all the prisoners were pardoned and released by July 4, 1957, in conjunction with the signing of the Agreement on Commerce between Japan and Australia.

Third, changes related to Germany occurred, which in the past had always worked to constrain the release of Japanese war criminals. It was decided that the US, Britain, and France should establish their own separate clemency screening organizations. Accordingly, on October 27, 1953, the US opened the Interim Parole and Clemency Board (consisting of three American and two German members) to attend to war criminals under the jurisdiction of both the military and the US high commissioner for Germany. When West Germany regained its sovereignty with the effectuation of the Bonn-Paris conventions on May 5, 1955, the Interim board evolved into the Mixed Parole and Clemency Board (consisting of one member each from the US, Britain, and France, and three from West Germany). The US Department of State began to consider it dangerous to continue detaining German war criminals in light of West Germany's rearmament, and its participation in the North Atlantic Treaty Organization (NATO).

As of March 1956, the US-related German minor prisoners were reduced to about thirty compared with 136 Japanese Class B and C prisoners. From the beginning, the number of detained German minor war criminals was smaller and their terms of imprisonment shorter compared to Japanese Class B and C prisoners.

Fourth, diplomatic relations between Japan and the Soviet Union were restored. After First Secretary Nikita Khrushchev on February 24, 1956, delivered what became known as the "criticism of Stalin" in a secret speech to a closed session of the 20th Party Congress limited to Soviet delegates, the Soviet Union's decision to release war criminals before completion of prison terms was, on July 25, conveyed to the first group of war criminals, including Sejima Ryūzō. Their repatriation ship arrived in the port at Maizuru, Kyoto on August 19.

Moreover, Article 5 of the Joint Declaration by Japan and the Union of Soviet Socialist Republics which was concluded on October 19, and came into effect on December 12, stipulated that "all Japanese citizens convicted in the

Union of Soviet Socialist Republics shall be released and repatriated to Japan." On December 26, all the Japanese detainees and war criminals returned to Japan. The United States was left behind even by the Soviet Union.

December 29, 1958

It was under these circumstances that the Kishi Cabinet was formed on February 25, 1957. Immediately before this, on January 30, an American soldier shot and killed a Japanese farm housewife in the training grounds of the US forces in Gunma Prefecture, an event which enraged the Japanese people. (This was the Girard Incident; Hayashi Itsurō and Sanmonji Shōhei, both of whom had been defense counsels at the Tokyo Trial, were requested by the US embassy to defend William Girard, the accused.) Kishi shrewdly took advantage of this rise in anti-US sentiment to request the newly assigned US ambassador to Japan Douglas MacArthur II (General MacArthur's nephew) to grant parole promptly to Class B and C prisoners and commute the sentences of Class A prisoners. He made the request on May 1, one month before his scheduled visit to the US.

Kishi's request for the commutation of sentences for Class A prisoners consisted of a reduction of the sentence by the actual days the prisoner had served so that he would complete the sentence and be released. Kishi was considering his close friend Kaya Okinori, who was planning to run for the next general election as an LDP candidate. While Kaya could run even during his parole, being paroled—that is, being on probation and serving his term outside of prison would have been humiliating to Kaya.

US secretary of state Dulles gave his assent to this proposal to commute the sentences of Class A prisoners. Furthermore, he even proposed a new procedure of entrusting the parole screening of Class B and C prisoners to the Japanese side, whose decision would be accepted by the US. This proposal secured presidential approval on June 18, 1957. In short, the US converted its stance toward the war criminal issue from a "judicial settlement" to a de facto "political settlement," while still retaining the façade of judicial screening.

That was the "last (third) change" in the US policy. At the Japan-US talks that commenced on June 19, both sides agreed on this procedure. This policy change was attributable to (1) a feeling of impatience on the part of the US for being the last country detaining Japanese war criminals and (2) the US intention to support Prime Minister Kishi so as to promote Japan's political stability. On all counts, however, it was virtually a fixed game.

How, then, did other concerned nations react when the US State Department sounded out their responses to the above proposal to commute the sentences of Class A prisoners? While some in France showed hesitation out of consideration for the impact it might have on the release of German war criminals (the US, Britain, and France ended up paroling or releasing all German minor war criminals by 1958), the nine countries concerned, including the Philippines, which had ratified the peace treaty in July 1957, agreed on commutations for ten Class A prisoners (excluding Minami Jirō, who had passed away in 1955, and Hashimoto Kingorō, who had died in 1957) on March 7, 1958.

Thus, all the Class A Japanese prisoners had their sentences reduced by the balance between their set prison term and the actual days they had served on April 7, 1958, allowing them to complete their prison terms and be released. On April 28, a ceremony to dissolve the defense team at the Tokyo Trial was convened at Matsumotorō restaurant in Hibiya Park, Tokyo. Kaya ran for the first general election as an LDP candidate after the merger of conservative parties and obtained the largest number of votes from voters in the 3rd electoral district of Tokyo. (Subsequently, Kaya served the Ikeda Hayato Cabinet as minister of justice for approximately a year beginning in July 1963.)

As for Class B and C prisoners, the last eighteen US-related prisoners were paroled on May 30, 1958 under the new procedure. A Sugamo Prison closing ceremony was convened on June 21, attended by Miyama Yōzō, deputy director of the Repatriation Relief Bureau, and others. Without intervention, it would not be until approximately 1980 that all the life imprisonment prisoners would complete their prison terms. Due to this, the sentences of Class B and C prisoners who had not completed their terms were, like their Class A counterparts, shortened to December 29, 1958. On this date, therefore, all the Japanese war criminals' sentences were over. The completion of the release of war criminals was, therefore, a hidden accomplishment of the Kishi Cabinet.

The Term "War Criminal" Losing Its Reality

One may wonder how the Japanese people viewed the paroles of Class A prisoners. On this issue, sociologist Hidaka Rokurō referred to "the affirmative reactions by the Japanese people to the release of Class A war criminals and the mass lifting of the purge."[26] The Japanese people in the 1950s, therefore approved of the release of war criminals, including Class A prisoners. If one recalls the emotional tendency among Japanese today to perceive Class A war criminals as "evil," the majority public opinion must have completely changed at some point.

Interesting, in this conjunction, was Prime Minister Satō Eisaku's remark in September 1970 that "after the Japan World Exposition in Osaka, there no longer is a pro–Japan-US security arrangement or an anti–Japan-US security arrangement."[27] Indeed, Japan in the 1950s and Japan in the 1970s were so totally different that one cannot help wondering what took place in the intervening 1960s.

First of all, Japanese society and its people underwent a tremendous change. Due to rapid economic growth, the Japanese people became affluent. More than 80 percent of the population perceived themselves as "middle-class," as having restored self-confidence, and as being positive regarding their current status. According to Hessell Tiltman, a British journalist, the Japanese in the 1960s indulged in the pursuit of material comfort, and their patriotism shifted toward "development of national land, industrial development, technological advancement . . . [and] a desire for the enhancement of national prestige as a peaceful and prosperous country."[28] From the mid-1960s, residents' campaigns also increased all over Japan.

Japanese over a certain age should recall that on March 24, 1970, ten days after the opening of the World Exposition in Osaka—and a week before the hijacking of Japan Airlines Flight 351 in the Yodogō Hijacking Incident—a funeral service was held for Rikiishi Tōru, a character from the comic book *Ashita no Joe*, at the Kodansha Auditorium in Tokyo. While he was indeed an extremely popular character, a funeral service for a fictional character was still quite an oddity. This incident might have reflected the spirit of the time in Japan as a new "major economic power."

---

26. Hidaka Rokurō, *Gendai ideorogī* [Contemporary Ideology] (Tokyo: Keisō Shobō, 1960).

27. Kusuda Minoru, *Kusuda Minoru nikki* [Kusuda Minoru Diary], ed. Iokibe Makoto and Wada Jun (Tokyo: Chūōkōron Shinsha, 2001).

28. H. Hessell Tiltman, *Nihon hōdō 30-nen* [Reporting on Japan for 30 Years], trans. Kase Hideaki (Tokyo: Shinchōsha, 1965).

Taking all of the above into consideration, one has to say that Satō Eisaku displayed sharp understanding of the current situation when he referred to the World Exposition in Osaka as a turning point. It was indeed a special national event for which even elementary school children were allowed to be absent from school. While those Japanese people who gathered in Osaka just to enjoy themselves boasted of the vested interests that they had acquired in the postwar days, they also intuitively loathed such concepts as "prewar days," "military," and "state." Through this process of transition, the term "war criminals," which was inseparable from those concepts, lost its reality. "War criminals," thus, came to connote simply a negative image, particularly in conjunction with the points that follow.

Like a Body Blow

Second, evaluation of the Pacific War became polarized.

The 1960s witnessed a rise in discussions about how to view the Pacific War among opinion leaders in Japanese press circles. The discussions polarized into war of aggression theory on the one hand, and war of self-defense theory on the other. All in all, it was reminiscent of the contention at the Tokyo Trial.

Those who were engaged in relief efforts for the war criminals and their families, including the Japan War-Bereaved Families Association, also began to join the argument that the war was one of self-defense, which later gave momentum to the argument for the enshrinement of war criminals at Yasukuni Shrine.

Nevertheless, the camp denouncing the aggressive war became the majority in Japan.[29] This denunciation of the war of aggression was an extension of the Peace Problems Discussion Group's (Heiwa Mondai Danwakai) argument for aversion to war, and its approval of the Tokyo Trial (see chapter 5, section 2). If this type of pacifist thinking were to be reflected in history education in schools, it would naturally take effect gradually. The judgments of the Tokyo Trial may not have had an immediate effect on society, but their overall gradual effect can be likened to repeated body blows.

---

29. Hatano Sumio, "Izoku no meisō" [War-Bereaved Families' Loss of Sense of Direction], in *Kioku toshite no Pāru Hābā* [Pearl Harbor as Memory], ed. Hosoya Chihiro, Irie Akira, and Ōshiba Ryō (Kyoto: Minerva Shobō, 2004).

Besides, somewhat later there also was the influence of international politics.

From around the 1970s, Japan's Asian neighbors began to criticize the "major economic power" Japan for its war responsibility. For instance, Chinese leaders, who felt threated by the expansion of Japan's wealth and the country's sense of self-confidence, repeatedly criticized Japanese militarism and aggression.[30]

Right-wingers in Japan, provoked by these criticisms, fought back against the war of aggression theory. Two books arguing against the Tokyo Trial were published in 1971. Kojima Noboru's *Tōkyō Saiban* (Tokyo Trial) and Richard Minear's *Victors' Justice: Tokyo War Crimes Trial* had the effect of encouraging the right-wingers' defense of the Pacific War as an act of self-defense, regardless of Minear's true intention. The left-wing camp in Japan felt a sense of crisis over the trend to deny Japan's war responsibility and began to use the Tokyo Trial as a "symbol of peace."

As a result of this combination of factors, it can be said that the majority of the Japanese people ended up perceiving war criminals in a generally negative light.

The Tokyo Trial That Cannot Be Settled as a Domestic Problem

While clemency can be considered the "institutionalization of forgetfulness" for the sake of progress, some criticize it as "lawful amnesia" and, therefore, a system that "sacrifices justice."[31] The clemency system is full of debatable points, but the daily *Asahi Shimbun* on January 5, 1955, approved the dissolution of "war criminals" as an "offensive name" and celebrated the completion of war criminals' release, stating, "It is of no use at this point to discuss the pros and cons of victors' judging the war responsibilities of the defeated in a military court."

It is true that the time is long past when the Allied Powers could gain interests from war crimes trials in international politics. After the restoration of Japan's sovereignty, war criminals became a symbol of "unequal relations"

---

30. Michael Schaller, *Altered States: The United States and Japan since the Occupation* (New York: Oxford University Press, 1997).

31. Martha Minow, *Between Vengeance and Forgiveness* (Boston: Beacon Press, 1998).

between sovereign nations and, therefore, the issue was written off. Thus, roughly thirteen years after the arrest of Tōjō Hideki, international politics, otherwise known as the Tokyo Trial, came to an end. The war crime issue also reached a "final solution."

For the Japanese government, the important thing was the release of prisoners from Sugamo Prison and its timing. It did not matter whether this was accomplished through parole or amnesty. The fact that a goal of Japan's foreign policy was accomplished merits a positive evaluation, but it cannot by any means be reduced to a straightforward "victory of Japanese diplomacy." While the former Allied governments felt bitter about Japan's tenacious pleading and the absurdly generous treatment of prisoners, they approved the release of Japanese war criminals in line with the reality of international politics.

Of particular note is that the US, which had been by far the most tolerant of Japan's conduct, never approved the granting of amnesty and adhered to its principle of a judicial solution until the end.

The obvious reason for this resolve of the US was to defend its own "justice." This basic US stance still persists today. During the Cold War, the US refrained from pressing Japan on its war responsibility, and despite Japan getting a little carried away and demanding the release, it concurred with requests for the release of war criminals as a realistic policy for solidifying the Western bloc. This sort of situation, however, could not happen again in post–Cold War days; this is a point about which Japanese people should be cautious. After all, the Tokyo Trial was an international issue; it was not one that could ever be settled as a domestic problem.

Afterword

By way of conclusion, I would like to explain briefly my personal view of the Tokyo Trial.

My stance is neither of the two traditional approaches of confirming or negating what happened in the Tokyo Trial. To reach an assessment of the Tokyo Trial, I believe that rather than judging the intentions of the Allied Powers in the trial, it is more useful to evaluate the trial's outcome as policy, from both the Allies' viewpoint and Japan's viewpoint.

I am highly critical of the Tokyo Trial as foreign policy on the part of the Allies. I say this not because the trial was "victors' justice." I take this stance because I believe the trial was a kind of "excessive justice" forcing the defeated to take responsibility for the war based on a highly political and crude "right or wrong" view of history. Such justice only aggravates the sense of humiliation and resentment on the part of the defeated.

In postwar Japan, the sense of humiliation actually increased as time passed, so the Japanese felt more humiliated long after the Tokyo Trial than they did during and immediately after the trial. Furthermore, divisions of opinion regarding the trial also became much more pronounced. From this, I conclude that the trial was a diplomatically dangerous, and highly imprudent policy on the part of the Allies.

Nonetheless, it would not be right to deny totally the validity of the Tokyo Trial. Seen from the point of view of Japan, I rather lean toward approval of the Tokyo Trial as an inevitable price that the war-defeated nation had to pay. My position differs from the traditional approach of approval of the trial in that it does not overestimate the trial from an idealistic stance.

First, it was impossible for Japan, the defeated, to evade painful accusations of one form or another regarding its responsibility for the war. Facing this truth, the Japanese shied away from the pursuit of responsibility on their part and, instead, accepted that of the victors. This was the path that Japan chose from among several options, and I do not intend to denounce Japan for making that choice. It should be recalled, however, that Justice Bernard Röling from the Netherlands said at the Tokyo Trial that a "one-sided indictment" was better than no indictment at all. Surely this remark should not be overlooked from the viewpoint of Japan's political culture. In international politics, inequity is normal. Consider, for example, the Nuclear Nonproliferation Treaty (NPT).

Second, Prime Minister Yoshida Shigeru accepted the Tokyo Trial out of a desire to eliminate the militarists from Japan, in cooperation with the US and Britain. I also recognize the significance of the trial for the same reason. Cooperation with the US, particularly, was indispensable to Japan. It had lost a war and possessed no natural resources of its own, and needed to obtain security and promote development through free trade. The Tokyo Trial was a prerequisite for the Allied policy of democratizing Japan and, as such, it made it easier for Japan to convert its postwar foreign policy to that of cooperation with the US. In other words, acceptance of the Tokyo Trial was a kind of "security" policy for Japan that helped smooth the transition to postwar politics and cooperation with the US.

The so-called "Tokyo Trial historical view" (in Japanese, *Tōkyō saiban shikan*), which has often been referred to, does not seem to be a particularly academic term. It is generally understood as a historical view, which the Tokyo Trial adopted, that evaluates prewar Japan in general as thoroughly "evil." To refute this stance today on the grounds that the Pacific War was an act of self-defense, in the manner of the group around Uzawa Fusaaki, the head of the Japanese defense panel, would be tantamount to replaying the court hearings in the domestic dimension or denying the legitimacy of the Tokyo Trial itself. Of course, after seventy years, the level of arguments would be more highly developed, but that would be all. What we should do instead is examine the Tokyo Trial critically and accept what must be accepted from the viewpoints of international relations and Japan's national interest.

To denounce the shortcomings of the Tokyo Trial would be an endless endeavor. Criticizing the trial itself on the grounds of its shortcomings, however, contributes nothing to Japan's interests today. In fact, a rehash of arguments about Japan's war responsibility would damage Japan's strength. Therefore, I am convinced that Japan should dauntlessly disclose to the world the fact of the sacrifices that Japan made as a result of the trial—this includes the prewar leaders as Class A war criminals and the 4,855 Class B and C war criminals who were tried and punished[1]—and do so without becoming sub-servient or self-deprecating.

In any event, the foregoing is merely my personal view, and I would not dare to ask for agreement from the general reader. Still, if this book has a message for its readers, it is that we should apply more coolheaded thinking to the Tokyo Trial. This is where discussion of the Tokyo Trial in Japan ought to begin today.

I have attempted to portray "the political history of the Tokyo Trial" as dispassionately and objectively as possible. In that respect, I quote novelist Nagai Kafū who praised British diplomat Ernest Mason Satow's 1921 book, *A Diplomat in Japan*, in his June 16, 1935, diary:

> [Satow's] observation is extremely impartial and his writing extremely candid, so much so that his reader can understand how time changes as if he were watching a great river flow from its bank. This is some-thing one can never expect from a book written by a Japanese. Any book on the Meiji Restoration written by a Japanese person is only full of bitterness, and obligatory praises of the conduct of royalists from the Satsuma and Chōshū clans, who are without exception adored and worshipped as heroes. In contrast, works by Westerners are devoid of narrow-minded moralistic judgments. Their main concern is to describe faithfully the facts, what has happened, satisfying readers with vivid impressions and profoundly deep emotions.[2]

Nagai's observation remains very much valid today.

Journalist Tokutomi Sohō also pointed out that, "The essence of history is not just to enumerate some facts but to make observations on their inter-relations, origins, causes, and effects, and to narrate them impartially and faithfully."[3]

---

1. Ministry of Health and Welfare, Repatriation Relief Bureau, ed., *Hikiage to engo 30-nen no ayumi* [Thirty-Year History of Repatriation and Relief Activities] (Tokyo: Ministry of Health and Welfare, 1977).

2. Nagai Kafū, *Tekiroku: Danchōtei nichijō* [Summary: The Danchōtei Diary] (Tokyo: Iwa-nami Shoten, 1987), vol. 1.

3. Tokutomi Sohō, *Tokutomi Sohō shūsengo nikki* [Tokutomi Sohō Postwar Diary] (Tokyo: Kodansha, 2007), vol. 4.

What Nagai and Tokutomi advocated as a method for portraying history is difficult to achieve, which makes such portrayals all the more valuable. While I am fully aware that this book falls far short of the standard proposed by these two literary giants, I have attempted as much as possible to eliminate "bitterness" and "moralistic judgments" and, instead, devote myself to a "faithful" description of the "facts" alone.

This book is based on my 2002 publication, *Tōkyō Saiban no kokusai kankei* (The Tokyo Trial and International Relations).[4] The content has been made easier to read for the general public, supplemented with previously unintroduced references and descriptions, and further enriched with two new chapters, chapters 7 and 8, which give an account of the release of Japanese war criminals.

For more detailed information and analysis as well as sources not in the footnotes, readers are encouraged to refer to my *Tōkyō Saiban no kokusai kankei* and "'Seigi' to 'jihi'" (Justice and Mercy).[5] I wish to add that chapters 7 and 8 of the current volume are part of study projects under Grant-in-Aid for Scientific Research (C)2 for 2001–2004 (JSPS KAKENHI Grant Number JP13620096) and the Grant-in-Aid for Scientific Research (C) for 2005–2008 (JSPS KAKENHI Grant Number JP17530129) funded by the Japan Society for the Promotion of Science.

After I published *Tōkyō Saiban no kokusai kankei* essentially for specialists, a number of mentors and friends suggested that I write another book on the Tokyo Trial for a wider audience. I was particularly encouraged by the enthusiastic advice of the late Professor Sakamoto Takao, who sadly passed away in 2002, since I had received my doctoral degree from Gakushūin University. I benefitted immensely from the invaluable advice of the late Professor Amakawa Akira, who sadly passed away in 2017, on the need for a chronological table and other details. Now that I have completed the

---

4. Higurashi Yoshinobu, *Tōkyō Saiban no kokusai kankei* [The Tokyo Trial and International Relations] (Tokyo: Bokutakusha, 2002).

5. Higurashi Yoshinobu, "'Seigi' to 'jihi': Kōwago no senpan shakuhō to Nichi-Bei kankei" [Justice and Mercy: War Criminals Releases and US-Japan Relations after the Signing of the Peace Treaty], ed. Amerika Gakkai [The Japanese Association for American Studies], *Amerika kenkyū* [American Studies] 35 (March 2001).

manuscript of this book, I sincerely hope I have somehow attended to these issues raised by my mentors.

While I was writing this book, I had an opportunity to report on my work in progress to a study group of alumni at the Matsushita Institute of Government and Management chaired by Noda Yoshihiko, a member of the House of Representatives and prime minister from 2011–2012. It was an invaluable experience for me to discuss my study with professional statesmen. The experience gave me a chance to reconsider the meaning of historical issues that are very much alive in contemporary Japan. Readers may detect the effect of this experience in these pages.

Mr. Aoyama Yū, who was an editor at Kodansha's Gendai Shinsho publishing department (Kodansha's new library of knowledge), first proposed publication of this book. Soon after the publication of *Tōkyō Saiban no kokusai kankei,* Mr. Aoyama contacted me and enthusiastically encouraged me to work on the present volume. I accepted without hesitation. However, time passed swiftly after that conversation on sports with Mr. Ueda Tesuyuki, then director of the Gendai Shinsho publishing department, and Mr. Aoyama in Ginza, Tokyo. Because Mr. Aoyama was transferred to another post, we could not work together on completion of this new book. I hope the final result might serve as a small token of gratitude to Mr. Aoyama, who first envisioned the project.

Mr. Yokoyama Tateki, then deputy director of the Gendai Shinsho publishing department, succeeded Mr. Aoyama and guided me through the entire process toward publication with his skillful management and strong support. A student of political science himself, Mr. Yokoyama warmly encouraged me at times, and made the work particularly pleasant for me. He also took the role of potential readers by giving timely advice on my choice of words and expressions when they were perhaps too clumsy for general readers. If this volume turns out to be not unduly difficult to read, it is owed to Mr. Yokoyama's fitting advice.

Last but not least, I wish to express my heartfelt appreciation to the supportive people at my publisher, Kodansha, for their generosity, from which I have greatly benefited.

Higurashi Yoshinobu
November 2007

Chronological Table

1919	Jun. 28	Treaty of Versailles signed
1941	Oct. 25	British prime minister Winston Churchill announces the war objective to punish Nazi war criminals
1943	Nov. 1	Moscow Declarations among Britain, the Soviet Union, and the United States announced
1944	Jan. 18	The United Nations War Crimes Commission (UNWCC) officially launched (Dissolved on Mar. 31, 1948)
1945	Apr. 12	US president Franklin D. Roosevelt passes away (succeeded by Harry Truman)
	Jul. 26	Britain, China, and the United States announce the Potsdam Declaration
	Aug. 8	Britain, France, the Soviet Union, and the United States sign the London Agreement with the Charter of the International Military Tribunal
	Aug. 14	Japan accepts the Potsdam Declaration
	Aug. 17	Suzuki Kantarō Cabinet resigns en masse and the Prince Higashikuni Cabinet formed
	Aug. 29	UNWCC adopts policy recommendations toward Japan
	Aug. 30	General Douglas MacArthur, Supreme Commander for the Allied Powers, instructs drafting of list of Class A war crimes suspects
	Sep. 2	Japan signs the Japanese Instrument of Surrender
	Sep. 11	Tōjō Hideki arrested (first directive to arrest war crimes suspects)
	Oct. 2	SWNCC 57/3, basic policy on Japanese war crimes trials, decided
	Oct. 8	General Yamashita Tomoyuki's trial in Manila commences (Yamashita sentenced to death by hanging on Dec. 7, 1945)
	Oct. 9	Shidehara Kijūrō Cabinet formed (en masse resignation of the cabinet on May 22, 1946)
	Oct. 18	Indictments for the Nuremberg Trials submitted
	Nov. 13	US Dachau Trials of German minor war criminals commence (concluded in Aug. 1948)
	Nov. 14	War crimes suspects start to be confined at Sugamo Prison
	Nov. 20	The Nuremberg Trial (International Military Tribunal) commences
	Dec. 1	First Ministry of Demobilization (formerly the Ministry of Army) and Second Ministry of Demobilization (formerly the Ministry of Navy) founded
	Dec. 6	American prosecution team including Joseph Keenan arrives in Japan
	Dec. 8	MacArthur sets up International Prosecution Section (IPS) within GHQ
	Dec. 18	Yokohama War Crimes Trials by the US (on Class B and C war criminals) commence

1946	Jan. 19	The International Military Tribunal for the Far East created by a special proclamation of General Douglas MacArthur The Charter of the International Military Tribunal for the Far East promulgated
	Feb. 2	British prosecutors arrive in Japan
	Apr. 1	Corps of American defense counsels for the Tokyo Trial formed
	Apr. 3	The Far Eastern Commission decides policy paper FEC 007/3 and not to indict the emperor of Japan
	Apr. 13	Soviet delegation arrives in Japan
	Apr. 29	Tokyo Trial indictments submitted
	May 3	The Tokyo Trial (International Military Tribunal for the Far East) commences
	May 4	Corps of Japanese defense counsels for the Tokyo Trial formed
	May 6	Procedures for arraignment by defendants begins
	May 17	Justice Radhabinod Pal from India arrives at the Tribunal
	May 22	First Yoshida Shigeru Cabinet formed
	Jun. 4	Prosecution starts presentation of evidence (Keenan's opening statement)
	Jun. 13	Justice Delfin Jaranilla from the Philippines arrives at the Tribunal
	Jun. 27	Defendant Matsuoka Yōsuke passes away during the trial
	Jul. 4	The Republic of the Philippines becomes independent
	Oct. 1	Judgment and sentencing at the Nuremberg Trials
	Dec. 9	Subsequent Nuremberg Trials by the US commence (concluded on Apr. 14, 1949)
	Dec. 11	United Nations General Assembly adopts Proposal 95 (I) on codification of the Nuremberg Doctrines
1947	Jan. 5	Defendant Nagano Osami passes away during the trial
	Jan. 24	Prosecution completes presentation of evidence
	Jan. 27	Defense's motion to dismiss prosecution (rejected on Feb. 3)
	Feb. 24	Defense starts counterevidence (Kiyose Ichirō's opening statement)
	Apr. 9	The Tokyo Tribunal exempts Ōkawa Shūmei from trial
	May 24	Katayama Tetsu Cabinet formed
	Aug. 15	India becomes independent
	Aug. 20	Relevant US government offices reach a tentative agreement to forgo a second international trial
	Aug. 30	Twenty-three Class A war crimes suspects are exempted from prosecution and released
	Oct. 9	Britain notifies the US of its nonparticipation in the second international trial

1948	Jan. 12	Defense completes counterevidence
	Jan. 13	Prosecution starts rebuttals
	Jan. 30	Defense starts surrebuttals
	Jan. 31	US Department of War notifies its policy to abandon a second Class A war crimes trial to MacArthur
	Feb. 11	Prosecution starts summation (through Mar. 2)
	Feb. 17	US Department of War announces that there will be no second international trial
	Mar. 2	Defense's summation commences
	Mar. 10	Ashida Hitoshi Cabinet formed
	Apr. 15	Prosecution's final argument
	Apr. 16	Conclusion of the Tokyo Trial
	May 31	First and Second Ministries of Demobilization reorganized into Repatriation Relief Agency's Demobilization Bureau
	Jul. 26	Judges decide on portions of the judgments (translation into Japanese starts)
	Jul. 29	New Zealand proposes FEC 314 on termination of trials on Japanese war criminals to the Far Eastern Commission
	Oct. 9	US National Security Council adopts NSC 13/2 (on prompt termination of Japanese war crimes trials)
	Oct. 15	Second Yoshida Shigeru Cabinet formed
	Oct. 19	The GHQ Trial indicts Toyoda Soemu and Tamura Hiroshi
	Nov. 12	International Military Tribunal for the Far East sentencing (reciting of the majority judgment starts on Nov. 4)
	Nov. 22	MacArthur convenes an advisory council on the Tokyo Trial sentences among the Allies
	Dec. 9	United Nations General Assembly adopts the Genocide Convention
	Dec. 23	Seven war criminals including Tōjō Hideki executed
	Dec. 24	Seventeen Class A suspects, including Kishi Nobusuke, are exempted from prosecution and released
1949	Jan. 8	Umezu Yoshijirō passes away during imprisonment
	Feb. 23	The GHQ Trial sentences Tamura Hiroshi to eight years hard labor
	Feb. 24	Far Eastern Commission adopts FEC 314/8 on termination of Class A trial The International Military Tribunal for the Far East closes
	Mar. 31	Far Eastern Commission adopts FEC 314/15 on recommendation of termination of Class B and C trials
	Jun. 3	Shiratori Toshio passes away during imprisonment
	Sep. 6	The GHQ Trial finds Toyoda Soemu not guilty

	Oct. 19	US Yokohama War Crimes Trials concluded
	Dec. 20	The US grants good-conduct credit to convicted German war criminals
	Dec. 25	Soviet Khabarovsk trial commences (sentencing on Dec. 30) GHQ announces commutation based on good conduct and confinement credit
1950	Mar. 7	GHQ issues Circular No. 5, Clemency for War Criminals, introducing parole system
	Jul. 23	Tōgō Shigenori passes away during imprisonment
	Nov. 3	Koiso Kuniaki passes away during imprisonment
	Nov. 21	Shigemitsu Mamoru paroled (first parole granted on Class A war criminal; Shigemitsu completes his prison term on Nov. 7, 1951)
1951	Jan. 31	US high commissioner John McCloy grants commutation for German war criminals sentenced by the Subsequent Nuremberg Trials
	Apr. 9	Australia's Class B and C trial on Manus Island concluded (end of Allied trials of Japanese war crimes)
	Sep. 8	Treaty of Peace with Japan signed
1952	Apr. 24	Sensō Jukeisha Sewakai (Aid Society for War Prisoners) established
	Apr. 28	Treaty of Peace with Japan comes into effect (supervisory authority over Sugamo Prison transfers from the Allied Powers to Japanese government)
	Jun. 12	House of Representatives adopts the first resolution on release of Japanese war criminals
	Aug. 5	Treaty of Peace Between Japan and the Republic of China comes into effect Kuomintang China Government completes release of Japanese Class B and C prisoners
	Aug. 22	Hiranuma Kiichirō passes away during imprisonment
	Sep. 4	US president Truman establishes Clemency and Parole Board for War Criminals
1953	Jan. 20	Dwight Eisenhower administration formed
	Oct. 27	US Interim Parole and Clemency Board founded
	Dec. 30	The Philippines completes release of Japanese Class B and C prisoners
1954	Jan. 3	Medical parole granted to Minami Jirō (passes away Dec. 5, 1955)
	Apr. 1	Repatriation Relief Bureau, Ministry of Welfare founded (Repatriation Relief Agency's Demobilization Bureau closed down)
	Apr. 22	France completes release of Class B and C prisoners
	Oct. 30	Medical paroles granted to Hata Shunroku (passes away May 10, 1962) and Oka Takasumi (passes away Dec. 4, 1973)
	Dec. 10	First Hatoyama Ichirō Cabinet formed

1955	Apr. 8	Medical parole granted to Shimada Shigetarō (passes away Jun. 7, 1976)
	Apr. 9	US National Security Council adopts NSC 5516/1 on prompt paroles of Japanese war crimes prisoners
	May 5	Effectuation of the Bonn-Paris conventions (West Germany regains sovereignty)
	Jun. 18	Medical parole granted to Araki Sadao (passes away Nov. 2, 1966)
	Sep. 7	Eight participating countries in the Tokyo Trial agree on release of Class A prisoners after 10-year imprisonment
	Sep. 17	Paroles granted to Hashimoto Kingorō (passes away Jun. 29, 1957), Kaya Okinori (passes away Apr. 28, 1977), and Suzuki Teiichi (passes away Jul. 15, 1989)
	Dec. 13	Parole granted to Hoshino Naoki (passes away May 29, 1978)
	Dec. 16	Paroles granted for Kido Kōichi (passes away Apr. 6, 1977) and Ōshima Hiroshi (passes away Jun. 6, 1975)
1956	Mar. 31	Parole granted to Satō Kenryō (passes away Feb. 6, 1975), completion of paroles for Class A prisoners
	Jun. 9	Beijing government opens special military tribunal on Japanese "war criminals" (through July 20)
	Oct. 19	The Japan-Soviet Joint Declaration of 1956 signed (effective Dec. 12)
	Dec. 26	Completion of return of Japanese "war criminals" and detainees from the Soviet Union
1957	Jan. 26	Shigemitsu Mamoru passes away
	Feb. 25	First Kishi Nobusuke Cabinet formed
	Dec. 24	Ōkawa Shūmei passes away
1958	Apr. 7	Ten Class A prisoners complete prison terms through commutation
	May 30	Parole granted to eighteen US-related Class B and C prisoners
	Dec. 29	All remaining Class B and C prisoners complete prison terms through commutation

List of References

Only those sources that are quoted in the text or that are related specifically to the text are listed. For other references, see the list in Higurashi Yoshinobu's *Tōkyō Saiban no kokusai kankei: Kokusai seiji ni okeru kenryoku to kihan* (The Tokyo Trial and International Relations: Power and Norms in International Politics).

English Publications

Allison, John M. *Ambassador from the Prairie*. Boston: Houghton Mifflin, 1973.

Bird, Eugene K. *The Loneliest Man in the World: The Inside Story of the 30-year Imprisonment of Rudolf Hess*. London: Secker & Warburg, 1974. Translated by Sasao Hisashi and Kaji Etsuko as *Shūjin Rudorufu Hesu: Imada gokuchū ni ikiru moto Nachi fukusōsai* (Tokyo: Shuppan-sha, 1976).

Bird, Kai. *The Chairman: John J. McCloy*. New York: Simon & Schuster, 1992.

Brackman, Arnold C. *The Other Nuremberg: The Untold Story of the Tokyo War Crimes Trial*. 2nd edition. New York: William Morrow & Co., 1988. Translated by Higurashi Yoshinobu as *Tōkyō Saiban: Mō hitotsu no Nyurunberuku* (Tokyo: Jiji Press, 1991).

Bontecou, Eleanor. *Papers of Eleanor Bontecou*. Harry S. Truman Presidential Library, Personal Papers and Organizational Records. Microfiche.

Buruma, Ian. *The Wages of Guilt: Memories of War in Germany and Japan*. London: Vintage, 1994. Translated by Ishii Shinpei as *Sensō no kioku: Nihonjin to Doitsujin* (Tokyo: TBS Britannica, 1994).

Buscher, Frank. *The U.S. War Crimes Trial Program in Germany, 1946–1955*. New York: Greenwood Press, 1989.

Cotler, Irwin, ed. *Nuremberg Forty Years Later*. Montreal: McGill-Queen's University Press, 1995.

Emmerson, John K. *The Japanese Thread: A Life in the U.S. Foreign Service*. New York: Holt, Rinehart and Winston, 1978. Translated by Miyaji Kenjirō as *Arashi no naka no gaikōkan: Jon Emāson kaisōroku* (Tokyo: Asahi Shimbunsha, 1979).

Davidson, Eugene. *The Trial of the Germans: An Account of the Twenty-Two Defendants before the International Military Tribunal at Nuremberg*. Columbia, MO: University of Missouri Press, 1997.

Department of Foreign Affairs and Trade, ed. *Documents on Australian Foreign Policy 1937–1949, Vol. IX: January–June 1946*. Canberra: Australian Government Publishing Service, 1991.

Fearey, Robert A. *The Occupation of Japan, Second Phase, 1948–1950*. New York: Macmillan, 1950. Translated by the Institute of Pacific Relations as *Nihon senryō: Sono seika to tenbō* (Tokyo: Kōbundō, 1951).

Fisher, Louis. *Military Tribunals and Presidential Power: American Revolution to the War on Terrorism*. Lawrence: University Press of Kansas, 2005.

Gaddis, John Lewis. *We Now Know: Rethinking Cold War History.* Oxford: Clarendon Press, 1997. Translated by Akagi Kanji and Saitō Yūsuke as *Rekishi toshite no Reisen: Chikara to heiwa no tsuikyū* (Tokyo: Keio University Press, 2004).

GHQ/SCAP records, Adjutant General's Office (AG) papers, Government Section (GS) papers, General Staff 2 (G2) papers, Legal Section (LS) papers, Far Eastern Commission (FEC) Papers. National Archives and Records Administration (NARA), Archives II. College Park, Maryland. Microfiche in National Diet Library, Tokyo.

Goldensohn, Leon. *Nuremberg Interviews.* New York: Alfred A. Knopf, 2004.

Greene, Joshua M. *Justice at Dachau: The Trials of an American Prosecutor.* New York: Broadway Books, 2003.

Hamilton, Alexander, James Madison, and John Jay. *The Federalist.* Edited by Goldwin Smith. New York: The Colonial Press, 1901. Translated by Saitō Makoto et al. as *Za Federarisuto* (Tokyo: Fukumura Shuppan, 1991).

Haffner, Sebastian. *The Meaning of Hitler.* Weidenfeld and Nicolson, 1979. Translated by Akabane Tatsuo as *Hitorā to wa nani ka* (Tokyo: Sōshisha, 1979).

Hankey, The Right Hon. Lord. *Politics, Trials and Errors.* Chicago: Henry Regnery Company, 1950. Translated by Hasegawa Saiji as *Senpan saiban no sakugo* (Tokyo: Jiji Press, 1952).

International Prosecution Section (IPS) Papers, GHQ/SCAP records, Archives: RG 331. National Archives Microfilm Publications, 1991. Copies in Modern Japanese Political History Materials Room (Kensei Shiryōshitsu), National Diet Library, Tokyo.

Johnson, U. Alexis, with Jef Olivarius McAllister. *The Right Hand of Power: The Memoirs of an American Diplomat.* New Jersey: Prentice-Hall, 1984. Translated by Masuda Hiroshi as *Jonson Beitaishi no Nihon kaisō: Ni Niroku Jiken kara Okinawa henkan, Nikuson shokku made* (Tokyo: Sōshisha, 1989).

Kay, Robin, ed. *Documents on New Zealand External Relations.* Vol. 3, *The Anzus Pact and the Treaty of Peace with Japan.* Wellington: Government Printer, 1985.

Kennan, George. *American Diplomacy, 1900–1950.* Chicago: University of Chicago Press, 1951.

Kesaris, Paul, ed. *Documents of the National Security Council.* Maryland: University Publications of America, 1980. Microfilm.

Krock, Arthur. *Memoir: Intimate Recollection of Twelve American Presidents from Theodore Roosevelt to Richard Nixon.* London: Cassell, 1968. Translated by Yagi Isamu as *Kaisō: Mokugeki shitekita Amerika-shi* (Tokyo: Hayakawa Shobō, 1970).

Link, Arthur S. et al., eds. *The Papers of Woodrow Wilson.* Vols. 56–57. Princeton: Princeton University Press, 1987.

MacArthur, General Douglas. *Papers of General Douglas MacArthur.* Blue Binders, War Crimes. MacArthur Memorial Archives, Norfolk, Virginia. Microfilm.

Maga, Tim. *Judgment at Tokyo: The Japanese War Crimes Trials.* Lexington: University Press of Kentucky, 2001.

Maogoto, Jackson N. *War Crimes and Realpolitik: International Justice from World War I to the 21st Century.* London: Lynne Rienner Publishers, 2004.

Mendelsohn, John. "War Crimes Trials and Clemency in Germany and Japan." In *Americans as Proconsuls: United States Military Government in Germany and Japan, 1944–1952*, edited by Robert Wolfe. Carbondale: Southern Illinois University Press, 1984.

Millis, Walter, ed. *The Forrestal Diaries.* New York: Viking, 1951.

Minear, Richard H. "In Defense of Radha Binod Pal." *The Japan Interpreter* 11, no. 3 (Winter 1977): 263–270. Translated as "Pāru hanketsu no igi: Ienaga kyōju e no hanron", *Misuzu* 190 (November 1975).

———. *Victors' Justice: Tokyo War Crimes Trial.* Princeton: Princeton University Press, 1971. Translated by Andō Nisuke as *Tōkyō Saiban: Shōsha no sabaki* (Tokyo: Fukumura Shuppan, 1998).

Minow, Martha. *Between Vengeance and Forgiveness: Facing History After Genocide and Mass Violence.* Boston: Beacon Press, 1998.

Nandy, Ashis. *The Savage Freud and Other Essays on Possible and Retrievable Selves.* Princeton: Princeton University Press, 1995.

Nye, Jr., Joseph. *Understanding International Conflicts: An Introduction to Theory and History.* 5th Edition. New York: Pearson Longman, 2005. Translated by Tanaka Akihiko and Murata Kōji as *Kokusai funsō: Riron to rekishi* (Tokyo: Yūhikaku, 2005).

Office of the Judge Advocate General (JAG). *War Crimes Branch Papers: General and Administrative Records 1944–1949.* National Archives and Records Administration (NARA), Archives II: RG 153. College Park, Maryland.

Reel, A. Frank. *The Case of General Yamashita.* Chicago: University of Chicago Press, 1949. Translated by Shimojima Muraji as *Yamashita saiban*, 3 vols. (Tokyo: Nihon Kyōbunsha, 1952).

Rix, Alan, ed. *Intermittent Diplomat: The Japan and Batavia Diaries of W. Macmahon Ball.* Carlton: Melbourne University Press, 1988.

Röling, B. V. A., and Antonio Cassese. *The Tokyo Trial and Beyond: Reflections of a Peacemonger.* Cambridge: Polity Press, 1993.

Schaller, Michael. *Altered States: The United States and Japan since the Occupation.* New York: Oxford University Press, 1997. Translated by Ichikawa Yōichi as *"Nichi-Bei kankei" to wa nan datta no ka: Senryōki kara Reisen shūketsugo made* (Tokyo: Sōshisha, 2004).

Smith, Jean Edward, ed. *The Papers of General Lucius D. Clay: Germany, 1945–1949.* Vol. 1. Bloomington: Indiana University Press, 1974.

Sutton, David N. "The Trial of Tojo: The Most Important Trial in All History?" *American Bar Association Journal* 36, no. 2 (1950): 93–96.

Taylor, Telford. *The Anatomy of the Nuremberg Trials: A Personal Memoir*. London: Bloomsbury, 1993.

———. *Final Report to the Secretary of the Army on the Nuremberg War Crimes Trials under Control Council Law No. 10*. New York: William S. Hein, 1997.

UK Foreign Office. *Foreign Office: Political Departments: General Correspondence from 1906–1966*. National Archives of the UK (TNA): FO 371/76250–76253, 84032–84035, 99509. Kew, London, 1949–1952.

UK Lord Chancellor's Office. *Lord Chancellor's Office and Lord Chancellor's Department: Registered Files*. The National Archives of the UK (TNA): LCO 2/2992. Kew, London, 1947–1948.

US Department of Defense. (III) File, Correspondence Files, 1943–1951, Army Headquarters, Department of Army, 1945–1957, File No. 22/431/33. Australian Archives, Victoria.

US Department of State. Central Decimal Files. National Archives and Records Administration (NARA), Archives II: RG 59; 1950–1954, 694.0024–0026, Boxes 3020–3022; and 1945–1949, 740.00116, Box 3632. College Park, Maryland.

———. *Foreign Relations of the United States [FRUS]*. Washington, DC: Government Printing Office, 1955–.

———. *Records Relating to Political Relations of Japan, 1950–1954; 1955–1959*. National Archives and Records Administration (NARA): RG 59, Decimal Files 611.9424 and 694.0024, Microfilm. Delaware: Scholarly Resources.

Japanese Publications and Documents

Abe Genki. *Sugamo nikki* [Sugamo Diary]. Tokyo: Tentensha, 1992.

Abe Kōbō. "Uragirareta sensō hanzainin" [Betrayed War Criminals]. *Kaizō* (April 1953).

Aikawa Yoshisuke monjo [Aikawa Yoshisuke Papers]. Modern Japanese Political History Materials Room [Kensei Shiryōshitsu], National Diet Library, Tokyo.

Aisin Gioro Pujie. *Fuketsu jiden: "Manshūkuo" kōtei o ikite* [Autobiography of Pujie: Life as Imperial Brother of the Emperor of Manchuria]. Translated by Maruyama Noboru et al. Tokyo: Kawade Shobō Shinsha, 1995.

Aisin Gioro Puyi. *Waga hansei: "Manshūkoku" kōtei no jiden* [My Life up to Now: Autobiography of the Emperor of Manchuria]. 2 vols. Translated by Ono Shinobu. Tokyo: Chikuma Shobō, 1977.

Ara Takashi, ed. *Nihon senryō: Gaikō kankei shiryōshū* [Occupation of Japan: Diplomacy-Related Documents]. 10 vols. Tokyo: Kashiwa Shobō, 1991.

Arai Toshio Shiryō Hozonkai [Arai Toshio Materials Preservation Society], ed. *Chūgoku Bujun senpan kanrisho shokuin no shōgen* [Testimonies of Officials at the Fushun War Criminals Management Center]. Tokyo: Nashinoki-sha, 2003.

Araki Sadao. "Sugamo danchō no ki" [Heartbreak Diary of Sugamo]. *Bungei shunjū* (November 1955).

Asahi Shimbun Shuzaihan [Asahi Shimbun Press Group], ed. *Sensō sekinin to tsuitō* [War Responsibility and Commemoration]. Tokyo: Asahi Shimbunsha, 2006.

Asahi Shimbun Hōtei Kishadan [Asahi Shimbunsha Court Reporters Group], ed. *Tōkyō Saiban* [The Tokyo Trial]. 3 vols. Tokyo: Tōkyō Saiban Kankōkai [Tokyo Trial Publishing Committee], 1962.

Awaya Kentarō. *Tōkyō Saiban ron* [Discussing the Tokyo Trial]. Tokyo: Ōtsuki Shoten, 1989.

———. *Tōkyō Saiban e no michi* [Road to the Tokyo Trial]. Vols. 1 and 2. Tokyo: Kodansha, 2006.

Chazono Yoshio, ed. *BC-kyū senpan Yokohama Saiban shiryō* [Documents on the Yokohama War Crimes Trials on Class B and C War Criminals]. Tokyo: Fuji Shuppan, 1985.

Chūgoku Kikansha Renrakukai [Association of Returnees from China], trans. and ed. *Kakusei: Bujun senpan kanrisho no 6-nen* [Awakening: Six Years at the Fushun War Criminals Management Center]. Tokyo: Shimpū Shobō, 1995.

Etō Jun. *Mō hitotsu no sengoshi* [Another Postwar Era]. Tokyo: Kodansha, 1978.

Fujiyama Ichirō. *Fujiyama Ichirō jiden: Utagoe yo hibike minami no sora ni* [Autobiography of Fujiyama Ichirō: Sing Out to the Southern Skies]. Tokyo: Kōjinsha, 1993.

Fujiwara Iwaichi. *F-kikan* [F-Organization]. Tokyo: Hara Shobō, 1966.

Gunji Nobuo. *Kaitei shinban bokushingu 100-nen* [100 Years of Boxing: Revised New Edition]. Tokyo: Jiji Press, 1976.

Hagiwara Tōru. *Kōwa to Nihon* [Peace Treaty and Japan]. Tokyo: Yomiuri Shimbunsha, 1950.

Hara Yoshihisa, ed. *Kishi Nobusuke shōgenroku* [Testimonies by Kishi Nobusuke]. Tokyo: Mainichi Shimbunsha, 2003.

Harada Kumao. *Saionji-kō to seikyoku* [Prince Saionji and Political Situations of the Time]. 9 vols. Tokyo: Iwanami Shoten, 1950.

Haruna Mikio. *Himitsu no fairu: CIA no Tai-Nichi kōsaku* [Secret Files: CIA Covert Operations in Japan]. Vol. 1. Tokyo: Kyodo News, 2000.

Hata Ikuhiko. *Gendaishi no taiketsu* [Confrontations in Contemporary History]. Tokyo: Bungeishunjū, 2003.

Hata Ikuhiko et al., eds. *Sekai sensō hanzai jiten* [World Encyclopedia of War Crimes]. Tokyo: Bungeishunjū, 2002.

Hatano Sumio. "Izoku no meisō: Nihon Izokukai to kioku no kyōgō" [War-Bereaved Families' Loss of Sense of Direction: Japan War-Bereaved Families Association and Conflicting Memories]. In *Kioku toshite no Pāru Hābā* [Pearl Harbor as Memory], edited by Hosoya Chihiro, Irie Akira, and Ōshiba Ryō. Kyoto: Minerva Shobō, 2004.

Hidaka Rokurō. *Gendai ideorogī* [Contemporary Ideology]. Tokyo: Keisō Shobō, 1960.

Higurashi Yoshinobu. "'Bunmei no sabaki' ga nokoshita enkon" [Grudges that "Trial of Civilization" Left Behind]. *This is Yomiuri* (October 1998).

———. "Paru hanketsu saikō" [Rethinking Pal's Judgment]. In *Nihon kindaishi no saikōchiku* [Reconstruction of Japanese Modern History], edited by Itō Takashi. Tokyo: Yamakawa Shuppansha, 1993.

———. "'Seigi' to 'Jihi': Kōwago no senpan shakuhō to Nichi-Bei kankei" [Justice and Mercy: War Criminals Releases and US-Japan Relations after the Signing of the Peace Treaty]. Edited by Amerika Gakkai [The Japanese Association for American Studies]. *Amerika kenkyū* [American Studies] 35 (March 2001).

———. *Tōkyō Saiban no kokusai kankei: Kokusai seiji ni okeru kenryoku to kihan* [The Tokyo Trial and International Relations: Power and Norms in International Politics]. Tokyo: Bokutakusha, 2002.

———. "Tōkyō Saiban kiroku no kōkan mondai (1) (2)" [Dispute over Publication of the Record of the Tokyo Trial (1) (2)]. *Hōritsu jihō* (March and April 2003).

Hirota Kōki Denki Kankōkai [Hirota Kōki Biography Publishing Committee], ed. *Hirota Kōki* [Hirota Kōki]. Tokyo: Ashi Shobō, 1992.

Hōmu Daijin Kanbō Shihō-Hōsei Chōsabu [Judicial System and Research Department, Secretariat of the Minister of Justice], ed. *Senso hanzai saiban gaishi yō* [Summary of Historical Overview of War Crime Trial]. Tokyo: Ministry of Justice, 1973.

Hosaka Masayasu. *Shōwa-shi nanatsu no nazo* [Seven Puzzles in Shōwa history]. Tokyo: Kodansha, 2003.

———. *"Yasukuni" to iu nayami* [Anguish Called Yasukuni]. Tokyo: Mainichi Shimbun-sha, 2007.

Hosoya Chihiro. *San Francisco kōwa e no michi* [Road to San Francisco Peace Treaty]. Tokyo: Chūōkōronsha, 1984.

———, ed. *Nihon to Amerika: Pātonāshippu no 50-nen* [Japan and the United States: Fifty Years of Partnership]. Tokyo: Japan Times, 2001.

Hosoya Chihiro, Andō Nisuke, and Ōnuma Yasuaki, eds. *Tōkyō Saiban o tou* [Questioning the Tokyo Trial]. Tokyo: Kodansha, 1984.

House of Representatives Legal Affairs Committee. *Senpan kankei shiryō* [War Criminal–Related Documents]. Tokyo: Committee on Judicial Affairs, n.d.

Igarashi Takeshi and Kitaoka Shinichi, eds. *Sōron, Tōkyō Saiban to wa nan datta no ka* [Contestation, What Was the Tokyo Trial]. Tokyo: Tsukiji Shokan, 1997.

Iguchi Haruo. "Taiheiyō Sensō shūketsu o meguru rekishi ronsō" [Historical Debate over Termination of the Pacific War]. In *Kioku toshite no Pāru Hābā* [Pearl Harbor as Memory], edited by Hosoya Chihiro, Irie Akira, and Ōshiba Ryō. Kyoto: Minerva Shobō, 2004.

Inagaki Takeshi. *Kakumeika Chandora Bōsu* [Chandra Bose, the Revolutionary]. Tokyo: Shinchōsha, 1986.

Inoue Tadao shiryō [Inoue Tadao Documents]. Yasukuni Kaikō Bunko [Yasukuni Archives].

Irie Yōko. *Fugi: Shinchō saigo no kōtei* [Puyi: Last Emperor of the Qing Dynasty]. Tokyo: Iwanami Shoten, 2006.

Ishida Yūji. *Kako no kokufuku: Hitorā go no Doitsu* [Overcoming the Past: Germany after Hitler]. Tokyo: Hakusuisha, 2002.

Itagaki Tadashi. *Yasukuni kōshiki sanpai no sōkatsu* [Summary of the Yasukuni Official Visit Issue]. Tokyo: Tentensha, 2000.

Itō Takashi, ed. *Satō Eisaku nikki* [Satō Eisaku Diary]. Vol. 1. Tokyo: Asahi Shimbunsha, 1998.

Itō Takashi et al., eds. *Shigemitsu Mamoru shuki* [Shigemitsu Mamoru's Personal Notes]. Vol. 2. Tokyo: Chūōkōronsha, 1988.

Kamishima Jirō. *Nichijōsei no seijigaku: Mijika ni jiritsu no kyoten o motomete* [Politics of Everyday Life: Seeking Self-Reliance Close to Home]. Tokyo: Chikuma Shobō, 1982.

Katō Shunsaku. *Kokusai Rengō seiritsu-shi: Kokuren wa donoyōni shite tsukurareta ka* [History of the Founding of the United Nations: How Was the United Nations Created?]. Tokyo: Yūshindō Kōbunsha, 2000.

Katō Norihiro, ed. *Nihon no mei zuihitsu* [Best Japanese Essays]. Supplementary issue 98. Tokyo: Sakuhinsha, 1999.

Kawabe Torashirō. *Ichigayadai kara Ichigayadai e* [From Ichigayadai to Ichigayadai]. Tokyo: Jiji Press, 1962.

Kawakami Isamu. "Sugamo Purizun hōkokusho" [Report from Sugamo Prison]. *Bungei shunjū* (December 1955).

Kaya Okinori. *Uzu no naka* [Inside the Whirlpool]. Private compilation, 1979.

Kido Kōichi kankei monjo [Documents Related to Kido Kōichi]. In *Kido-ke monjo* [Kido Family Documents], Microfilm. Chiba: National Museum of Japanese History.

Kido Kōichi Nikki Kenkyūkai, ed. *Kido Kōichi nikki* [Kido Kōichi Diary]. Vol. 2. Tokyo: University of Tokyo Press, 1966.

——, ed. *Kido Kōichi nikki: Tōkyō Saiban-ki* [Kido Kōichi Diary: Tokyo Trial Period]. Tokyo: University of Tokyo Press, 1980.

Kishi Nobusuke et al. *Kishi Nobusuke no kaisō* [Memoir of Kishi Nobusuke]. Tokyo: Bungeishunjū, 1981.

Kirichenko, Alexey. "Tōkyō Saiban e no Kuremurin himitsu shirei" [Kremlin's Secret Directive to the Tokyo Trial]. Translated by Kawamura Suguru. *Seiron* 398 (July 2005).

Kita Hiroaki. *Gunritsu hōtei: Senjika no shirarezaru "saiban"* [Courts-Martial: The Unknown "Trials" of Wartime]. Tokyo: Asahi Shimbunsha, 1997.

Kitaoka Shinichi. *"Futsū no kuni" e* [Toward a "Normal Country"]. Tokyo: Chūōkōron Shinsha, 2000.

———. *Nihon no jiritsu: Tai-Bei kyōchō to Ajia gaikō* [Japan's Independence: Cooperation with the United States and Diplomacy in Asia]. Tokyo: Chūōkōron Shinsha, 2004.

Kiyose Ichirō. *Hiroku Tōkyō Saiban* [Secret Record of the Tokyo Trial]. Tokyo: Yomiuri Shimbunsha, 1967.

Kodama Yoshio. *Shibafu wa fumaretemo: Sugamo senpan no kiroku* [Even If Our Lawn Is Stepped on: Records of the Sugamo War Criminals]. Tokyo: Shin Yūkan Shimbunsha, 1956.

Kojima Noboru. *Tōkyō Saiban* [The Tokyo Trial]. Tokyo: Chūōkōron Shinsha, 2007.

Kokkai kaigiroku [National Diet Session Record]. http://kokkai.ndl.go.jp/.

Komiyama Noboru, ed. *Gensui Hata Shunroku gokuchū gokugai no nisshi* [Field Marshal Hata Shunroku's Diary in and out of Prison]. Private compilation, 1992.

Kōsaka Masataka et al. *Rekishi no tenkanten de kangaeru* [A Thought at a Turning Point of History]. Tokyo: Kodansha, 1994.

Kusuda Minoru. *Kusuda Minoru nikki: Satō Eisaku sōri shuseki hishokan no 2000-nichi* [Kusuda Minoru Diary: The 2000 Days of Prime Minister Eisaku Sato's Chief of Staff]. Edited by Iokibe Makoto and Wada Jun. Tokyo: Chūōkōron Shinsha, 2001.

Kyōdō Tsūshinsha Shakaibu [Kyodo News Social Affairs Department], ed. *Chinmoku no fairu* [Silent Files]. Tokyo: Kyodo News, 1996.

Maruyama Masao. "Gunkoku shihaisha no seishin keitai" ["Thought and Behaviour Patterns of Japan's Wartime Leaders"]. In *Gendai seiji no shisō to kōdō* [Thought and Behaviour in Modern Politics]. Expanded edition. Tokyo: Miraisha, 1964. Originally published in *Shinchō*, 1949. Translated by Ivan Morris in Maruyama Masao, *Thought and Behaviour in Modern Japanese Politics* (London: Oxford University Press, 1963).

Matsumura Kenzō. *Sandai kaikoroku* [Three Generation Memoir]. Tokyo: Tōyō Keizai Shinpōsha, 1964.

Matsumoto Shigeharu. *Shōwa-shi e no ichi shōgen* [A Testimony to Shōwa History]. Tokyo: Mainichi Shimbunsha, 1986.

Matsutani Sei. *Nihon saiken hiwa: Tōkyō Saiban ya saigunbi nado, dōran no hanseiki o ikita moto shushō hishokan no kaisō* [Secret Stories on Japan's Reconstruction: Recollections of a Former Secretary to the Prime Minister Who Lived through Half a Century of Turmoil, including the Tokyo Trials and Rearmament]. Tokyo: Asagumo Shimbunsha, 1983.

Mikuriya Takashi. *Tennō to seiji: Kindai Nihon no dainamizumu* [The Emperor of Japan and Politics: The Dynamism of Modern Japan]. Tokyo: Fujiwara Shoten, 2006.

Mikuriya Takashi et al., eds. *Tokugawa Yoshihiro shūsen nikki* [Tokugawa Yoshihiro Diary after the End of the War]. Tokyo: Asahi Shimbunsha, 1999.

———. *Urabe Ryōgo jijū nikki: Shōwa Tennō saigo no sokkin* [Diary of Grand Chamberlain Urabe Ryōgo: Last Aide of the Shōwa Emperor]. Vol. 5. Tokyo: Asahi Shimbunsha, 2007.

Ministry of Foreign Affairs, ed. *Gaikō kiroku* [Diplomatic Record]. 7th release on "Preparatory works toward signing of the San Francisco Peace Treaty" (B'4.0.0.2) and "Japan's preparatory measures for the San Francisco Peace Treaty" (Peace Treaty documents) (B'4.1.0.14). Diplomatic Archive of the Ministry of Foreign Affairs, 1982.

———. *Gaikō kiroku* [Diplomatic Record]. 14th release on "Miscellaneous matters related to handling of Japanese war criminals after effectuation of the peace treaty" and "Handling of Class A war criminals" etc. (D'1.3.0.3). Diplomatic Archive of the Ministry of Foreign Affairs, 1998.

Ministry of Foreign Affairs, Treaties Bureau, Legal Affairs Division, ed. *Heiwa Jōyaku no teiketsu ni kansuru chōsho* [Protocol of the Signing of the Peace Treaty]. Vol. 3. Diplomatic Archive of the Ministry of Foreign Affairs, 1967.

Ministry of Health and Welfare, Repatriation Relief Bureau. *Hikiage engo no kiroku* [Record of Repatriation Relief Activities]. Vols. 2–3. Tokyo: Ministry of Health and Welfare, 1955–1963.

———. *Hikiage to engo 30-nen no ayumi* [Thirty-Year History of Repatriation and Relief Activities]. Tokyo: Ministry of Health and Welfare, 1977.

Mitarai Tatsuo, ed. *Minami Jirō* [Minami Jirō]. Private compilation, 1957.

Mitsui Takaharu. "Kīnan kenji no yanushi" [Landlord of Prosecutor Keenan]. *Bungei shunjū* (June Special Issue, 1952).

Miyama Yōzō. *Haikyo no Shōwa kara: Teikoku rikugun sōsō no ki* [From Ruined Shōwa: Funeral Service for the Imperial Army]. Edited by Kai Katsuhiko. Tokyo: Kōjinsha, 1989.

Mizuno Tetsuo. *Haruka naru heiwa ni: Sugamo no yogen* [Toward Faraway Peace: The Prophecy of Sugamo]. Tokyo: Tōkō Shoin, 1952.

Momose Takashi. *Jiten Shōwa sengoki no Nihon* [Encyclopedia of Japan in the Postwar Era]. Edited by Itō Takashi. Tokyo: Yoshikawa Kōbunkan, 1995.

Mōri Kazuko. *Nit-Chū kankei: Sengo kara shinjidai e* [Japan-China Relations: From the Postwar to a New Era]. Tokyo: Iwanami Shoten, 2006.

Mutō Akira. *Gunmu kyokuchō Mutō Akira kaisōroku* [Memoir of Mutō Akira, Director of the Military Affairs Bureau]. Edited by Jōhō Yoshio. Tokyo: Fuyō Shobō, 1981.

Nagai Kafū. "Danchōtei nichijō" [Danchōtei Diary]. In *Kafū zenshū*, vol. 25. Tokyo: Iwanami Shoten, 1994.

———. *Tekiroku: Danchōtei nichijō* [Summary: The Danchōtei Diary]. 2 vols. Edited by Isoda Koichi. Tokyo: Iwanami Shoten, 1987.

Nair, Aiyappan Pillai Madhavan. *Shirarezaru Indo dokuritsu tōsō: A.M. Nairu kaisōroku* [Unknown Struggle for Indian Independence: Memoirs of A.M. Nair]. Translated by Kawai Shin. Tokyo: Futōsha, 1983. Originally published as *An Indian Freedom Fighter in Japan: Memoirs of A. M. Nair* (Telangana: Orient Longman, 1982).

Naitō Masao. "Pāru hanji 'igi hanketsu' no kyokō" [Myth of Judge Pal's "Dissenting Judgment"]. *In-Pa kai kaihō* [Indo-Pakistan Society, Tokyo University of Foreign Studies] 16 (2006).

Nakajima Takeshi. *Pāru hanji: Tōkyō Saiban hihan to zettai heiwa-shugi* [Justice Pal: Criticism of the Tokyo Trial and Absolute Pacifism]. Tokyo: Hakusuisha, 2007.

Narahashi Wataru. *Gekiryū ni sao sashite: Waga kokuhaku* [Rowing against the Torrent: My Confession]. Tokyo: Tsubasa Shoin, 1968.

National Diet Library, Research & Legislative Reference Bureau, ed. *Shinpen Yasukuni Jinja mondai shiryōshū* [Newly Compiled Documents on the Yasukuni Shrine Issue]. Tokyo: National Diet Library, 2007. http://www.ndl.go.jp/data/publication/document2007.html.

NHK Special. "Pāru Hanji wa nani o toikaketa no ka" [What Question Did Justice Pal Pose?]. Broadcast August 14, 2007.

"NHK Hōdō no Kiroku" Kankō Iinkai ["NHK News Record" Publishing Committee], ed. *NHK hōdō no 50-nen: Gekidō no Shōwa to tomo ni* [Fifty Years of NHK Reporting: Through the Turbulent Shōwa Era]. Tokyo: Kondō Shoten, 1988.

Nishida Shunichi. "Bōrei to natta Sugamo senpan" [Sugamo War Prisoners Who Became Ghosts]. *Kaizō* (February 1954).

Nishimura Kumao. "Sanfuranshisuko no omoide" [Reminiscences of San Francisco]. *Chūō kōron* (May 1957).

Nitta Mitsuo, ed. *Kyokutō Kokusai Gunji Saiban sokkiroku* [Stenographic Record of the International Military Tribunal for the Far East]. 10 vols. Tokyo: Yūshōdō Shoten, 1968.

Nomura Masao. *Sabakareta Nihon* [Japan Tried]. Tokyo: Kadokawa Shoten, 1956.

Oda Bunji. *Sugamo senpan keimusho tokuyūgo jiten* [Dictionary of Special Terminology Used by Inmates of Sugamo Prison]. Tokyo: Seifū, 1986.

———. *Kanshu ga kakushi totte ita Sugamo Purizun mikōkai firumu* [Unpublicized Photos of Sugamo Prison Taken Secretly by a Prison Guard]. Edited by Chazono Yoshio. Tokyo: Shōgakukan, 2000.

Ogata Taketora Denki Kankōkai [Ogata Taketora Biography Publishing Committee], ed. *Ogata Taketora* [Ogata Taketora]. Tokyo: Asahi Shimbunsha, 1963.

Ōkawa Shūmei Kenshōkai [Ōkawa Shūmei Memorial Association], ed. *Ōkawa Shūmei nikki: Meiji 36-nen–Shōwa 24-nen* [Ōkawa Shūmei Diary: Meiji 36–Shōwa 24]. Tokyo: Iwasaki Gakujutsu Shuppansha, 1986.

Ōno Katsumi. *Kasumigaseki gaikō: Sono dentō to hitobito* [Kasumigaseki Diplomacy: Its Traditions and People]. Tokyo: Nihon Keizai Shimbunsha, 1978.

Osaragi Jirō. *Osaragi Jirō haisen nikki* [Osaragi Jiro's Diary after the War Defeat]. Tokyo: Sōshisha, 1995.

Pal, Radhabinod. *Heiwa no sengen* [Declaration of Peace]. Edited by Tanaka Masaaki. Tokyo: Tōzai Bunmeisha, 1953.

———. *Nihon muzairon: Shinri no sabaki* [The "Japan Not Guilty" Argument: Judgment of the Truth]. Edited by Tanaka Masaaki. Tokyo: Taiheiyō Shuppansha, 1952.

———. *Senshi o yaburu: Nihon wa muzai nari* [Breaking War History: Japan Is Not Guilty]. Translated and edited by Yoshimatsu Masakatsu. Tokyo: Nihon Shoseki Insatsu Tōkyō Shisha, 1952.

———. *Tōkyō Saiban genten: Eibunban Pāru hanketsusho* [Original Pal Judgment at the Tokyo Trial in English]. Tokyo: Kokusho Kankōkai, 1999.

Pal, Satyabrata. "Mago ga akasu Tōkyō Saiban: Pāru hanji no kigai" [Tokyo Trial Disclosed by Pal's Grandson: Justice Pal's Grit]. Translated by Tagawa Yasugo. *Seiron* 417 (December 2006).

Prime Minister's Office, Pension Bureau. *Onkyū seidoshi* [History of the Pension System]. Tokyo: Ministry of Finance Printing Bureau, 1964.

Roos, John. *Sugamo jinmon chōsho* [Record of Interrogation at Sugamo Prison]. Supervised by Higurashi Yoshinobu, translated by Yamada Hiroshi. Tokyo: Yomiuri Shimbunsha, 1995.

Saitō Shizuo. *Gaikō* [Diplomacy]. Tokyo: Simul Shuppankai, 1991.

Sakamoto Kazuya. "Heiwa Jōyaku to 'Tōkyō Saiban jutaku' ronsō ga kaku gaikōshi-teki shiten" [Diplomatic Historical Perspective Missing in the Debate on the Peace Treaty and the "Acceptance of the Tokyo Trial"]. *Seiron* (September 2005).

Sakamoto Takao. *Rekishi kyōiku o kangaeru: Nihonjin wa rekishi o torimodoseru ka* [Thinking about History Education: Can the Japanese Reclaim Their History?]. Tokyo: PHP Institute, 1998.

———. *Shōchō tennō seido to Nihon no raireki* ["Emperor as Symbol" System and Japan's Historical Trial]. Tokyo: Toshi Shuppan, 1995.

———. *Towareru Nihonjin no rekishi kankaku* [Historical Sense of the Japanese in Question]. Tokyo: Keisō Shobō, 2001.

Saki Ryūzō, ed. *Nihon no mei zuihitsu* [Japan's Best Essays]. Supplementary issue 91. Tokyo: Sakuhinsha, 1998.

Sanematsu Yuzuru. *Sugamo* [Sugamo]. Tokyo: Tosho Shuppansha, 1972.

Sanmonji Shōhei. "Kyokutō gunji saiban" [International Military Tribunal for the Far East]. Vol. 3, *Kataritsugu Shōwa-shi* [Showa History to Be Recorded], ed. Hoshina Zenshirō, et al. Tokyo: Asahi Shimbunsha, 1990.

Sasakawa Ryōichi. *Sugamo nikki* [Sugamo Diary]. Tokyo: Chūōkōronsha, 1997.

Satō Kenryō. *Daitōa Sensō kaikoroku* [Memoirs of the Greater East Asia War]. Tokyo: Tokuma Shoten, 1966.

Satō Seizaburō. *Sasakawa Ryōichi kenkyū: Ijigen kara no shisha* [Study of Sasakawa Ryōichi: Emissary from Another Dimension]. Tokyo: Chūōkōronsha, 1998.

Sawa Kunio. "Tōkyō Saiban wa haisha e no hōfuku datta" [The Tokyo Trial Was Retaliation against the Defeated]. *Seiron* (February 2006).

Sawada Jirō. "Haisen kara kikoku made" [From War Defeat to Return Home]. *Chūkiren* (inaugural issue, 1997).

Sejima Ryūzō. *Sejima Ryūzō kaisōroku: Ikusanga* [Memoir of Sejima Ryūzō: Long and Lonely Journey]. Tokyo: Fusōsha, 1996.

Sengo Kyōsei Yokuryū-shi Hensan Iinkai [Committee for Compilation of the Postwar History of Forced Internment], ed. *Sengo kyōsei yokuryū-shi* [Postwar History of Forced Internment]. Vol. 5. Tokyo: Public Foundation for Peace and Consolation, 2005.

Sensō Jukeisha Sewakai [Aid Society for War Prisoners], ed. *Gyōmu hōkoku* [Activities Report]. Private compilation, n.d.

Shida Yukio. *Shiberia yokuryū o tou* [Questioning Detention in Siberia]. Tokyo: Keisō Shobō, 1987.

Shigematsu Kazuyoshi, ed. *Sugamo Purizun no ikō ni tou: Senpan no omokage to yūshū no hibi, hiroku shashin dokyumento* [Questioning the Remnants of Sugamo Prison: The Vestiges of War Criminals and Days of Imprisonment, Secret Photo Documents]. Tokyo: Maki Shobō, 1981.

Shigemitsu Mamoru. *Sugamo nikki* [Sugamo Diary]. 2 vols. Tokyo: Bungeishunjū Shinsha, 1953.

Shimamura Saburō. *Chūgoku kara kaetta senpan* [War Criminals Who Returned Home from China]. Tokyo: Nit-Chū Shuppan, 1975.

Shimanouchi Tatsuoki. *Tōkyō Saiban* [The Tokyo Trial]. Tokyo: Nippon Hyōronsha, 1984.

Shimoda Takesō. *Sengo Nihon gaikō no shōgen: Nihon wa kou shite saiseishita* [Testimonies on Postwar Japanese Diplomacy: How Japan Was Reborn]. Vol. 1. Tokyo: Institute of Public Administration, 1984.

Shindō Eiichi et al., eds. *Ashida Hitoshi nikki* [Ashida Hitoshi Diary]. Vol. 2. Tokyo: Iwanami Shoten, 1986.

Shirai Yoshio. *Za chanpion* [The Champion]. Tokyo: Tokyo Shimbun Publishing, 1987.

Suetsugu Ichirō. *"Sengo" e no chōsen* [Challenge to "Postwar Era"]. Tokyo: Rekishitosho-sha, 1981.

Sugamo Hōmu Iinkai [Sugamo Legal Affairs Committee], ed. *Senpan saiban no jissō* [The Facts of the War Crime Trial]. Reprinted edition. Tokyo: Sugamo Senpan

Saiban no Jissō Kankō Iinkai [The Sugamo Facts of the War Crime Trials Publication Group], 1981.

Sugawara Yutaka. *Tōkyō Saiban no shōtai* [The True Nature of the Tokyo Trial]. Tokyo: Jiji Press, 1961.

Sugimoto Ken. *Kaigun no Shōwa-shi: Teitoku to shimbun kisha* [Shōwa History of the Imperial Japanese Navy: An Admiral and a Newspaper Reporter]. Tokyo: Bungeishunjū, 1985.

Tajiri Akiyoshi. *Tajiri Akiyoshi kaisōroku: Hansei o kaketa Chūgoku gaikō no kiroku* [Memoirs of Tajiri Akiyoshi: A Record of a Life in China's Diplomacy]. Tokyo: Hara Shobō, 1977.

Takagi Kiyohisa. *Tōa no chichi Ishiwara Kanji* [Ishiwara Kanji, Father of East Asia]. Tokyo: Tamairabo, 1985.

Takamatsunomiya Nobuhito Shin'nō Denki Kankō Iinkai [Nobuhito, Prince Takamatsu Biography Publishing Committee], ed. *Takamatsunomiya Nobuhito Shin'nō* [Nobuhito, Prince Takamatsu]. Tokyo: Asahi Shimbunsha, 1991.

Takemae Eiji. *GHQ no hitobito: Keireki to seisaku* [People of GHQ: Career and Policy]. Tokyo: Akashi Shoten, 2002.

Takeyama Michio. *Shōwa no seishin-shi* [Intellectual History of Shōwa]. Tokyo: Shinchōsha, 1956.

Tamura Yoshio, ed. *Hiroku Daitōa senshi* [Secret Record of the Greater East Asia War]. Vol. 6. Tokyo: Fuji Shoen, 1954.

Tanaka Nobumasa, Tanaka Hiroshi, and Hata Nagami. *Izoku to sengo* [War-Bereaved Families in Postwar Days]. Tokyo: Iwanami Shoten, 1995.

Tanaka Nobumasa. *Yasukuni no sengoshi* [Postwar History of Yasukuni Shrine]. Tokyo: Iwanami Shoten, 2002.

Tanaka Ryūkichi. *Haiin o tsuku: Gunbatsu sen'ō no jissō* [To Pinpoint the Reason for Defeat: The Reality of Warlordism]. Tokyo: Chūōkōronsha, 1988.

Tatai Yoshio. *Ketsudan shita otoko: Kido Kōichi no Shōwa* [A Determined Man: Shōwa Era of Kido Kōichi]. Tokyo: Bungeishunjū, 2000.

Tatamiya Eitarō. *Hashimoto Kingorō ichidai* [Life of Hashimoto Kingorō]. Tokyo: Fuyō Shobō, 1982.

Taya Chikako. *Sensō hanzai to hō* [War Crimes and Law]. Tokyo: Iwanami Shoten, 2006.

Tiltman, H. Hessel. *Nihon hōdō 30-nen* [Reporting on Japan for 30 Years]. Translated by Kase Hideaki. Tokyo: Shinchōsha, 1965.

Tobe Ryōichi. "Shōwa Tennō to shin Tōjō Hideki" [Emperor Shōwa and His Subject Tōjō Hideki]. *Shokun!* (July 2004).

Tōgō Kazuhiko. "Shushō no sanpai ni moratoriamu o" [Moratorium on Prime Ministers' Visits to Yasukuni]. *Ronza* (September 2006).

Tōgō Shigehiko. *Sofu Tōgō Shigenori no shōgai* [Life of My Grandfather Tōgō Shigenori]. Tokyo: Bungeishunjū, 1993.

Tōgō Shigenori. *Jidai no ichimen* [An Aspect of the Time]. Tokyo: Chūōkōronsha, 1989.

Tokugawa Yoshihiro. *Jijūchō no yuigon* [The Last Testament of a Grand Chamberlain]. Tokyo: Asahi Shimbunsha, 1997.

Tokutomi Sohō. *Tokutomi Sohō shūsengo nikki: Ganso yume monogatari* [Tokutomi Sohō Postwar Diary: A Tale of Heroism]. 4 vols. Tokyo: Kodansha, 2006–2007.

Tōkyō Saiban Kenkyūkai [Tokyo Trial Research Committee], ed. *Kyōdō kenkyū Paru hanketsusho* [Collaborative Research on the Pal Judgment]. Tokyo: Kodansha, 1984.

Tominaga Shōzō. *Aru B/C-kyū senpan no sengoshi: Hontō no sensō sekinin to wa nani ka* [Postwar History of Some Class B and C War Criminals: Looking into True War Responsibility]. Tokyo: Suiyōsha, 1977.

Toyoda Kumao. "Haisōki" [A Record of a Debacle]. *Chūō kōron* (September 1996): 80–104.

———. *Sensō saiban yoroku* [Additional Records of the War Crimes Trials]. Tokyo: Taiseisha, 1986.

Twenty-First Century Forum, ed. *Sengo o koeru* [Overcoming the Postwar Era]. Kyoto: Sagano Shoin, 1995.

Uematsu Keita. *Kyokutō Kokusai Gunji Saiban* [International Military Tribunal for the Far East]. Tokyo: Jinbutsu Ōraisha, 1962.

Ugaki Kazushige. *Ugaki Kazushige nikki* [Ugaki Kazushige Diary]. Vol. 3. Edited by Tsunoda Jun. Tokyo: Misuzu Shobō, 1971.

Ushida Kumi, trans. "Uēku-tō kaidanroku" [Record of the Discussion on Wake Island]. *Seiron* 417 (December 2006).

Ushijima Hidehiko. *Nonfikushon tennō Akihito* [Nonfiction Report on Emperor Akihito]. Tokyo: Kawade Shobō, 1990.

Ushimura Kei. *"Shōsha no sabaki" ni mukiatte: Tōkyō Saiban o yominaosu* [Facing "Victors' Justice": Rereading the Tokyo Trial]. Tokyo: Chikuma Shobō, 2004.

———. *Saikō "seiki no isho" to Tōkyō Saiban* [Rethinking the "Will of the Century" and the Tokyo Trial]. Tokyo: PHP Institute, 2004.

———. "Nihon o bengo shita Amerika-jin wa hangyakusha ka" [Is an American Who Defended Japan a Traitor?]. *Shokun!* (December 2006).

Ushimura Kei, Higurashi Yoshinobu, and Nakamasa Masaki. "Tōkyō Saiban no 'hikari to yami'" ["Light and Darkness" of the Tokyo Trial]. *Shokun!* (May 2007).

Wakatsuki Reijirō. *Kofūan kaikoroku* [Kofūan Memoir]. Revised edition. Tokyo: Yomiuri Shimbunsha, 1975.

Watanabe Kazuhide. *Kyojin Nakajima Chikuhei* [Nakajima Chikuhei the Giant]. Tokyo: Hōbunshorin, 1955.

Yabe Teiji Nikki Kankōkai, ed. *Yabe Teiji nikki* [Yabe Teiji Diary]. Vol. 2, *Keyaki no maki*. Tokyo: Yomiuri Shimbunsha, 1974.

Yamada Munemutsu et al. *Gendai no hakken* [Discovery of Contemporary Times]. Vol. 6. Tokyo: Shunjūsha, 1960.

Yamamoto Shigeru. *Kān hakase no shōzō* [Portrait of Dr. Cahn]. Tokyo: Bēsubōru Magajin-sha, 1986.

Yokota Kisaburō. "Tōkyō hanketsu no kaibō" [Anatomy of Tokyo Sentences]. *Nihon kanri hōrei kenkyū* 26 (May 1992).

———. *Watashi no isshō* [My Life]. Tokyo: Tōkyō Shimbunsha, 1976.

Yodogawa Nagaharu. *Yodogawa Nagaharu jiden* [Autobiography of Yodogawa Nagaharu]. Vol. 1. Tokyo: Chūōkōronsha, 1988.

Yomiuri Shimbun Sensō Sekinin Kenshō Iinkai [Yomiuri Shimbun War Responsibility Verification Committee], ed. *Kenshō sensō sekinin* [Verifying War Responsibilities]. 2 vols. Tokyo: Chūōkōron Shinsha, 2006.

Yoshida Shigeru. *Nihon o kettei shita 100-nen: Tsuketari, omoidasu mama* [Japan's Decisive Century: A Brief History]. Tokyo: Chūōkōron Shinsha, 1999.

Yoshiura Kameo. *Sugamo Purizun kaiwai* [Round about Sugamo Prison]. Private compilation, 1956.

Index

Note: The abbreviation 't' refers to a table. Page numbers in *italics* refer to photographs/illustrations.

A

ABCD encirclement, 168, 169t

Abe Genki, 181, 190, 262, 263, 264

Abe Kōbō, 311

Abe Nobuyuki, 98

Acheson, Dean G., 54, 200

ACJ. *See* Allied Council for Japan

Act No. 103 (execution of sentences and clemency) (1952), 314, 318, 333

Act on Special Aid to the Wounded and Sick Retired Soldiers and War-Bereaved Families, 18

Adenauer, Konrad, 282, 284, 300

Agreement on Commerce (Japan/Australia) (July 4, 1957), 342

Aichi Kiichi, *317*

Aikawa Yoshisuke, 94, 260, 312, 323, 334, 338

Aisin Gioro Pujie, 328

Aisin Gioro Puyi, 93, 119, *120*, 121–22, 162, 173, 186, 221, 328

Akihito, Crown Prince, 316, 320

Allied Control Council, 219

Allied Council for Japan (ACJ), 112, 122

Allied Powers/Forces, 37, 50, 51, 52–53, 99, 197–98, 255, 326, 340, 347: arguments for US initiative/cooperation among Allies, 52–53, 54, 55, 62; Class A/B/C war crimes, 22–23; defeated nations policy, 38, 40, 41–42, 43, 48; establishment of legitimacy of, 36, 45, 191, 304–5; good vs evil historical view, 36; policy of recording history, 43–45; Tokyo Trial as 'foreign policy', 349; unconditional surrender policy, 48, 49

Allison, John, 296, 299, 304, 323–24, 325, 332

Almond, Major General Edward, 285

Amakawa Akira, 271, 352

American Section (of American defense counsels), 148

amnesty and pardons, 120, 290, 297–98, 313, 321, 323, 324, 325, 329, 348

Amō Eiji, 126, 262, 264

Andō Kisaburō, 262, 263, 264

Anti-Comintern Pact, 111t, 162, 169t

ANZUS Pact (1951), 304

Aoki Kazuo, 18, 19, 262, 263, 264, 312, 338

Araki Sadao, *107*, 151, *152*, *154*, 161, 170, 293, *317*: selection as defendant, 93, 95t, 97; charges, 105t; parole, 322, 323, 326, 331, 334–35, 336–37; counts charged and sentence, 225, 226t, 236, 309

Arima Yoriyasu, 257

Arita Hachirō, 312, *317*

Army Department (Imperial Headquarters), 188

Army War College, 95–96t, 97

Asahi Shimbun, 9, 78, 113, 229, 347: opinion poll on trial (2006), 12–13

Asanuma Inejirō, 316

Ashida Hitoshi, 98–99, 192, 218, 227

Atlantic Charter (1941), 24–25, 40–41

atomic bombings and tests, 30, 191, 237, 241, 246, 324, 328, 333

Attlee, Clement Richard, 58, 60, 211, 246

Auschwitz concentration camp, 23

Australia, 12, 127, 168, 197, 198, 200, 213, 236, 289: argument for prosecuting emperor, 59–61, 62, 64, 66, 86–87; drafting of peace treaty, 298, 299, 304, 310; release of war criminals, 322, 323, 326, 341–42; Subsequent Tokyo War Crimes Trials, 264, 275, 276t

Awaya Kentarō, 98, 257

B

Baba Tsunego, 138

Bajpai, Girija Shankar, 199, 200

Ballantine, Joseph W., 125–26

Ball, William Macmahon, 112

Basic Initial Post Surrender Directive to Supreme Commander for The Allied Powers for The Occupation and Control of Japan (JCS 1380/15) (November 3, 1945), 36, 70

Bassiouni, M. Cherif, 284–85

Bataan Death March, 209–10

Benelux countries, 269

Berendsen, Carl, 65, 66

Berlin Blockade, 269

Bernard, Henri, 195, 205t, 209, 213, 214, 215, 350: separate dissenting opinion 236, 237, 238, 239

Bernays, Colonel Murray C., 24, 80, 82

Betts, Brigadier General Edward C., 255

Bevin, Ernst, 60, 62, 211, 212

biological weapon warfare, 276, 329

Bird, Kai, 284

Blakeney, Major Benjamin Bruce, 121, 123, 124, 147, 148, 158, 160, 176, 310

Blewett, George G., 118, 129, 142, 160

Bonn-Paris conventions (May 5, 1955), 342

Bormann, Martin, 84

Borton, Hugh ("Borton draft"), 266, 267, 297

Bose, Rash Behari, 202

Bose, Subhas Chandra, 244, 246

Brackman, Arnold C., 9–10

Brannon, John G., 129, 145, 175, 178, 222

Britain, 12, 144, 197, 210, 244, 249: argument for active involvement in trials, 61–62; Atlantic Charter, 41; attempts to prevent break up of trial, 211–13, 214; argument for summary execution, 57–58; drafting of peace treaty, 298–301, 304, 307, 310; economic blockade of Japan, 126, 168; identifying defendants, 64, 82, 85–86, 87, 89; India and, 245–46; Japan's surrender, 47, 62, Nuremberg Trial, 256; punishment of suspected war criminals, 41, 46, 47; release of war criminals, 322, 326, 342; Subsequent Tokyo War Crimes Trials, 257, 265, 272, 275, 276t

British Commonwealth, 211, 213, 235, 259–60, 299, 303–4, 323; identifying defendants, 85, 86, 90; indictments, 101, 106; opinion of Kennan, 111–12, 127, 259; opinion of Webb, 206, 207–8, 213

Brooks, Alfred, 129, 156, 157, 158

Bureau of Far Eastern Affairs (US State Department), 321

Bureau of Naval Affairs (Ministry of the Navy), 164

Byrnes, James F., 197, 199, 200, 256

C

Cabinet Information Bureau, 262

Cabinet Order 201 (July 31, 1948), 218

Cabinet Planning Board (Japan), 95–96t, 139, 160, 162, 165

Cairo Declaration (November 27, 1943), 47

Canada, 12, 51, 62, 200, 272, 275, 322: justice for, 197, 198, 205t, 206, 211, 212, 213

Carpenter, Colonel Alva C., 257, 260, 266, 285–86

Casablanca Conference (January 1943), 48

Caudle, Charles, 159

Central China Area Army, 96t, 157, 163, 234

Central Liaison Office (Shūsen Renraku Kanjikai) (Japan), 131, 132, 138, 139, 144

Chakravorty, B. N., 250–51

Charter of the International Military Tribunal for the Far East (1945), 22–23, 24, 46, 49, 100, 167, 199, 238–39: attempts to amend, 147, 148, 201; promulgation of, 82–85

Cherry Blossom Society (Sakurakai), 116, 153, 221

Chiba Shigeru (professional baseball player), 293

Chief Defense Counsel, 147

Chifley, Joseph Benedict, 59, 213

China Expeditionary Army, 262

China, Kuomintang, 290, 310, 321, 322, 327–29: Subsequent Tokyo War Crimes Trials, 273, 275, 276t

China, People's Republic of (PRC), 12, 13, 62, 153, 346–47: anti-Japanese sentiment, 20, 37; charges, 90, 105, 120, 126; justice for, 208, 213; indictments, 100, 101; punishment for suspected war criminals, 41, 43, 47; response of Japan to Tokyo Trial, 165, 168, 197, 198, 235

Chinese Civil War, 273

Chiyonoyama (sumo grand champion), 292

Chō Isamu, 117

Chūbu Nihon Shimbun, 232

Churchill, Winston, 41, 58, 269–70

Ciano, Gian Galeazzo, 159

CIC (Counter-Intelligence Corps), 68

CIE. *See* Civil Information and Educational Section

Circular No. 5 (Clemency for War Criminals) (March 7, 1950), 288–91, 292, 318

civilian population: inhumane acts/persecution, 27

Civil Information and Educational Section (CIE) (GHQ/SCAP), 113, 190–91

"Civilization's Justice" theory, 30–38

Class A ("A-kyū") war criminals and suspects, *11*, 12, 13, 55, *67*, 71, 132, 144, 174, 180: arguments for release of war crimes prisoners 318–21; British argument for summary execution, 57–58; commutation system (clemency), 251, 280, 282–88, 289, 290, 291, 343, 344–45; defense counsels, 140; definition of, 21–26; detention of war crimes suspects, 281–82; distinction between Class B/C and, 20–27; drafting of peace treaty and, 295–99; employment outside prison, 334–35; enshrinement of, 13–20, 338; executions, 7–8, 9, 229, 266, 298; finalization of Article 11 in peace treaty, 299–301; good-conduct/confinement credits, 283, 285, 286–87, 293, 294, 318; handling/ punishment, 41–42, 46, 50, 56, 70, 71–73; handling of remains/disposal of ashes, 7–8, 9; impact on families of, 310–13; indictments against, 99–104, 105t, 106, 216–18; Japan's acceptance of peace treaty, 297, 299, 300, 305–306; medical paroles, 326, 329–31; parole system (clemency), 288–294, 299, 308, 309t, 310, 319, 322, 323, 335–36, 339–40; perception as "symbols of Japan's war responsibility", 20, 21, 31; perception as 'victims of war', 14, 16, 285, 293, 310–11, 316; petition asserting invalidity of Tokyo Trial, 63–64; plausibility of "Replacement Theory", 98–99; policy of defense of individual defendants, 141–42, 143, 148–49, 174, 180, 181; political activities after release, 331, 337, 343; public abhorrence and disillusionment toward, 181–82, 347; public sympathy and opinion toward, 313–16, 344–46; reason for special weight given to, 24–25; responsibility of cabinet members, 242, 262, *263*, 265;

selection of "heavyweight" defendants, 89–94, 95–96t; show of "magnanimity" toward, 287–88; Subsequent Tokyo War Crimes Trials, 254, 257–58, 259, 260–61, 270, 272–73, 275; Ten-Year Rule, 331, 336; transfer and parole of, 266, 280–82, 285–87, *286*, 287; treatment of prisoners at Sugamo Prison, 291, *292*, 293; trip to Kōrakuen Ball Park, 313–15; validity of sentences under domestic laws, 336–38

Class B/C war criminals and suspects 15–17, 55, 57, 63, 72–73, 104, 127, 260, 267, 310–11: commutation system (clemency), *286*, 289, 291, 293, 310, 320, 321, 324, 341, 342, 343, 344–45; definition of, 26–27; distinction between Class A and, 20–27; drafting of peace treaty, 301, 306, 307–8; hierarchy of responsibility, 29; parole system (clemency), 310, 315, 319–20, 331, 339; sentences, 218, 232, 235, 264, 312; Subsequent Tokyo War Crimes Trials, 261, 263, 264–65, 270–73, 274–75, 276t; Ten-Year Rule, 325–26, 339

classical realism, 243

Clay, General Lucius D., 76, 255

Clemenceau, Georges Benjamin, 34–35

clemency. *See* commutation system; parole system

Clemency and Parole Board for War Criminals, 321, 325, 326, 335

Cold War, 124–25, 172, 187, 248, 254, 265, 271, 282, 297, 348: release of war criminals, 336, 339, 340

Coleman, Captain Beverly M., 146–48

Cole, Roger, 157

command responsibility (Yamashita standard), 73

Committee on the Cabinet of the House of Representatives, 302

communism, 116, 130, 187, 230, 241, 249, 268, 298, 323, 331, 332

Communist Party (China), 327–29

Communist Party (Japan), 75, 90–91, 225

Communist Party (Soviet Union), 88, 94, 122, 124

commutation system (clemency): arguments for release of war crimes prisoners, 318–21, 333; China and, 326–29; final policy change from United States, 342–44; "gradualist approach to release", 291, 292, 308, 319, 321, 323, 325; international issue, 347–48; "radicalist approach to release", 290, 298, 318–19, 320, 324, 329–41; response to arguments for release, 321–23; Ten-Year Rule, 324–26, 331, 339; transfer of war criminals, 280, 282–88, 297, 298, 300, 308–309, 310, 313; US-Japan relations and, 323–24

Comyns-Carr, Arthur, *86*, 99, 100, 118, 184, 185, 189, 192, 259

conference (handling of war criminals) (October 16, 1945), 57–58

conspiracy argument, 45, 52, 145, 192, 193, 238; conspiracy-based historical view, 50, 81–82; indictments against Class A war criminals, 103, 104, 106, 151–61, 216–18; Kiyose's opening statement for defense, 166–67; legal merit and use of, 79–80, 216; majority judgment's view of history, 220–22; Nuremberg Trial, 230; policy issues around indictments, 99–100; prosecution's establishment of facts by evidence, 111t; rebuttals to summaries of the defenses for defendants, 161–66; selection of "heavyweight" defendants, 89, 90, 231

Constitution of Japan (May 3, 1947), 89, 228, 307

Control Council Court (October 18, 1946), 256

conventional war crimes, 22, 26, 27, 100, 104, 224, 230, 241, 272, 275

Council of Allied Ambassadors to Japan, 266

Counter-Intelligence Corps (CIC), 68

courts-martial (*gunritsu hōtei*), 27, 31

Cramer, Major General Myron C., *195*,

205t, 210, 213, 214, 232, 234, 236

crime of murder, 23, 56, 150, 155, 162, 206, 284; addition to list of charges, 100–102, 103–104, 105, 106, 216, 223

crimes against humanity, 38, 50, 51, 55, 150, 166, 192, 204, 224: Class B/C crimes, 26–27, 28–29; essence of, 28; list of charges, 100–102, 104; Nuremberg Trial, 230; special weight of Class A crimes, 24–25; Subsequent Tokyo War Crimes Trials, 256, 273

crimes against peace 90, 127, 150, 156, 220, 340: basic policy of punishment, 35, 49, 50, 52, 55; charter of the tribunal, 82–85; justices and, 203, 204, 206, 209; Class A/B/C crimes, 20–22, 24, 25; dissenting opinions, 237, 241, 243, 244; policy issues around indictments, 100, 101, 103; reduced significance of, 273–74; sentences, 231–32, 236, 238; Subsequent Tokyo War Crimes Trials, 256, 258, 259–60

Criminal Affairs Bureau (Ministry of Justice), 139

Criminal Law of Japan, 289

criminal organizations, 46, 82, 84, 256

Cunningham, Owen, *149*, 158

Cutter, Colonel R. Ammi, 50–51, 52

D

Dachau Trials, 269, 280, 281, 283

Daigo Fukuryūmaru (Japanese fishing boat), 324

Dai-Nihon Bengoshikai Rengōkai (federation of bar associations), 141

Dai-Nihon Genron Hōkokukai (Japanese-Speech Patriot Association), 261

Dai-Nihon Seijikai (Great Japan Political Society), 70–71

death sentences, 100, 251, 281, 283, 284, 329, 340–41: decisions on sentences, 225, 226t, 227–28, 230–36, 238. *See also* life

imprisonment; sentencing

Declaration by the Allied Nations, 41

defense counsels, *129*, 267–68, 344: closing arguments, 191–94; conflicts of interest among defendants, 174; defendants' motions to dismiss prosecution, 150–51; delaying tactics, 171–72, 173; Japan, 140, *142*, *143*; presentation of counterevidence, 168, 169t, 171, 172, 176, 215; summaries of the defenses for defendants, 151–61, 173; United States, 144–47, *148*, *149*, 150; use of evidence, 170–71

Defense Department (United States), 325

demilitarization policy (Occupation authority), 14–15, 36, 248

Demobilization Bureau (Repatriation Relief Agency), 15, 291, 305, 306, 308, 311, 313, 318

Dening, Esler Maberley, 314

Derevyanko, Lieutenant General Kuzma Nikolayevich, 122

Dohihara Kenji, *107*, 147, 149, 221: charges, 105t; selection as defendant, 93, 95–96t, 97; death sentence, 17, 225, 226t, 233, 235; summary/rebuttal of the defense for, *156*, 151, 161–62, 174

Dominions Office (United Kingdom), 59

Dönitz, Karl, 340

Dulles, John Foster, 296, 298, 304, 322, 323, 324, 335, 343

Dutch East Indies, 105, 111t, 127, 217

E

East-West Study Group (Colloquium on Peace Affairs) (Heiwa Mondai Tōgikai), 228

Eden, Anthony, 321

education authority: Japan, 115

Eguchi Wataru, 119

Eighth Army (United States), 7, 8, 9, 73, 266, 286, 294

Eighth Route Army (Bālù-jūn), 327

Eisenhower, General Dwight D., 24, 49, 65, 322, 325–26, 335

Emmerson, John K., 74–75

emperor of Japan. *See* Hirohito, emperor of Japan

End-of-War Settlement budget, 140

Enomoto Shigeharu, 313

espionage, 28, 327, 329

Etō Jun, 31

European Theater Mortuary Number One (US Army), 9

Evatt, Herbert Vere, 59, 239

Everson, Frederick, 259

executions, 8, 14, 32, 70, 72, 229, 288, 341: argument for summary execution, 42, 57–58, 80; completion of trial, 266, 268, 270; reconsideration of, 281, 284, 311

F

Fahy, Charles, 255, 256

Falco, Robert, 146

Far Eastern Commission (FEC), 200, 201, 290, 295: selection of defendants, 60, 61, 62–64, 65, 66; Subsequent Tokyo War Crimes Trials, 266, 271–73, 275

Fearey, Robert Appleton, 182

FEC. *See* Far Eastern Commission

FEC 007/3 (international policy) (April 3, 1946), 63–66, 88, 89, 201, 258, 273, 275

FEC 314 (termination of trials) (July 29, 1948), 271–72, 273, 274, 275, 277

Federalist Papers, 240

Fellers, Brigadier General Bonner, 65, 184

First Ministry of Demobilization (formerly Ministry of the Army), 15, 76, 138–39

Fite, Katherine B., 259

foreign ministers conference (Moscow) (December 1945), 62

Foreign Ministry (Australia), 88

Foreign Ministry (China), 91

Foreign Office (United Kingdom), 260, 330, 336: British stance on trial, 58–59, 61–62

Foreign Relations Committee (US Senate), 297

Fortune (magazine), 71

Fourteen Points, 40

France, 12, 44, 46, 62, 101, 300, 310, 331: justice for, 195, 197, 205t, 209, 213, 214, 215; justice's separate dissenting opinion, 236, 237, 238, 239; release of war criminals, 321, 322, 342, 345; selection of defendants, 89, 90; Subsequent Tokyo War Crimes Trials, 256, 257, 269, 272, 275, 276t

Fraser, Peter, 65, 213

Freeman, James, 158

French Indochina, 63, 111t, 164, 217, 333

Frierson, Major Luther, 7

Fujiwara Ginjirō, 94, 312

Fujiyama Aiichirō, 312

Fujiyama Ichirō, 292

Fundamentals of National Policy (*Kokusaku no kijun*) (1936), 221, 233

Furness, George A., 123–24, 158

Furumi Tadayuki, 328

Fushun War Criminals Management Center (China), 327–28

G

Gaddis, John Lewis, 33

Gairdner, Lieutenant General Charles Henry, 62, 211

Gascoigne, Alvary, 172, 189, 190, 212, 229

General Headquarters, Supreme Commander for the Allied Powers (GHQ/SCAP), 135, 140, 145, 190: basic policy on Japan, 29, 52–53, 54, 63; power of Occupation Forces, 130–31; release of war crimes suspects, 280–82, 288–90, 294; Subsequent Tokyo War Crimes Trials, 254, 257, 261, *263*, 264–65; selection of defendants, 65, 66, 70, 75, 78

General Treaty for Renunciation of War as an Instrument of National Policy. *See* Kellogg-Briand Pact (Pact of Paris) (1928)

Geneva Convention (1929), 127, 160, 165

genocide, 23, 28

Genyōsha (Dark Ocean Society), 82

Germany, Federal Republic of (West Germany), 300, 316; commutation system, 282–85, 289–90, 315, 325, 341–42, 344

Gestapo (State Secret Police, Nazi Germany), 46, 82

GHQ/SCAP. *See* General Headquarters, Supreme Commander for the Allied Powers

Girard Incident (January 30, 1957), 343

Golunsky, Sergei Alexandrovich, 94, 95, 98, 112, 122, *123*, 198

good-conduct/confinement credit, 283, 285, 286, 287–88, 293, 294, 318

Göring, Hermann, 8, 89

Gotōda Masaharu, 302

Gotō Fumio, 262, 263, 264, 338

Greater East Asia Co-Prosperity Sphere, 81, 193

Gross, Ernest A., 260

Guangdong, 101, 155, 276t

Guider, Captain John W., 146–47

guilt. *See* war guilt

H

Haffner, Sebastian, 28

Hagen, George, 289, 291, 293–94

Hamaguchi Osachi, 116

Hamilton, Alexander, 240

Handy, General Thomas T., 282, 283

Hankou, 101, 155

Hara Chūichi, 312, 330

Harada Kumao, 182

Harbin Special Agency, 95t, 161

Harris, E. Richard, 151, 153

Hasegawa Kazuo, 292

Hashida Kunihiko, 72

Hashimoto Kingorō: charges, 105t, 116, 117; closing arguments for the defense, 192, 193; parole, 331, 336–37, 344; selection as defendant, 93, 95t, 97, *107*; sentence, 226t, 310; summary/rebuttal of the defense for, *152*, *156*, 162

Hata Shunroku, 194, *292*: charges, 105t; parole, 322, 326, 330, 337; sentence, 226t, 233, 238, 310; selection as defendant, *107*, 93, 95, summary/rebuttal of the defense for, *156*, 153, 162, 174

Hatoyama Ichirō, 106, 294, 331–33, 336–37

Hayashi Itsurō, 141, 143, 236, 192–94, 312, 313, 343

Henderson, Loy Wesley, 200–201

Hess, Rudolph, 230, 340

He-Umezu Agreement (1935), 160–61

Hidaka Rokurō, 344

Higashikuni Naruhiko, Prince, 114, 130, 133

Higgins, Carlisle Wallace, 112

Higgins, John, 210

Higurashi Yoshinobu, 23, 93, 103, 105t

Hiranuma Kiichirō, 17, 229, 310: charges,

105t, 106, *107*; selection as defendant, 93, 95t, 97; sentences, 226t; summary/rebuttal of the defense for, 149, *152*, *154*, 162, 174

Hirohashi Tadamitsu, 69

Hirohito, emperor of Japan, 9, 160, 163, 227, 266, 323, 338–39: Australian argument for prosecution of emperor, 59–61; evasion of emperor issue, 184–87; international agreement not to prosecute, 65–66; as issue for prosecutors, 86–88; non-indictment of, 55, 99, 183–84, 238; United States' argument for sparing, 64–65; argument of war responsibility of, 75, 84, 85, 134, 137, 181, 238, 239, 276

Hirose Saburō, 328

Hiroshima, 30, 237

Hirota Kōki, 9, 63, *107*: charges, 105t; death sentence, 17, 225, 226t, 227, 229, 233, 234, 235–36, 238, 265; selection as defendant, 90–91, 93, 95t; summary/rebuttal of the defense for, 149, 151, *152*, 153, *156*, 160, 168, 169, 171, 174

Hodgson, Lieutenant Colonel Joseph V., 51, 52, 64

Home Ministry (Japan), 139

Hōmufu (Ministry of Legal Affairs, later Hōmushō [Ministry of Justice]), 318

Honda Kumatarō, 262, 264, 266

Honjō Shigeru, 72, 92, 155

Honma Masaharu, 26, 124

Hori Shigeru, 319

Hoshina Zenshirō, 133

Hoshino Naoki, *107*, *152*, 174, 178, *317*, 336: charges, 105t, 162; selection as defendant, 93, 95t, 97; sentence, 226t, 309; summary of the defense for, 153

house arrest, 71, 257, 261, 262

House of Councillors (Japan), 18, 306, 315, 320, 323, 338: Committee on the Cabinet, 87; Committee on Judicial Affairs, 14

House of Representatives (Japan), 68, 76, 114, 127, 139, 141, 294, 302, 315, 320, 332, 337, 338, 353

Howard, Joseph, *129*, 156

Hozumi Shigetaka, 141, 142

Hull, Cordell, 126, 176

Hull note, 176, 246

Humphreys, T. Christmas, 90

Hunk, Walter, 340

Hu Yaobang, 20

I

ICC (International Criminal Court), 28, 243

Ichigayadai, *11*, 106, *107*

Ichikawa Ennosuke II (Ichikawa En'ō I), 292

Ichimada Hisato, 312

ICJ (International Court of Justice), 307

Ienaga Saburō, 249

Iguchi Sadao, 144, 299–300, 327

Ikeda Shigeaki, 71, 257

Imamura Hisa, 14

Imamura Hitoshi, 14, 26

Imperial General Headquarters (Japan), 70, 123, 327

Imperial Household Agency, 16

Imperial Japanese Army and General Staff, 15, 106, 134, 160, 221, 235, 260, 265: charges, 116, 117, 123; selection as defendant, 77, 78, 97

Imperial Japanese Navy, 19, 157, 159, 164, 183, 221, 227, 234: defense of state/defense of individuals, 175, 176, 177–79; response to Tokyo Trial, 134, 137, 139

INA (Indian National Army), 245

India, 12, 61, 62, 209, 231, 246, 322: justice

for, 198, 199–200, 201–4; interpretation of Pal's judgment, 237, 240–252; Subsequent Tokyo War Crimes Trials, 272, 275

Indian National Army (INA), 245

Indian National Congress, 246

Instrument of Surrender (September 2, 1945) (Japan), 49, 55, 62, 197, 199, 200, 201, 206

Interim Parole and Clemency Board (United States), 342

International Court of Justice (ICJ), 307

International Criminal Court (ICC), 28, 243

International Defense Section, 147

international law, 24, 27, 28, 46, 48, 243, 267, 274, 307–8: "norm of justice" 33, 35

International Military Tribunal. *See* Nuremberg Trial

International Military Tribunal for the Far East. *See* Tokyo Trial

international morality, 35

International Prosecution Section (IPS), 112, 117, 197, 257, 259: selection of defendants, 68–70, 77, 78, 79–80, 82, 85, 86, 87, 90, 93, 102

international relations and diplomacy, 267–68, 293, 346, 347, 348

interrogations, 77, 78, 79, 85, 91, 92, 117, 133

Inukai Takeru, *115*, 306, 320

IPS. *See* International Prosecution Section

Iraq War (2003), 243

Irie Keishirō, 139

Irie Sukemasa, 239

Ishibashi Tanzan, 138

Ishihara Hiroichirō, 262

Ishii Shirō, 276

Ishiwara Kanji, 91–93, *94*, 117, 221, 264, 324

Itagaki Seishirō, 18, *107*, 117, 184, 202: charges, 105t; death sentence, 226t, 233, 235; majority judgment, 221, 223; selection as defendant, 91, 92, 93, 95t, 97; summary/rebuttal of the defense for, 153, *154*, 162, 174

Italy, 28, 34, 97, 159, 162, 166, 298

Itō Nobumi, 114

Itō Seiichi, 175, 178

Iwamura Michiyo, 70, 262, 263, 264

J

Jackson, Justice Robert H., 54, 255, 256

JAG. *See* Judge Advocate General (JAG) (United States)

Japanese Military Academy (JMA), 91, 95–96t, 106, 119, 132, 134, 174

Japanese Naval Academy (JNA), 74, 96t, 134

Japanese Naval Aviation Preparatory School (Tsuchiura), 74

Japanese-Soviet Neutrality Pact (April 1941), 111t, 124, 169t, 223

Japan Federation of Bar Associations, 141, 307, 312

Japan-Germany-Italy Tripartite Pact, 97, 99, 111t, 231, 298: defendants' involvement in, 155, 158–59, 164, 165, 166

Japan War-Bereaved Families Association (Nihon Izokukai), 14, 346

Japan World Exposition (Osaka), 346

Jaranilla, Delfin, *195*, 205t, 209, 213, 214, 236, 237

Jasper, Karl, 34

JCS 1023/10 (directive, basic policy on German war criminal trials) (July 8, 1945), 25

JCS 1067 (US Joint Chiefs of Staff directive) (May 11, 1945), 49

JCS 1380/15 (Basic Initial Post Surrender

Directive to Supreme Commander for The Allied Powers for The Occupation and Control of Japan) (November 3, 1945), 36, 70

JCS 1512 (October 6, 1945). *See* SWNCC 57/3 (policy paper)

JCS 1779 (directive, German reconstruction) (July 15, 1947), 269

JCS. *See* Joint Chiefs of Staff (JCS) (United States)

Jiang Zemin, 13

Jinja gōshi jimu kyōryoku yōkō (Yasukuni Shrine Guideline on Enshrinement Administration Cooperation), 16

Jinja Honcho (Association of Shinto Shrines), 303

Jiyū Minshutō (Liberal Democratic Party) (LDP), 336

JMA. *See* Japanese Military Academy

JNA. *See* Japanese Naval Academy

Joint Chiefs of Staff (JCS) (United States), 25

Joint Chiefs of Staff's Directive on the Identification, Apprehension and Trial of Persons Suspected of War Crimes. *See* SWNCC 57/3 (policy paper)

Joint Declaration (Japan/Soviet Union) (October 19, 1958), 342

Judge Advocate General (JAG) (United States), 37, 79, 205t, 210

Judge Advocate Section (JAS) (General Headquarters of Far East Command), 281

Judicial Affairs Bureau (First Ministry of Demobilization), 139

Judicial System and Research Department (Minister's Secretariat of Ministry of Justice), 181–82

Justice Department (United States), 77, 325

justices, 52, 62, 63, 77, 79, 299, 301–303: appointment of, *195*, 196–204, 205t, 206, *207*, 208; drafting/writing of judgement, 215–18, 219, 237; final points of contention, 216–18; identifying defendants, 83, 85–86 ; internal strife with group, 110–12; interpretation of Pal's judgment, 237, 240–52; issues with producing a unified judgement, 210–11; judgment seen as disadvantageous precedent, 264–65; majority group/minority group, 213–14, 215–16, 218, 219–20, 230, 237, 237, 239–40; majority judgment's view of history, 220–22; Nuremberg-like judgement, 218–20; separate opinions of, 236–40; varied stances of, 208–10; war as consequence of international politics, 223–24. *See also* defense counsels; prosecution counsels

K

Kades, Charles L., 48

Kaigo Tokiomi, 113, *114*

Kaishintō (Constitutional Reform Party), 294, 307, 314–15, 331

Kamikawa Hikomatsu, 138

Katō Masuo, 102–3

Katō Takahisa, 313

Kawabata Yasunari, 225, 231

Kawabe Torashirō, 119

Kawakami Isamu, 314

Kawashima Yoshiko, 118

Kaya Okinori, 70, *107*, *152*, 155, 163, 178, 265, 291, *317*: charges, 105t; parole, 336, 337, 343, 344; selection as defendant, 93, 95t, 97; sentence, 226t, 310

Kellogg-Briand Pact (Pact of Paris) (1928), 150, 208, 220, 303: dissenting opinions, 237, 239, 241, 243; wars of aggression, 43, 45, 46, 47

Kelsen, Hans, 196

Kennan, George F., 47, 58, 88, 198, 266, *267*, 268, 270–71

Keenan, Joseph Berry, 62, 119, *120*, 200, 223, 232, *253*, 320: as chief prosecutor, 77, *86*, 191–92, 205; defense counsels, 144, 145; logic of the prosecution, 125, 126, 127; made sport of, 188–89, 190; opening statement at trial, 110–12; selection of "heavyweight" war criminals, 83, 85, 86–88, 98, 100; Subsequent Tokyo War Crimes Trials, 257, 259, 261; war responsibility of emperor, 183–85, *186*, 187

Kenworthy, Aubrey S., 188

Keynes, John Maynard, 44

Khabarovsk Trial (December 25, 1949), 120, 122, 276

Khrushchev, Nikita, 342

Kido Kōichi, 78, 89, *107*, 118, *292*: charges, 105t, 130; defense counsel, 142, 148, 149; defense of state/defense of individuals, 183, 184, 186; parole, 334, 336; selection as defendant, 91, 93, 96t, 97, 99; sentence, 226t, 227, 233, 235, 238, 310; summary/rebuttal of the defense for, *152*, *154*, 155, 161, 163, 171, 180–81

Kido Kōichi nikki (court evidence #3340), 183

Kimura Heitarō, 17, *107*, 117, 163, 174; charges, 105t; defense counsel, *154*, 155–56; selection as defendant, 93, 95t, 97; death sentence, 225, 226t, 233, 235

Kimura Shiroshichi, 285

Kirichenko, Alexey, 88

Kishi Nobusuke, 70, 202, 254, 259, 262, 312, 332, 338: parole, 302, 338, 342, 343, 344

Kiyosawa Kiyoshi, 36

Kiyose Ichirō, 214, 233, 312: defense counsel, 141, *142*, 143, 148, 150; opening statement for the defense, 166–67, 171; parole of war criminals, 332, 336–37; selection of defendants, 93, 96t

Kodama Kikan (Kodama Agency), 262, 264

Kodama Yoshio, 174, 262, 264

Koiso Kuniaki, 17, 103, *107*, 261, 309, 312: charges, 105t; selection as defendant, 93, 96t, 97; sentence, 226t, 233; summary/rebuttal of the defense for, *152*, *156*, 163

Koizumi Junichirō, 13, 302

Kojima Noboru, 98, 99, 347

Kokuryūkai (Black Dragon Society), 91, 262

Kokusui Taishūtō (Patriotic People's Party), 262

Konoe Fumimaro, 72, 153, 159, 163, 221, 233

Koo, V. K. Wellington, 51, 52

Korean War, 288, 291, 296, 333

Korea, Republic of, 13

Kuhara Fusanosuke, 71, 261

Kuomintang (KMT) (Chinese National Party), 273, 276t, 290, 309t, 310, 321, 322

Kurusu Saburō, 125

Kusaba Tatsumi, 123

Kuzuu Yoshihisa, 262, 264

Kwantung Army (Japan), 42–43, 72, 117, 123, 221, 276: defendants' ranks in, 92, 93, 95–96t, 155, 157, 161, 162, 165, 166

Kyodo News Agency, 7, 8, 102–3

Kyushu Imperial University, 218, 339

L

Ladybird, HMS, 153, 162, 163

Landsberg Prison (Federal Republic of Germany), 282, 283

Lansing, Robert, 35

Laurel, Jose, 70

Lawrence, Jeffrey, 210

Lazarus, Aristides, *149*, 153, 184

League of Nations, 81

Leftist Socialist Party, 315, 320

Legal Affairs Councilors' Office (later Office for Investigation of War Criminals), 133, 135, 138

legal positivism, 242, 248

Legal Section (LS) (General Headquarters), 147, 285, 286, 289, 290, 311, 318: Subsequent Tokyo War Crimes Trials, 257, 260, 261, 264, 265, 266, 268

Leipzig War Crimes Trials, 304, 313

Levin, Michael, 129, 155, 160

liaison committee on war crimes trials (Sensō Saiban Renraku Iinkai) (First Department of Central Liaison Office), 139

Liaison Conference (Imperial Headquarters and Government) (Japan), 164, 175

life imprisonment, 73, 238, 309, 329: charges and sentences, 226t, 230, 231, 233, 235; commutation system, 283–84, 289, 293; political advantage of, 340–41. See also death sentences; sentencing

Liutiaogou Incident (Mukden Incident) (September 18, 1931), 92, 111t, 116, 162, 166, 221

Lloyd George, David, 34

Logan, Jr., William, 118, 129, 148, 149, 155, 180, 181, 185, 186, 192, 194

London Agreement (Nuremberg Charter) (August 8, 1945), 46, 48, 49, 63, 82, 83, 84, 100, 131, 192, 219, 237

London Conference (June–August 1945), 54

London Naval Treaty, 116

Lopez, Pedro, 127

M

MacArthur, General Douglas, 36, 172, 184, 185, 190, 223, 245, 253, 285: appointment of justices, 197, 198–99, 200, 204, 205, 212, 216; charges, 98, 100, 112, 127, 151; Charter of the International Military Tribunal for the Far East, 82, 83, 86, 147, 198; formation of framework for Tokyo Trial, 48, 50, 53, 54, 65; Occupation Policy, 68, 71, 77; prosecution of emperor, 64–65, 87; right of veto, 88; Subsequent Tokyo War Crimes Trials, 260, 261, 262–63, 265; SWNCC 57/3 (policy paper), 54–56, 60, 61, 62, 63

MacArthur II, Douglas, 343

Maeda Tamon, 113, 114

Mainichi Shimbun, 109, 181

major war criminals, 26, 46, 199, 255, 256, 282–83, 290

Malmédy massacre (December 17, 1944), 46, 281

Manchukuo, 81, 221, 328, 329: logic of the defense, 153, 158, 162, 165, 166, 169t; selection of defendants, 93, 95t, 111t, 120, 121

Manchurian Incident, 43, 55, 99, 148, 244, 247, 322: conspiracy-based historical view, 106, 110, 121, 123, 125, 136, 221; selection of defendants, 79, 81, 83, 97, 111t, 113, 115, 116, 117; summaries of the defenses for defendants, 153, 155, 156, 157, 158, 159, 163, 164, 165

Manchurian Industrial Development Company, 260

Manmitsu dai-nikki (classified documents on Manchurian Incident), 78

Mansfield, Alan J., 86, 87, 88, 127

Manus Island Trial, 276t, 280

Maogoto, Jackson, 44

March Incident (March 1931), 116, 158

Marco Polo Bridge Incident, 111t, 166

Marshall, General George C., 68, 267

martyrdom, 8, 50, 190, 192, 311

Maruyama Masao, 146, 181

Masaki Hideki, 217

Masaki Jinzaburō, 93, 98, 217, 260

Matsudaira Nagayoshi, 19

Matsudaira Tsuneo, 155

Matsudaira Yoshitami, 19

Matsui Iwane, 17, 93, 96t, 105t, *107*, *152*, *156*, 157, 163, 192: death sentence, 226t, 231, 233, 234, 235, 242

Matsumoto Shigeharu, 134, 139

Matsumura Kenzō, 68

Matsumura Tomokatsu, 123

Matsuoka Yōsuke, 17, 19, 22, 103, 151, *152*, 159, 174, 223, 225: charges, 105t; selection as defendant, 93, 96t, 97

Matsutani Sei, 134, 150, 310

Mattice, Floyd, 155, 156

McCloy, John J., *44*, 49, 51, 53, 56, 57, 71, 197: commutation system, 282, 283–84

McDermott, Edward, 159

McDougall, Edward Stuart, *86*, *195*, 205t, 206, 211, 213, 214, 244

McManus, Lawrence, *129*, 151

medical paroles, 326, 329–31

Meiji Constitution, 113, 173, 183, 242

Mei Ju-ao, *195*, 205t, *207*, 208, 213, 214, 329

Mendelsohn, John, 283

Menon, P. Govinda, 112, 202

Menzies, Robert G., 276, 342

Metternich, Klemens, 40

Mikasa Takahito, Prince, 316

militarism, 37, 136, 163, 198, 211, 256, 298, 347: formation of framework for Tokyo Trial, 47, 59, 74, 75; Subsequent Tokyo War Crimes Trials, 328, 329

Military Affairs Bureau (Army Ministry), 96t, 97, 117, 118, 156, 157, 158, 164, 235

Military Pension Act, 76

Military Service Law, 76

Mill, John Stewart, 229

Mimura Osamu, 87

Minami Jirō, *107*, 116, 121, 221: charges, 105t; parole, 322, 323, 326, 330, 344; selection as defendant, 93, 96t, 97; sentence, 226t, 229, 310; summary/rebuttal of the defense for, *152*, *156*, 157, 164

Minear, Richard H., 243, 347

Ministry of the Army. *See* First Ministry of Demobilization

Ministry of Foreign Affairs (Japan), 95–96t, 118, 159, 312, 319: drafting of peace treaty, 296, 298, 301–2, 303, 305–6, 308; Japanese response to Tokyo Trial, 131, 132, 133, 134, 135, 137–39, 140, 141, 143; Pearl Harbor, 175, 176, 179; Subsequent Tokyo War Crimes Trials, 262, 277

Ministry of Justice (Japan), 139, 140, 333

Ministry of Legal Affairs (Japan), 337–38

Ministry of the Navy. *See* Second Ministry of Demobilization

Ministry of Welfare (later Ministry of Health, Labour and Welfare), 14, 15, 18, 132

minor war criminals, 26, 28, 29, 57, 255, 283, 342, 343

Minshutō (Democratic Party of Japan), 301–2, 332

Misora Hibari, 292

mixed military courts, 263

Mixed Parole and Clemency Board, 342

Miyake Shōtarō, 141

Miyama Yōzō, 132, 187, 344

Morgan, Roy L., 102

Morgenthau, Jr., Henry, 42, *43*, 58, 80

Mōri Hideoto, 139

Morishima Gorō, 174

Morishima Morito, 103

Moscow Declaration on Atrocities (November 1, 1943), 26, 41, 42 murder. *See* crime of murder

Murthy, Narasimha, 249

Mutō Akira, 17, *107*, 118, 219, 222: charges, 105t; death sentence, 226t, 233, 234, 235; selection as defendant, 93, 96t, 97; summary/rebuttal of the defense for, *152*, *154*, 157, 164, 178

Mutual Defense Assistance Agreement, 325

N

Nagai Kafū, 74, 351–352

Nagano Osami, 17, 18, 19, 22, *107*, 151, 176, 179, 183, 225, 234: charges, 105t; selection as defendant, 93, 96t

Nagasaki, 30, 237

Nagasu Kazuji, 217

Naigai Hōsei Kenkyūkai (Research Group on Domestic and Overseas Laws and Politics), 138, 141, 143

Nair, Aiyappan Pillai Madhavan, 202

Nakamura Toyoichi, 131–33, 135, 138, 144, 145

Nakasone Yasuhiro, 20, 302, 303

Nandy, Ashis, 244

Nanjing Incident (Nanjing Massacre), 27, 127, 153, 156–57, 163, 234, 238, 242, 265: charges against defendants, 101, 104, 105

Napoleon (I), 238

Narahashi Wataru, 75, 133, 225

Naruse Banji, 320

National Archives and Records Administration (United States), 7

nationalism and ultranationalism, 191, 192, 194, 228–30, 240, 268

National Mobilization Plan (Japan), 160

National Offenders Rehabilitation Commission, 318, 319–20, 333

National Security Council (NSC), 270, 335

Naval War College, 96t, 97

Nazi party, 46, 70, 84, 106, 166

Nazi war criminals, 58, 70, 76, 80, 82: treatment of, 12, 25, 26, 28, 29, 37, 38, 40, 41

Nehru, Jawaharlal, 248, 249, 250, 251

Netherlands, 12, 35, 62, 310, 322, 349–50: charges, 90, 101, 105, 127; release of war criminals, 331, 336, 341; response of Japan to Tokyo Trial, 168, 197, 208, 213, 237; Subsequent Tokyo War Crimes Trials, 275, 276t

Neurath, Konstantin von, 340

New York Times, 167, 284

New Zealand, 12, 59, 65: drafting of peace treaty, 298, 299, 304; release of war criminals, 322, 326; Subsequent Tokyo War Crimes Trials, 271–73, 275

NHK (Japan Broadcasting Corporation), 171, 191

Nicaragua, 307

Nihon Izokukai (Japan War-Bereaved Families Association), 14, 346

Nihon Jiyūtō (Japan Liberal Party), 106, 315, 321, 331

Nihon Minshutō (Japan Democratic Party), 331

Nihon Shakaitō (Japan Socialist Party), 106

Nihon Shinpotō (Japan Progressive Party), 106

Nikitchenko, Major-General Iona Timofeevich, 146

Nine-Power Treaty, 43, 47

Nippon Times, 190, 251

Nish, Ian, 202

Nishi Haruhiko, 140, 175, 179

Nishimura Kumao, 295, 302, 303

Nishio Toshizō, 262, 264

Nishiyama Tsutomu, 252

Noda Yoshihiko, 302

Nomonhan Incident (Battle of Khalkhin Gol) (1939), 94, 95, 101, 111t, 123, 150, 160, 166, 169t, 217, 223

Nomura Kichisaburō, 126

Nomura Masao (judicial correspondent), 78, 168, 181

non-combatant civilians: illegal killing, 56

North Atlantic Treaty Organization (NATO), 342

North China Area Army, 262

North China Buffer State Strategy, 111t, 160

Northcroft, Erima Harvey, 92, *195*, 205t, 206, 208, 211, 213

Northeast Asian Affairs Division (US State Department), 266, 296, 324, 325

Northern Expansion Doctrine (*Hokushin-ron*), 221

Nosaka Sanzō, 225

"not guilty" concept, 244, 247

NSC (National Security Council), 270, 335

NSC 13/2 (directive, basic policy on Japan) (October 9, 1948), 270, 271, 274

NSC 5516/1 (US-Japan policy) (April 9, 1955), 335

Nuclear Nonproliferation Treaty (NPT), 350

Nugent, Lieutenant Colonel Donald R., 113

Nuremberg Doctrine, 206, 208, 209, 210, 211, 212, 213, 214, 218, 232, 248

Nuremberg Trial (International Military Tribunal), 12, 30, *39*, 70, 106, 132, 146, 172, 198, 210, 273: charges/counts, 102, 104; comparison with Tokyo Trial, 121–22, 140, 144, 192, 197, 205, 241, 288; "conspiracy argument", 216; establishment of Subsequent Nuremberg Trials, 254–57, 269–70, 282; executions, 8, 9; genocide, 23; identifying defendants, 89; judgment of Tokyo Trial, 219; precedent for policies for Tokyo Trial, 23, 25–26, 28, 29, 38; precedent for prosecution of emperor, 51, 52, 60; precedent for Tokyo Trial, 43–45, 48, 52, 53, 54, 55, 62, 63, 79, 81, 83, 84; public opinion toward war crimes trials, 269–70; sentences, 227, 230, 231, 232, 340

O

Oberkommando der Wehrmacht (OKW) (Supreme Command of the Armed Forces) (Nazi Germany), 47

Occupation Policy, 137, 140, 185, 189–90, 217, 248, 258: definition of charges, 68, 76, 85, 124; formation of framework of Tokyo Trial, 54, 56, 59, 62, 64–65; power of Occupation Forces, 130–31; release of war crimes suspects, 280, 281, 309t, 311, 319, 337; seen as "prison without bars", 295–96; shift in policies, 276t, 277

October Incident (1931), 158

Ogasawara Islands, 71

Ogata Sadako, 132

Ogata Taketora, 71, 241, 261

Ōhashi Nami, *115*

Okada Keisuke, 184

Oka Takasumi, *107*, 145, 147: charges, 105t; medical parole, 326, 330; selection as defendant, 93, 96t, 97; sentence, 226t, 238, 310; summary/rebuttal of the defense for, *152*, *154*, 164, 175, 177, 178

Ōkawa Shūmei, 22, 106, 116, 117, 174, 221, 225: charges, 105t; dismissal of, *109*, 151; selection as defendant, 93, 96t, 97; sentence, 262, 264; summary/rebuttal of the defense for, *152*, 158, 164, 174, 179–80

Okazaki Katsuo, 135, 319

OKW (Oberkommando der Wehrmacht) (Supreme Command of the Armed Forces) (Nazi Germany), 47

Ōmori Prisoner of War Camp, 71

Ōno Katsumi, 130–31

Ono Seiichirō, *143*

Orlando, Vittorio Emanuele, 35

Osaragi Jirō, 225, 228

Ōshima Hiroshi, 77, *107*, 140, *292*, 336: charges, 105t; selection as defendant, 93, 96t, 97; sentence, 226t, 231, 236, 310; summary/rebuttal of the defense for, 149, *152*, *156*, 158, 159, 164, 165

Ōta Saburō, 145

Ott, Eugen, 93

Ōuchi Hyōe, 113, *114*

P

Pacific War (Greater East Asia War) (1941–1945), 27, 41, 104, 111t, 148, 173, 175, 223, 247, 337: Ballantine's review of, 125–26; polarization of evaluation, 346–47

pacifism, 72, 174, 180, 228, 346

Pact of Paris. *See* Kellogg-Briand Pact (1928)

Pakistan, 246, 295, 322

Pal, Radhabinod, *195*, 236, 307: announcement of resignation, 203–4, 205t; anti-Western imperialism, 244–45, 248; drafting/writing of judgment, 201–2, *207*, 209, 211, 213, 214, 218; Indian government and, 248–52; legal methodology/fact-finding, 242–47; misinterpretation of dissenting opinion, 247–48; separate dissenting opinion, 237, 239, 240–42, 302

pardons. *See* amnesty and pardons

Paris Peace Conference, 34, 104

parole system, 285, 288–94, 299, 308, 322, 323, 324, 325: Class A war crimes suspects, 330, 331, 335–36; as "judicial measure", 338–40

"Pāru Hanji wa nani o toikaketanoka" (What Did Justice Pal Question?) (NHK TV program) 201

Patrick, William, *195*, 222, 240: drafting/

writing of judgment, 203, 204, 205t, 206, *207*, 208, 209, 210, 211, 212–13, 214

Peace Problems Discussion Group (Heiwa Mondai Danwakai), 346

peace treaty. *See* Treaty of Peace with Japan (San Francisco Peace Treaty)

Pearl Harbor, 26, 212, 223, 234, 243: charges, 90, 97, 100, 104, 124; conflict between Ministry of Foreign Affairs/Imperial Japanese Navy, 174–78, 179; formation of framework of Tokyo Trial, 54, 56, 57, 79; protection of honor of Imperial Japanese Navy, 177–78; summaries of the defenses for defendants, 157, 158, 159, 160

People's Commissariat for Foreign Affairs (Soviet Union), 94, 198

People's Rally for Obtaining Food (1946), 106

Persico, Joseph E., 8–9

Philippines, 12, 127, 310, 321, 322, 344: drafting/writing of judgment, 198, 201, 209, 213, 236; selection of defendants, 62, 90, 101, 105; sentencing, 235; Subsequent Tokyo War Crimes Trials, 272, 275, 276t

planning memorandum (September 11, 1945) (War Crimes Office), 79

"Points of Responses to War Responsibility and so forth" (executive board of the Central Liaison Office [Shūsen Renraku Kanjikai]), 133–34

Police and Public Security Bureau (Home Ministry) (Japan), 139

Policy Planning Staff (PPS) (US State Department), 266–67

Policy of the United States in Regard to the Apprehension and Punishment of War Criminals in the Far East. *See* SWNCC 57/3 (policy paper)

Politburo (Central Committee of Communist Party) (Soviet Union), 88, 94, 122, 328, 329

Political Advisor's Office (US State Department), 75

political elites: Japan, 71–73, 75–76

Port Arthur, 110

Potsdam Declaration/Conference, 131, 150: Article 10 interpretation, 40, 47–48, 49, 131, 150, 301; drafting of peace treaty, 298, 301, 305, 306; formation of framework for Tokyo Trial, 40, 47, 48, 49, 51, 60

PPS 28 (policy paper), 267, 270

PRC. *See* China, People's Republic of

Prisoner-of-War Information Bureau (Ministry of the Army) (Japan), 158, 262

prisoners of war: treatment of, 27, 42, 118, 127, 264, 277; summaries of the defenses for defendants, 156, 157, 159, 160, 162, 163, 164, 165, 233

Prison Law (1953), 314, 334

Privy Council (Japan), 78, 95t, 162

prosecution counsels, 215, 222, 234, 240, 259, 267–68; closing arguments, 191; establishment of facts by evidence, 111t; rebuttals to summaries of the defenses for defendants, 161–67, 173

protest movements, 218

Public Offices Election Act (1950), 337

Public Officials Pensions Law, 320

Q

Qin Dechun, 161

R

Radford, Admiral Arthur W., 332

Raeder, Erich, 340

Reagan, Ronald, 307

Red Army (Soviet Union), 124

Red Cross Convention, 160

Reich Cabinet (Nazi Germany), 46

Relief Bureau, 15, 18

Repatriation Relief Agency (Demobilization Bureau), 15, 291, 305, 306, 308, 311, 313, 318

Research Institute of National Policy, 123

right of self-defense, 45, 167, 189

Rikiishi Tōru (comic book character), 345

Rikken-Seiyūkai (Association of Friends of Constitutional Government), 261

Robinson, James J., 177

Röling, B.V.A., *195*, 205t, 208, 211, 213, 214, 215, 244, 350: sentences, 224, 225, 230, 232, 236; separate dissenting opinion, 237, 238–39, 248, 302

Rome Statute of the International Criminal Court (the Rome Statute) (July 17, 1998), 28

Roosevelt, Franklin D., 38, 41, 42, 46, 47, 48, 77, 160, 270

Royall, Kenneth Claiborne, 263, 281

Rushdie, Salman, 81

Russo-Japanese War, 59, 110, 122, 177, 245

S

Sackett, Benjamin E., 117

Saha Shakaitō (Leftist Socialist Party), 315

saijin meihyō (list of Class A/B/C enshrinement candidates), 16, 17, 18

Saionji Kinmochi, 180

Sakamoto Takao, 28, 228, 307

Sakurakai (Cherry Blossom Society), 116, 153, 221

Sandusky, Arthur A., 91

San Francisco Peace Treaty. *See* Treaty of Peace with Japan

Sanmonji Shōhei, 312, 313, 343

Sasakawa Ryōichi, 109, 118–19, 190, 196–97, 262, 315

Satō Eisaku, 202, 321, 346

Satō Kenryō, 79, *107*, 117, *292*, 336: charges, 105t; selection as defendant, 93, 96t, 97; sentence, 226t, 238, 310, 331; summary/rebuttal of the defense for, *152*, *154*, 158, 164, 174, 182

Satow, Ernest Mason, 351

Sawamoto Yorio, 177

SCAP Circular No. 5. *See* Circular No. 5

SCAPIN 550 (Removal and Exclusion of Undesirable Personnel from Public Office), 314

Schirach, Baldur von, 340

Schutzstaffel (SS), 46, 82

Scott-Fox, Robert David J., 58

Sebald, William Joseph, 113, 229, 290

Second Hague Conference (1907), 56

Second Ministry of Demobilization (formerly Ministry of the Navy), 15, 76, 134, 138, 139

Second Sino-Japanese War, 27, 55, 81, 83, 99, 127, 148, 247: selection of defendants, 106, 111t, 118; summaries of the defenses for defendants, 153, 155, 157, 160, 162, 163, 165

Section for Investigation of War Criminals (First Department of Central Liaison Office) (formerly Legal Affairs Councilor's Office), 138

Section for War Criminals (First Department of Central Liaison Office), 138, 144

Sejima Ryūzō, 122–23, 327, 342

"Senpan no kaishō hōsaku (an)" (Ways and Means to Resolve the War Criminal Issue), 319

Senpan Shakuhō Iinkai (Committee for the Release of War Criminals), 312

Sensō Jukeisha Sewakai (Aid Society for War Prisoners), 312, 323

"Sensō sekinin ni kansuru ōtō yōryō (an)" (Outline of Responses to War Responsibility), 133–34

sentencing, 72, 173, 215, 225, 239, 344: Nuremberg Trial, 230, 283; reaction of Japanese people to, 227–30. *See also* death sentences; life imprisonment

SFE (Subcommittee for the Far East), 50, 53, 55

Shawcross, Attorney General Hartley William, 43, *44*, 61–62, 184, 185, 201

Shiba Katsuo, 176

Shidehara Kijūrō, 75, 76, 78, 91, 106, 130, 133, 156, 159: as a witness, 114, *115*, 116

Shigemitsu Mamoru, 31, 89, *107*, 130, 140, 146, 185, 193–94, 221, 307: charges, 105t; logic of the prosecution, 121, 123, 125, 127; parole, *279*, 290, 293–94, 309; political activities after parole, 331, 332, 336, 337; selection as defendant, 93, 94, 96t, 97, 98; sentence, 225, 226t, 227, 229, 231, 233, 234, 238; summary/rebuttal of the defense for, 149, *152*, *154*, 158–59, 164–65, 173, 174, 178, 181, 265

Shimada Shigetarō, 70, *107*, 145, 183, *292*, 314: charges, 105t, medical parole, 329–30; selection as defendant, 93, 96t, 97; sentence, 226, 234, 236, 238, 310; summary/rebuttal of the defense for, *152*, 159, 165, 176–78, 179

Shimanouchi Tatsuoki, 119

Shimizu Kōnosuke, 114, *115*, 116

Shimoda Takesō, 136

Shinobu Junpei, 138, 139

Shirai Yoshio (boxing world champion), 316

Shiratori Toshio, 17, 22, 106, *107*, 309: charges, 105t; selection as defendant, 93, 95t, 97; sentence, 226t, 231, 341; summary/rebuttal of the defense for, *152*, 159, 164, 165

Shōden bribery scandal, 218

Shōriki Matsutarō, 260, 312

Siberian Intervention, 122, 277

Simon, John Allsebrook, 43

Simpson, Gordon, 281, 283

Six-Power Conference (London) (March 1948), 269

Smith, David F., 168, *169*, 170, 174

Snow, Conrad, 321

Sone Eki, 135

Southern Expansion Doctrine (*Nanshin-ron*), 111t, 221

Soviet Union, 12, 148, 150, 158, 184, 187, 197, 322: aims for the Tokyo Trial, 123–24; charges, 88–89, 104, 111t, 120; justice for, 208, 210, 213; commutation system (clemency), 288, 290, 323, 326–27, 336; diplomatic relations with Japan, 342; formation of framework for Tokyo Trial, 41, 44, 46, 51, 54, 58, 62, 66; Germany and, 269; majority judgment, 223; Nuremberg Trial, 256; paradox of Cold War, 124–25; selection of "heavyweight" defendants, 93, 94, 95, 98; Stalin's witness, 122–23; Subsequent Nuremberg Trials, 255, 257; Subsequent Tokyo War Crimes Trials, 264, 272, 275, 276; United States and, 198–99, 254

Spandau Prison (West Berlin), 282, 340

Special Far Eastern and Pacific Committee, 51, 52

Speer, Albert, 340

Stalin, Joseph, 88, 122–23, 198, 326, 342

State Defense Committee (Soviet Union), 122

State Department (United States), 29, 38, 100, 199, 201, 223, 247, 282; draft of peace treaty, 295, 296–98; formation of framework of Tokyo Trial, 48, 50, 53, 54, 61; release of war criminals, 322, 324, 325, 337, 341–42, 343–44; Second Tokyo Trial, 256, 257, 260, 267

State-War-Navy Coordinating Committee (SWNCC), 50, 54, 69

stenographic records, 153, 215

Stimson Doctrine, 43, 47

Stimson, Henry L., 47, 57, 80, 210, 229, 282: "Victors' Justice" theory 30, 31, 37, 42, *43*, 44, 45, 46

Streicher, Julius, 97

Sturmabteilung (SA) (Nazi Germany), 46

Subcommittee for the Far East (SFE), SWNCC, 50, 53, 55

submarine warfare, 165

Subsequent Nuremberg Trials (United States), 269, 283

Subsequent Tokyo War Crimes Trials, 254–60: argument for completion of trial, 266, *267*, 268, 271–73; avoidance of Class A trial, 260–61; Class B/C War Crimes Trials, 258–59, 265, 276t; GHQ trials, *263*, 264; termination of all trials, 274–75; trial of former cabinet members, 262–64. *See also* Tokyo Trial

Sugamo Prison, 16, 21, *279*, 314: commutation system (clemency), 286–87, 289, 291, *317*, 330, 341, 344, 348; "de facto release measures", 333–35; detention during trial, 69, 71, *72*, *107*, 109, 180, 181; former cabinet members, 262–63; post-sentencing, 227, 235, 266

Sugawara Yutaka, 102, 170

Sugiyama Hajime, 238

suicides: war criminals, 8, 50, 68, 69–70, 92, 123, 185, 187

Sumatra, 157, 164, 235, 276t

Suma Yakichirō, 262

summary execution: war criminals, 42, 57–58, 80

Supreme Commander for the Allied Powers. *See* General Headquarters, Supreme Commander for the Allied Powers (GHQ/SCAP)

Supreme Court (United States), 54, 64, 87, 136, 151, 255

Supreme Military Council (Japan), 70

surrender. *See* Instrument of Surrender (Japan)

Suzuki Teiichi, *107*, 142, 149, 194, *292*: charges, 105t; members of cabinet, 262–63; parole, 336; selection as defendant, 93, 96t, 97; sentence, 226t, 310; summary/rebuttal of the defense for, *152*, *154*, 160, 165, 178, 265

Suzuki Tōmin, *114,* 115

SWNCC (State-War-Navy Coordinating Committee), 50, 54, 69

SWNCC 57/1 (August 24, 1945), 50, 52, 53, 64

SWNCC 57/3 (policy paper), 25, 77, 79, 82, 85, 201: formation of framework of Tokyo Trial, 55–56, 57, 59, 60, 61, 62, 63, 65, 66

T

Tada Hayao, 262, 264, 266

Taisei Yokusankai (Imperial Rule Assistance Association), 71, 82, 166

Taiyuan War Criminals Management Center (China), 327

Tajiri Akiyoshi, 133

Takagi Yasaka, 138

Takahashi Sankichi, 262, 264

Takamatsu Nobuhito, Prince, 19, 312, 316

Takarabe Takeshi, 178

Takayanagi Kenzō, 135, 138, 139, 141, 142, 143, 148, 167: closing arguments of the defense, 192, 193, 194

Takazawa Hiroaki, 7

Takeyama Michio, 225

Takigawa Yukitoki, 113, 114

Tamura Hiroshi, 93, 262, *263*, 264

Tanaka Giichi, 100, 102, 103, 220, 221

Tanaka Masaaki, 251

Tanaka Memorandum, 102, 103

Tanaka Ryūkichi, 98–99, *115, 117,* 118–19, 164, 185

Tani Masayuki, 262, 263, 264, *317*, 331–32

Taoka Ryōichi, 138

Tatekawa Yoshitsugu, 117, 221

Tatsumi Ryūtarō, 292

Tavenner, Jr., Frank S., 125, 149

Taylor, Colonel Telford, 255, 256, 269

Teigin Bank robbery incident, 218

Ten-Year Rule, 325–26, 331, 339

Terashima Ken, 262, 263, 264

Thailand-Burma Railway, 163, 164, 235

Third Hague Convention (Relative to the Opening of Hostilities) (1907), 110

Thorpe, Brigadier General Elliot R., 68–69, 71

Tiltman, Hessell, 345

Tobe Ryōichi, 183

Tochinishiki (sumo grand champion), 292

Tōgō Fumihiko, 147

Tōgō Shigehiko, 178

Tōgō Shigenori, 17, 19, 70, *107*, 121, 137, 140, 147, *152*, *154*, 291, 293: charges, 105t; majority judgment, 222, 223; selection as defendant, 93, 96t, 97; sentence, 219, 226t, 227, 238, 293; summary/rebuttal of the defense for, *152*, *154*, 160, 175, 177, 178, *179*, 265

Tōjō Hideki, 7, 9, 21, 56, 75, 77, 82, 85, 126: abortive suicide attempt, 68–70; charges, 105t, 106, 131, 141, *142*, 148; cabinet members, 262–63; cross-examination of, 185–90, 227; death sentence and execution, 17, 226t, 233, 234, 266, 309, 341; last act of service to emperor, 184–85; response of Japan to trials, 174, 176, 184, *186*; selection as defendant, 90, 91, 93, 100, *107*, 108, 117, 96t, 97; summary/rebuttal of the defense for, *152*, *154*, 155, 160, 161, 162, 163, 164, 165, 173, 178, 180, 182

Tokugawa Yoshichika, 114, *115*, 116

Tokugawa Yoshihiro, 18, 19, 69

Tokutomi Sohō, 21, 71, 75, 110, 121, 167, 174, 261, 351

Tokyo Absentees' Family Society (Tōkyō Rusu Kazokukai), 14

Tokyo Charter. *See* Charter of the International Military Tribunal

Tokyo Trial, 7, 9, 12, 13, 16, 21, 48, 106, 108, 150, 273, 288: acceptance as Japan's security policy, 136–39; call for independence/impartiality/neutrality, 196, 201, 239–40; chronological table, 354–58; conclusion of trial, 215, 270, 276t; documentation as evidence, 78–79; drafting of policy on 'conspiracy', 80; emergence of anti-American sentiment, 268; 'foreign policy' of Allied Powers, 349; international/domestic issue, 347–48; Japanese "unified opinion", 133, 136, 137–39; Japanese witnesses, 113–17, *179*; jurisdiction/legitimacy of, 193, 204, 205, 219, 240, 304–5, 306, 349, 350; lack of knowledge of Anglo-American law, 140, 146; language barriers/translations, 77, 84, 139–41, 173, *217*; need to avoid "ritualized revenge", 241; obsession with proving atrocities, 126–28; perception as Anglo-American court, 64, 101, 102, 113; prolongation of trials, 171–73; publication of records, 288; public opinion strategy, 190–91; racial factors, 244–45; scheme for Japanese-initiated court, 132; security policy in international politics, 38, 350; seen as 'greatest hypocrisy in history', 71; spiritual restoration of Japanese people, 19; "symbol of peace", 347. *See also* Subsequent Tokyo War Crimes Trials

Tominaga Kyōji, 94

Toyoda Kumao, 134, 175, 227, 308

Toyoda Soemu, 262, *263*, 264

translators, *217*

Treaty Bureau (Ministry of Foreign Affairs) (Japan), 94, 131, 132, 139, 295–96, 302, 305

Treaty of Peace Between Japan and the Republic of China, 321

Treaty of Peace with Japan (San Francisco Peace Treaty), 286, 292, 313: Article 11 in treaty, 295, 299–305, 307, 308–9, 314–15, 318, 319; British Commonwealth and, 303–5; draft by Britain, 298–99; draft by US State Department, 295, 296–98; Japan's reaction and acceptance, 305–8; provision of commutation system (clemency), 308–9, 310, 313, 318

Treaty of Versailles, 35, 40, 45, 313

Truman Doctrine, 125

Truman, Harry S., 46, 54, 73, 99, 112, 125, 127, 172, 184, 321: writing/drafting of judgment, 246, 255, 288, 295

Tsugita Daizaburō, 133

Tsukuba Fujimaro, 18

Tsurumi Yūsuke, 139

U

Ueda Kenkichi, 95

Ugaki Kazushige, *115*, 163, 165, 168, 182, 268, 312

Uha Shakaitō (Rightist Socialist Party), 315

Ukai Nobushige, 138

UK Liaison Mission (UKLIM) in Japan, 62, 172, 212

Umezu Yoshijirō, 17, *107*, 121, 123, 147, 309: charges, 105t; selection as defendant, 94, 96t, 98; sentence, 226t, 341; summary/rebuttal of the defense for, *152*, 160, 165, 174

United Nations, 33, 41, 44, 132, 135, 273, 274, 298, 336, 339

United Nations War Crimes Commission (UNWCC), 50–52, 131, 212

United States, 12, 24, 25, 38, 126, 168, 187, 213, 322: American defense counsels, 144–47, *148*, *149*, 150, 170, 171; appointment of justice for, 197, 199;

arguments for US initiative/cooperation among Allies, 53, 54, 55, 61, 85; atomic bombings and tests, 30, 191, 237, 241, 324; basic policy toward Japan, 49–50; charges, 86, 89, 106; commutation system (clemency), 280–81, 291, 292, 310, 339; Dachau Trials, 280–81; demands for further arrests of war crimes suspects, 70–71; drafting of peace treaty, 295, 296–98, 299–301; economic/military threat to Japan, 188–89; formation of framework for Tokyo Trial, 41, 42, 46, 47, 58–59, 62; "New Look" policy, 325; policy shift toward trials, 270–71; policy toward Germany, 255, 256, 269; release of war criminals, 341–42, 348; "soft peace" policy, 296–97, 298, 304; Soviet Union and, 198–99, 254; Subsequent Tokyo War Crimes Trials, 260, 275, 276t

United States European Command, 283

UNWCC. See United Nations War Crimes Commission

Urabe Ryōgo, 338

US Castle Bravo (thermonuclear weapon test at Bikini Atoll), 324

US High Commissioner for Germany, 282, 283, 315, 342

Ushiba Nobuhiko, 140

Ushimura Kei, 161, 247

US-Japan Treaty of Commerce and Navigation, 188

Uzawa Fusaaki, *129*, 141, 143, 192, 193, 194, 350

V

Van Meter, Captain Donald S., 108

"Victors' Justice" theory, 40, 48, 85, 132, 224, 237, 241, 243, 285: call for independence/impartiality/neutrality, 196–98, 199, 202; civilisation's justice versus, 30–34, 36, 38; defense counsels, 141, 145, 146; perception of trial as 'revenge', 285, 305, 306, 340–41, 349

Victory in Europe Day (V-E Day) (May 8, 1945), 46

Vincent, John Carter, 199

vivisection experiments (Kyushu Imperial University), 218, 339

Vyshinsky, Andrey Yanuaryevich, 94

W

Wakatsuki Reijirō, 113, 114, *115*

Walker, Lieutenant General Walton, 266

war: criminalization of, 46, 56, 71, 125, 150, 189, 220, 241, 273, 274; justices' stances on, 205, 207, 208, 209, 214, 237, 238, 239

War Crime Affairs Bureau (Foreign Office) (United Kingdom), 58

War Crimes Branch (Civil Affairs Division [CAD], US War Department) (United States), 257, 259, 260

War Crimes Modification Board, 283

War Crimes Trials Countermeasures Committee, 133, 135, 138

war criminals: handling/ punishment, 41, 46, 49–50, 56, 70, 71–73; use of term, 20–21, 49, 74. *See also* Class A ("A-kyū") war criminals and suspects; Class B/C war criminals and suspects

War Criminal Clemency Advisory Board, 283

War Criminals Relief Movement, 310–13

War Department (United States), 37, 38, 45, 197, 288: Dachau Trials, 280–82; formation of framework for Tokyo Trial, 50, 54, 56, 64, 65, 79, 80; Subsequent Tokyo War Crimes Trials, 256, 258, 259, 261, 271

war guilt, 45, 76, 130, 190, 298–99, 300, 304, 336

War Guilt Information Program (June 3, 1946), 190

Warren, Major Franklin, 147, *148*, 151, 153, 157

war responsibility, 190, 192, 265, 297, 320, 336: charges, 100, 132, 133, 137, 142; demarcation between militarists and 'the people', 37; drafting of peace treaty, 297, 298, 299; responsibility of emperor, 184–88; formation of framework of Tokyo Trial, 21, 28, 31, 34, 35, 43, 45; official posts and, 164–66; release of war criminals, 346–47, 348, 349, 350; victors' pursuit of, 75–76

wars of aggression, 25, 33, 124, 162, 168, 191, 243: charges, 79, 80, 82, 83, 92, 101, 106, 114; conspiracy-based historical view (*Tōkyō Saiban shikan*), 81–82, 126, 350; definition of, 242–44; natural law argument, 208, 209–10, 216; polarized evaluation of Pacific War, 346–47; post-WWI change in understanding of, 34–35

"war of self-defense" argument, 241, 337, 350: closing arguments of the defense, 191, 192, 193, 194; polarized evaluation of Pacific War, 346–47; response of Japan to Tokyo Trials, 141–42, 143, 149, 153, 156, 167–68, 176–77, 182, 189

war tactics: sanctioned justice, 30

wartime felony, 27

"War Trial Report" (NHK radio program), 191

Washington Naval Treaty, 126

Washington Post, 284

Watanabe Hamako, 315

Watanabe Kazuhide, 72

Watsuji Tetsurō, 139

Webb, Chief Justice William F., *195*, 209, 225, 238, 245: appointment, 203, 205t, *207*, 208, 212; charges, 108, 121, 124; drafting/writing of judgment, 215, 219; recall of, 213, 214; response of Japan to Tokyo Trial, 147, 151, 167, 168, *169*, 170, 172, 173–74, 184, 186; sentencing, 226, 231, 232, 236; separate opinion, 236, 238–39, 248

Weber, Max, 31

Weir, Brigadier General John M., 64

Wilhelm II, Kaiser, 34, 35, 60

Williams, George, 153

Willoughby, Major General Charles A., 57, 71, 257

Wilson, Woodrow, 24–25, 34, 35, 40

witnesses and witness statements, 114–23, 215

Wood, Edward Frederick Lindley, 200

World War I, 34–35

Wright of Durley, Lord, 51, 212

X

Xiang Zhejun, *101*

Y

Yabe Teiji, 78, 102, 139, 167

Yalta Conference and Agreement, 54, 88

Yamada Otozō, 276

Yamaichi Securities Co., Ltd., 334

Yamamoto Eisuke, 178

Yamamoto Kumaichi, 175

Yamanashi Katsunoshin, 312

Yamaoka, George, 82, *129*, 147, *148*

Yamashita Tomoyuki, 26, *27*, 57, 72, 73, 104, 144

Yamazaki Iwao, 130

Yanagiya Kingorō, 292

Yanai Hisao, 140

Yasukuni Shrine, 13n5, 14–22, 338–39, 346

Yasukuni Shrine Veneration Association, 15, 18

Yodogawa Nagaharu, 74

Yodogō Hijacking Incident (1970), 345

Yokohama Prison, 71

Yokohama War Crimes Tribunals/Trials, 73, 144, 146, 218, 232, 263, 275

Yokota Kisaburō, 211, 217, 218

Yokusan Seijikai (Imperial Rule Assistance Political Association), 166

Yomiuri Shimbun, 8, 20, 110, 114, 115, 181, 231, 260, 336, 337

Yonai Mitsumasa, 65, *115*, 162, 184

Yoshida Shigeru, 78, 106, 218, 228, 263: charges, 130, 134–36, 137; drafting of peace treaty, 296, 298; parole, 315, 319, 320, 321, 323–24, 331, 332, 334, 350

Yoshimatsu Masakatsu, 251

Yoshimoto Takaaki, 139

Yoshimura Matasaburō, 305, 310

Yoshino Sakuzō, 116

Yoshizawa Kenkichi, 132

Yoshizumi Masao, 133

Young, Colonel Edward H., 260

Z

zaibatsu, 116, 123, 137

Zaryanov, Major General Ivan M., 124, *195*, 205t, *207,* 208, 213, 214, 216, 236

Zhanggufeng Incident (Battle of Lake Khasan) (1938), 94, 95, 158, 217, 223

Zhang Zuolin Assassination Incident (Huanggutun Incident) (1928), 102

Zhou Enlai, 37, 329

About the Author

Dr. Higurashi Yoshinobu is professor of Japanese political history and foreign policy in the Faculty of Law at Teikyo University. He was born in Tokyo in 1962. He received his BA in Law from Rikkyo University in 1986, MA in History from Rikkyo University in 1988, and PhD in Political Science from Gakushuin University in 2000. At Kagoshima University, he has served as assistant professor (1993–1994), associate professor (1994–2004), and subsequently professor (2004–2012) in the Faculty of Law, Economics and the Humanities. He is the author of *Tōkyō Saiban no kokusai kankei* [The Tokyo War Crimes Trial and International Relations] (Tokyo: Bokutakusha, 2002), which was awarded the Yoshida Shigeru Prize in 2003 and published as a Chinese-language edition in 2016 (Shanghai: Jiao Tong University Press). His most recent books are *Tōkyō Saiban* [The Tokyo Trial] (Tokyo: Kodansha, 2008), awarded the 2008 Suntory Prize for Social Sciences and Humanities (History and Civilization category) and translated into Chinese in 2017 (New Taipei: Gusa Press), and *Tōkyō Saiban o tadashiku yomu* [Correctly Reading the Tokyo War Crimes Trial] (Tokyo: Bungeishunjū, 2008), co-authored with Dr. Ushimura Kei. Other works include his translation of Arnold C. Brackman's *The Other Nuremberg* into Japanese (*Tōkyō Saiban*, Tokyo: Jiji Press, 1991), and his supervision of the Japanese edition of John G. Roos's *In a Prison Called Sugamo* (*Sugamo jinmon chōsho*, Tokyo: Yomiuri Shimbunsha, 1995).

（英文版）東京裁判

The Tokyo Trial: War Criminals and Japan's Postwar International Relations

2022年3月27日　第1刷発行

著　者　　日暮吉延
英　訳　　公益財団法人日本国際問題研究所
発行所　　一般財団法人出版文化産業振興財団
　　　　　〒101-0051 東京都千代田区神田神保町2-2-30
　　　　　電話　03-5211-7283
　　　　　ホームページ　https://www.jpic.or.jp/

印刷・製本所　　大日本印刷株式会社

© 2008 Higurashi Yoshinobu
Printed in Japan
ISBN 978-4-86658-230-6